TRADE POLICY, INDUSTRIALIZATION, AND DEVELOPMENT

WIDER

Studies in Development Economics embody the output of the research programmes of the World Institute for Development Economics Research (WIDER), which was established by the United Nations University as its first research and training centre in 1984 and started work in Helsinki in 1985. The principal purpose of the Institute is to help identify and meet the need for policy-oriented socio-economic research on pressing global and development problems, as well as common domestic problems and their interrelationships.

Trade Policy, Industrialization, and Development:

New Perspectives

Edited by

Gerald K. Helleiner

*A study prepared for the
World Institute for Development Economics Research (WIDER)
of the United Nations University*

CLARENDON PRESS · OXFORD

1992

Oxford University Press, Walton Street, Oxford OX2 6DP
Oxford New York Toronto
Delhi Bombay Calcutta Madras Karachi
Petaling Jaya Singapore Hong Kong Tokyo
Nairobi Dar es Salaam Cape Town
Melbourne Auckland
and associated companies in
Berlin Ibadan

Oxford is a trade mark of Oxford University Press

Published in the United States
by Oxford University Press, New York

© *United Nations University 1992*

World Institute for Development Economics Research (WIDER)—
The United Nations University 42 C, 00100 Helsinki, Finland.

All rights reserved. No part of this publication may be reproduced,
stored in a retrieval system, or transmitted, in any form or by any means,
electronic, mechanical, photocopying, recording, or otherwise, without
the prior permission of Oxford University Press

British Library Cataloguing in Publication Data
Data available
ISBN 0-19-828359-8

Library of Congress Cataloging in Publication Data
Trade policy, industrialization, and development : new perspectives /
edited by Gerald K. Helleiner.
p.   cm.—*(WIDER studies in development economics)*
"*A study prepared for the World Institute for Development*
Economics Research (WIDER) of the United Nations University."
Papers presented at a conference at WIDER in Helsinki in Aug.
1988.
Includes index.
1. Developing countries—Commercial policy—Congresses.
2. Developing countries—Industries—Congresses.   3. Economic
development—Congresses.   4. International trade—Congresses.
I. Helleiner, Gerald K.   II. World Institute for Development
Economics Research.   III. Series.
HF4055.T73   1991   382'.3'091724—dc20   91–15325
ISBN 0-19-828359-8

Typeset by Best-set Typesetter Ltd.

Printed in Great Britain by
Bookcraft (Bath) Ltd.
Midsomer Norton, Avon

PREFACE

FOR the greater part of the postwar period developing countries have striven to diversify, and particularly to industrialize, their economies as the surest way to accelerating their economic growth. The policies adopted to achieve these ends have, however, aroused intense controversy. The mainstream view in academic circles in Western countries, and the view taken also by the Bretton Woods institutions, has been that only industrialization based on 'outward-oriented' trade policies has the best chance of resulting in efficient economic growth and development. By contrast, industrialization based on 'inward-oriented' policies, which promote domestic industries behind protectionist barriers, is likely, it is argued, to result in resource misallocation, high-cost production, and limited growth rates, particularly in developing countries with small domestic markets.

One objection to this postulated opposition between inward and outward orientation in trade policies has been that historically most countries, whether developing or developed, which have successfully built an export trade in industrial goods have done so only after an initial phase of 'inward' production for their domestic markets. Thus, the two phases are best viewed as sequential, rather than as alternative.

There has also been a growing recognition that trade policy orientation is by no means uniquely related to export performance. The slow-down in world economic growth during the 1980s in particular has resulted in a wide dispersion of export growth rates among countries with export-oriented policies. Clearly, trade policy orientation has been only one among many domestic policies and domestic structual changes which have influenced export performance, while changes in the global economic environment have also influenced, often dramatically, the growth potential of individual developing countries.

The search for more satisfactory explanations of the complex interrelationships between the export sector and domestic economic growth has led in recent years to attempts to broaden existing trade theory by incorporating the more important institutional, structural, and other features of developing countries' economies. Thus, the influence of oligopolistic markets, the role of foreign enterprises and intra-firm trade, the nature and effects of externalities in domestic industrial development, the acquisition and use of modern technologies and economies of scale, are all necessary elements of a wider understanding of the interrelated processes of export and domestic growth.

The WIDER research project on which this book is based aims to elucidate these various interrelationships, both by theoretical enquiry and by a number of case-studies of industrial development in Third World countries. As Professor Helleiner says, in his introductory essay, 'There is certainly far more to the analysis of trade policy than the dichotomous characterizations that have been so emphasized in much of the mainstream literature in recent years—in terms of so-called "inward" or "outward" orientation. There is also far more to industrialization policy than simply trade policy.' Indeed, the emphasis on the inward–outward dichotomy has obscured the relevance of other forces both in the private sector and in the nature of government support for technological, infrastructural, and human development.

This volume should contribute to a better appreciation of the actual problems and constraints of industrialization and growth in developing countries, as well as pointing the way to useful further lines of research in this important area.

Lal Jayawardena
Director, WIDER

Helsinki
October 1989

EDITOR'S PREFACE

THIS volume arose from a research project undertaken under the auspices and with the support of the United Nations University's World Institute for Development Economics Research (WIDER). Its first stage involved an exploratory workshop conducted at the University of Toronto in April 1987 in which all of the authors represented in this volume participated together with a number of others. The workshop led to a major conference at WIDER in Helsinki in August 1988. This conference was attended by a much larger number of participants. Earlier versions of the chapters in this volume were presented at the conference, together with others not published here. (A full list of the participants and their papers can be obtained from WIDER.)

I should like to thank WIDER, and particularly its Director, Lal Jayawardena, and Hema Perera, Jan Johansen, and Liisa Roponen for the wonderful support they offered throughout the project and particularly at the time of the Helsinki conference. Rodney Schmidt and Jennifer Johnson provided invaluable assistance in the preparation of this volume for publication; both deserve the reader's thanks.

G.K.H.

Toronto
June 1989

CONTENTS

List of Contributors	xi
1. Introduction GERALD K. HELLEINER	1

PART I: MAJOR ISSUES: THE STATE OF KNOWLEDGE

2. Learning and Productivity Change in Developing Countries HOWARD PACK	21
3. Firm (or Plant) Size in the Analysis of Trade and Development R. ALBERT BERRY	46
4. Market Structure and Trade in Developing Countries NORMAN LEE	89
5. Externalities, Development, and Trade FRANCES STEWART and EJAZ GHANI	122
6. Closing the Productivity Gap: Does Trade Liberalization really Help? DANI RODRIK	155
7. Marketing Manufactured Exports from Developing Countries: Learning Sequences and Public Support DONALD B. KEESING and SANJAYA LALL	176

PART II: CASE-STUDIES—COUNTRIES AND INDUSTRIES

8. Foreign Direct Investment and Patterns of Industrialization and Trade in Developing Countries: The Brazilian Experience WINSTON FRITSCH and GUSTAVO H. B. FRANCO	197
9. High-Technology Exports and Strategic Trade Policy in Developing Countries: The Case of Brazilian Aircraft RICHARD BALDWIN	225
10. International Competition and Market Penetration: A Model of the Growth Strategy of the Korean Semiconductor Industry CHANG-HO YOON	254

11. Total Factor Productivity in Automobile Production in Argentina, Mexico, Korea, and Canada: The Impacts of Protection 279
LEONARD WAVERMAN and STEVEN MURPHY

Index 317

CONTRIBUTORS

DR RICHARD BALDWIN
Graduate School of Business, Columbia University, New York, NY USA

DR ALBERT BERRY
Department of Economics, University of Toronto, Toronto, Ontario, Canada

DR WINSTON FRITSCH
Departamento de Economia, PUC-RJ, Pontificia Universidade Catolica do Rio de Janeiro, Rio de Janeiro, Brazil

DR GUSTAVO FRANCO
Departamento de Economia, PUC-RJ, Pontificia Universidade Catolica do Rio de Janeiro, Rio de Janeiro, Brazil

EJAZ GHANI
The World Bank, Washington, D.C., USA

STEVEN MURPHY
Centre for International Studies, University of Toronto, Toronto, Ontario, Canada

MR DONALD KEESING
World Bank, Washington, DC, USA

DR SANJAYA LALL
Institute of Economics and Statistics, Oxford, UK

PROFESSOR NORMAN LEE
Faculty of Economics and Social Studies, University of Manchester, Manchester, UK

DR HOWARD PACK
Department of City and Regional Planning, Economics, Public Policy and Management, University of Pennsylvania, Philadelphia, PA, USA

DR DANI RODRIK
Kennedy School of Government, Harvard University, Cambridge, MA, USA

MS FRANCES STEWART
University of Oxford, International Development Centre, Oxford, UK

MR LEONARD WAVERMAN
Department of Economics, University of Toronto, Toronto, Ontario, Canada

PROFESSOR CHANG-HO YOON
Korea University, Department of Economics, Seoul, Korea

1
Introduction*

G. K. Helleiner

THE appropriate role of trade policy in industrialization has long been controversial. Mainstream economic theory has always emphasized the importance of comparative advantage for the attainment of overall efficiency at both national and global levels. Emphasis upon comparative advantage may not always, however, imply free trade policy, as has traditionally been suggested. The historical experiences of such countries as Germany, Japan, the United States, and, more recently, Korea suggest that governmental interventions in trade and in other spheres may sometimes assist efficient industrialization and development processes. At the same time, there now exists a whole panoply of reasons why more activist trade policies may be theoretically justifiable. Most of these theoretical arguments have been based upon 'second-best' reasoning in which it is conceded that an alternative policy-mix in which trade policies play a minor role would be preferable if only it were attainable; political and other constraints, institutional rigidities, and the like necessitate resort to interventionist trade policies, even though they are known to be theoretically less than optimal, in pursuit of welfare improvements. More recently, in the literature on so-called 'strategic' trade policy, a new theoretical case for governmental intervention in trade has been built, on the basis of assumptions alternative to those traditionally dominant in the literature (Brander and Spencer 1985; Krugman 1986a). While these alternative assumptions, relating particularly to market structure and learning phenomena (see the simple exposition in Chapter 10), are certainly subject to challenge, and policy conclusions are highly sensitive to their details, they seem not wholly unreasonable approximations of reality in at least some cases. Whatever the merits of these newer theoretical arguments, as seen in the academic institutions of the industrialized world where these issues are hotly debated, there still seems to be a great deal of life left in the 'older' trade policy debates in the developing countries.

Apart from the new strategic arguments, the principal arguments for (objectives of) an activist trade policy can be grouped under five headings:

1. Economic efficiency
2. Risk aversion and/or national security

---

* I am grateful to Dani Rodrik, Frances Stewart, and Chang-ho Yoon for comments on an earlier version.

3. Internal income redistribution, either in pursuit of distributional equity, in response to powerful interest groups and rent-seekers, or to meet government revenue requirements
4. Macroeconomic objectives, notably full employment and capacity utilization, and balance in external payments
5. Improvement in international terms of trade.

Activist arguments relating to industrialization objectives are typically found under the first three headings. Particular attention is directed in this volume to the issues involved in the pursuit of economic efficiency. The principal strands of the arguments for government intervention that are based upon economic efficiency objectives are: (*a*) the 'infant-industry' argument; (*b*) 'externalities' arguments, including those favouring the entire infant manufacturing sector, because of its purported positive effects elsewhere in the economy; and (*c*) the purported need to offset the negative incentives for industry created by already existing product or factor market 'distortions'. (For good surveys of the main issues in traditional trade policy debates, see Chenery 1961, and Krueger 1984.)

Carlos Diaz-Alejandro effectively summarized the state of the debate on these matters a few years ago, as follows:

In the trade and development literature there has existed for a long time, going back at least to John Stuart Mill, a striking difference between the rigor of formal proofs on the static advantages of free trade, typically involving careful assumptions and *caveats*, and the impetuous enthusiasm with which most of the professional mainstream advocates free or freer trade policies, on both static and dynamic grounds, for all times and places. (1975, p. 96)

At the same time, he argued,

The leap from vague qualitative arguments to impetuous policy advocacy is no monopoly of the orthodox.... [Some economists] casually invoke this or that imperfection to justify just about any level of protection or any other policy that happens to come into the head of a policy maker to whom they wish to be sympathetic. (p. 115)

Again,

[I]t is easy to see that different assumptions regarding the availability, effectiveness and real costs of different policy instruments can yield a disconcerting variety of heterodox conclusions. By now any bright graduate student, by choosing his assumptions regarding distortions and policy instruments carefully, can produce a consistent model yielding just about any policy recommendation he favored at the start. To reach his conclusion, moreover, he need not introduce development targets additional to static efficiency. The conclusion, of course, applies a fortiori when other targets are brought in. (p. 97)

On the one hand, then, we have caution and *caveats* as theoreticians grope their way towards more realistic models, with those on the frontier typically the most conscious of how much remains to be explored. On the other hand, despite widespread professional agnosticism about their developmental efficacy, advocates of both liberal and interventionist orientations continue to press for various kinds of trade policy reform.

In recent years, pressures upon developing countries to liberalize their trade policies have sharply increased (Helleiner 1990). There can be little doubt that a good deal of governmental intervention in trade has 'misfired' in developing countries. At the same time, both governments and international institutions prefer simple rules to complex ones. So do analysts of government behaviour who most fear its capture by special interest groups (for example Krugman 1987). The new orthodoxy of trade liberalization— in the sense of shifting from direct controls to market instruments of policy, and toward uniformity of inter-industry incentives—offers what seems to be a simple, familiar, and universally applicable policy rule. But the models from which the rule is derived are subject to challenge; and the empirical evidence as to the impact of such policy reform is limited.

Only very rarely, in any case, is the trade policy choice anything so bald as choice between free trade and 'protectionism'. The general case is rather that of *partial* trade policy reform—frequently also undertaken in conjunction with major macroeconomic policy changes—where the analysis of its effects is more complex and the results less clear. As the assumptions and approaches of specialists in industrial organization are increasingly transferred to the arena of international trade, one can expect some transfer as well of their characteristic caution—even agnosticism—as to the effects of partial policy changes.

Strictly speaking, trade policy relates purely to the inter-industry or inter-sectoral structure of incentives (and sometimes direct controls) *within* the tradables sector. Policy relating to the *overall* relative price of tradables as against non-tradables, which can also influence the levels of exports and imports, is better considered a matter of macroeconomic policy, notably exchange-rate policy (although the same effect can obviously be achieved by a combination of import tariffs and export subsidies). Trade policy therefore influences the *structures* of production and consumption of tradable goods and services, and thus the levels and composition of exports and imports. Other non-trade governmental policies—differentially subsidizing or taxing particular trade or tradable activities—may also influence the incentive structure; unless specifically directed at exports or imports these are probably best excluded from the category of 'trade' policies but they may none the less be important elements in 'industrial' policies. In the context of many developing countries, and some industrialized ones as well, trade policies can be best understood as a subset of industrialization policies.

Twenty years have elapsed since the enormously influential OECD empirical study of trade and industrialization experience and policies in developing countries by Little *et al.* (1970). That study, together with those of Bhagwati and Krueger for the US National Bureau of Economic Research (NBER) a few years later (1978), strongly supported traditional liberal trade policy verities for the developing countries. Considerable knowledge and experience with trade policies and industrialization have since accumulated, not least in the 'newly industrializing countries' (NICs). While the World Bank has directed research attention to some of the key policy issues in this realm during the 1980s its research seemed to many to have been slanted in an 'orthodox' direction from its outset and did not, in any case, seriously address many of the most interesting questions—in particular, those relating to the role and implications of market imperfections as well as governmental ones.

The research project that generated this WIDER volume began as an investigation of the development policy implications of the so-called 'new' or 'strategic' trade theories. These theories—emphasizing the roles of scale, learning, and market structure—have been said by many (for example Krugman 1986*b*; Rodrik 1988) to be more relevant to the developing countries, above all because of their small and imperfect markets, than to the industrialized world for which most of the writing on them has been intended. Some expressed an early concern that these 'new' approaches might provide a convenient rationale for familiar 'old' policies that could be particularly costly in small countries (for example Dixit 1987). These seemed important matters to sort out. As it evolved, however, the project adopted a much broader and more eclectic approach. (A smaller and more narrowly focused research project addressing the original questions, relating purely to the relevance of strategic considerations to developing-country trade-policy formation, is now planned at WIDER.)

The bulk of the recent 'new' trade theory literature has been on 'strategic' trade policy and the efficacy of subsidies as credible threats in industries where there is potential for learning, first-comer advantages, and quasi-rent-earning. It is important to consider the applicability of this literature to some developing-country cases, and this volume therefore contains case-studies exploring these approaches in the Korean semiconductor and Brazilian civil aircraft industries. There are probably early limits, however, to the potential for strategic trade policy in this narrow sense in most developing countries. A good deal of the 'older' trade and investment policy debate in small and/or developing countries has nevertheless always revolved around the questions of scale economies, learning, externalities, oligopoly and small-numbers bargaining, and the 'shaping of comparative advantage' that are now in fashion in much of the mainstream literature. Interest in the possible applicability of the new trade theories to developing-country trade seemed to make it an opportune time for the launching of further *empirical* research on some of these old and key questions.

This volume has no policy axe to grind. As the reader will see, its authors do not possess a uniform set of judgements on trade and industrialization policy questions: some lean more towards faith in markets and others have greater hope for constructive governmental inputs. They are united only in the seriousness with which they view the need to confront the tenets of available trade theories with the empirical reality in the developing countries. They all seek to draw appropriate trade policy conclusions for developing countries from the increased information and extended methodological and theoretical tool-box now available.

The traditional policy conclusion of the orthodox trade economist—that free, or at least fairly liberal, trade policies are best for development—may still be correct. Indeed some argue that the debate has already been 'settled' in that very way (for example Balassa 1990; Bhagwati 1987*a*). But, if that is the case, that conclusion can no longer be based, without considerable further examination, upon theory that so neglects or severely plays down such real-world phenomena as oligopoly, learning-by-doing, externalities, scale economies, domestic non-price or institutional constraints, and foreign ownership. The empirical significance, theoretical implications, and policy relevance of these realities are matters that must be squarely addressed rather than simply assumed away. There is certainly far more to the analysis of trade policy than the dichotomous characterizations that have been so emphasized in much of the mainstream literature in recent years—in terms of so-called 'inward' or 'outward' orientation. There is also far more to industrialization policy than simply trade policy. These would have seemed banal and obvious things to say had there not been such inordinate attention paid to the role of anti-export bias in trade policies in recent writing on industrialization, from Little, Scitovsky, and Scott through the World Bank's *World Development Report, 1987*.

How is it best to begin a systematic reconsideration of the relationships between trade policy, industrialization, and development? An essential and obvious early step is a review of the most relevant literature relating to the developing countries, with particular emphasis on empirical studies. This volume begins with state-of-the-art surveys of some of the major issues raised by the 'new' trade theories—learning, scale, market structure, externalities, and certain institutional influences upon trade performance. It then presents a series of somewhat 'structuralist' or 'new' trade-theory-oriented case-studies of particular developing countries and particular industries. I hope that these may stimulate empirically oriented readers to undertake the many more such studies that are obviously now required.

In the sphere of trade policy the gap between theoretical explorations of alternative possibilities and detailed knowledge of actual experience has recently grown disturbingly wide. There are by now likely to be much higher social returns from further empirical research upon recent trade and industrialization experience, drawing upon the insights of the current theoretical literature, than from elaborations and refinements of the available theoretical literature itself (though such theoretical research must also obviously continue). In order to try to contribute to the development of the empirical literature which is now so needed the remainder of this introduction is written not only in conventional terms, as a framework for and summary of the chapters that follow, but also, less conventionally, as a guide to the issues that require more research attention. It is organized in the same way as the volume itself—according to (*a*) major issues, and (*b*) country and industry case-studies.

1. MAJOR ISSUES

Learning

The *infant-industry* argument posits that in certain circumstances governmental support for an industry may be justified on a temporary basis to permit it to 'mature' to the point where it can stand on its own feet. In order for this to be theoretically defensible the discounted present value of the future social benefits from the industry must exceed those of the costs during the period of governmental (social) support. It is not enough, that is, to demonstrate that learning takes place in protected industries. Moreover, there must be reasons for believing that private decision-makers are unlikely themselves to act in such a way as to generate the potential excess of social benefits over social costs. One possibility is that the industry in question generates future positive externalities that cannot be captured by the owners. These externalities may be external to the firms but within the industry, or within the industrial sector as a whole, or they may be enjoyed by the national economy outside the industry in question. In the last case the argument sometimes converts into an externality-based argument for governmental intervention on behalf of manufacturing in general. The first-best policy for such externalities is to direct pin-pointed subsidies (or taxes) at the source of the positive (negative) external effects (Baldwin 1969). If these are already provided or if there are no such externalities, the infant-industry argument requires that governmental decision-making in the social interest be governed by factors different from those governing private decisions. There are several such possibilities: (*a*) the government may possess more information about future potential profitability, perhaps because it also knows about others' or its own investment programmes (it is also possible, of course, that bureaucrats, in fact, know less than market participants); (*b*) governments may be less risk-averse than individual private decision-makers because of their much wider (social) portfolio; and (*c*) governments may employ a lower rate in the discounting of the future since they are obliged, in their planning of development, to take a longer view of national interests. Governments may also be legitimately concerned about interactions between learning and market concentration (Dasgupta and Stiglitz 1988).

The optimal instrument of government policy for the support of 'infants' in such cases is, in any case, a production subsidy, not a trade policy intervention that unnecessarily also influences consumption. If the correct instrument is chosen the current costs to society are theoretically reduced and intervention is more likely to be defensible. It is obviously still possible for the present value of future benefits to exceed that of costs even when the latter are unnecessarily inflated by the choice of a second-best policy instrument. Efforts to measure such benefits and costs have, alas, been virtually non-existent. There have been very few efforts even to relate learning to trade or subsidy policies in a systematic manner. One such analysis of Turkish experience found no evidence of greater cost reductions in more heavily protected industries than in others (Krueger and Tuncer 1982); but that is not exactly what is at issue in the debate over the efficacy of infant-industry protection. There can be little question but that the long length of time over which many industries have enjoyed subsidies or protection creates a presumption that the *ex post* benefits have often fallen short of the costs (unless, perhaps, there has been a steady flow of positive externalities). The infant-industry argument has certainly frequently been abused. On the other hand, subsidies and trade barriers do sometimes come down as well as rise, and the record of the past, even if effectively demonstrated to have been a bad one, need not be relevant to the deployment of the appropriate policies in the here and now, or in the future.

The efficacy of governmental intervention via subsidies or trade policy based upon the time-worn infant-industry argument hinges critically upon the degree to which learning and therefore productivity improvement (cost reduction) occurs with experience and/or time. The same is true of governmental interventions motivated by the newer 'strategic' arguments. More broadly still, the relationship between learning or productivity improvement and governmental trade (and other) policies ought to be of far greater interest to developing-country policy-makers than the possible benefits from the essentially once-for-all static reallocation of resources that trade theory traditionally emphasizes. It is therefore important to survey what is known from empirical evidence on these links, as Howard Pack does in Chapter 2, and to reconsider the theoretical arguments that relate to these matters, as Dani Rodrik does in Chapter 6. Other authors also address these issues in this volume, most notably Richard Baldwin, Chang-ho Yoon, and Leonard

Waverman and Steven Murphy in their industry case-studies, Albert Berry in his survey of scale issues, and Donald Keesing and Sanjaya Lall in their analysis of learning in export marketing.

Pack particularly emphasizes the need for more studies that elucidate the social returns from alternative instruments for the acquisition of technology. Despite the conceptual and measurement problems associated with the concept of total factor productivity (TFP) he also calls for further research on the determinants, or at least concomitants, of rapid TFP growth at the industry level, about which there is still surprisingly little known. Is there, for instance, any relationship between TFP improvement either at the industry or the country level, and firm size? market structure? foreign participation in ownership? foreign licensing? threshold factors like per capita income or skill base? exposure to external competition? factor-intensity? macroeconomic conditions? liberalization episodes? Does the stability of incentives matter? Are long-run effects adequately captured in short-period measurements and analyses? Can one decompose technical change and TFP improvement into more specific elements, for example adaptation of existing technique, improved skill base, 'pure' learning-by-doing, etc.? What, in fact, has been the experience in specific industries and countries in respect of the time-path and the concomitants of the acquisition of indigenous 'technological mastery'?

Rodrik argues that, even in theory, the relationships between trade policy and growth in technical efficiency are dubious, that many of the arguments used by liberalizers lack sound theoretical underpinnings, and that the relevant empirical evidence is lacking. He also notes the expanding number of cases of developing-country trade liberalization which may now be carefully studied, always seeking to identify the particular role played by trade rather than macroeconomic policy reform. There is evidently room for *much* more empirical research into these matters.

Scale

Scale and scope economies have always figured prominently in the literature of industrial organization. They have also traditionally played an important role in trade policy debates in small and/or developing countries where limited domestic market size raises obvious questions as to minimum efficient scale plants (Eastman and Stykolt 1967; Harris 1985; Dixit 1987). Modern trade theory has resurrected their importance in mainstream literature (Helpman 1984). Allowing for scale economies has significantly increased the estimated social returns from trade liberalization in some recent studies, although the outcome could, in principle, also turn out otherwise (Harris and Cox 1983; Rodrik 1988).

Current mainstream explanations of international trading patterns draw heavily upon the concept (if not much hard evidence) of scale economies. The current conventional wisdom has it that North–South trade is predominantly inter-industry and Heckscher–Ohlin in character (that is it is based upon different factor endowments), whereas North–North trade is predominantly intra-industry trade, driven by product differentiation and scale economies. The potential for intra-industry South–South trade has also frequently been noted. Despite evidence that this is not always the case, the view that developing countries are most likely to export standardized products nevertheless continues to dominate. More careful and detailed analysis of developing countries' success (and further potential) in the export of differentiated 'niche' goods and services benefiting from scale economies would almost certainly be fruitful.

Arguments for governmental trade policy interventions based upon domestic factor market distortions also frequently relate, in large part, to the differential structure of factor prices faced by large and small firms. Their different technologies or choice of techniques also imply that differing firm size structures will generate different income distributions; thus distribution-related arguments for governmental interventions may also require knowledge of the significance of differences in firm size. Indeed in development debates there has long been intense interest in differences in firm size, *particularly* because of their implications for employment and distributional equity. Large firms may also be more powerful political actors than small ones, so that there may be indirect longer-run implications for development via the influence upon governmental policies wielded by differing firm size structures.

Albert Berry surveys the overall state of knowledge about the interrelationships between firm (or plant) size and trade policies in Chapter 3. What is striking about his survey of the role of firm (or plant) size in trade performance and development is how limited our knowledge is. Intra-industry heterogeneity of firms—particularly in respect of size and choice of technique—is typically very great. Yet we are uncertain as to either the implications of trade policies for the intra-industry size composition of output or their consequent effects. Scale or scope economies may be important in particular developing country industries but Berry guesses that in a wide range of cases they may be non-existent or small. In manufacturing for export, however, the requirements of international marketing and quality control, and the need to stay abreast of global technical change all seem to imply a certain minimum scale and capital intensity (see also Chapter 7). Unless ways are found of encouraging small firms to network or co-operate in exporting, more outward-oriented trade policy may therefore not directly generate the developmental effects that many expect.

Market Structure

Market structure features prominently in the 'new' trade theories. Indeed their central feature is the incorporation of some of the insights of industrial organization analysis into the consideration of trade policies. The empirical literature on market structure in the manufacturing sector in developing countries is somewhat spotty. Norman Lee effectively surveys what there is in Chapter 4.

There is probably more room for manageable, fresh empirical research of a purely descriptive character, under the general heading of market structure than under the headings of scale, learning, or externalities. Both at the national and the international level there are both inadequate data on and inadequate analyses of non-competitive circumstances. Lee reminds us that measurements of market concentration, contestability, ease of entry and exit, are not without serious problems in the mainstream literature; but even the crudest measurements are infrequently available in developing-country circumstances. Further measurement problems arise in attempting to develop similar measures for industries at the global level. The degree to which national markets are truly segmentable one from another, the appropriate definition of international (or global) industries, the treatment of the enormous variety of coalitions and inter-firm links (majority ownership; joint ventures; technology, management, and marketing contracts; co-production schemes; long-term contracts; informal market-sharing; cartels; etc.) are among the areas of difficulty. What is now the role of price competition versus non-price competition in the international industries of greatest interest to developing countries? Have product characteristics (locations or 'addresses' in characteristics space (Lipsey and Dobson 1987)) played or are they likely to play an important role in developing countries' penetration of global markets in these industries?

Another dimension of market structure that has featured prominently in industrialization debates in small and/or developing countries is the role of foreign ownership, and therefore intra-firm trade. In Chapter 8 Winston Fritsch and Gustavo Franco assess emerging trends in manufacturing and manufactured goods trade in Brazil, and draw implications that are potentially of much wider relevance. They argue that the behaviour of transnational corporations, driven by a logic that encompasses global profit calculations rather than purely national considerations, has been an important, though certainly not the only important, determinant of recent Brazilian trading patterns.

A further dimension of market structure research thus relates to the phenomenon of intra-firm trade (which, of course, has its own definitional difficulties). Where is it found? What difference does it make? What are the emerging links between trade policies, investment policies, and the character of international trade and investment flows, including VERs, VIEs, and 'quid pro quo DFI' (Bhagwati 1987*b*)? More broadly, what influence does industrial organization in all its complexity have upon differential export performance across countries, and within countries, over time?

Externalities

The possibility that manufacturing industries generate positive externalities and that they therefore deserve special governmental support through trade policy and other instruments has long rationalized protectionist practices in countries with weak industrial sectors. The empirical literature on the presence or, better, the size of such externalities—whether positive or negative—is nevertheless quite limited. Economists continue to find it extremely difficult to measure such effects even where, as in the case of environmental pollution, there is fairly universal agreement that they are likely to be important. Richard Baldwin's case-study of strategic trade policy in the Brazilian civil aircraft industry (Chapter 9) innovates in its incorporation of positive training externalities into its social benefit-cost analysis. Frances Stewart and Ejaz Ghani present a survey, inevitably largely taxonomic rather than empirical, of externality issues and their relationship to trade policies for development in Chapter 5. On the basis of their account, it seems safe to say that of all the relatively neglected trade policy issues that are highlighted in this volume, externalities pose the greatest difficulties for empirical research and practical policy-makers. It is nevertheless important to pose the questions to which they give rise.

Is there real content in the concept of 'basic' or 'strategic' (not in the game-theoretic meaning) industries? Can one identify measurable positive externalities from various kinds of industrial activities in 'successful' developing-countries' experiences? Are there analogous examples in the industrialized countries' historical record? Can one pursue this question, say, with reference to current claims for informatics in Brazil or India, or other similar cases? (The chapter by Stewart and Ghani includes material on the Silicon Valley experience in the US that is suggestive of the type of evidence one would be seeking.) What about improved measurement of such qualitative matters as 'linkage' effects, training effects, managerial experience, etc.?

Institutional Influences

Incentive structures, as modified by governmental trade, exchange rate, and other policies, are obviously of major importance to trading and industrialization performance. Not only is the overall degree of neutrality of these incentive structures as between exporting and import-competing activities relevant to performance but so also are their dispersion among different activities within these categories, their stability and predictability over time, and their transparency.

No economist would dream of minimizing the importance of incentive structures. But these are not the only determinants of trade or other economic performance. Structural and institutional features of economies, often unique to particular industries or countries, may seriously limit the capacity of economic actors to respond to incentives, sometimes affecting some significantly more than others, for example large firms as against small. Development is a process in which increasing numbers of actors find it possible to respond to economic and other opportunities. More 'structurally' and 'institutionally' orientated economists place considerable emphasis upon non-price constraints and policy measures in the course of the development process. In the context of the current keen interest in export-oriented industrialization it is especially important to analyse the institutional/structural requirements of policies that pursue it. To do this requires assessment of policy failures as well as successes in this realm. In Chapter 7 Donald Keesing and Sanjaya Lall survey experience in this non-price arena. They argue, as many do, the importance of free access to inputs. But they also argue that public support for knowledge acquisition in the specific case of export marketing is socially justifiable; this, they say, must be carefully designed and sequenced if it is to succeed. Empirical research into the non-price dimensions of successful exporting has been relatively neglected by trade economists but, significantly, not by the business schools. Further research, such as that of Levy on the comparative structural characteristics of exporters in Taiwan and Korea (1988) and that of Rhee *et al.* in Korean global market entry (1985), could also be very useful.

2. CASE-STUDIES—COUNTRIES AND INDUSTRIES

Case-studies are sometimes derided as too partial and too 'anecdotal' to contribute to the development of general knowledge. In this field, however, as indeed in all of economics (if economists are honest with themselves) there are *no* universal truths. Carefully structured comparative studies of countries and industries can play an important part in the development of understanding and relevant theory. Part II of this volume contains case-studies that indicate some of the possibilities for further study. In the first study the authors Winston Fritsch and Gustavo Franco highlight certain 'structural' characteristics of a particular national economy and their impact upon trade experience, exploring provocatively the links between foreign direct investment and trade performance in Brazil. Evidently there is *much* more of such 'structural' research to be done at the level of country case-studies.

There has recently been a whole research industry built upon demonstrating the virtues of 'liberalizing' trade in developing countries (Choksi and Papageorgiou 1986; Papageorgiou *et al.* 1986). Granting that the incentive structure *is* usually biased against exports and that effective subsidies in import-competing industries *are* typically over-differentiated and irrational, there are still a great many issues deserving of greater research exploration. Not least are the likely (simulated) effects of wholesale liberalization in circumstances of market imperfections, scale economies, and foreign ownership, where they have not yet taken place; and as suggested earlier, careful analysis of the effects where they have.

Distrust of the capacity of governments to 'pick winners', or, more to the point, to create them (see Chapter 5) leads most mainstream economists to recommend against an 'active' industrial policy that targets assistance to particular industries or firms, as opposed to generalized support for training, research, etc. Certainly there are reasons for doubt as to the capacity of governments to assemble and process the information that would be required, as Chang-ho Yoon argues in Chapter 10. Governments are also susceptible to pressure from interest groups. And the record of governmental intervention in this sphere includes some monumental disasters. But recitation of the many government mistakes in this sphere does not constitute analysis. Despite mainstream presumptions, for which there is sound theoretical and empirical backing, there do exist examples of apparent success; and they deserve study. Moreover, some of the apparent short-term 'failures' may have generated happier longer-run results (Westphal 1982). Why have some governments achieved significantly better (or worse) 'batting averages' in their selection of winners than others? Analysis of the Korean experience—in terms of the efficiency and welfare implications of alternative approaches—may be particularly rewarding. What have been the principal, and the most effective and ineffective, instruments of developing-country governments' industrial, trade, and investment policies? If governmental interventions are temporary, at what point in the firm's or industry's life are they most productive? Also of interest is the degree to which apparent import liberalization in developing countries has, as in industrialized countries, led to increased use of alternative firm-specific and industry-specific governmental policy instruments.

The potential and problems of second-best or strategic export subsidies, which are likely to be of increased importance in the 1990s, certainly also deserve more attention than they have thus far received. Do the GATT and the emerging 'countervail' system really rule export subsidies out? What about alternative devices for encouraging 'infant firms' to develop export activities? *Is* it as difficult for 'late-comer' developing countries to pick likely medium-term 'winners' as it is for those trying to operate on the technological frontier?

In the rest of Part II a small sample of industry case-studies is presented. As has been noted above, Richard Baldwin and Chang-ho Yoon have here deployed the approaches of those who have analysed strategic trade policy in the industrialized countries to analyse, respectively, the civil aircraft industry in Brazil and the semiconductor industry in Korea. Baldwin's chapter is illustrative of the methodology rather than suggestive of strong policy conclusions; but his calibration of a model of an oligopolistic Brazilian export industry indicates that, taking account of labour-training effects, government subsidies may have been justified. Yoon demonstrates how a private Korean firm, evidently *without* direct governmental support, successfully penetrated a high-technology oligopolistic global industry by filling a market 'niche' left in consequence of investment 'wars' among leading US and Japanese firms seeking to capture an advantage in the next stages of technological and product development.

Leonard Waverman and Steven Murphy present a very useful and original alternative approach to industry-level analysis. By comparing appropriate measures of TFP in the same (automobile) industry across several countries (Argentina, Mexico, Korea, and Canada) and over time they are able to estimate industry-level costs of protection (they are high), establish whether TFP growth rates are related to trade policy regimes (they are not), and investigate the links between TFP growth, international competitiveness, and social benefit. (Their more complete analysis of productivity in the international automobile industry will be made available in a separate WIDER monograph.)

There is clearly room for many more detailed case-studies of the evolution of individual industries both at the national and at global levels. Industrial adjustment processes have been the subject of a great deal of attention in the industrialized countries during the past decade. There is still, however, a dearth of careful industry-level analyses of firm and industry behaviour in response to international competitive pressure. The detailed industrial organizational and trade (and investment) compositional effects of the NICs' increasing penetration of Northern markets for particular products, the 'strategic' behaviour of threatened firms (and governments), and the time-profile of change in different industries and countries, all could benefit from further analyses. Is there, for instance, an optimal speed of adjustment? On what country or industry-specific factors might it depend? Within developing countries, the 'transitional' experience of domestic industries and labour markets in episodes of trade liberalization deserve similar expanded analysis. Developing countries' industries face 'exit' issues as well as the 'entry' problems upon which the development literature has tended to focus.

In this context, it is noteworthy that 'the international division of labour'—whether in its neoclassical or its radical version—has typically been interpreted in narrow geographic and static terms. International trade theory has concentrated upon the location of production of *known products*. It has had very little to say about the comparative advantages of particular nations' *firms* (regardless of where they locate their activities), these firms' *life cycles*, or the generation of *new products*. US-owned transnational corporations have done much better in international competition in recent years than have firms with a US geographic location (Lipsey and Kravis 1985). Governments in rich nations and poor seek success for 'national champion' firms (sometimes state-owned) no less than for particular industries. It may be fruitful to analyse carefully the evolution of some of the successful large industrial firms in the developing countries, particularly those that export.

The importance of product differentiation and the finding of 'niches' in characteristics space cannot be over-emphasized in small countries. Yet in the developing-country trade literature these issues rarely surface. As has been seen, the assumption seems to be that developing countries can only sell standardized and homogeneous products; yet the evidence is by now very much to the contrary. Defining 'industries' appropriately may therefore be a crucial part of the design of industry-level research.

Quantitative modelling is often appropriate and possible at the industry level. Partial analysis of inter-country and/or inter-firm rivalry and strategic behaviour under varying assumptions regarding learning curves, behavioural rules (conjectural variations), etc. has been productive in several industrialized-country studies, and in those by Baldwin and Yoon in this volume. There is room not only for further simulations of this type but also for more careful and detailed micro-level research on the functioning of individual firms and industries both in developing countries and in the wider context of the global market-place.

REFERENCES

BALASSA, BELA (1990), 'Outward Orientation', in Hollis Chenery and T. N. Srinivasan (eds.), *Handbook of Development Economics* (North-Holland, Amsterdam).

BALDWIN, ROBERT (1969), 'The Case against Infant-Industry Tariff Protection', *Journal of Political Economy*, 77, pp. 295–305.

BHAGWATI, JAGDISH (1978), *Foreign Trade Regimes and Economic Development: Anatomy and Consequences of Exchange Control* (Ballinger, Cambridge, Mass.).

——(1987a), 'Outward Orientation: Trade Issues', in Vittorio Corbo, Morris Goldstein, and Mohsin Khan (eds.), *Growth-Oriented Adjustment Programs* (International Monetary Fund/World Bank, Washington, DC), pp. 257–90.

—— (1987b), 'VERs, Quid pro Quo DFI and VIEs: Political Economy Theoretic Analysis', *International Economic Journal*, 1/1.
BRANDER, J. A., and SPENCER, B. J. (1985), 'Export Subsidies and International Market Share Rivalry', *Journal of International Economics*, 18, pp. 83–100.
CHENERY, H. B. (1961), 'Comparative Advantage and Development Policy', *American Economic Review*, 51 (Mar.), pp. 18–51.
CHOKSI, A., and PAPAGEORGIOU, D. (eds.) (1986), *Economic Liberalization in Developing Countries* (Blackwell, Oxford).
DASGUPTA, PARTHA, and STIGLITZ, JOSEPH (1988), 'Learning-by-Doing, Market Structure and Industrial and Trade Policies', *Oxford Economic Papers*, 40/2, pp. 246–68.
DIAZ-ALEJANDRO, C. F. (1975), 'Trade Policies and Economic Development', in Peter Kenen (ed.), *International Trade and Finance, Frontiers for Research* (CUP, Cambridge).
DIXIT, AVINASH (1987), 'Trade Strategies for Small Countries', *Scandinavian Journal of Economics*, 83/3, pp. 349–68.
EASTMAN, H. C., and STYKOLT, S. (1967), *The Tariff and Competition in Canada* (Macmillan, Toronto).
HARRIS, RICHARD G. (1985), *Trade, Industrial Policy and International Competition* (University of Toronto Press, Toronto).
—— and COX, D. (1983), *Trade, Industrial Policy and Canadian Manufacturing* (Ontario Economic Council, Toronto).
HELLEINER, G. K. (1990), 'Trade Strategy in Medium-Term Adjustment', WIDER, *World Development* (June), mimeo.
HELPMAN, ELHANAN (1984), 'Increasing Returns, Imperfect Markets, and Trade Theory', in W. Jones and P. B. Kenen (eds.), *Handbook of International Economics*, 1 (North-Holland, Amsterdam), pp. 325–66.
KRUEGER, A. O. (1978), *Liberalization Attempts and Consequences* (National Bureau of Economic Research, New York).
—— (1984), 'Trade Policies in Developing Countries', in R. W. Jones and P. B. Kenen (eds.), *Handbook of International Economics*, 1 (North-Holland, Amsterdam), pp. 519–69.
—— and TUNCER, BARAN (1982), 'An Empirical Test of the Infant Industry Argument', *American Economic Review*, 72/5, pp. 1142–52.
KRUGMAN, PAUL (ed.) (1986a), *Strategic Trade Policy and the New International Economics* (MIT Press, Cambridge, Mass.).
—— (1986b), 'New Trade Theory and the Developing Countries', (WIDER), mimeo.
—— (1987), 'Is Free Trade Passé', *Journal of Economic Perspectives*, 1/2, pp. 131–44.
LEVY, BRIAN (1988), 'Korean and Taiwanese Firms as International Competitors: The Challenges Ahead', *Columbia Journal of World Business*, Spring.
LIPSEY, RICHARD, and DOBSON, WENDY (eds.) (1987), *Shaping Comparative Advantage* (C. D. Howe Institute, Toronto).
—— and KRAVIS, IRVING B. (1985), 'The International Competitiveness of U.S. Firms' (Working Paper 1557, National Bureau of Economic Research, New York).

LITTLE, IAN, SCITOVSKY, TIBOR, and SCOTT, MAURICE (1970), *Industry and Trade in Some Developing Countries: A Comparative Study* (OUP, Oxford).

PAPAGEORGIOU, DEMETRIS, MICHAELY, MICHAEL, and CHOKSI, ARMEANE (1986), 'The Phasing of a Trade Liberalization Policy: Preliminary Evidence' (paper presented to the American Economic Association convention, Dec.), CPD Discussion Paper, 1986–42 (World Bank, Washington, DC).

RHEE, YUNG WHEE, ROSS-LARSON, B., and PURSELL, G. (1985), *Korea's Competitive Edge, Managing the Entry into World Markets* (Johns Hopkins University Press for the World Bank, Baltimore).

RODRIK, DANI (1988), 'Imperfect Competition, Scale Economies, and Trade Policy in Developing Countries', in R. E. Baldwin (ed.), *Trade Policy Issues and Empirical Analysis* (University of Chicago, Chicago).

WESTPHAL, L. E. (1982), 'Fostering Technological Mastery by Means of Selective Industry Promotion', in M. Syrquin and S. Teitel (eds.), *Trade, Stability, Technology and Equity in Latin America* (Academic Press, New York).

WORLD BANK (1987), *World Development Report, 1987* (World Bank, Washington, DC).

PART I

Major Issues:
The State of Knowledge

2

Learning and Productivity Change in Developing Countries*

Howard Pack

1. INTRODUCTION

The topic of this chapter, learning and technical change in manufacturing, is the most recent incarnation of an issue that has a long history in development economics—the relation between education and growth. Much of the newest literature that considers growing technical competence in manufacturing firms to be a result of purposive effort by firm managers disregards earlier analysis of the returns to formal education and on-the-job training of workers and managers (OECD 1964; Psacharopoulos 1985). The latter studies provide measures that have been placed into a conventional growth-accounting framework. The new literature on technical change at the firm level cannot so easily fit into growth accounting; while it can be viewed as an effort to explain the determinants of the 'residual', most of the underlying studies do not have such a motivation.[1] Rather, they are best understood as asking: (*a*) how the production function for a given product comes into being in a particular country; and (*b*) what permits the growth of efficiency in the initially established production function. While the second objective might be thought of as similar to explanations of the residual, very few of these studies explicitly undertake growth accounting rather than describe the methods adopted by firms to improve efficiency. An important potential connection to normative analysis is thus missed.

This chapter has the following structure. Section 2 reviews some of the major findings of the literature on micro-level technical change in less developed country (LDC) manufacturing. Section 3 evaluates the normative implications of this research. Section 4 reviews and attempts to explain the results of growth-accounting exercises of the manufacturing sector in LDCs. Section 5 reviews some of the issues posed by new theories of international trade. Conclusions are presented in Section 6.

---

* Helpful comments on an earlier draft were received form G. Helleiner, G. Franco, D. Rodrik, and F. Stewart.

2. A REVIEW OF THE LITERATURE ON FIRM-LEVEL TECHNICAL CHANGE

The new literature on technical change in LDCs had a simultaneous flowering in a number of locales, particularly Latin America and India. Katz and his co-workers and Lall sought to document that industrial firms in LDCs were active participants in the industrialization process.[2] Rather than simply purchasing foreign equipment and using it according to prevailing norms, an indigenous effort was undertaken, particularly in large firms, that changed the method of production. Machine performance was altered to increase potential output, the production process was changed to allow for the use of local raw materials with different properties, and new products were developed. Most of the changes documented were incremental rather than major technological breakthroughs. Cumulatively, they had a substantial impact on the imported manufacturing process and the products available—altering the received technology to make it relevant for local conditions. The documentation of this indigenous technical change is intrinsically interesting and provides a good antidote to the view, implicit in international trade theory and microeconomics, of a uniform international technology costlessly available to everyone.

These efforts replicated the vast literature in the economic history of the developed countries concerned with the process of industrialization. The documentation of minor technical change has been a staple of these studies. Landes's well-known book (1969) provided detailed descriptions of similar changes and related them to the larger framework of the Industrial Revolution. For many major industry sectors technical change and the complex interaction of technology and economics have been exhaustively documented (Hughes 1970). Those familiar with standard economic history would hardly be surprised by the results obtained in the new industrialization literature. Many LDC manufacturing firms have inevitably emulated technical trajectories that were established in the early industrializing nations. Having purchased equipment from developed countries, they inevitably encountered both technical and economic problems not found in the country of origin of the equipment and responded to the differing conditions. While it is reassuring that the challenge–response paradigm receives another confirmation, it is difficult to see how it could have been otherwise. Only rigid disciples of dependency theory, whose familiarity with technology appears limited to the nuances of espresso machines, could confidently assert the technical incompetence and incapacity to learn of their compatriots.

2.1 The Economic Significance of Technical Change in LDCs

One major difference between the new technology studies and those of previous economic historians is immediately apparent. When the latter documented a cost-saving innovation, the development of a new product, or a better method of utilizing local resources, they could usually be sure that the innovation improved social welfare. Factor and product markets were largely undistorted. Product or process innovation that was successful implied that consumer or producer surplus at shadow prices was improved. Since the firms examined were at the technical frontier and there were no alternative sources of these products in other countries, or transportation costs were very high, private and social profitability were closely (but not perfectly) related.[3]

In contrast, the new studies in LDCs provide an interesting economic history of technical evolution and the basis for a richer paradigm about technological development than the one derived from the history of the developed countries (Dahlman and Westphal 1982; Katz 1984). They do not, however, lend themselves to an assessment of the economic significance of the phenomena so assiduously described. Most of the documented innovation has occurred in countries that have followed intensive import-substitution strategies.[4] Given the resulting price distortions, private returns are not of particular interest; unfortunately, the social rate of return on innovative activity has not been calculated. Assuming that there were gains in consumers' surplus from improved processes, some could have been achieved in a less costly manner by removing restrictions on imports, whether they took the form of tariffs or quotas.

Moreover, the emphasis in the recent technical change studies on the firm rather than the industry makes it difficult to evaluate the significance of the reported innovative activity. The increased producers' surplus stemming from improved efficiency might have been still greater had there been general incentives to induce all firms to meet foreign competition. The intense spotlight documenting the effort of a few firms leaves one in the dark about the extent of innovation. Was it characteristic of the entire industry within which the firms operated or was it an isolated phenomenon? Given the variation in intra-industry productivity that is a feature of all estimates of best-practice production functions in LDCs,[5] the extent of such technical efforts is an important question. An attempt to assess, retrospectively, whether the Mill–Bastable (M–B) criterion (that the discounted present value of the social gains must exceed those of the social costs) was satisfied on an industry-wide basis has not been undertaken in any of the studies, although initial costs of protection (and those of perhaps misdirected innovative efforts) are well known.

One partial indicator that the M–B criterion may have been satisfied is the growth of total factor productivity (TFP) in an industry or sector. However, almost all of the technical change studies examine the history of only one or two firms. Even if they experienced growth in TFP, as Katz *et al.* (1987) convincingly document for an Argentine rayon firm, such growth may not have diffused throughout a generally inefficient sector. The improved efficiency for one or two firms lowers the real resource cost of production for them but may not lead to any gain in consumers' surplus, and the total welfare improvement may well be very small. Thus, even though the industry was not the focus of attention in the various firm studies, an evaluation of the social significance of innovation necessarily requires industry- or sector-wide analysis.

2.2 The Contrast with the East Asian NICs

In contrast to the intensive study of process innovation in some countries characterized by import-substituting industrialization (ISI), there is less documentation of what happened in the case of the East Asian newly industrializing countries (NICs). This gap does not necessarily imply that similar efforts were not undertaken—they may simply not have been studied. Nevertheless, my suspicion is that further research would turn up a significantly different picture from that characterizing India and some Latin American import-substituting countries. Most of the innovative activity in the latter countries, carefully studied by various authors, was a response to the limits imposed by ISI policies.[6] Foreign-exchange shortages led firms to attempt to increase the output from existing machinery or to substitute domestic for imported raw materials. While there was some product innovation, many of these products, particularly in Argentina, were sold within the protected Latin American Free Trade Area.[7]

In East Asia the availability at international prices of traded inputs—machinery, raw materials, and intermediates—precluded the need for unique, site- and material-specific innovations that were not purchasable on the world market (Keesing and Lall, Chapter 7 this volume). Thus, the Koreans and Taiwanese were able to marshall their technical abilities to product innovations that satisfied world demand, to evaluating potential suppliers of technology, and to choosing appropriate modes of technology transfer. During the 1960s and much of the 1970s, firms in the Gang of Four appear to have spent greater effort at perfecting products, for example by achieving improved fit of clothing, greater durability of finishes, stronger stitching, and introducing new materials such as velcro. Moreover, they frequently entered new product areas, an achievement that was important to their growth (see Section 4.3).

In Korea much of the relevant knowledge came from foreign purchasers of these products (Westphal et al. 1984). Buyers of Gang of Four exports established resident buying-offices that provided advice on quality control and design changes (Keesing and Lall, Chapter 7 this volume). Calling the knowledge so obtained 'product innovation' would be an exaggeration; yet the economic value (at shadow prices) is clear. Moreover, such a transfer of knowledge is likely to have a very high rate of return given the relatively small costs incurred by local producers. While the absorption of knowledge about Western sizes, quality requirements, and new designs certainly required real resources, they are likely to have been small compared with the costs incurred in the process-innovation efforts in the ISI countries.

Roughly, the development process in the East Asian countries appears to have been one in which initial isoquants were inherited from a fairly robust industrial past or obtained by transfer of simple technologies from more industrialized countries. These were slowly improved over time. Firms met export demand by growing along the expansion path dictated by their slightly altered isoquants and changing relative factor prices.[8] This is not to imply that the process was simply the result of market forces. There was considerable government direction of this effort (Pack and Westphal 1986; Wade 1990), particularly with respect to new capital and technology-intensive industries. But the major pattern in the Gang of Four was that an initial set of technologically simple industries grew vigorously, providing foreign exchange for the acquisition of still more equipment and raw materials; only after industrialization was well launched did substantial (and necessary) efforts begin to stimulate new domestic technological development. In contrast to the import-substituting countries, much of this next stage was pursued through technology licensing rather than indigenous research. The Gang of Four, like Japan before them, were quite willing to be 'dependent' on imported machinery and production knowledge though to varying degrees they insisted on contracts that provided a substantial amount of domestic learning.

In some instances firms in India and Latin America could not purchase relevant technology. Companies on the technology frontier in the industrialized countries had not been forced to utilize the local raw materials and were certainly not interested in some of the (socially) appropriate product innovations in countries with lower incomes and smaller markets. With respect to appropriate product innovations, net social benefits from local innovation may have occurred in so far as such products were not available on the world market. (Border prices are not of much help in the assessment of the value of innovations in non-traded products.) However, the technical change studies emphasize process rather than product innovation and the former certainly requires a social benefit-cost justification. However, most authors who describe technical change in the internally oriented Latin American countries claim that the net benefit of innovation is very difficult to estimate. Often it is asserted that their 'dynamic' nature makes it impossible to measure benefits while joint costs make it very difficult to estimate costs for individual products in multiproduct firms. Hence, no social evaluation is possible of the benefits and costs of the documented technical change.

A variety of research strategies is in fact available to meet these problems, but none has been pursued (Mansfield 1977). This gap not only precludes a test of whether innovation effort meets the standard welfare criterion, but also prevents an examination of another important question, namely whether some of the development of knowledge locally, where it was similar to that purchasable in international markets, was the least-cost method of acquiring specific capability. For example was local development cheaper than licensing of technology or entering into joint ventures?

Most studies of Japanese industrial development and more recently of the Gang of Four document the considerable purchase, particularly through licensing, of relevant foreign technology. Part of the difference in behaviour may be the near obsession in many of the inward-oriented economies with the possibility of excessive royalty payments for technology licences.[9] Even if this were the case, an issue rarely investigated empirically,[10] licensing still might have been a more cost-effective path to the acquisition of relevant technological capacity. While many analysts of LDC technical development reject this option, arguing that it does not generate sufficient 'dynamic' indigenous learning, they never calculate the benefits and costs of the alternative methods of technology acquisition; nor do they document the superiority of domestic efforts relative to licensing.[11] The concern with learning often has unfortunate parallels with earlier views of the desirability of ISI. While learning is to be fostered—witness the important role the government played in Japan, Korea, and Taiwan—the relative effectiveness of alternative instruments that can be employed is a critical issue requiring investigation.[12]

3. NORMATIVE ANALYSIS

One of the features of the technology studies is the sole emphasis on the technical improvement in manufacturing processing without regard for factor and product prices. One does not learn whether the firms being studied are capable of competing on the world market given their current productivity. *A fortiori* there is no effort to provide measures of the ability to compete in an undistorted environment using domestic resource cost (DRC) measures. It may be the case that even with unimproved initial levels of productivity, import liberalization that permitted inputs to be purchased at international prices would have permitted competition in international markets. If not, then the relevant issue is whether the technical progress of the firms is sufficiently rapid to offset the growing technical efficiency of more productive firms in the rest of the world. Competitiveness at world prices is always a relevant issue unless it can be shown that the 'dynamic' benefits are very great. Indeed, despite extensive intervention,

South Korea clearly used the ability to export after a limited period of protection as the criterion to decide whether government programmes should be initiated and when they should be terminated (Pack and Westphal 1986).

To assess competitiveness, it is necessary to know whether the firms' progress is as fast as that of major competitors, whether changes are occurring in factor proportions employed, and what is happening to the level of factor prices. A focus solely on the absolute technical performance of local enterprise conveys little meaningful information to permit determination of whether industries have improved their relative standing in the world.

A useful format for viewing these issues is provided by Nishimizu and Page (1986). They decompose the domestic resource cost (DRC) and show that changes in it over time reflect four additive effects: changes in the shadow price of primary factors, changes in world prices which themselves reflect movements in total factor productivity in major trading nations, gains from improved factor choice, and the rate of growth of domestic total factor productivity (TFP). The decomposition is:

$$DRC^* = S_L w^* - S_K r^* - p^* + [S_L - a_L]L^* \\ + [S_K - a_K]K^* - TFP^*, \qquad (1)$$

Where asterisks denote rates of growth, S_i denotes the share of labour, L, or capital, K, at shadow prices, p is the world price, and a_i the share of each factor at market prices.

Assuming that factor shares at market prices are not too different from those at shadow prices and that changes in relative factor prices are small, equation (1) simplifies to

$$DRC^* = -p^* - TFP^*. \qquad (2)$$

If the long-run growth of TFP abroad is reflected in changing prices for foreign products, movements in DRC depend solely on the relative rate of growth of domestic factor productivity versus that of major trading nations. Unfortunately, despite their insights, many of the studies documenting technical change provide no systematic measures either of total factor productivity in the firms (or industry) undergoing technical change nor of the rates of productivity growth in similar foreign industries. Research by Teitel and Thoumi (1986) suggests that some of the learning generated during the import-substitution period has begun to generate exports in Argentina and Brazil. Some of the exporting industries are those that Katz and his co-workers investigate. Exports, even if they are efficient, do not demonstrate that the initial deadweight loss incurred during the learning period was justified; Teitel and Thoumi provide evidence that sufficient learning has occurred so that DRC has been falling as a result of the differential productivity movements shown in equation (2).

The literature on micro-technical change underlines an important point which is easy to overlook in the reigning condemnation of ISI. Underlying ISI policies was the possibility, and hope, that learning would result in downward shifts in industry supply curves. The studies of technical change suggest that improved productivity may in fact have occurred, partially vindicating the expectations of ISI advocates. Such learning may not, however, have resulted in increasing competitiveness in world markets (taken on faith that local TFP growth exceeded foreign) if the protective regime did not encourage firms to compete in the international market. Improved technological capability, measured by greater TFP, was offset in many cases by the continued high cost of traded inputs, by a protective regime which permitted owners of primary inputs successfully to obtain returns greater than warranted by their productivity in a competitive system,[13] by short production runs and the ensuing higher costs generated by reliance on small domestic markets, and so on.[14] If the fruits of extensive learning are to lead to widely diffused social benefits, trade liberalization is required to ensure some reduction in prices. Otherwise the benefits of the technological change in the oligopolistic industries studied by Katz and others may yield rents to innovators but fail to provide benefits to domestic consumers or downstream manufacturers who are potential exporters.

4. SECTORAL PRODUCTIVITY GROWTH IN LDCs

A considerable literature exists on TFP growth in developing countries.[15] Studies of productivity growth in LDCs, like those in the industrialized countries, have relied mainly on growth accounting. While many trenchant criticisms of this method exist (Griliches and Jorgenson 1967; Nelson 1973, 1981) it is difficult to devise an implementable alternative framework for analysing the relevant issues.

Despite the imperfections in TFP measurement, sustained learning at an industry-wide level should be reflected in the growth of measured total factor productivity. Many articles elucidate the methods of computation, their pitfalls, and difficulty of interpretation, particularly within the context of developed countries (Nadiri 1970; Nelson 1981). One problem with measuring TFP in developing countries is the relatively short time-periods for which the requisite data are available. Whereas in the developed countries (DCs), time-series for fifty or more years are not uncommon, LDC data for even twenty years are relatively rare. Such short time-series may be unduly influenced by changing capacity-utilization levels, especially where an attempt is made to build large-scale plants to take advantage of scale economies, but sales are limited to the domestic market so that capacity-utilization increases over time. Cyclical variations are also difficult to deal with and merge into the capacity-utilization problem. In addition, utilization can increase if countries embark on an outward-oriented policy that augments foreign exchange, and allows firms to purchase intermediate inputs necessary for greater output with a fixed plant.

4.1 Measuring the Importance of TFP Growth

Most studies calculate the share of the growth of total output, Q, accounted for by TFP, or TFP^*/Q^* where asterisks denote rates of growth. Using this measure, successful performance is indicated by a high share of output growth that cannot be attributed to primary input growth. While this is a useful approach, there are cogent reasons for also examining the rate of growth of TFP rather than its share in output. For example many of the more successful NICs exhibit a high rate of labour-force growth, a high rate of saving, and an initially low capital/output ratio. These jointly imply a high rate of growth of weighted primary inputs, perhaps 9 per cent per year. If the country achieves a growth of TFP of 3 per cent per year, exceeding that of the change in world-best practice, it is doing quite well in terms of equation (2). Nevertheless, its value of TFP^*/Q^* is 25 per cent, a figure that many of the existing studies of the *relative* importance of TFP growth would consider to be on the low side. However, to conclude from a calculation of TFP^*/Q^* that 'technical progress' is unimportant would be unwarranted. The absolute rate of growth of TFP is a magnitude of interest in the assessment of the performance of economies under different regimes alleged to be more or less conducive to learning. Indeed, in evaluating regimes strictly on their technical performance this may be preferable to measures of TFP^*/Q^*.[16]

4.2 TFP and the Trade Regime

Table 1 presents a set of estimates of TFP growth rates compiled by Nishimizu and Page on two-digit branches in manufacturing (1987).[17] Several observations may be made.

Consider the widely held view that countries with a neutral trade regime will exhibit a higher rate of growth of productivity than those with a protectionist regime. I have shown elsewhere that it is very difficult to confirm this as a general tendency with the evidence currently available, although Korean experience provides confirmation in *one* country (Pack 1988). Here, however, I concentrate on productivity measures for those countries for which micro-studies of technical change discussed above have concluded that rapid learning is occurring. The import-substituting countries whose learning processes in manufacturing have been subjected to considerable scrutiny have not done particularly well. Argentina, India, and

Table 1. Total factor productivity growth by country and industry

	USA 1960–79	Japan 1960–79	Argentina 1956–73	Chile 1960–81	Korea 1960–77	India 1959–79	Singapore 1970–9
Food	1.31	−1.24	−0.82	0.12	5.26	0.24	0.62
Beverages	1.31	−1.24	−0.82	4.74	5.26	−0.90	1.73
Tobacco	−0.68	−1.24	2.83	2.26	5.26	−0.64	3.22
Textiles	1.92	0.31	−0.27	0.19	4.51	0.30	−3.23
Fabricated textiles	1.09	1.01	−0.27	−1.33	1.62	0.30	−2.11
Leather and footwear	0.25	0.69		−2.07	2.80	0.27	−6.50
Wood and products	0.09	1.88	−1.66		5.62	−0.19	−6.57
Furniture and fixtures	0.26	0.95	−1.66	6.57	4.88	0.96	−2.44
Paper and products	−0.16	0.84		2.91	4.52	0.12	2.18
Printing and publishing	0.58	−0.08		0.08		0.01	−1.36
Rubber	2.59	0.59	1.42	−1.50	5.88	−0.81	−1.57
Chemicals and products	1.21	2.44	3.22	−0.18	4.49	−0.36	2.30
Petroleum and coal	−1.79	−3.16		3.69	0.68	0.26	1.49
Non-metallic minerals	0.07	1.20	1.52	3.29	4.53	−0.50	1.44
Ferrous metals	−0.59	0.90	0.55	0.35	1.87	−0.55	3.41
Non-ferrous metals	−0.59	0.12	0.55		1.87	−0.55	−13.87
Metal products	0.50	1.91		5.04	6.01	−0.55	−3.59
Non-electrical machinery	0.36	1.29	6.49		5.73	−0.03	−3.28
Electrical machinery	1.58	3.28	3.28	−1.91	7.25	0.24	−0.04
Transport equipment	0.65	1.41	6.49		5.10	−0.27	1.27
Precision instruments	0.81	2.63			7.25		

Sources: Nishimizu and Page (1987) and Tsao (1985).

Mexico, countries for which firm-level learning has been documented in the studies mentioned earlier, often show negative TFP*. In a few sectors the two Latin American countries show values of TFP* that exceed those of their major trading partner, the US, but this is not a frequent occurrence. The same is true of India when compared with two of its major competitors, Japan and Korea.[18]

In the few sectors in which Argentina and Mexico have experienced TFP growth in excess of the comparable US industry, the technology studies cited do not differentiate between the laggard firms in each sector catching up with best practice within the country and best practice itself being improved as the technically efficient local firms move toward international best practice. Handoussa et al. (1986) have explored this phenomenon in Egypt by obtaining estimates of best-practice frontiers. Their study demonstrates that rapid TFP growth in many Egyptian sectors was attributable solely to improved capacity utilization in low-productivity firms rather than to increasing technical proficiency of the best-practice firms. While the intra-country diffusion of best practice is of considerable importance, it is not the type of technical progress that the micro-studies have attempted to demonstrate.

A major issue that pervades the literature is the alleged beneficial effect of a neutral trade regime relative to one that generates greater profitability from sales in domestic markets. The limited data at the two-digit level shown in Table 1 leave this question moot. South Korea clearly does well; at least one study (Kim and Kwon 1977) has shown, however, that for a considerable part of the period studied, increasing capacity utilization was a major source of measured growth in TFP (though this, of course, is one potential benefit of export orientation). The only other largely outward-oriented country in the sample was Singapore and the results there hardly confirm the view that outward orientation inevitably yields large efficiency gains.[19] In Taiwan, data for the entire manufacturing sector show TFP^*/Q^* equals 25 per cent (Kuo 1983). The evidence on TFP growth is still uneven in coverage across countries and over time; it does not provide strong confirmation for the a priori views of many economists about the superiority of trade neutrality in this respect, certainly not sector by sector.[20] Nevertheless, as Chenery (1986) has shown, the *economy-wide* productivity performance of economies with more neutral trade regimes has been superior to that of the inward-looking ones. Two processes that may underlie this phenomenon are these economies' high initial levels of TFP and their ability to avoid declining terms of trade for manufactured products.

High initial levels of TFP
The poor performance of individual sectors in Singapore,[21] the good, but not spectacular rate of growth of manufacturing-wide TFP in Taiwan of

3 per cent per annum (Kuo 1983), and the mixed performance in individual Korean sectors suggest some problem of interpreting the measured TFP growth rates. It seems unlikely that when plants in Singapore and Taiwan were established, the initial *level* of TFP was high relative to existing international best practice. In Singapore, this is probable because much of the investment was undertaken by multinational corporations (MNCs). Although Taiwan had lower participation of MNCs in its industrial sector, it had benefited from the migration from the mainland of many managers and technicians. If this view is correct, it implies that available TFP growth measures in the East Asian NICs may be deficient, not capturing the rapid initial spurt of productivity growth that permitted a high TFP level to be obtained quickly when industries were established. Such an index-number problem typically does not arise in the developed countries except in new products which are inevitably a small part of most two-digit sectors. While the same measurement problem exists in ISI countries, it may be conjectured that it is not quantitatively important, given the low level of TFP in many countries even after many years of production experience (Pack, 1984, 1987).[22]

Avoiding declining terms of trade
Export orientation increases industry's ability to absorb rapid increases in primary factors.[23] For the two great success stories, South Korea and Taiwan, the stylized facts of growth include both a rapid growth of productive inputs and a fairly high overall rate of TFP growth. Is the success of these two attributable to export orientation and the greater productivity it generated or has the question been incorrectly phrased?

Consider the Korean case. Over a period of 17 years its manufacturing sector realized average annual rates of growth of capital stock and labour of 13 per cent and 5.3 per cent respectively. Had the manufacturing sector been oriented towards the domestic market, the allocation of new factors inevitably would have been to products with lower marginal returns than were obtained by exporting to new markets—the domestic terms of trade would have been less favourable than the world terms of trade. Importsubstituting countries have typically been unable to absorb much smaller additions to their stock of factors without running into severely diminishing returns due to the inability of the domestic market to absorb the additional output. Thus, the proper measure of the contribution of export orientation is the difference in realized TFP growth relative to that which would have occurred had the domestic market been the major destination of output.

While it is difficult to implement empirically, this counterfactual scenario provides the most appropriate framework for understanding the importance of export orientation. The absence of large differences in measured TFP growth in manufacturing as between import-substituting and export-oriented economies is not particularly relevant. The ability of the latter to maintain high marginal returns in the face of a rapid absorption of factors from lower-productivity uses in both agriculture and the urban informal sectors is a major source of the success of the export strategy. The structural transformation measured by Chenery and Kuznets and predicted in the Lewis model occurs without the rapidly growing manufacturing sector facing deteriorating terms of trade that would probably occur in the closed economy. Viewed from this perspective, the advantage of export orientation is allocative—factors can be moved rapidly from low-productivity to high-productivity sectors without the latter encountering diminishing returns; and, given the size of the world market, the whole process can proceed much more quickly.[24]

The initially established levels of TFP are an important component of the success of the NICs. The benefit from reallocation of resources depends critically on high levels of productivity in manufacturing. In contrast, in the ISI countries, the manufacturing sector offered high rates of remuneration based not on productivity but on the rents afforded by protection. When factors are transferred to a protected sector, the social gains are limited.

In addition, there is a macroeconomic gain from export orientation, namely the ability to avoid stop-go policies that more frequently appear in the inward-oriented countries and which may have an adverse impact on productivity growth. While the increasing average utilization rates that characterize export-oriented economies do not, of themselves, lead to a more rapid growth rate of potential output, they do generate higher short- and medium-term growth rates. The greater output obtained in the short term allows some flexibility in dealing with the diverse problems encountered in rapidly changing economies. Workers may be more willing to accept change in location, occupation, and industry, and capitalists more willing to expand into new sectors in a more rapidly growing industrial sector than in one subject to 'stop-go' policies. More generally, it is possible that a stable macroeconomic environment, including relative price stability, conservative fiscal and monetary policies, and appropriate exchange-rate policies has been more important than such details of the trade regime as the absence of quotas in explaining the success of the East Asian countries. While in principle it is possible to discriminate between these alternative sources of superior performance, the correlation of macro-policy and trade regime across countries makes this a difficult enterprise.

Finally, two cautionary notes about the normative significance of total productivity growth are apposite. First, it is possible that such growth has undesirable implications for employment and income distribution if, for example, it is labour-saving in an economy that exhibits substantial dualism and slow growth of productive employment opportunities. This is an old and perhaps obvious point, but, particularly in light of the fact that none of the TFP studies cited above attempts to estimate the bias of technical change, faster growth is not necessarily better with some social welfare functions.[25] Secondly, under some conditions, TFP may be too high. It is well known that investment in excess of the 'golden rule' rate can be detrimental in the sense that additional investment decreases future consumption possibilities. Once it is noted that achieving TFP growth may require a sacrifice of current consumption, a similar possibility exists that investment in productivity-enhancing activities may be excessive. Some of the recent economic dissatisfaction in Korea seems to be an expression of discontent of this type though other factors are undoubtedly involved. While TFP growth is critical for successful economic performance, no theorem exists to demonstrate that it does not run into diminishing social returns.

4.3 TFP, Education Levels, and the Production Function

It is often suggested that their high levels of education played an important role in the rapid structural transformation of the East Asian super-exporters (Scitovsky 1985); yet most economy-wide estimations of the sources of growth in East Asia have found that, though TFP^*/Q^* for the entire economy is as high as 40 per cent, changing education levels are not an important contributor to aggregate growth. Although education by sector is not available, I will argue that high education levels have, in fact, been quite important in obtaining rapid growth in manufacturing.

Existing approaches to evaluating the contribution of education to growth derive measures of changes in education over time and use them as independent variables in production functions or to adjust the nominal labour force. Typically, the contribution of education or the quality-adjusted labour force is then calculated within the framework of an *assumed* production function, usually Cobb–Douglas. For some of the East Asian countries, however, the major contribution of education may have been to alter the constellation of economic opportunities. Methods of production that would have been technically infeasible became viable because of the presence of highly educated managers and technicians. Changes in the method of production were particularly important as these economies experienced a rapid change in relative factor proportions.

The rate of growth of output when the underlying production function is CES in form is:

$$Q^* = TFP^* + \alpha K^* + (1 - \alpha)L^* + \tfrac{1}{2}\alpha(1 - \alpha)\,[(\sigma - 1)/\sigma]\,[K^* - L^*]^2. \quad (3)$$

The first three terms provide the familiar Cobb–Douglas explanation while the last introduces a correction if σ, the elasticity of substitution, differs significantly from unity. If capital grows much more rapidly than labour, labour may act as a brake on output growth. However, the greater the ease with which capital can be substituted for labour, the less is any such restrictive effect; a higher σ slows the onset of diminishing returns to the more rapidly growing factor.[26]

It is thus of some importance in analysing the growth process of the Gang of Four, particularly Korea and Taiwan, where TFP*/Q* for manufacturing is 25 to 40 per cent, depending on the period, to discriminate between a Cobb–Douglas production function which imposes a particular value of σ and a more general approach that allows the data to choose this parameter. Estimation of CES production functions for each country suggests that the value of σ may be greater than unity, but it is impossible to decide between this estimate and the Cobb–Douglas form in terms of the usual statistical criteria because of the high degree of multicollinearity and the high value of R^2. Suppose, however, that the true elasticity in the East Asian countries is, in fact, greater than unity. What are then the implications for the interpretation of their growth patterns?

Unless $K^* - L^*$ is quite large, a non-unitary value of σ results in minor adjustments to the rate of growth yield by the Cobb–Douglas. But rapid growth in the capital/labour ratio describes the situation in Korea, Singapore, and Taiwan where the rates of increase of the two primary factors were the following for the manufacturing sector:[27]

	K^*	L^*
Korea (1960–77)	13.0	5.3
Singapore (1970–9)	14.3	8.4
Taiwan (1961–80)	14.8	6.6

Part of increasing output ascribed in studies of the sources of growth to TFP growth may be attributable to the ease with which the manufacturing sector substitutes capital for labour if the underlying production function is CES with σ > 1: in effect the higher elasticity of substitution economizes on the more slowly growing factor and has the same effect as a Hicks labour-saving innovation. Thus, for the manufacturing sector high education levels may assume great importance. What is the behaviour that forms the basis for this explanation of the East Asian growth process?

In a paper written with Larry E. Westphal (1986) it was argued that

most of the technology introduced during industrialization is transferred in one way or another from industrially more advanced countries. But because *industrialization adds to the variety of products produced and processes used in a country, it does in fact involve technological change in the sense of gaining mastery over products and processes that are new to the local economy* . . . much technological change consists of assimilating and adopting foreign technology. (p. 105)

The production function of a country which mainly imports its equipment thus depends on its ability to search for and modify alternative foreign production processes. In Figure 1, rather than continuing to move along the unit isoquant AA as factor proportions change, a firm or industry can move along BB. The dashed isoquant, the envelope of AA and BB, exhibits a higher elasticity of substitution than AA alone. The presence of a highly educated group facilitates this shift in the production process and is reflected in a greater value of σ.

Learning issues can also be clarified within this framework. Most learning is likely to be localized; countries are more efficient in using techniques similar to their current ones than those that differ substantially in their capital/labour ratio or degree of automation.[28] As they move away from their current endowment, say R, in Figure 1, they may have to move along $B'B'$ rather than along BB. If the presence of a substantial core of highly educated managers and technicians makes learning easier, a firm moving from R to the more capital-intensive region will not spend as much time along $B'B'$—it will more quickly move to BB. Westphal et al. (1984) have argued that Korea acquired substantial ability in production engineering during the period of rapid industrial growth after 1965. Other researchers

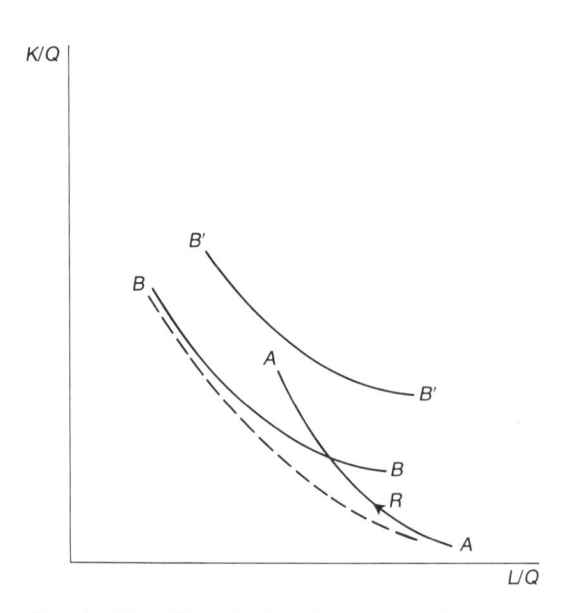

FIG. 1. The effect of education on growth

aver that the same holds for Taiwan and Hong Kong. The significance of such learning is particularly important in a situation of rapidly changing factor proportions where successful adaptation and assimilation also increase the short-term elasticity of substitution.

I have interpreted the move from AA to BB (rather than moving along AA or moving to $B'B'$) as a feasible response to changes in relative factor scarcity where there exists a large educated managerial group. Another dimension of flexibility, also reflected in the move from AA to BB, is a shift among products from those with intrinsically more labour-intensive production methods to those with more capital- or technology-intensive attributes.[29] In both Korea and Taiwan a systematic shift has occurred in the factor intensity of the industry-mix, dictated by changing relative factor endowment.[30] But the feasibility and efficiency with which this shift is undertaken depends on managerial abilities that are presumably at least partly the product of formal education.[31] Investigating new products, identifying market niches, and marketing are not activities likely to be undertaken successfully by managers who have simply learned on the job.[32] Thus, education may lie behind a high elasticity of substitution because of its favourable impact both on the ability to scan and implement new technologies and on the flexibility of the product-mix.

These considerations may explain why labour-force adjustments explain little of aggregate Korean growth (Kim and Park 1985).[33] This interpretation implies that purely domestic decisions, namely substantial public and private expenditure on education, constituted a necessary complement of the neutral trade policies and stable macroeconomic policies. While export orientation would have avoided the adverse price impact on the manufacturing sector of a slowly growing non-industrial economy, if a lower level of education had existed the efforts to transform the sectoral structure rapidly via exports would have led to a decline in marginal productivities and hence a rise in costs, slowing or aborting the export expansion.

This benefit conferred by education is not specific to trade regimes. It is possible that an inward-oriented economy undergoing rapid structural change would benefit from it in a similar way as did Israel until 1967 while it was primarily engaged in ISI (Pack 1971). In the absence of fast-growing exports, a rapid sectoral transformation in which technology assimilation and absorption become critical issues will only become relevant when investment/GNP ratios are very high and lead to rapidly growing GNP per capita and the typical Engel efffects. Rapid growth is possible in import-substituting countries but their high investment ratios are often associated with high marginal capital/output ratios and low aggregate growth rates. Thus, a country like Argentina may not have derived as much benefit from its highly educated labour force as was possible.

5. THE NEW TRADE THEORIES AND OTHER EMERGING ISSUES

Many of the chapters in this volume consider the implications of the new trade theories for the developing countries. In production processes characterized by static scale economies or steep learning curves, the resulting static or dynamic increasing returns may provide justification for intervention under the rubric of 'import substitution as export promotion'. There are also other arguments for intervention, particularly in oligopolistic industries in which rents are earned.[34] These rents are most likely to exist in industries in which even most of the advanced NICs are unable to compete, given the enormous research costs and the relatively short product lifecycles. The new trade theories rest on a number of assumptions about production and research processes including the extent of static increasing returns stemming from lumpy initial investment, the slope of learning curves, and the extent to which R & D is encouraged by the size of the local market as opposed to (subjectively) less certain foreign markets. Scale economies are addressed in some detail by Albert Berry in Chapter 3; they will therefore not be considered here. Other empirical issues including the identification and size of the rents obtainable in particular markets lie beyond the purview of this chapter.

5.1 Research and Development and Market Structure

The Schumpeterian hypothesis that greater R & D incentives exist if discoveries are more appropriable as a result of concentrated market structure has received little empirical confirmation in the literature on the industrial countries.[35] R & D may also be encouraged by industrial protection as it becomes possible to allocate R & D over larger quantities.[36] While it is possible that ISI and the ensuing appropriability generated by an oligopolistic industrial structure encourages research, this has not been systematically shown for LDCs. Nevertheless, Katz, Lall, and others have documented that R & D does occur under protectionist regimes, although much of this innovation addresses problems generated by the ISI policy itself.

5.2 Learning Curves

The remaining empirical issue relevant for the new trade theories is the existence of steep learning curves as a result, for example, of increasing yields of semiconductor chips being obtained from a given wafer as cumulated output grows. Unfortunately, except for the early progress curves estimated by Hirsch (1952), Alchian (1955), and others for airframe production, the literature for the DCs is largely based on non-systematic guesses, even for well-defined products where the technological base of learning curves is well understood.[37] To address subtle but important questions such as whether learning curves for LDCs in a given sector differ according to import or export orientation of the sector or government policy is thus impossible at this time.

5.3 The Reversal of Comparative Advantage

While strategic trade policy has received considerable scrutiny, it appears relevant for only a few industries in a handful of developing countries. A different set of issues, relevant to many LDCs, has begun to emerge, though the evidence is as yet too tentative to allow an evaluation of its quantitative importance. Briefly, the argument is that the advent of new technologies such as those based on microprocessors and laser beams is about to shift static comparative advantage in sectors such as clothing, textiles, and automobile production back towards the developed countries.[38] In terms of Figure 1, the isoquant map is being extended in a more capital-intensive direction and simultaneously shifting inwards. Even with large differences in relative factor prices, particularly higher wage rates, comparative advantage may revert back toward the developed countries in some of the goods on which the success of the Gang of Four was based.

Two examples are germane. Many layers of cloth for suits of different sizes can now be cut by a laser beam rather than by a highly paid skilled labourer; robots and flexible manufacturing systems can replace many workers in car manufacturing. While the evidence is so far necessarily tentative as the technologies are still in the development stage, preliminary estimates such as those of Wheeler and Mody suggest that even a country like South Korea may have considerable difficulty in remaining competitive despite lower wages than richer countries. This process implies that the elasticity of substitution is decreasing in given production processes, a view often suggested in the past. While a new technological epoch may yield such an outcome, the continuation of significant factor-substitution possibilities in many sectors two centuries after the first Industrial Revolution suggests caution in drawing strong inferences with respect to this question. Nevertheless, given the prevailing wisdom of export orientation, a new generation of countries desiring to emulate the policies of the Gang of Four and to evolve along a 'natural' trajectory of comparative advantage, may find the route more difficult.

6. CONCLUSIONS

Firm-level micro-studies have provided much useful knowledge of conditions in LDCs; and technical change studies have provided innovative and interesting documentation of a complex process of change. The next research task is demonstration of the normative significance of recorded technical change; this necessitates the linkage of future studies of firm-level technical progress to industry-wide analysis including the evolution of total factor productivity. Future research needs to analyse whether, from a policy perspective, stimulation of indigenous technical activity is to be preferred to the purchase of internationally available technology. The requisite policies are, of course, not mutually exclusive. Productive absorption of foreign technology requires some set of domestic skills and its purchase needs to be selective and informed by some domestic capability. The interventionist East Asian technology policy suggests one possible mix of purchase and local activity (Pack and Westphal 1986; Wade 1990). Other sequences may be better in other contexts.

One set of fascinating questions remains an open research area. How have countries like Korea learned entirely new technologies, such as those required to produce automobiles, in a relatively short time and well enough quickly to become major exporters? Why have relatively advanced industrial countries such as India and Yugoslavia failed in this dimension? Is it again the adverse impact of ISI policies or is there an explicit technological dimension that requires explanation?[39] The licensing of technology and some joint production are known to have been important in Korea. What lessons can be learned from this?

This chapter has focused on the experience of semi-industrialized countries for this is the group for which a fair amount of information is available. Yet there is a large set of countries, mainly in sub-Saharan Africa, that are much less industrialized. What lessons does this chapter hold for them? It is now a commonplace that the ultimate constraint on the development of the least developed countries is the limited supply of skilled and educated persons. In the long run this is a critical issue and the discussion above of the role of education in the East Asian NICs highlights its importance. The conventional wisdom about short-run policies suggests movement towards a low level of uniform effective protection. While a useful guide-line, such policies should be accompanied by some more precisely honed intervention, for example to improve technical capability of plant managers and technicians.[40] Unfortunately, the existing literature on learning and productivity offers little guidance about specific interventions to increase the rate of TFP growth. This absence does not reflect adversely on this body of research. It is also impossible to infer from the vast literature on technical change in the developed countries any specific policies that might enable them to resume their historic growth rates of total factor productivity. In both cases the gaps in knowledge are powerful arguments for further carefully defined research.

REFERENCES

AHLUWALIA, ISHER (1985), *Industrial Growth in India* (OUP, Delhi).

ALCHIAN, ARMEN (1955), 'Reliability of Progress Curves in Airframe Production', *Econometrica* 21, pp. 679–93.

ATKINSON, A. B., and STIGLITZ J. E. (1969), 'A New View of Technological Change', *Economic Journal*, 79, pp. 573–8.

BRANDER, J. A., and SPENCER, B. J. (1985), 'Export Subsidies and International Market Share Rivalry', *Journal of International Economics*, 18, pp. 83–100.

CHENERY, HOLLIS (1986), 'Growth and Transformation', in Chenery *et al.* (1986), pp. 13–36.

—— ROBINSON, SHERMAN and SYRQUIN, MOSHE, (eds.) (1986), *Industrialization and Growth: A Comparative Study* (OUP, New York).

—— and SYRQUIN MOSHE, 'Typical Patterns of Transformation', in Chenery *et al.* (1986), pp. 37–8.

CONTRACTOR, FAROK (1980), 'The Profitability of Technology Licensing by U.S. Multinationals', *Journal of International Business Studies*, 11/2, pp. 40–64.

DAHLMAN, CARL J., and WESTPHAL, LARRY (1982), 'Technological Effort in Industrial Development—An Interpretative Survey of Recent Research', in Frances Stewart and Jeffrey James, *The Economics of New Technology in Development Countries* (Frances Pinter, London).

DIAMOND, PETER, MCFADDEN, DANIEL, and RODRIGUEZ, M. (1978), 'Measurement of the Elasticity of Substitution and the Bias of Technical Change: An Impossibility Theorem', in Melvyn Fuss and Daniel McFadden (eds.), *Production Economics: A Dual Approach to Theory and Application* (North-Holland, Amsterdam).

FRANSMAN, M., and KING, K. (eds.) (1984), *Technological Capability in the Third World* (Macmillan, London).

GREENE, W.H. (1983), 'Simultaneous Estimation of Factor Substitution, Economies of Scale, Productivity, and Non-Neutral Technical Change', in A. Dogramaci (ed.), *Development in Econometric Analysis of Productivity* (Lluwer-Nijhoff, Boston, Mass.).

GRILICHES, ZVI, and JORGENSON, DALES W. (1967), 'The Explanation of Productivity Change', *Review of Economic Studies*, 34, pp. 249–83.

HANDOUSSA, H., NISHIMIZU, M., and Page, J. M., jun. (1986), 'Productivity Change in Egyptian Public Sector Industries after the "Opening", 1973–79', *Journal of Development Economics*, 20, pp. 53–74.

HELLEINER, GERALD K. (1979), 'World Market Imperfection and the Developing Countries', in W. R. Cline (ed.), *Policy Alternatives for a New Industrial Economic Order* (Overseas Development Council, Praeger, New York), pp. 357–90.

HIRSCH, WERNER A. (1952), 'Manufacturing Progress Functions', *Review of Economics and Statistics*, 34, pp. 143–55.

HUGHES, JONATHAN (1970), *Industrialization and Economic History* (McGraw-Hill, New York).

KAMIEN, MORTON I., and SCHWARTZ, NANCY L. (1975), 'Market Structure and Innovation: A Survey', *Journal of Economic Literature*, 13 (Mar.), pp. 1–37.

KATZ, JORGE (1984), 'Domestic Technological Innovations and Dynamic Comparat-

ive Advantage: Further Reflections on a Comparative Case Study Program', *Journal of Development Economics*, 16/1 and 2, pp. 13–37.
——(ed.) (1987), *Technology Generation in Latin American Manufacturing Industries* (Macmillan, London).
——and ALBIN, EDUARDO (1976), *Technology and Industrial Exports: A Microeconomic Analysis of Argentina's Recent Experience* (Inter-American Development Bank, Washington DC), mimeo.
——GUTKOWSKI, MIRTA, RODRIQUES, MARIO, and GOITY GREGORIO (1987), 'Productivity and Domestic Technological Search Efforts: The Growth Path of a Rayon Plant in Argentina', in Katz (1987).
KIM, Y. C., and KWON, J. K. (1977), 'The Utilization of Capital and the Growth of Output in a Developing Economy: The Case of South Korean Manufacturing', *Journal of Development Economics*, 9, pp. 265–78.
——and PARK, J. K. (1985), *Sources of Economic Growth in Korea: 1962–82* (Korea Development Institute, Seoul).
KUO, S. (1983), *The Taiwan Economy in Transition* (Westview Press, Boulder, Col.).
KUO, W. (1974), 'Technical Change, Foreign Investment, and Growth in Taiwan's Manufacturing Industries, 1952–70', Industry of Free China.
LALL, SANJAYA (1984), 'India's Technological Capacity: Effects of Trade, Industrial Science and Technology Policies', in Fransman and King (1984), pp. 225–44.
——(1985), *Multinationals, Technology and Exports* (Macmillan, London).
——(1987), *Learning to Industrialize* (Macmillan, London).
LANDES, DAVID (1969), *The Unbound Prometheus* (CUP, London).
MANSFIELD, EDWIN (1977), *The Production and Application of New Industrial Technology* (Norton, New York).
MOKYR, JOEL (1985), *The Economics of the Industrial Revolution* (Rowman & Allanheld, Totowa).
MYTELKA, LYNN (1978), 'Licensing and Technology Dependence in the Andean Group', *World Development*, 6/4, pp. 447–60.
NADIRI, M. I. (1970), 'Some Approaches to the Theory of Measurement of Total Factor Productivity: A Survey', *Journal of Economic Literature*, 8 (Dec.), pp. 1137–77.
NELSON, RICHARD (1973), 'Recent Exercises in Growth Accounting: New Understanding of Dead End', *American Economic Review*, 73, pp. 462–8.
——(1981), 'Research on Productivity Growth and Productivity Differences: Dead Ends and New Departures', *Journal of Economic Literature*, 19 (Sept.), pp. 1029–64.
——and PHELPS, E.S. (1966), 'Investment in Humans, Technological Diffusion and Economic Growth', *American Economic Review*, 56, pp. 69–75.
NISHIMIZU, MIEKO, and PAGE, JOHN M., jun. (1986), 'Productivity Change and Dynamic Comparative Advantage', *Review of Economics and Statistics*, 68/2, pp. 241–7.
————(1987), 'Economic Policies and Productivity Change in Industry: An International Comparison' (World Bank, Washington, DC.), mimeo.
——and ROBINSON, SHERMAN (1984), 'Trade Policies and Productivity Change in Semi-Industrialized Countries', *Journal of Development Economics*, 16, pp. 177–206.

NORDHAUS, WILLIAM (1969), *Invention, Growth, and Welfare* (MIT Press, Cambridge, Mass.).
OECD (1964), *The Residual Factor and Economic Growth* (Organization for Economic Co-operation and Development, Paris).
PACK, HOWARD (1971), *Structural Change and Economic Policy in Israel* (Yale University Press, New Haven, Conn.).
—— (1984), 'Total Factor Productivity and Its Determinants', in G. Ranis *et al.* (eds.), *Comparative Development Perspectives* (Westview Press, Boulder, Col.).
—— (1987), *Productivity, Technology, and Industrial Development* (OUP, New York).
—— (1988), 'Industrialization and Trade', in H. B. Chenery and T. N. Srinivasan (eds.), *Handbook of Development Economics* (North-Holland, Amsterdam).
—— and WESTPHAL, LARRY E. (1986), 'Industrial Strategy and Technological Change: Theory vs. Reality', *Journal of Development Economics*, 22, pp. 87–128.
Pratten, C. F. (1971), *Economies of Scale in Manufacturing Industry* (CUP, Cambridge).
PSACHAROPOULOS, GEORGE (1985), 'Returns to Education: A Further International Update and Implications', *Journal of Human Resources*, 20/4, pp. 583–604.
ROSENBERG, NATHAN (1976), *Perspectives on Technology* (CUP, London).
SCITOVSKY, TIBOR (1985), 'Economic Development in Taiwan and South Korea: 1965–1981', *Food Research Institute Studies*, 19, pp. 215–64.
TEITEL, SIMON (1984), 'Technology Creation in Semi-industrial Countries', *Journal of Development Economics*, 16/1–2, pp. 13–37.
—— and THOUMI, FRANCISCO E. (1986), 'From Import Substitution to Exports: The Manufacturing Exports Experience of Argentina and Brazil', *Economic Development and Cultural Change*, 34/3, pp. 455–90.
TSAO, YUAN (1985), 'Growth Without Productivity: Singapore Manufacturing in the 1970s', *Journal of Development Economics*, 19, pp. 25–39.
WADE, ROBERT (1990), *Governing the Market: Economic Theory and Taiwan's Industrial Policies* (Princeton University Press, Princeton, NJ).
WESTPHAL, L., RHEE, Y. W., and PURSELL, G. (1984), 'Sources of Technological Capability in South Korea', in Fransman and King (1984), pp. 179–300.
WHEELER, DAVID, AND MODY, ASHOKA (1990), *Automation and World Competition* (Macmillan, London).

NOTES

1. Many of the major contributions to this literature are contained in: Fransman and King (1984); Lall (1985, 1987); Katz *et al.* (1987); *Annals of the American Academy of Political and Social Science*, Nov. 1981; *Journal of Development Economics*, Oct. 1984; and *World Development*, May/June 1984.
2. Although many of the studies of Latin America were published in 1987, most of the working papers were available by 1977. Some of the papers in Lall's 1985 book of essays were published in the mid-1970s.
3. Some divergence between private and social profitability may have been generated by real external economies. Interestingly, economic historians, who are not defenders of defunct government policies, have rarely emphasized their importance, causing one to wonder about the emphasis on real external eco-

nomies by many analysts of current technological development. E.g. in a recent volume of essays that reviews the state of knowledge about the Industrial Revolution there are two entries in the index on external economies and an examination of these reveals only a perfunctory interest in them (Mokyr 1985). Rosenberg (1976), examining the interaction between machinery-producers and purchasers, provides an important exception to the general neglect of external economies. It may be that the omission reflects the difficulty of demonstrating these in a quantitatively convincing manner rather than anecdotally. While they may be important, and observed government actions with respect to industrial policies in some LDCs can be viewed as an effort to benefit from them (Pack and Westphal 1986), demonstration of their empirical as opposed to theoretical significance has proved to be a formidable task.

4. Teitel (1984) is concerned with this issue.
5. For a survey of many of these studies see Pack (1988).
6. See Teitel (1984).
7. This does not imply that most Latin American exports were within the free trade area; rather, the exports of new products of Argentine firms whose technical evolution was examined was often to countries within LAFTA (Katz and Albin 1976).
8. Chenery and Syrquin document the unusually high percentage of manufacturing growth in Korea and Taiwan that had its ultimate source in exports (1986).
9. See e.g. Mytelka (1978).
10. See, however, Contractor (1980). For a survey of many of the issues see Helleiner (1979).
11. The later chapters of Lall (1985) make a similar point.
12. For evidence of the inadequacy of purely domestic learning in India see Lall (1987).
13. Thus encouraging resources to flow to sectors not on the basis of their domestic resource costs but on the basis of market rates of return.
14. On the importance of product diversity as a source of high cost see Pack (1987).
15. For references see Chenery (1986), Nishimizu and Page (1987), and Pack (1988).
16. Using a neoclassical growth model, in which the entire economy and individual sectors are close to a golden age growth path, rich countries with slow rates of labour-force growth (though augmented by Harrod-neutral technical change) and somewhat faster capital growth are likely to be characterized by a high value of TFP^*/Q^*, or were until 1973. At the other end of the spectrum, the poorer countries will exhibit a value for L^* between 2.5 and 3.5, perhaps a similar value of K^*, and a low residual. For these, TFP^*/Q^* will be very low.

Middle-income NICs may experience not only technical progress, but rapid capital accumulation as well, e.g. by providing incentives for domestic saving and making foreign commercial financing easier; this will reduce the importance of TFP^*/Q^* as the denominator will grow more quickly than in either richer or poorer countries. Rapid intermediate-term growth in the capital/labour ratio will occur though diminishing returns to capital will eventually slow this process. Thus, primary factor accumulation will be a substantial contributor to growth in fast-growing NICs even where they achieve high rates of technical

change. If technical progress results from capital-embodied technical change, TFP may assume a larger role in the intermediate term.
17. The figures from Singapore are from Tsao (1985).
18. For a recent exhaustive analysis of Indian performance see Ahluwalia (1985).
19. While it is tempting to re-examine the underlying data for Singapore since the results are so far from a priori expectations, a similar re-evaluation would be no less appropriate for all countries. Perhaps Argentina, Brazil, and Mexico also have data flaws, understating their productivity growth.
20. A more thorough discussion of these issues is given in Pack (1988).
21. Tsao (1985) presents a discussion of Singapore.
22. Given the substantial role of MNCs in the manufacturing sector of Argentina, Brazil, and Mexico, a disaggregated investigation of both the level and rate of growth of TFP in these economies would be of considerable interest.
23. Part of this section is derived from Pack (1988).
24. Benefits from reallocation of factors among sectors implies a disequilibrium in which the marginal product of factors is not initially equal across sectors, a widely noted phenomenon in all LDCs.
25. It is, unfortunately, not an easy matter simultaneously to estimate the elasticity of substitution and the bias of technical change. See Diamond *et al.* (1978) for the case of the CES, and Greene (1983) for the case of more flexible functional forms.
26. $\partial Q^*/\partial \sigma = \frac{1}{2}\alpha (1 - \alpha) [K^* - L^*]^2/\sigma^2$ which is positive.
27. The sources for these figures are: Korea: Nishimizu and Robinson (1984); Singapore: Tsao (1985); Taiwan: Kuo (1983).
28. Atkinson and Stiglitz (1969) call this localized technical progress.
29. The capital intensity would be captured by α in the Cobb–Douglas case and the distribution parameter in the CES case.
30. The Rybczynski effect of trade theory.
31. Nelson and Phelps (1966) argue that education is primarily productive in a rapidly changing technical environment. Their argument can be extended to a changing product environment.
32. On the importance of these activities see Keesing and Lall, Ch. 7 this volume.
33. No studies have been done of the manufacturing sector alone using the Denison method for labour-force adjustments.
34. Brander and Spencer (1985).
35. For a review of the developed-country literature see Kamien and Schwartz (1975).
36. See Nordhaus (1969) and Rodrik, Ch. 6 this volume.
37. For references to what is known see Wheeler and Mody (1990).
38. An exhaustive empirical analysis of these issues is contained in Wheeler and Mody (1990).
39. Evaluation of the Yugo and various Hyundai models in publications such as *Consumer Reports* suggest large differences in technical knowledge.
40. These and related issues about the reorganization of industry are discussed in Pack (1987), chs. 8 and 9.

3

Firm (or Plant) Size in the Analysis of Trade and Development

R. Albert Berry

1. INTRODUCTION

Early neoclassical models of international trade emphasized differences in factor endowments as the source of gains from trade and explained the income distribution impacts of trade in terms of its price effects on relatively scarce and relatively abundant factors. The core mechanisms of such models and the core propositions generated from them continue to be central to our thinking about trade and development, having recently benefited from a resurgence of support for the merits of 'outward-oriented' growth strategies, and some empirical evidence suggesting that export orientation can improve income distribution in developing countries by raising the labour share (for example Fields 1984), or more precisely, the 'lower-income labour' share. Those models, in simplest guise, assumed common technology across the trading countries along with the constant returns to scale underpinning pure competition among identical firms in any given industry. Industries were thought of as self-contained so that the input–output structure of the economy was not a focus of attention.

Since then the implications of economies of scale, differing technology across countries, and imperfect factor and product markets have all been drawn out, the latter in considerable detail. Input–output analysis has permitted students to take account, albeit imperfectly, of indirect as well as direct inputs used in exports and import substitutes. No comparable progress has been made toward the incorporation of intra-industry heterogeneity, a complication probably of particular relevance for the less developed countries (LDCs)[1] where such heterogeneity is often striking and where evidence suggests intra-industry relationships between the trade stance of a firm (exporter, domestic seller, etc.) and such features as its capital intensity. The heterogeneity in question may reflect product market imperfections, similar to those contemplated in some of the new trade theory. But it may have other origins (imperfect factor markets, differential access to or ability to use or create improved technology, variance in age) as well. In many industries it takes the form of a wide and related variance in firm size, technology in use, factor proportions, and factor productivities. The variance is considerably greater in some industries than others, and the 'average' (if one may use the term) technology in operation differs much more from the counterpart developed-country technology in some industries than in others, with this difference being inversely related to the modernity of technology in the LDC industry (see Nelson 1968). The most widely commented reason for the observed heterogeneity and the correlation between technologies, factor proportions, and productivities on the one side and firm or plant size on the other, is the apparently marked variance in factor prices across firms of different sizes, with labour costs typically rising with size and capital costs more likely to fall (though in this case the relationship may be much more complicated). A competing hypothesis is that many production functions are non-homothetic, such that larger size (whatever its sources) implies a higher profit-maximizing capital intensity. Finally, it has been argued that some firms simply have better technology than others, whether because they are better run, or have better access to such technology, or for other reasons.[2] Transport costs and imperfect domestic product markets also play a role.

Intra-industry heterogeneity exists in all sectors but with somewhat different implications for trade. This chapter focuses on manufacturing, the major sector in which Heckscher–Ohlin principles would be most expected to hold and where economies of scale are often significant. It is the major sector of import-substituting in LDCs and an increasingly important export sector. In mining and agriculture a country's competitive situation is largely determined by natural resource endowments rather than relative abundances of labour or capital so there is no strong presumption that exports will be labour-intensive. Most branches of agriculture appear to be characterized by few if any economies of scale, but a strong negative correlation between size (of farm) and labour intensity parallels that in manufacturing, so many of the same issues do arise.

Whatever its origins, the fact of heterogeneity has several major implications. First, since economic efficiency (total factor productivity with factors valued at social opportunity cost) may vary considerably across firms within a given industry, and may not be well correlated with private profits, a firms's ability to compete internationally need not signal its economic efficiency, let alone that of the industry of which it is a part. Attempts to identify groups of potentially efficient export or import-competing firms should possibly be guided less by industry or product and more by firm size or type of technology. Secondly, the effects of trade on the level and composition of labour demand and on income distribution must evidently be described rather differently when factor proportions are as closely related to firm size as to industry. The optimistic implication of the Heckscher–Ohlin model that a labour-abundant country following its comparative advantage and hence exporting labour-intensive goods will benefit from a better income distribution need no longer follow.[3] If large firms tend to do the exporting—a widely noted tendency (see, for example, Adar and Hirsch

1974; Tyler 1976; Auquier 1980; Glesjer, *et al.* 1980)—and tend to be capital-intensive, the result could be just reversed. This might seem unlikely given the general presumption that import-substituting activities are significantly more capital-intensive than exports, but if outward orientation raises the production of tradables relative to non-tradables as well as the ratio of exportables to import substitutes, it could happen. In any case the capital intensity of exports would reduce any distributional benefits from trade even if it did not reverse them.

Early development thinking tended to give little recognition to intra-industry heterogeneity and to accept, explicitly or implicitly, that modern technology was 'desirable' and that economies of scale were a frequent feature of industry, or at least that diseconomies of scale were not. Small-scale manufacturing was generally not part of the model in terms of which people thought about development problems. A general questioning of these ideas has followed from the well-known fact that small-scale manufacturing tends to have much higher labour/capital ratios than does large-scale industry (LI) and that it generates most of the sector's employment in the majority of LDCs, and the less universally but still fairly widely held view that under conditions of labour abundance it is often more efficient economically than is LI.[4] Studies indicate that it can show great flexibility, good innovative capacity, high savings and reinvestment rates, and rapid growth, though the necessary and sufficient conditions for this are not yet well understood. It can also contribute to a lessening of the inefficiency (and perhaps the excessive capital intensity) of large firms by competing with them; there exist many cases in which the initial monopoly position of an import-substituting firm was later eroded as small and medium-sized firms entered into competition with it. One upshot of the changing views is that support for micro-enterprise has become popular in some of the international agencies. The World Bank, meanwhile, has focused its non-LI attention on small and medium-sized factories rather than on the very small micro-enterprises.

The ongoing debate on the question of size and efficiency in LDCs began before many countries had achieved much success in the manufactured-export field or had indeed given a great deal of thought to that possibility. The dominant policy syndrome was import-substituting industrialization; the gradually heightening awareness that protection tended to generate large-scale, capital-intensive monopolies or oligopolies of questionable efficiency was one of the inputs to the spreading view that smaller size might be associated with better performance. As export potential was demonstrated by an expanding group of LDCs, a new twist was given to the size–efficiency issue. It was quickly confirmed that larger manufacturing firms were generally more successful at the exporting game. To the extent that this represented basic economies of scale either in production or in the export-marketing process it constituted an important argument in favour of large size. It also raised the question of the degree to which export involvement would induce or force large firms to be more efficient and labour-intensive under the presence of international competition. On the other hand there were questions as to how much of the less successful export record of small firms was the result of policy bias (their lack of access to inputs necessary to achieve export success), and to what extent the export-marketing problem facing small firms could be alleviated or overcome by commercial intermediaries of one sort or another.

The last decade or so has seen a rethinking of the role of small enterprise in developed as well as developing countries. In most industrial countries the majority of new employment has been generated in smaller firms, many of which are successful exporters. There is much talk of the decline of the long production run in favour of production flexibility. Several socialist countries, for example Hungary and Yugoslavia, are looking to small private firms as a source of both dynamism and exports. Do such trends have longer-run implications for the role of small and medium industry (SMI) in developing countries, or more importantly for the potential contribution they can make as generators of employment and income for low-income workers?

Despite positive qualitative assessments of SMI that are now quite general, the importance of its potential contribution remains ambiguous and the importance of designing policies in its support even more so. The former ambiguity results from the fact that it has not yet been possible to bring *ex post* evidence, cross-country or other, to bear successfully on the question of how much substitutability there is between smaller and larger enterprise. Accordingly it is not possible to look at a country's industrial structure and present a defensible quantitative estimate of how much greater the SMI sector could become without running into diminishing returns for want of complementary larger enterprises. In cases where a lot of SMI is engaged in subcontracting relationships with LI there might not be much scope for raising the ratio of SMI product to LI product. In other cases that scope might be much greater. Another source of uncertainty about SMI is the lack of convincing analysis of how its presence affects income distribution, after due account is taken of indirect as well as direct effects. Finally, the impact of possible policy tools on the sector is ill-understood; few countries have made a very serious effort to foster its growth, and few studies document carefully the results of such attempts.

The remaining sections of this chapter elaborate on some possible implications of intra-industry heterogeneity in LDCs for the effects of trade in general and for specific trade-related policies such as management of the exchange rate and liberalization. Before turning to those issues, we briefly review the character of the heterogeneity under discussion, and note several severe empirical impediments to convincing analysis of its implications.

The impact of economies of scale and scope on the size distribution of firms and on firm-level efficiency[5] is one key issue; where such economies are important, size variability would be expected to have efficiency implications. If production economies of scale or of scope are quite important in a wide range of industries, it would be unlikely that SMI could make a major contribution to growth or to the balance of payments. Economies of scale or scope in international marketing would further decrease SMI's potential role on the export but not the import-substituting side.

It is important, though, to remember that the existence of production economies of scale does not guarantee that large firms will tend to be economically more efficient than smaller ones. First, the potential productivity of large firms could be greater because of technical economies of scale, but if X-efficiency is lower in those firms their actual efficiency might not exceed that of smaller firms. Secondly, if larger firms face more distorted factor prices than smaller ones, (for example above-equilibrium wages and below-equilibrium costs of capital, a commonly held view), they may be less efficient that the smaller firms even though they reap the benefits of economies of scale. Thirdly, the production function in some industries may be non-homothetic in such a way that with a high ratio of wages to cost of capital large firms are more efficient whereas when that ratio is low small firms are more efficient.

Although most economic comparisons between smaller and larger firms (or plants) are couched in static terms, it is also important to take account of firm dynamics. Frequent entry and exit (characteristic of small firms) implies a sort of flexibility on the one hand, but exit implies a cost, for example capital discarded, or workers displaced, which is not taken into account in static comparisons. Infrequency of exit by large firms can however imply heavy subsidization costs to white elephants. Where growth is a function of efficiency, one would expect size and efficiency to be correlated though the source was not true economies of scale—a matter difficult to allow for in statistical estimates of economies of scale. Where smaller firms grow systematically, the appropriate comparison between small and large involves differences over two growth patterns rather than between two specific sizes.

The above qualifications notwithstanding, it is reasonable to assume that widespread economies of scale lower the likelihood that SMI can make a major contribution to growth or to the balance of payments, and raise the likelihood that SMI firms owe their existence to some 'protective' market distortions. It is hence useful to consider briefly the evidence on economies of scale and its practical implications (Section 2) before we turn to data on the nature of intra-industry heterogeneity (Section 3) and to its implications (the remaining sections).

Measurement of economies of scale is a major empirical challenge in any assessment of SMI's potential, but there are others. Estimation of the output, employment, or income-distribution effects of trade involves consideration both of how efficiency and factor proportions vary across existing groups of producers, but also of how efficiency and factor proportions of each group may be affected by trade. An exported good or service involves output not only of the last sector which had something to do with its production, for example agriculture or manufacturing, but of all the sectors which contributed, including commerce, transportation, etc. Its final cost and hence competitiveness depend on the efficiency of each sector involved, as does its impact on factor demand. The quantity so exported is the domestic value added, that is the value of the export *minus* the value of imported inputs.[6] The economies of scale which contribute to competitiveness are those of all the sectors involved.

Unfortunately data are seldom if ever fully adequate to a static assessment of factor utilization in net exports. Since both X-efficiency and factor proportions may vary widely within sectors, use of sectoral averages to build up estimates of the inputs used in net exports can be seriously misleading. A general equilibrium analysis which aspires to measure the final effect of an increase in certain exports on factor use and factor prices is much harder still, since it involves specification of the various linkages from export production, and knowledge of when changes in economic demand or supply of factors or goods lead to quantity changes and when to price changes. The most that can be hoped for here is to identify some of the major linkages and indirect effects.

A final serious data problem involving analyses of factor proportions is the inadequate evidence on capital and on the mix of labour skills. Many studies rely on proxies for the level of capital inputs, such as installed horsepower, but there is good reason to believe that such proxies are not very good ones. Labour productivity, also used as a proxy for the K/L ratio, is likely to be even weaker, since it is a positive function of both the K/L ratio and the level of X-efficiency.

2. ECONOMIES OF SCALE: A NOTE ON THE EVIDENCE

The clarity of the concept of economies of scale in economic theory stands in contrast to a serious fuzziness with respect to measurement and a lack of much in the way of theoretical or empirical grounding for prediction of the extent of such economies (see Gold 1981). Economies of scale are usually defined as cost savings from a higher level of output with both product and basic technology held constant. Economies of scope refer to cost savings resulting from the joint production of a range of goods or services. Economies of size (which is what most statistical analyses measure) can derive from economies either of scale or of scope, not to mention any other advantages of size. Economies of scale are likely to be relevant at the plant level; economies of scope may be more relevant at the firm level.

The empirical evidence on any and all of these 'economies' remains seriously inadequate (a convenient sampling of findings is found in Shepherd 1979). In some cases the nature of the technology makes it clear that important economies of scale exist, but their magnitude is hard to pin down. Those conclusions reached by comparing observed costs of different-sized firms or plants face severe identification problems when they try to sort out cost savings associated with scale from those due to other possible sources. A different set of problems plagues analyses based on engineering data, for example lack of familiarity with how an operation would be run at a different scale from the one being used. The 'survivor technique'—the third major approach to the analysis of economies of size—has its own drawbacks but also contributes new insights. What has not been easy is a satisfactory integration of the evidence generated by these three approaches.

In developed countries, as in LDCs, a wide range of firm and plant sizes pass the survivor test, a fact which led Stigler to conclude that 'the long run marginal and average cost curves of the firm are customarily horizontal over a large range of sizes' (1958, p. 56). Saving (1961) reported that sixty-four of the ninety-one US industries for which he was able to make 1947–54 survivorship estimates had minimum optimal plant sizes requiring the production of not more than 1 per cent of the industry's value added.

Following the train of thought associated with the survivor technique, one may ask the meaning of the persistence of many small or medium plants and firms in industries where it is generally believed, sometimes with supporting engineering evidence, that economies of scale or scope are important. Perhaps that latter evidence is somehow erroneous. Perhaps it is accurate, but the process of firm growth or shrinkage is gradual so that though the optimal size for each firm in the long run can be approximated by engineering or cost evidence on economies of scale, the optimal position in the short run cannot be. Probably the optimal technology differs somewhat according to various exogenous characteristics of a firm, and optimal size is a function of technology. Certainly size varies by the vintage of technologies and many firms with non-frontier technologies should not change technology and hence size until the existing plant has been depreciated. Optimal size is also a function of size of market, which in turn reflects transport costs, etc. (In that case higher returns of bigger firms constitute an economic rent like that on well-located real estate.) These various reasons would suggest that even under well-functioning markets the optimal size of different plants or firms in a given industry at a given point of time could vary considerably.

An additional interpretation must be borne in mind in industries where the dominant position of the largest firm(s) is fostered by considerable economies of scale and shored up by impediments to the entry or growth of small firms, for example via product differentiation, advertising, preferential access to capital, etc.; the large firms may not risk curtailment of their oligopoly profits by expanding output (though they could do so at low cost) nor can other firms grow to where they replicate that efficiency. In these circumstances the first-best option from the standpoint of efficiency—the expansion of large firms' output—is blocked, and smaller firms with higher costs are 'efficient' in the sense that they provide the best attainable utilization of resources in the industry. Where policy can weaken impediments to entry, the likelihood of a first-best resource allocation can be improved. Where this is not the case, the survival of small firms suggests that their use of resources is superior to any feasible alternative.

The presence of serious market imperfections such as are found in LDCs complicates survivor technique interpretations, since they create the possibility that private efficiency differs markedly from social efficiency for any given firm(s). Indeed survival, in spite of low returns to resources used, may actually signal market imperfections impeding the transfer of those resources to higher pay-off uses. Where factor market imperfections are very important, even the relative *private* efficiency of plants or firms of different sizes is hard to measure. What one needs to make the most of the survivor approach in LDCs is independent evidence on the degree of market imperfections favouring one type of firm against another. Survival could then be taken as an indicator of social efficiency as long as the surviving firm was not a net beneficiary of market imperfections *vis-à-vis* its rival types of firms. Thus, if one believes that the differentials in wage costs in favour of small firms are not as large as the capital-market and other biases favouring large firms, survival implies relative efficiency.[7] If one believes the distortions in favour of small firms are stronger than the opposite ones, survival does not necessarily imply effective use.

Assessing the economic importance of economies of scale, scope, or size for developing countries requires evidence on the flexibility of output structure. If one begins with decent industry-level data on economies of scale, in order either to quantify the lost output associated with non-optimal-sized plants or firms, or (when the efficiency-maximizing firm size performs less well on some other count such as employment generation) to assess the trade-off between those losses and employment or poverty-reduction gains, it is necessary to specify the range of international trade patterns acceptable to the country and the extent to which this trade increases its capacity to choose among alternative firm sizes and factor proportions without loss of output or income. I have seen no such attempt to trace out the opportunity locus created for a country between output and employment, in consequence of economies of scale cum non-homotheticity of the production function.[8] The nature of the locus would turn substantially on the question of whether the size range most marked by economies of scale is also the range within which the L/K ratio falls most markedly with size. Most existing estimates of economies of scale provide only the former size range but not the latter.

As is probably to be expected, engineering data tend to show greater cost reductions with size than do cost or profit data. The nature of such engineering data normally involves holding technology constant (in some sense) across size; sometimes, therefore, other lower-cost technological options will exist for lower levels of output, so that the 'true' envelope curve would show less downward slope than that for the fixed technology.[9] The broader the product definition the more likely this is. The data may tend to underestimate non-production costs of larger-sized plants or firms where, for example, managerial diseconomies of scale set in (rising real costs) or rents are taken out in the form of unnecessary perks, luxurious working conditions, etc., as well as in higher profits.

While engineering data may tend to overstate economically attainable economies of scale, cost data could show a bias in either direction. Understatement of such economies could result from competitive pressures, which would be expected to eliminate a higher share of actual or latent smaller firms than large ones, leading to a weaker observed size–cost relationship than that implied in the technology. If at each size, firms (actual or potential) are distributed around a median cost level, larger firms with costs well above average would not be competed out of existence while the comparable small firms would be, leaving a differentially selected set of relatively efficient (*vis-à-vis* the universe) small firms. Often large firms can use market power to get cheaper inputs than rivals, a factor which would work in the opposite direction, tending to make the cost curve steeper than the economies-of-scale curves.

Most of the empirical work on economies of scale has been undertaken in industrialized countries. Despite the evident need to reinterpret the results *vis-à-vis* the LDC context, it is worth reviewing. Scherer, who believes that well-executed engineering estimates do provide the best single source of information on the cost–scale question (Scherer *et al.* 1975, p. 94), concludes for the US that

First, with the exception of the refrigerator-freezer industry, the optimal plant sizes tend to be quite small relative to the national market.... Second, the long-run cost curves in most industries are much less steep at suboptimal plant scales than one is led to believe by typical textbook illustrations. (Scherer 1980, p. 94)

In half the industries the elevation of unit costs at an output level of one-third the minimum optimal scale (the smallest scale at which minimal unit costs are attained) was found to exceed that minimal cost by 5 per cent or less.

Evidence from large developed countries to the effect that economies of scale are less significant than seems often to be assumed is however not inconsistent with their being very important in the lower size range relevant in LDCs. The most useful industrial-country evidence for these latter countries would involve smaller output levels than usually reported on; even then it might provide only rough guidance in the case of those industries with marked factor substitutability because the relative social opportunity costs of factors in LDCs differ greatly from factor prices in industrial countries, and cost savings in the latter case need not translate into social cost savings in the former. There should therefore be a premium on the accumulation of LDC data which reflect such factor substitutability when it exists. As in the case of industrial countries, it is important to check the degree of consistency among the various measures of economies of scale, scope, or size, to interpret the discrepancies which emerge, and in the case of the cost, profit, or survivor measures to adjust as much as possible for those factors contributing to success which do not have to do with scale of production or of management. As has been seen, in LDCs there is the additional and difficult problem that social costs may differ markedly from private costs.

The empirical evidence on economies of scale, scope, or size in LDCs is limited, and no such impressive interpretative literature exists as for the US and some other industrial countries. Pre-investment or engineering data for industries like cement, steel and other metal products, and various chemicals show quite marked economies of scale (for example cost declines of 30–60 per cent) over size ranges which would be relevant in many LDCs. Consistent with expectations, the economies are less marked (for example 20 per cent) in branches like spinning of coarse cloth (Teitel 1975 pp. 98–9).

Data on costs and/or profits by size are much more of a mixed bag than are the engineering data. Most such data, and especially the statistical analysis of them, come from industrial countries and usually, as with those on US corporations, refer to firms which would be large or very large by the standards of many developing countries. Scherer (1980, p. 92) presents after-tax profit-rate data (unfortunately before-tax data would be better for present purposes) for various sub-periods in the 1960s and 1970s; the maximum profit-rate gap between the smallest and largest groups distinguished (assets of 10–25 million and assets of over 1 billion respectively) was from 9.9 per cent for the former to 13.5 per cent for the latter in 1963–5 while the minimum gap was from about 12 to 13.2 per cent in 1975–7.[10] On an industry-by-industry level Marcus found that the relationship between firm size and profitability in the US was erratic, with some industries characterized by positive relationships, others negative ones, and others none at all (Marcus 1969).

While developed-country data are mainly from corporations, in LDCs other ownership forms have considerably higher shares of total output, and trade-offs between efficiency and employment are likely to involve the size range where proprietorships or limited companies dominate. Estimates of total factor productivity, based on quantum figures on inputs and outputs, are perhaps the main source of *ex post* evidence on the implications of scale. Useful unit-cost data are scarce, and estimates of profits are usually derived by residual analysis of census information rather than obtained from detailed firm-level data. Almost all the evidence refers to plants rather than firms. Available profit data (more precisely, rough estimates of the rate of return to capital) tend to show no systematic relation to plant size. In India (1974–7 data) the proxy presented by Little *et al.* (value added less the wage bill divided by capital) was essentially constant (between 0.26 and 0.28) over the broad range from ten to 499 workers though it was substantially lower (0.19) for plants with above 500 workers.[11] In Colombia (1976 data) Cortes *et al.* (1987, p. 73) report no systematic relationship between size and rate of return though for plants of 100–199 workers the same ratio as Little *et al.* employed was a little lower (27.2 per cent) than for either smaller or larger plants (both about 32 per cent). In Korea the pattern is just the reverse, with the ratio twice as high for establishments of 100–199 workers as for smaller ones and falling off, though less dramatically, for larger ones also.[12]

Thus, if we may judge by the sparse and undoubtedly rough figures available, the generally positive relationship between profits and size observed among US corporations does not seem to characterize LDC plants. Even were such a link to show up, it would not necessarily reflect technical economies of scale. Since most large firms are multi-product, and since in many industries technologies change rapidly, cost analysis is likely to be very far from an *ex post* test of the extent of technology-specific economies of scale characterizing the industry.[13] In basic cement, perhaps so, but in most industries not. Both size and profitability often reflect the good management or good luck associated with the manufacturing of a good product.

Profitability, especially of larger firms, can also reflect their market power. In the US context Porter (1974, pp. 214, 218–27) has argued that where bigger firms earn higher profits they typically do so less because they are more efficient or lucky than because they possess more market power than smaller ones. He distinguishes strategic groups within an industry, where each group consists of firms following similar strategies in terms of the key decision variables.[14] Entry can be easy into one strategic group but difficult into another.

Economies of scale are most significant in protecting the firm that has a large share, is vertically integrated, has a captive distribution and service network, or uses national advertising media.... there can coexist stable market shares among the leading branded firms in the industry, on the one hand, protected by high entry barriers, and rapid entry and exit (or turnover) among small unadvertised or private label producers, on the other hand. (Porter 1974, p. 216)

Porter explains the empirical finding that level of concentration in an industry has a less positive effect on profits of small firms than on those of large firms.[15]

If the leading firms operate in strategic groups protected by mobility barriers, insulated from intergroup rivalry and with superior bargaining power over suppliers and customers relative to smaller firms, then the relation between size and profitability would be positive. However, the relationship could go the other way if smaller firms in the industry followed specialist strategies achieving high product differentiation and great technical know-how in their particular product niches, while the large firms followed broad line strategies achieving lower product differentiation and there were few economies of scale in the industry. (Porter 1974, p. 220)

Measurement of total factor productivity (TFP) represents in part an attempt to focus on the technical input–output relationships, thereby avoiding some of the complications involved in interpreting cost and profit data. Again there are no unqualified generalizations emerging from such analyses, a fair number of which have been carried out in LDCs. If there is a pattern of any frequency, it is probably that TFP reaches a maximum somewhere in the middle size range rather than at the bottom or the top. Thus, for Korea, Ho (1980, pp. 64–5) reports that in about two-thirds of the four-digit branches he studied, the peak occurred in the range of 50–500 employees, while it occurred at a smaller size for about a quarter and in the largest size range for about 13 per cent. Cortes et al. (1987, p. 104) found a positive relationship between size and the 'technical efficiency ratio' (defined as the ratio of a firm's output/input ratio to the corresponding ratio for a firm on the efficiency frontier) among small and medium metal-working firms and a quadratic relationship among food-processing firms. Little et al. found a varying relationship between size and technical efficiency in the four industries surveyed, but no tendency toward the quadratic pattern just cited, nor toward a clear dichotomy with larger firms faring better or less well, though in three of the four industries large firms of 100 or more workers had higher TFP indexes than small firms of under ten workers. Marked differentials in social benefit/cost ratios in favour of smaller firms of less than fifty workers are reported by Liedholm and Mead for ten of twelve industry cases in Sierra Leone, Jamaica, and Honduras (1987, p. 73).

The probable non-comparability of available studies, and the possibility that most of them suffer from significant input-measurement problems may explain the lack of any clear pattern relating size to TFP. In any case it is clear that more research would be necessary to establish any solid generalizations, let alone to probe further the causal connection between size and TFP. Only a few studies have included size as one of several independent variables to test for its separable effect on TFP (or profits or cost levels, for that matter). In their analysis of Indian industries Little et al. (1987, p. 201) found size to be unrelated to technical efficiency in four of the five industries analysed; in the machine-tool industry a significant positive association was found, though based on their econometric analysis of average production functions, they suspect this association is probably not so much due to technical economies of scale as to better organization of production and more complete mastery of the technical possibilities of the production process. In four of the five industries the frontier or best-practice firms were more skill-intensive and smaller than the average firm in the sample; in machine tools they were much larger than average.[16] Cortes et al. (1987, p. 105) also found that size had no significant explanatory power when it appeared together with other determinants of TFP.[17]

To summarize, neither the evidence on the relation of size to unit costs or profits nor the implications of survivor analysis suggest a prevalence of economies of scale, scope, or size in LDC manufacturing. But neither do these data clearly contradict such a possibility, given the alternative interpretations to which they are open. The fact that size structure tends to vary across industries in very much the same way from country to country suggests systematically greater economies of size in some industries than in others; yet the fact that average size tends to be several times greater in developed than developing countries (see Banerji 1978, p. 161) suggests that other factors as strong as or stronger than any such universally relevant economies of size are at work also. Engineering data indicated significant economies in some industries. A best guess, based on their presence in certain industries, is that scale economies are of substantial importance overall, but that they are not nearly universal enough or strong enough to offset the presumption that small and medium-scale firms make a major contribution to economy-wide efficiency, and *a fortiori* to employment creation.

3. INTRA-INDUSTRY HETEROGENEITY IN LDCs: ILLUSTRATIVE EVIDENCE

In the primary sector, which provides the bulk of exports from most Third World countries, size of enterprise varies widely. Minerals tend to be produced by large establishments (often foreign ones), partly because their extraction tends to require large amounts of capital and partly because the rents involved are large and draw the attention of powerful groups. Agricultural exports vary widely in factor proportions and in the distribution of income and rents, from cases where they are produced by small family-farmers (cocoa in Ghana, coffee in parts of Colombia, fruit and vegetables in some countries) to others where they involve quite modern capital-intensive processes.[18] Again, if rents are large, this fact alone is likely to influence the technology and the size of establishment since what the rich and powerful want they often get.[19] For manufacturing it is possible to generalize a little more and to begin to address some of the interesting issues and concerns surrounding the character of international trade.

As indicated above, manufacturing industries in LDCs are usually characterized by a particularly wide range of technologies, factor proportions, and firm (or plant) sizes. The full range of factor proportions and of labour productivity in manufacturing is usually immense, from the virtual absence of capital and very low labour productivity of the marginal self-employed producer of some non-durable consumer goods to the modern heavy-industry firm. Not only are there striking differences between the large firms and the rest in most branches of industry, but the 'non-large' firms are often very heterogeneous among themselves, with very small 'informal'-sector establishments as well as small and medium-sized factory-sector units. It is important not to lump all of these non-large producers together since (a) subsets of them may compete with each other as well as or instead of competing with large producers, and (b) where one should draw the line between smaller and larger establishments (if indeed a dichotomy is useful at all) depends on the empirical relationship between size and the variable of interest in a particular discussion, for example the labour/capital ratio if the issue is employment or income distribution. If labour intensity were to fall discretely between informal establishments and very small factories, that could be the relevant distinction.

Also important, though less central to the concerns of this chapter are various sources of heterogeneity among larger firms. Both multinationals and state enterprises are almost always large, by the standards of the country. Each responds to somewhat different pressures from those affecting large national private firms, and each tends to be prominent in some industrial branches but not in others. Though these three categories of large firms do not differ dramatically among themselves in terms of employment generation, that is, all are much less labour-intensive in the aggregate than small firms, it would be of interest to know how they differ in other relevant dimensions, such as the extent to which they subcontract, and their success in developing or adapting new technologies and where relevant, diffusing them.

Much of our organized information on the variance of input/output ratios within industries comes from factory-sector data organized by employment size of firm plant. Those ratios are, as noted, significantly correlated with size, though since the correlation is not perfect, data organized by size tend somewhat to understate the variances in question. Aggregate data from India and Colombia show a fairly typical three-to-one ratio between the capital intensity of the largest firms (over 500 workers) and those of 10–19 workers.[20] When firms are ranked by output or (especially) by capital the gap becomes more marked (Cortes et al. 1987, p. 118). The size–factor proportions relationship varies a great deal from industry to industry, as revealed in Table 1 which reports the evidence for five industries in India. It is unclear whether the variance of the capital/labour ratio across all manufacturing firms depends more on product, that is, industry, or on the set of variables related to size,[21] sophistication of technology, and other correlates.[22] The same ambiguity holds whether the ratio in question is physical capital to number of workers, or some perhaps more relevant indicator of capital intensity like inputs of physical plus human capital to inputs of unskilled labour.

Another correlate of firm size and technology is import intensity, that is, the relative importance of imported raw materials and capital goods. In Colombia, as of 1964 when foreign exchange was in scarce supply, the share of intermediate inputs which were imported varied from about 10 per cent for plants of under twenty workers to 26 per cent for those of 200 or more

Table 1. Mean capital/labour ratios in four Indian industries ('000s rupees per worker)

Size of firms (no. of workers)	Printing	Machine tools	Soap	Shoes	Metal casting
<5	2.35	—	8.17	0.64	3.00
	(1.11)		(7.43)	(0.54)	(0.00)
5–9	6.39	3.69	5.77	0.49	30.29
	(7.38)	(0.91)	(3.55)	(0.58)	(8.73)
10–24	9.60	5.42	5.67	0.45	35.04
	(10.17)	(11.68)	(2.86)	(0.40)	(49.07)
25–49	6.34	3.14	5.68	0.72	26.46
	(4.19)	(2.04)	(0.92)	(0.62)	(21.20)
50–99	10.47	3.45	6.73	—	18.03
	(3.65)	(1.64)	(4.88)		(20.17)
>100	14.27	7.40	6.44	5.53	35.11
	(12.51)	(7.31)	(3.59)	(4.13)	(31.28)

Note: Figures in parentheses are standard deviations.
Source: Little et al. (1987, pp. 156–7).

workers (Todd 1983, p. 215). By 1976 when foreign exchange was less scarce the gap in observed import intensity was a little smaller, ranging from 14 per cent for the former group to 29 per cent for the latter. When firms are ranked by output the gap is considerably greater; in 1976 import intensity was about 5 per cent for those small firms (size defined by output) with the same share of output as the firms with under twenty workers, and around 28 per cent for the comparable large-firm group.

It has been widely observed that most LDC manufactured exports come from relatively large establishments, and that the export/output ratio tends to be higher for large firms than for smaller ones. It remains true, however, that the net balance-of-payments impact of larger firms is in many countries more negative than that of smaller ones; one might guess that the only exceptions are the few countries with high aggregate export to output ratios in manufacturing. As of 1970, when Colombia's manufacturing export boom was under way, Diaz-Alejandro's figures indicated that even the largest exporters were characterized by significant balance-of-trade deficits. Diaz-Alejandro noted the strong tendency for both manufactured exports and imports to be highly concentrated in a fairly small number of large, high-wage firms and observed that neither the 'trade-deficit' nor the large average size of the major exporters 'fits well with an image of firms producing labour-intensive, manufactured exports: rather, many of the same companies which have benefited, and still are benefiting from import intensive import substitution, now seem to benefit from the newest export promotion policies' (1983, p. 269).

How widespread is this pattern and how does it change over time as the industrial sector grows and matures? Korea provides an interesting case, given its spectacularly successful record as an exporter of manufactures. As in the case of Colombia, many firms which started as import-substituters became successful exporters. Larger firms export a much higher share of output and purchase a much higher share of raw materials abroad (Table 2). In Malaysia too the export share of output was markedly higher (27 per cent) in large firms (100 workers and over) than for smaller ones (about 11 per cent) as of 1973 (Bruch 1980, p. 433).

If large firms tend to be more capital-intensive than smaller ones, and if manufactured exports come mainly from large firms, does this imply that LDC manufactured exports tend to be capital-intensive? Not necessarily, since those exports come mainly from fairly labour-intensive industries and may sometimes draw on more labour-intensive subcontractors.[23] But, if we may judge from the admittedly imperfect data from Colombia, the possibility certainly exists (see Berry and Diaz-Alejandro 1980, pp. 156–7). I have not yet seen evidence which deals in fully adequate detail with this issue, though Silber's study in the Brazilian context goes some way. Using data on firms from eighty-seven four-digit manufacturing sectors, he pre-

Table 2. Export and import patterns of manufacturing enterprise, by size, Korea, 1975

Size of enterprise (No. of workers)	Sales going abroad (%)	Raw materials and parts acquired abroad (%)
5–9	2	8.2
10–19	6	15.1
20–49	17	33.6
50–99	26	41.0
100–199	29	43.1

Source: Ho (1980, pp. 16, 20). His source is the Medium-Small Industry Bank, *Report on the Status of Medium-Small Industries, 1975*, Tables 1.18 & Table 2.21.

sented wage and electricity-consumption data separately for exporters and non-exporters.[25] For these sectors as a group (accounting for 75 per cent of manufactured exports in 1974), the export/sales ratio rose with size to a peak of 8.6 per cent for firms of 250–499 workers, falling thereafter to 5.1 per cent for the largest category (Table 3), suggesting the possibility of relationships between non-monotonic size and export tendency relationships. Average production wages were about 50 per cent higher in exporters than in non-exporters and the consumption of electricity per employee was over twice as high. Unfortunately almost all of the largest firms do some exporting, but do not on average have it as a major activity, so the factor proportions involved in their exports could differ from their average factor proportions,[26] rendering such overall comparisons between exporters and non-exporters misleading. The size category exporting the highest share of its sales had well below average production wages and electricity consumption per employee. Still, there is no doubt that Brazil's manufactured exports are quite capital-intensive relative to the country's factor proportions, if not to the manufacturing sector's factor proportions; the labour productivity of manufacturing was about three times that of the economy in 1974, and that of exporters somewhat higher again. (The figures of Table 3 do not include the smallest establishments of fewer than five workers.)

Given the complexities of breaking into large developed-country markets, it would not be surprising if small and medium-sized exporting firms focused especially on other LDC markets. This pattern was recently noted in the case of Colombia where as of 1980–1 no more than 2.5 per cent of exports of a sample of small and medium-sized firms went to the US or the European Common Market,[27] while those regions took a much higher share of total manufactured exports. The composition of such exports by sector

Table 3. A comparison of wages and electricity consumption per employee, by exporting and non-exporting firms and by firm size, 87 four-digit industries, Brazil, 1974

No. of employees	Average production worker wage			Electricity consumption per employee			Exports as % of sales		Total exports (%)	Firms exporting (%)
	All	Exporters	Non-exporters	All	Exporters	Non-exporters	All[a,b]	Exporters		
5–19	5 202	4 893	5 210	1 267	1 513	1 261	0.41	16.0	0.6	2.2
20–49	6 367	5 812	6 436	1 967	2 299	1 926	1.46	13.3	2.0	10.0
50–99	6 722	6 958	6 657	2 652	2 394	2 722	2.35	11.0	3.0	20.4
100–249	7 211	7 397	7 082	4 751	5 452	4 261	4.69	11.4	10.2	39.4
250–499	7 558	7 655	7 433	7 192	7 651	6 600	8.61	15.3	18.1	56.0
500–999	8 192	8 259	7 992	11 595	12 466	8 972	7.73	10.3	16.7	73.8
1 000–1 999	8 799	9 050	6 932	9 154	9 537	6 300	7.05	8.0	20.1	86.5
≥2 000	12 922	13 242	9 928	14 117	14 585	14 602	5.06	5.6	28.7	88.5
All[c]	9 349	10 505	7 091	9 374	11 484	5 255	5.29	8.0	100.0	15.2

[a] Assumes the same ratio of sales/worker between exporters and non-exporters in each size class of firms.
[b] Estimate.
[c] Excludes firms of fewer than 5 employees, which are included in Silber's tables.

Source: Calculated from Silber (1987), Table 1–3.

would be of interest; possibly the sectors are not particularly labour-intensive ones.

An important aspect of export capability in most manufacturing sectors is the level of technology. Larger firms may fare better than small ones in export markets because of economies of scale in production, economies of scale in export marketing, public policies which discriminate in their favour or in which there are economies of scale, and more time/experience in business permitting a build-up of expert skills. They may also benefit from better access to productive technologies,[28] which could involve either better capacity to search for or implement existing technologies and/or better research skills to develop new products or processes or to adapt existing ones.

Among large firms it is useful to distinguish between multinationals and national firms. The importance of multinationals in the manufactured exports of many LDCs reflects the advantage of proprietary information, as well as of special access to (their own or other) marketing networks abroad. When multinationals license their technology rather than engage directly in production in the LDC, their most likely licensees are medium or large firms (by the size criteria of the LDC); in any case when proprietary knowledge is involved, as it tends to be in the earlier phases of the product cycle, export capacity is likely to reflect access to such information. When LDC exports are in the later stages of the product cycle and the technology is relatively stable and widely known, the combination of long runs and cheap labour provides the competitive edge so, whether MNCs or national firms, the exporters are likely to be large. It is also generally accepted that larger national firms have the edge over small ones in terms of benefiting from technological change, though there may be a middle range with some advantage *vis-à-vis* the very large.

How much technological improvement can occur in small firms under favourable conditions and with effective government support remains a matter of speculation. Certainly an earlier view that smaller industry is technologically stagnant has been debunked by accumulating evidence to the contrary. The picture emerging from Taiwan of modest-sized but quite agile exporting firms, operating in a context of strong support from service firms and the government (for example Levy 1988a), raises interesting issues about the potential for reconciling the advantages of smallness with the needs for technological advance and flexibility. There are at least some conceptual grounds for a certain amount of optimism. Where smallness is associated with well-functioning markets and the degree of specialization which such markets permit, it is less implausible that small firms would invest in improving technology. Where products are marketed abroad, technological diffusion among producers should also occur more easily, since the reticence to allow 'competitors' to acquire one's advances should be moderated.[29] Further, if the frequent allegation that large firms adopt inappropriate technology is valid and the phenomenon quantitatively significant, small firms may not need to generate as much technological change to make as much of an economic contribution as their larger counterparts. The danger of the adoption of new technology so inappropriate that its use lowers national income is clearly much less for exporters than for protected import-substituters, but the concern that larger firms tend to adopt less than optimal technology does remain.

Pack has highlighted the contrast between the indigenous learning by mainly large import-substituting firms, most studied for India and Latin America, a learning which mainly responded to conditions imposed by import-substituting industrialization (ISI) policies and consequent foreign-exchange shortages and involved mainly input substitution and process innovation, and what he suspects was a greater focus by the East Asian countries on product innovations for world markets *cum* technology licensing (Pack, Chapter 2 this volume). Assuming this contrast to be a valid one,[30] it would be worth while to ask which sort of innovation can be more easily undertaken by smaller firms or for them, for example by government.

In considering the export potential of small firms, Bruch (1980, p. 430) identified three categories of clear potential: the processing of spatially dispersed natural resources; traditional products using labour-intensive indigenous technology and protected by the special characteristics of the product or the special skills involved, for example batik cloth in South-East Asia; and products which cannot be standardized or specialized products with small total markets. In most countries the first two categories probably offer rather limited potential; the potential of the third one thus becomes the major question.

4. EFFECTS OF TRADE UNDER INTRA-SECTOR FIRM HETEROGENEITY

4.1 Economic Aspects

Intra-sector heterogeneity expands the range of possible effects of rapid export growth. Perhaps the most pessimistic scenario would be found in a labour-abundant country with a low investment propensity, where the import-substituting sector (defined as that with the activities whose resource absorption falls as that of the export sector rises)[31] was not very capital-intensive, and where export market were not very buoyant. Labour abundance implies that the optimal level of capital intensity would be low and heightens the probability that excessively capital-intensive technologies would be adopted. With sufficiently inappropriate factor proportions, such an export sector could slow the country's growth as well as aggravate income inequality. Such a negative outcome would be less likely if the country's labour abundance were less marked, since available technologies would not be so inappropriate. Or if the investment propensity were high, any initial loss due to inappropriate technology could be erased as growth raised the capital/labour ratio and previously inappropriate technology became appropriate.[32] Finally, when the 'import-substituting' activities which lose resources when exports expand are very capital-intensive, it is unlikely that an economy would suffer efficiency or equity loss from export growth, even if the export sector is rather capital-intensive. Knowing exactly which sectors suffer shrinkage in this way, after all of the general equilibrium dust has settled, is of course very difficult.

While theoretically possible, it seems improbable that an inefficient export sector would substantially slow overall growth. The more serious concern raised by the existence of inter-industry heterogeneity is that the income-distribution effects of trade in manufactured goods may not after all be positive as suggested by Heckscher–Ohlin-type theory, since exports come mainly from larger firms of above-average capital intensity for their industries. No very useful analysis has yet been undertaken to allow one to predict the indirect effects of the expansion of a large firm into the international market; such prediction would require a well-developed industrial organization model. The exports may simply involve an increase in the large firm's own output or it may open up space in the domestic market, which could be filled by a similar firm or alternatively by a small labour-intensive one. It may involve subcontracted production of inputs by more labour-intensive firms.

It also requires a sophisticated model to judge which outputs would rise were less resources used to produce exports. The tendency to presume that exports (manufactured or primary) ultimately compete for resources with the sort of large-scale capital-intensive industries which are viewed as synonymous with the ISI strategy may be wide of the mark.[33] For one thing, that type of import substitution tends to be import-intensive and hence, as far as the balance of payments is concerned, more complementary with exports than a substitute for them (Diaz-Alejandro 1965). Those economic activities which are fostered by a shortage of exports and hence of foreign exchange for imports of intermediate and capital goods are likely to be more labour-intensive and smaller scale than those which come in the wake of an abundant supply of imports. Labour intensity of import substitutes may also be encouraged by the small size of the domestic market. It is possible that capital-intensive production of exports is encouraged by the need to reap economies of scale, achieve high quality, etc., while the captial-intensive production of importables has been more the result of policy than any exogenously given factors. More research is clearly needed in this area; in most developing countries import-substitution policy has virtually disregarded employment and income-distribution goals, with India being perhaps the only major exception (Mazumdar 1988, pp. 2–4).

In short, when exports are produced in a relatively capital-intensive way (contrary to the more conventional assumption) and they facilitate capital-intensive production for the domestic market rather than discouraging it (as the more usual way of looking at this issue would imply), and where the 'really import-substituting activities', that is, activities to which resources are shifted when imports fall, are in fact relatively labour-intensive, the scope for negative distributional effects is obvious. The exports may lead to a shift of resources from non-tradables (or non-tradeds) to both exports and certain import substitutes, while the extra foreign exchange goes to new imports, tourism abroad, capital flight, or whatever.

Whether the expected direction of the income-distribution effects of trade on a country are likely often to be reversed by consideration of the type (for example size) of firm producing the exports or import substitutes may remain a matter of guesswork for some time. Possibly more empirical light can be thrown on the equally important issue of whether trade structure and level matters much to distribution in the first place. Serious attempts to relate trade policy or structure to distributional outcomes via either cross-country or time-series analysis are few. Analysis of trade's distributional effects in single-country general equilibrium models has tended to support the view that it is an unimportant determinant of distribution, or at least that plausible modifications in the level and structure of trade are not important (for example Bourguignon 1986). This result seems reasonable when one notes that over the last several decades the share of value added which is exported has typically been in the range of say 5–20 per cent of GDP in developing countries[34] and the directly employed workers a somewhat smaller share of the labour force.[35] Except for the new dramatically successful East Asian exporters, the manufactured-export sector appears not to have made a very large direct contribution to employment,[36] even though the production of manufactured exportables has systematically been more labour-intensive than that of manufactured importables (Tyler 1976, p. 174; Krueger et al. 1984). If exporting firms do tend generally to be more capital-intensive than non-exporters in the same industry, however, most studies may have somewhat overestimated the employment creation associated with such exports.[37]

The initial optimism of a good number of economists as to the employment and income-distribution potential of export orientation (excluding minerals since they create so few jobs) probably reflected an inadequate recognition of the fact that labour productivity in modern manufacturing is usually well above the economy-wide average, including a number of important non-tradables sectors. It may also owe something to the fact that

Taiwan, the country on which the strongest case can be and has been built,[38] is in many structural respects quite atypical of most LDCs. While even in that case the impressive equality the country has achieved is probably due less to its export success than to its prior thoroughgoing agrarian reform,[39] few would question that export growth has also played an important role (as argued by Kuo *et al.* 1981). The evolution of income distribution shows no such recognizable benefits, however, in most of the other export-oriented countries. In Korea, though the income-distribution data are less solid than in Taiwan, the current view is that inequality rose substantially in the 1970s, after being similar to that of Taiwan during the mid-1960s (Koo 1984). This increase, and the resulting difference in inequality *vis-à-vis* Taiwan, has been explained in terms of the greater prevalence of large firms in Korea than in Taiwan (Scitovsky 1985, p. 218), the increasing capital intensity pursued as part of the outward-oriented industrialization strategy and the heavy credit and other subsidies to that capital-intensive export sector (Hong 1981, p. 33). In Brazil the export sector is much less dominant so one would expect its character to be less important as a determinant of income distribution. Although the worsening characteristic of the 1960s may have ended in the 1970s, inequality remained at one of the highest levels anywhere. Such examples lead one to hypothesize that the steady-state distributional impact of a high degree of outward orientation is in most cases probably modest in scope, that it depends on the setting, and that it depends on what policies are used to encourage exports. Part of the setting, certainly, is the size structure of firms in general and of exporting firms in particular, and the extent of factor market imperfections or other contributors to widely differing factor intensities by firm size. Among the policy considerations are the inducements to exports and whether these do or do not fall differently on different types of firms.

4.2 Political Economy Considerations

As we have seen, firm heterogeneity complicates the purely economic analysis of the impact of trade on a country. To understand its implications more fully, it is important to assess the role of policy in creating or influencing heterogeneity, and the extent to which policy favours one sort of firm over others. On the first count, minimum-wage legislation and the right to strike or other union-supportive legislation are commonly viewed as contributing to the positive relation between wages and firm size, while subsidized credit from development banks to large firms contributes to the negative relation between the cost of borrowed capital and firm size. On the second, to the extent that government policy favours the rich and powerful, one would expect it to reflect the interests of the large when these are in conflict with the small. In many developing countries trade policy has gone through first a relatively open period during which indigenous artisan or small-scale industry was damaged or (for some industries) eradicated by imports while free trade ideology was widely touted, and then a later period of import-substituting industrialization in which protection was directed at the more capital-intensive and large-scale industries which had not developed on their own. In those countries which have moved toward an outward-oriented strategy, policy has also tended to benefit larger firms more than small ones.

A model in which small enterprise has little or no political clout, while large enterprise does, can explain a good deal of the oft-commented perverseness of the ISI process. A rational protective system might, in a growing economy, seek to nudge into existence industries that are somewhat more capital-intensive than typical of the sector at any given point of time; but in many cases protective systems have gone well beyond what would have seemed reasonable in this regard. Various interpretations for such behaviour have been offered.[40] The fact that the protected capital-intensive industries were composed of large firms whose owners presumably had clout has been relatively neglected. It is striking to note that local prices of goods produced in small firms (shoes, clothing, furniture) are often highly competitive in world terms while those of goods produced by large firms (iron and steel, sometimes textiles, chemicals) are not. When comparative advantage lies in small agriculture and small industry, the exchange rate is often systematically overvalued; few countries have made serious attempts to get their small-enterprise goods into world markets, though the potential (after some organizational work) may seem obvious. Most countries give favoured import treatment to new capital equipment, most of it purchased by large capital-intensive firms, but look less kindly on and sometimes actually prohibit the importation of used machinery, which can so greatly benefit SMI.

5. OUTWARD ORIENTATION, FIRM SIZE, AND ALTERNATIVE PATHS TO DEVELOPMENT?

Though it is possible to conceive of situations in which export expansion does not contribute to economic growth, the empirical evidence has thrown up numerous cases of successful outward orientation so that the natural presumption now is that it does make sense in many countries to pursue such a strategy, at least to some degree. The contrast between Taiwan and Korea highlights the fact that manufactured-export-led growth can be pursued successfully with reliance mainly on quite large firms (the Korean route) or with relatively small ones (Taiwan). Both export and GDP growth performances have been nearly identical in the two cases, while as noted above the income-distribution experiences show a marked contrast in

Taiwan's favour. Under the Korean approach the focus is on high volume, high productivity manufacture of standardized products, whereas the smaller Taiwanese firms emphasize flexibility and rapid response in market niches for non-standardized products (Levy 1988b). Levy interprets the two countries' different approaches to the international market as a reflection of a different firm size structure within manufacturing, due in turn to Korea's lower stage of development when the two began their post-war drives to industrialization, the resulting greater degree of market failure in Korea, and the Korean response of internalizing the relevant transactions within large-scale enterprises (including large-scale trading companies).[41]

Two questions immediately follow. How accessible is the Taiwan route to other LDCs, and how much difference does the route chosen make? Dealing with the first question requires a look both at the character of international markets and at the domestic degrees of freedom a country has in determining the size structure of its manufacturing firms or of those which export. At present it would appear that in a number of industries product and technology change is placing a premium on supplier flexibility, a fact which could augur well for smaller, more agile firms. On the domestic side, the limited cross-country evidence leaves it unclear whether Korea's size structure of manufacturing firms at the onset of industrialization was more or less typical than was Taiwan's.[42]

As to the second question, only a very careful comparison of income-distribution patterns, trends, and determinants between the two countries would permit a confident guess as to how much difference size structure has made, and within that more general question, how much difference the size structure of exporters has made. While of probably increasing importance in the production of Korean manufactured exports, subcontracting seems to have been significantly more important in Taiwan. The lower wages and other advantages of small and medium-sized subcontractors which have figured prominently in the Japanese experience may have been recently accentuated for large Korean exporters by the pressure to lower costs resulting from the appreciation of the yen.[43] This may account for part of the rapid recent expansion in their number (Levy 1988b, p. 4). Where the export producers are themselves large, as in Korea, subcontracting presumably lowers the overall capital/labour ratio of the export activity. In the Taiwanese case, the existence of a strong network of small, flexible firms with which exporters can subcontract allows the exporters themselves to be smaller and to set up with limited capital, thus probably lowering capital/labour ratios through two separate routes. The system also provides the overall flexibility for which the Taiwanese export sector has become noted. One may speculate that the expertise concentrated in many parts producers in Taiwan is ultimately more effectively used when their sales are directed to different buyers over the course of time, in response to the differential success of those buyers in selling goods requiring these inputs. Where component production is in-house, the specialized machinery and skills may be less well used when the internal need diminishes. The effective network of small firms in Taiwan, based on the combination of well-developed entrepreneurial skills, and smoothly functioning markets, has also permitted considerable gains based on innovation and specialization in R & D (Levy 1988b, p. 15).

A contrast has developed also in the trading system by which the Taiwanese and Korean manufactures are moved on to the world market. Very large firms like those in Korea typically handle their own marketing (directly or through large trading companies) whereas the smaller-scale middleman comes into his own when smaller firms produce the exports or buy the imports, as in Taiwan. Though his role may make the distribution of trade-related income less egalitarian than the distribution of income generated in the direct production of exports, the effective middleman may be the key to achievement of a fairly progressive income distribution in the export sector.[44] Japan's famous trading companies remained central to Japanese trade until fairly recently. When their role in Japanese trade was finally diminished by the dominance of large manufacturing firms, they shifted their focus increasingly to trade between third countries, among which Korea and Taiwan have been prominent. In Taiwan from the late 1960s on these Japanese companies were joined and to some degree supplanted by US and European importers who set up offices in Taipei to deal with local manufacturers, including many small ones (Scitovsky 1985, p. 238). Subsequently (or perhaps concurrently) there was a proliferation of small traders trying to uncover export opportunities for small Taiwanese manufacturers. In 1973 the value of industrial exports per trader was 70 per cent higher in Korea than in Taiwan, and in 1984 it was nearly four times as high (Levy 1988b, pp. 4, 7). Korea meanwhile pushed the development of its own large trading companies, which gradually squeezed out the Japanese who had been important in the 1960s, and became central movers on the trade scene in their own right (Levy 1988b, p. 239). Currently there are eight authorized general trading companies in Korea, seven of which belong to the upper-ranking *jaebols* (conglomerates of a number of firms, most of which are large and operate in diverse and highly concentrated markets); it can be presumed that their important role in export promotion involved the large producers—in fact, most were the in-house marketing arms of those conglomerates. The eighth general trading company is a subsidiary of the Korea Trader's Association specially organized to promote exports of small and medium-sized firms; but its exports account for only 2 per cent of the total for the eight trading companies (Lee 1988, p. 28).

Overall firm size structure is a likely determinant of the size structure of exporters. Current policy on access to imports could also be rather important. Keesing and Lall (Chapter 7, Section 3) note that the four most dramatic Asian export success stories are 'the only developing economies offering quick, easy duty-free access to imported inputs in any location'. Normally access to imported inputs and capital equipment is subjected to bureaucratic processes and barriers for all firms, but in a way biased against the small firms. In several cases small and medium-sized firms have performed particularly well just after devaluations and the easing of controls on imports; perhaps the same removal of biases which leads to good growth of output for the domestic market could create the potential for good export performance when other conditions, for example good marketing networks, are also met. Keesing and Lall also emphasize both the 'enormous difficulties and the lack of relevant knowledge of the local entrepreneurs when they first begin exporting to major industrial economy markets' and the potentially important role of export-promoting organizations when instead of having a multi-purpose general service character (the usual pattern) they concentrate marketing and related assistance on a small number of the more promising export products and within a short (say three to five year) timeframe (Lec 1988). Given the desirability of a directed focus, there is no obvious reason why smaller and (especially) medium-sized producers could not share in the benefits of such assistance more than appears often to be the case now.

Not only entrepreneurial skills but also efficient provision of inputs, services, and information are necessary to make networks of small firms work effectively. The gaps in these respects remain striking in many countries. One optimistic note is that with the rapid expansion of education in nearly all Third World countries, one of the major prerequisites for a blossoming of a dynamic small-firm system may increasingly be met. If countries can with reasonable dispatch lay the groundwork for such a system they might at least have some choice among outward-orientation paths. If they cannot, the desirability of outward orientation and the optimal degree to which it should be pursued become more delicate decisions.

6. RECONSIDERING THE EFFECTS OF SPECIFIC TRADE-RELATED POLICIES

Just as firm heterogeneity has implications for the overall effects of trade on an economy, it is likely to affect the impact of specific trade-related policy tools such as the exchange rate, the structure of protection, etc. A number of areas can be considered using as backdrop a fairly common trade-policy syndrome which might be referred to as the 'biased intervention' package, including an overvalued exchange rate and a foreign-exchange rationing system; the overvaluation means that the recipients of the rationed foreign exchange are being subsidized, and the rationing procedure is biased in favour of large firms and existing (as opposed to new) firms.[45] The structure of import controls and export subsidies is also usually biased in favour of LI and against SMI. These various biases are plausible results of the greater political clout of LI and of the not infrequent belief within government bureaucracy that LI contributes more to an economy than does SMI.

6.1 Devaluation and Import Liberalization

Rationing is likely to discriminate against smaller firms both because they have less political power than larger ones *and* because the administrative costs of dealing with bureaucracy create greater problems for them.[46] Devaluation and associated higher prices for imports *coupled* with the better access implicit in price rather than administrative rationing are likely to be a net boon to SMI firms because their total import bill is relatively small (they are less dependent on imported raw material inputs and, being less capital-intensive, need fewer imports of machinery and equipment) but some imports may be important to them. A few cases have been noted suggesting such a positive impact of devaluation cum improved access. The Philippine devaluation of 1962 was followed by several years of unusually dynamic SMI growth. After Colombia's 1967 adoption of a floating exchange rate led to an expanded supply of foreign exchange and better SMI access to it, that sector underwent a dramatic boom, with high profits and employment growth of 8–10 per cent annually in the 1970s (Cortes *et al.* 1987, chs. 2, 6).

Devaluation typically has the direct effect of equalizing access to foreign exchange among firms, and, eventually (if it 'holds') the indirect effect of increasing the total supply of foreign exchange via an increase in the level of exports. The impact of liberalization, which refers to decreases in the protectionist intervention of the government against imports, on SMI cannot be predicted in so general a sense since it depends on the previous structure of protection and how that structure is altered. In most countries the playing-field is tilted against SMI in various ways so it is a reasonable presumption that the removal of all interventions would tend to improve its situation relative to LI, but liberalizations are usually partial so the outcome clearly depends on what changes are made. If tariff or quota protection is reduced from earlier levels but the disproportionate power of the LI sector is brought to bear, the weight of liberalization may fall more heavily on import-competing small enterprise. And even if the structure of liberalization is not biased against SMI in this way, there are reasons to worry that the transition process following on any sharp change in the incentive structure, in access to foreign exchange, or in import competition may create more dangers for it than for LI.

Mature LI firms tend to have reasonable levels of economic reserves with which to weather economic turbulence. They usually have a more diversified product line and often a more diversified set of markets, based on the good regional average at home and more foreign outlets. They are often able to draw on the public purse when necessary since they are well connected politically and can argue that the demise of their firm will have major perverse effects on output, employment, etc. SMI firms contrast in each of the above respects. Many are forced to operate under tight financial and working-capital constraints as they grow towards a more efficient size range. Some have not yet developed a *modus operandi* which can protect against external shocks. Few are likely to have decent access to credit or to public sector assistance at times of stress. Accordingly it is quite possible that SMI establishments which are presently or could soon become quite efficient will fold under the stress of policy change (especially when it is abrupt), while LI firms survive because of their better defence mechanisms. The dynamics set off by changed conditions must be studied with care to answer these questions.[47]

The liberalization experience of the Southern Cone countries of Latin America in the second half of the 1970s highlights the non-neutral role of government in the context of abrupt policy change. Policy reforms substantially deregulated the product, financial, and foreign-exchange markets. Early in these experiments, when the domestic currency was overvalued, large firms were the ones to benefit from cheap foreign loans. When large real devaluations occurred, pushing the real interest rates on foreign-currency-denominated loans strongly positive, many large firms survived only because the authorities *de facto* took the foreign-denominated loans on to the public books (Tybout 1985). Because of unequal access, both to the original loans and to the subsequent bail-out, success over the liberalization-stabilization period was related to firm size. Comparable experiences appear to have occurred in a number of other countries. Whether and to what degree large firms sustain shocks better for reasons of internal resilience, greater diversity, and better capitalization (that is, reasons other than their preferential access to government and to the financial system) is unclear and has been little studied in the context of recent economic turn-downs.

Sometimes liberalization is accompanied by other policies as part of a broader package. Since 1980 Korea has implemented pro-competition policies at the same time as trade liberalization (Lee 1988), and it is intriguing to consider their relative roles in the very rapid increase in the number of small and (especially) middle-sized establishments and the rapid increase in subcontracting activity of these firms during this period (Lee, n.d.).

6.2 The Potential of SMI as a Motor of Growth under Fiscal and Balance-of-Payments Crisis Conditions

The current near universality of balance-of-payments problems in the Third World has created a situation in which most LDCs urgently need to increase their production of tradables, both exports and import substitutes; their recent slow growth has also accentuated the need to create more productive jobs and to worry about poverty problems. The fiscal crisis makes capital an increasingly scarce resource. This change in conditions makes the economic characteristics of SMI particularly attractive; it is labour-intensive, in many ways exceptionally flexible, and an economizer of imports. The only striking disadvantage, unless it is less efficient than LI (sometimes true and sometimes not), is in the export markets.

In any case, a beleaguered country with employment and balance-of-payments crises could hardly ask for a better present than a dynamic SMI sector needing little capital and few imports, to grow but able to create a considerable amount of productive employment. Several possible hurdles may, however, stand in the way. First, it remains to be seen whether the best that SMI can do is to reflect the dynamism of the economy as a whole, or whether it can itself be a major motor of overall growth, or at the least swim against an otherwise backward-flowing tide. If it can only fulfil the first role, for example because it requires rapidly expanding demand in order to grow fast, its potential contribution to many LDCs at the present difficult juncture is greatly reduced. Secondly, it remains unclear which policy variables can most contribute to SMI success, either in normal times or (especially) in times of economic crisis. Thirdly, it may be very difficult for both economic and political reasons to provide any reasonable level of resources to SMI in times of crisis. Though it might use both foreign exchange *and* credit more productively than LI at such a time, it may be least likely to get the resources then because LI, always first at the trough, most needs them then. How many governments will cut back on the supply of foreign exchange to import-intensive large firms operating far below capacity and with large, restive work-forces, in order better to provide for small-scale firms which have not traditionally had much of a claim on those resources?

Trade-related policy variables would probably be central to the creation of a positive context for SMI to achieve its potential in such circumstances. Use of an equilibrium exchange rate so that price rationing substitutes for administrative rationing would probably be important, but hard to achieve since it is precisely under conditions of balance-of-payments strain that countries resort to the latter. More feasible, perhaps, if frequent government bias against it could be overcome, would be easy entry for second-hand machinery. Finally, a protective structure which took account of

SMI's interests by keeping its imported inputs no more protected than other industrial inputs, and which took care not to liberalize imports competing with its output could be important. While liberalization might be appropriate if done gradually, the greater vulnerability of SMI to shocks would need to be taken into account.

7. POLICY BIAS BETWEEN SMALL AND LARGE ENTERPRISE

The vast literature on trade policy has greatly advanced our understanding of the nature and degree of policy bias between the production of tradables and non-tradables and between the production of exportables and importables. Some components of policy bias are, at least in some circumstances, relatively easy to measure and compare among themselves (for example effective protection rates, exchange-rate disequilibria, etc.), while others (suasion, discretionary management of foreign exchange, various types of licensing) are not.[48] Given the lack of attention to issues of firm size either in economic theory or in industrial and trade policy, it should not be surprising that the effort to measure policy bias in that context has been much less, usually confined to comments on how much wages and capital costs differ by firm or plant size. Measurement (when attempted) has not generally been very sophisticated. Conceptual distinctions are sometimes required which have no obvious counterparts on the trade policy side.

Most discussions of size-related bias refer to biases which affect the overall potential of firms, not their potential for exporting or for substituting for imports. For present purposes one would aspire to distinguish firm or plant size-related policy bias by destination of production. Attention is often focused on the impact of policy bias not only on relative profitability of small versus large firms but also on the factor proportions of each and the related extent to which the biases affect social returns differently from private returns. The combination of underpriced capital and overpriced labour is assumed to induce large firms to be excessively capital-intensive while the opposite distortions have the opposite effect for the smallest firms. The usual assumption of higher-cost capital for smaller enterprise is clearly an over-simplification as is any concept involving a perfectly elastic supply of funds for any enterprise. In the small-enterprise case, some borrowed capital is often cheap (where special programmes exist), and some own funds are probably cheap because of poor alternative uses, but the basic problem is lack of access, that is, a quantity problem rather than a price one. Finally, it is recognized that not all of the higher-price or more restricted credit access of small firms can be attributed either to government policy bias, or to discrimination by banks; part (perhaps most) is due to the higher real costs, in most financial systems, of providing loans to small enterprise. Similarly in the case of the labour market, while it is generally accepted that some part of wage differentials between large and small firms is policy-related (effects of minimum wages, legislated fringe benefits, etc.), another part may be due to union power (possibly indirectly attributable to public policy, but clearly not so simply as through wage legislation), and another part to profit-maximizing behaviour on the part of large and small firms.

Complications notwithstanding, available evidence does give some idea of the factor price differentials across size categories. Blue-collar workers tend to earn two to three times more in large firms than in quite small ones, with the precise size–age profile and the total gap varying somewhat from country to country.[49] Capital-cost differentials vary much more from case to case and according to which size groups are being compared; where informal capital-market charges are compared to those of the formal market, the gap is again often two or three to one or even more, but as noted above it is not very helpful to think of any single lending rate as reflecting 'the' price of capital for any firm. With the range of figures thrown around in such discussions and the complication introduced by lack of access in the case of capital, it is not yet possible to generalize as to the 'net bias', if one wants to call it that, by size as far as the impact on profits is concerned. There seems little doubt that relative factor prices often differ enough to affect the choice of technology, where the production function permits.[50]

Observed factor price differentials reflect aspects of size-related policy bias along with other influences. Other types of size-related policy biases have to be sought in tax systems (different aspects of which work both for and against the small), in foreign-exchange allocation, in licensing procedures, in various types of institutional support, and elsewhere. As with the analysis of bias among trade-related output categories, the quantification of some of these components is difficult because of their frequent intangibility, the lack of appropriate data, etc. In most countries more data are classified by trade-related categories than by size; comparatively little effort has thus far been expended in the latter direction.[51] Reducing all the components of firm size bias to a single number, equivalent say to a product price differential of x per cent, is seldom possible except by judgement and guesswork; but then this is the usual case with trade-related categories of bias as well.

Much small-scale production is of traditional products for local consumption. In some cases (including cheaper clothing and furniture) small firms have a strong comparative advantage in the sense that they experience little trouble competing with imports, but costs of marketing, lack of product standardization, and so on have impeded exports. Export-promoting programmes usually focus on large firms, from special export credits (whether they go through the regular formal-sector financial institutions or specialized ones), to access to imported inputs, tax provisions, etc. On the import-substituting side, protection tends to be highest for the more capital-intensive large-firm sectors; since up to a point this could be a natural result of a desirable transition towards more capital-intensive products, and it might be necessary to distinguish the results of that transition from a true size bias, as where larger firms in a given industrial category receive more protection for their specific product items than do the smaller firms. Although a first guess might be that anti-small-firm bias is greater in the case of exportables and importables than in non-tradables, it is subject to the qualifications discussed above, as well as the additional major complication (also common to trade-bias analysis) that large firms both compete with and are complementary to small firms. Were the relationship exclusively competitive, the concept of policy bias and the allocative and other effects thereof would be conceptually straightforward enough. Where complementarity is the main relationship, the effects of bias are much less and again relatively straightforward. (An anti-small-firm bias in export policy might have little impact if large exporters are closely tied to small subcontractors.) When both relationships are common, the issue becomes difficult. For example in assessing anti-small-firm bias in capital markets, such bias as affects small firms which are complementary to large ones (for example subcontractors) may be of little relevance either to the small firms or to economy-wide efficiency; what matters is the bias faced by small firms competing with large ones. Since capital-cost differentials can vary greatly across industrial branches, as could other components of overall policy bias, the calculation of that bias should focus selectively on the competitive cases. An average calculation could be quite misleading.[52]

Just as one may ask whether there is more intra-industry than inter-industry variance in factor proportions or in total factor productivity, one may wish to know whether policy biases tend to be greater across firms with differing factor proportions or sizes, or across firms belonging to different industrial branches. The ratio of private to social factor prices varies widely across firms; very high (or low, even negative) rates of effective protection are frequently accompanied by negative real interest rates to selected (usually) large firms. A static calculation of misallocation costs (output forgone) might well come out lower for the technology or size-related misallocation since the labour and capital-cost differentials by size tend partially to offset each other.[53] Factor-proportions effects (and the associated income-distribution impact) of having the 'wrong' size structure could, however, be more serious than those of having the 'wrong' industries. The question of intra-industry factor substitutability has long been debated; discussion of the more complicated question of intra- or inter-industry factor substitutability in the production of exports is just beginning.

CONCLUSIONS

Because it is hard to assess the potential of labour-intensive and/or small enterprise to play an important role in a healthy development process, it is hard to know how best or how much to support and encourage such activities. The safest advice might be to focus first on policy-based market distortions which hamper such activities, for example on unequal access to foreign exchange or to capital.[54] When the case seems strong, pro-labour-intensive interventions designed to 'level the playing-field' could be pursued. But ultimately one must recognize that our understanding of firm behaviour and industrial structure does not provide solid grounds for believing that market solutions are near-optimal ones; if the potential of labour-intensive activities is to be reaped, strong and co-ordinated intervention/support policy might be needed; this will not become apparent until we have a better grip on the issues and a chance to see the effects of a few such support programmes.[55]

A strong support strategy involving many resources would be risky at this time given the uncertain pay-off. It would be especially risky in a world where export performance is of great importance if exports and labour intensity simply do not easily mix. Much more needs to be learned about the direct and indirect labour intensity and the income-distribution implications of LDC exports and about the variables which determine those outcomes. Perhaps policy packages can be designed to achieve good distributional and balance-of-payments outcomes simultaneously. Perhaps this can be achieved only in certain types of countries or at certain levels of development. Where the primary problem in exporting from labour-intensive firms lies in the quality of the labour (for example difficulty in achieving quality standards or the flexibility which comes with trained, educated labour) the goals may be jointly attainable in countries with a specially skilled labour force (for example Taiwan) or at later stages of development when such skills have finally been generated.[56] Rapidly rising levels of education may make the dual goals increasingly attainable in general. Countries with policies which support both tradables and labour-intensive production should with time learn more about the intersection of these domains, and become increasingly adept at adding positive interventions to a more passive set of policies related to factor proportions. If time and experience reveal little chance to pursue the twin goals simultaneously, then their conflict will have to be accepted and increasingly incorporated consciously into policy.

REFERENCES

ADAR, ZVI, and HIRSCH, SEEV (1974), 'Firm Size and Export Performance', *World Development*, 2/7, pp. 41–6.
ADELMAN, IRMA, and ROBINSON, SHERMAN (1978), *Income Distribution Policy in Developing Countries: A Case Study of Korea* (Stanford University Press, Stanford, Calif.)
ANDERSON, DENNIS (1982), 'Small Industry in Developing Countries: A Discussion of Issues', *World Development*, 10/11 pp. 913–48.
AUQUIER, ANTOINE A. (1980), 'Size of Firms, Exporting Behaviour and the Structure of French Industry', *Journal of Industrial Economics* (Symposium on International Trade and Industrial Organization, (ed.) Richard E. Caves), 29/2, pp. 203–17.
BANERJI, RANADEV (1978), 'Average Size of Plants in Manufacturing and Capital Intensity: A Cross Country Analysis of Industry', *Journal of Development Economics*, 5/2, pp. 155–66.
BERRY, A. (1988), 'International Trade and Income Distribution in Peru since 1870: Some Hypotheses', (University of Toronto, Toronto), mimeo.
BERRY, A., and DIAZ-ALFJANDRO, CARLOS F. (1980), 'The New Colombian Exports: Possible Effects on the Distribution of Income', in R. Albert Berry and Ronald Soligo (eds.), *Economic Policy and Income Distribution in Colombia* (Westview Press, Boulder, Col.).
BOURGUIGNON, FRANCOIS (1986), 'Income Distribution and External Trade: The Case of Costa Rica' (École Normale Supérieure, Paris), mimeo.
BRUCH, MATHIAS (1980), 'Small Establishments as Exporters of Manufactures: Tentative Evidence from Malaysia', *World Development* 8/5 and 6, pp. 429–42.
CORTES, MARILUG, BERRY, ALBERT, and ISHAQ, ASHFAG (1987), *Success in Small and Medium-Scale Enterprises: The Evidence from Colombia* (OUP, Oxford).
DIAZ-ALEJANDRO, CARLOS F. (1965), 'On the Import Intensity of Import Substitution', *Kyklos*, 18, pp. 495–511.
—— (1983), 'Trade and the Import Control System in Colombia: Some Quantifiable Features', in A. Berry (ed.), *Essays on Industrialization in Colombia* (Arizona State University, Tempe, Ariz.)
ESCANDON, JOSÉ F. (1981), 'Analisis de los Factores que Han Determinado el Desarrollo de la Pequeña Empresa en Colombia: Una Interpretacion Historica', *Coyuntura Economica*, 11/3, pp. 113–39.
FEI, JOHN C.H., KUO, SHIRLEY W.Y, and RANIS, GUSTAV (1979), *Growth with Equity: The Taiwan Case* (OUP, Oxford).
FIELDS, GARY (1984), 'Employment, Income Distribution, and Economic Growth in Seven Small Open Economies', *Economic Journal*, 94 (Mar.), pp. 71–83
FINGER, J.M. (1975), 'Trade Overlap and Intra-Industry Trade', *Economic Inquiry*, 13/4, pp. 581–9.
GLESJER, HERBERT, JACQUEMIN, ALEXIS, and PETIT, JEAN (1980), 'Exports in an Imperfect Competition Framework: An Analysis of 1,446 Exporters', *Quarterly Journal of Economics*, 94/3, pp. 507–24.
GOLD, BELA (1981), 'Changing Perspectives on Size, Scale, and Returns: An Interpretive Survey', *Journal of Economic Literature*, 19 (Mar.), pp. 5–33.

GOMEZ, LEONARDO VILLAR (1986), 'Caracteristicas de las Exportaciones Colombianas de Manufacturas: Un Analisis Empirico Sobre Intensidad en Mano de Obra', *Revista Cambio y Progreso*, 1/2, pp. 39–87.
HO, SAMUEL P.S. (1980), 'Small Scale Enterprises in Korea and Taiwan' (Staff Working Paper 384, World Bank, Washington, DC).
HONG, WONTACK (1981), 'Trade, Growth and Income Distribution: The Experience of the Republic of Korea' (Working Paper 3, Overseas Development Council, Washington, DC).
KOO, HAGEN (1984), 'The Political Economy of Income Distribution in South Korea: The Impact of the State's Industrialization Policies', *World Development*, 12/10, pp. 1029–38.
KRUEGER, ANNE O., GARY, HAL B., MONSON, TERY, and AKRASANEE, NARONGCHAI (eds.) (1984), *Trade and Employment in the Developing Countries: 1, Individual Studies* (University of Chicago Press, Chicago).
KUO, SHIRLEY W.Y., RANIS, GUSTAV, and FEI, JOHN C.H. (1981), *The Taiwan Success Story: Rapid Growth with Improved Distribution in the Republic of China, 1952–1979* (Westview Press, Boulder, Col).
LEE, KYU-UCK (n.d.), 'The Relationship between Small or Medium Firms and Large Firms in Korea', mimeo.
—— (1988), 'International Trade and Industrial Organization: The Korean Experience' (WIDER, Helsinki), mimeo.
LEVY, BRIAN (1988a), 'Transactions Costs, the Size of Firms and Industrial Policy: Lessons from a Comparative Case Study of the Footwear Industry in Korea and Taiwan', mimeo.
—— (1988b), 'Korean and Taiwanese Firms as International Competitors: The Challenges Ahead', *Columbia Journal of World Business*, 23/1, pp. 43–51.
LIEDHOLM, CARL, and MEAD, DONALD (1987), 'Small Scale Industries in Developing Countries: Empirical Evidence and Policy Implications', Department of Agricultural Economics, International Development Paper, 9 (Michigan State University, East Lancing, Mich.)
LITTLE, M.D., MAZUMDAR, DIPAK, and PAGE, JOHN M., jun. (1987), *Small Manufacturing Enterprises: A Comparative Analysis of India and Other Economies* (OUP, Oxford).
MARCUS, M. (1969), 'Profitability and Size of Firm', *Review of Economics and Statistics*, 51 (Feb.), pp. 104–7.
MAZUMDAR, DIPAK (1988), 'Import Substituting Industrialization and Protection of the Small Scale: The Indian Experience in the Textile Industry' (Working Paper, World Bank Economic Development Institute, Washington, DC).
MELLER, P., and MARFAN, M. (1981), 'Small and Large Industry: Employment Generation, Linkages, and Key Sectors', *Economic Development and Cultural Change*, 29/2, pp. 263–74.
MORRISON, C. (1985), 'Domestic Income Distribution and the Structure of Foreign Trade' (École Normale Supérieure, Paris), mimeo.
NELSON, RICHARD R. (1968), 'A Diffusion Model of International Productivity Differences', *American Economic Review*, 59/3, pp. 1214–48.
PORTER, MICHAEL E. (1974), 'The Structure within Industries and Companies' Performance', *Review of Economics and Statistics*, 61/2, pp. 214–27.

Rayment, P.B.W. (1976), 'The Homogeneity of Manufacturing Industries with Respect to Factor Intensity: The Case of the United Kingdom', *Oxford Bulletin of Economics and Statistics*, 38/2, pp. 203–10.

Saving, J.R. (1961), 'Estimates of Optimum Size of Plant by the Survivor Technique', *Quarterly Journal of Economics*, 75 (Nov.), pp. 569–607.

Scherer, F.M. (1980), *Industrial Market Structure and Economic Performance*, 2nd edn. (Houghton Mifflin, Boston, Mass.).

—— Beckenstein, Alan, Kaufer, Erich, and Murphy, R.D. (1975), *The Economics of Multi-Plant Operation: An International Comparisons Study* (Harvard University Press, Cambridge, Mass.).

Schmitz, Hubert (1982), 'Growth Constraints on Small Scale Manufacturing in Developing Countries: A Critical Review', *World Development*, 10/6, pp. 429–50.

Schumacher, E.F. (1974), *Small is Beautiful* (Sphere Books, London).

Scitovsky, Tibor (1985), 'Economic Development in Taiwan and South Korea: 1965–81', *Food Research Institute Studies*, 19/3, 215–64.

Shepherd, William G. (1979), *The Economics of Industrial Organization* (Prentice-Hall, Englewood Cliffs, NJ).

Silber, Simao Davi (1987), 'Aggregation and the Theory of International Trade', *Anais, XV Encontro Nacional da ANPEC*, 1 (Salvador, Brazil).

Stigler, George J. (1958), 'The Economies of Scale', *Journal of Law and Economics*, 2 (Oct.), pp. 54–71.

Teitel, Simon (1975), 'Economies of Scale and Size of Plant: The Evidence and the Implications for the Developing Countries', *Journal of Common Market Studies*, 13/1 and 2, pp. 92–115.

Todd, John (1983), 'Plant Size, Factor Proportions, and Efficiency in Colombian Industry', in A. Berry (ed.), *Essays on Industrialization in Colombia* (Arizona State University, Tempe, Ariz.).

Tybout, James R. (1985), 'A Firm Level Chronical of Financial Crises in the Southern Zone' (Development Research Dept., World Bank, Washington, DC).

Tyler, William G. (1976), *Manufactured Export Expansion and Industrialization in Brazil* (Mohr, Tübingen).

Wade, Robert (1988), 'The Rise of East Asian Trading States—How They Managed Their Trade', (World Institute for Development Economics Research), mimeo.

World Bank (1987), *World Development Report, 1987* (World Bank, Washington, DC).

NOTES

1. Such heterogeneity has been widely noted both in developed and developing countries. For the US Finger reported that as of 1963 about 40% of variation among 4-digit SITC categories in physical and in human capital intensity was within 3-digit SITC groups (Finger, 1975, p. 584). His main point in adducing these data was to argue that the literature attempting to explain 'overlapping trade' (exports and imports of the same 'product' or product category) as inconsistent with conventional factor abundance explanations of trade is off the

mark, since a closer examination reveals the extent of trade overlap is quantitatively similar to the extent of factor proportions variance which occurs within product categories. Some slippage in the analysis may have resulted from the fact that the author approximated physical capital intensity by non-wage value added per worker and human capital intensity by the average wage (p. 581).

For the UK, Rayment concluded that within-sector variance was 50% of the total variance across firms in wage and non-wage value added per head (1976, pp. 203–4).

2. The exact role played by size, however defined, in the existence of the observed high variance of factor proportions and productivities across firms is not necessarily central to the present discussion. If there is a more relevant correlate of factor proportions, it could be substituted for size in much of the discussion to follow without seriously affecting the argument. This is not to deny that the frequency and degree of economies of scale is important to these issues.
3. This point has been made by a number of authors. A particularly detailed discussion, based on Brazilian data, is Silber (1987). Such discussions fall within the long tradition begun by the Leontief paradox finding that US exports were more labour-intensive than its imports. But, as Silber notes, the lengthy set of hypotheses put forward to explain Leontief's finding has seldom included intra-industry heterogeneity.
4. A widely read study of the merits of smallness in general (not just in manufacturing) is Schumacher (1974). Important studies, besides those cited elsewhere in this chapter, include Schmitz (1982) and Anderson (1982).
5. For definitions, see p. 51.
6. Most statistics on the sectoral composition of exports, their directions, and their factor intensities refer only to the last 'producing' sector. Debates on the share of a country's exports which are manufactured are a result of arbitrary classification of some exports as manufactured and others as non-manufactured when the conceptually relevant measure is the share of domestic value added by each sector involved. Use of this measure would probably significantly change the figures on both the composition and the direction of exports for a number of countries.

The factor intensity of exports also requires the data of each contributing sector; unfortunately since factor proportions may vary widely within sectors, use of sectoral averages can be seriously misleading, as noted elsewhere.
7. Perhaps the most realistic way to view the relationship among the various distortions is to consider some of those from the capital market as the primary or 'more exogenous' distortions, and the wage differentials as derivative of the already existing cost advantages of large firms, but then to recognize that should the large firms lose too many of their advantages, public policy will find some way to re-establish their favourable position, by some sort of subsidy/distortion or other.
8. Were the production function for a specific industry typically homothetic, with economies of scale up to a certain (fairly large) size, there would be no output–employment trade-off since large firms would generate more output per unit of captial and the same amount of employment.

9. In principle, lower-cost options might also exist for higher levels of output but one suspects that most engineering data refer to modern and large-scale-oriented technologies.
10. Such comparisons may mislead due to variations across size categories in the accounting conventions involving depreciation, a tendency of smaller owner-managers to pay themselves inflated salaries to avoid double taxation, or several other differences.
11. Little, et al. (1987). The variable capital appears to be book value of all real assets (p. 113, n. 15) but this is not entirely clear.
12. Reported by Little et al. (1987, p. 109) on the basis of data from Ho (1980).
13. In fact, as noted above, few LDC data are available by firm, so the multi-product multi-plant firm usually cannot be analysed at all.
14. These variables are: 'degree of vertical integration, level of fixed costs, breadth of product line, extent and media composition of advertising, outlays on R & D as a percentage of sales, geographically served markets, nature of distribution channels employed, presence of in-house servicing capacity and so on.' (Porter 1974, p. 215).
15. It could alternatively reflect the fact, if it is one, that concentration reflects true economies of scale, so that small firms would not be expected to have high profits.
16. Little et al. (1987) used a 3-factor translog production function, distinguishing two labour categories—skilled and unskilled. The broad labour categories probably led to some biases.
17. In either of these studies it could be that size facilitated some of the firm characteristics associated with efficiency but neither analysis was in sufficient depth to probe all such possibilities.
18. Such differences are emphasized in Morrison (1985).
19. Many export products appear to be produced on large farms although there is no technical reason for this to be the case. See, regarding the Peruvian case, Berry (1988).
20. Indian data are presented in Little et al. (1987, p. 117); Colombian data are from Cortes et al. (1987, p. 67).
21. As the standard deviation figures in each size cell of Table 1 indicate, firm size measured by number of workers does not explain nearly all of the variance of the capital/labour ratio within a given industry.
22. I have not yet seen a decomposition analysis to assess the relative contribution of inter-industry and intra-industry variance to overall variance of factor proportions in manufacturing in an LDC. Delicate definitional issues would arise with respect to the appropriate boundaries of product categories; if they are defined too broadly, what would appear as intra-industry variance would really reflect product differences; if too narrowly the opposite would be true. Relevant data from industrialized countries are cited in n. 1 above.
23. I have not seen statistical evidence on the labour intensity of such subcontractors. Kyu-Uck Lee ('The relationship between Small or Medium Firms and Large Firms in Korea', mimeo, n.d.) implies that they are relatively labour-intensive in Korea, while presenting evidence that about 42% of the value of the 1984 shipments of small and medium firms (SMFs) (21–300

full-time workers being the basic demarcation though apparently it does not apply to all branches) was subcontracted. This share rose sharply in the early 1980s as did the number of small and medium firms. Some subcontracting was with general trading companies, however, so without more figures it remains unclear how to interpret the extensive subcontracting in which these SMFs were engaged.

25. Unfortunately it would have been more useful had the firms been classified into several categories by the export/sales ratio.
26. Silber undertakes an analysis of variance for several variables and reports considerable variance, e.g. of wage levels and of electricity consumption per worker, within industrial branches, but the implication of his results is not clear (1987, pp. 340–1).
27. Gomez (1986, p. 63). The small and medium firms were a sample of which 93% had assets of under 35m pesos or about $US700.
28. This hypothesis underlies R. R. Nelson's stylized view of differences between larger and smaller firms, as expounded in Nelson (1968).
29. Larger firms are typically concerned with reaping the monopoly profits of any advances they make. This tendency may partly explain the coexistence of significant observed learning and innovation at the firm level in various import-substituting industries with the lack of significant total factor productivity gains at the industry level, phenomena reviewed by Pack, Ch. 2.
30. Cortes et al. (1987, ch. 5) comment on the considerable product innovation for local markets by smaller firms which developed in the wake of the first and larger import-substituters in several Colombian industries. If such a pattern is common, Pack's contrast would have to be modified.
31. With less exports and hence less imports, resources could be transferred into production of more or less those same import items, or the demand patterns could involve their substitution by domestically produced items of considerably lower capital intensity, such as food. This issue is part of the broader question of how the presence of trade impinges on the structure of demand.
32. If the export sector utilizes foreign capital which would not have been available to the economy in the absence of the opportunities in that sector inappropriateness of technology does not lead to the same perverse effects discussed above.
33. In which case empirical comparisons between manufactured exports and manufactured imports whose production might be substituted, which usually lead to the conclusion that the former are less capital-intensive, are not convincing.
34. Based on the share of exports in final demand as reported in World Bank (1987), pp. 210–11, with allowance for fairly low use of imported inputs in the production of the exports.
35. An interesting relatively detailed model of the determination of income distribution in Korea is presented by Adelman and Robinson (1978). The model distinguishes among firm size categories producing the same goods but with different factor proportions, finding that size distribution was not an important determinant of distribution (p. 186) and that the impact of trade policy on distribution followed mainly from its effect on the agriculture/non-agriculture

terms of trade (p. 192). The validity of these conclusions for Korea depends, of course, on the quality of the model. Their extension to other countries, say countries with substantially more unequal income distribution and greater factor-intensity differences gaps among firms, could also not be taken for granted. Thus far no model that I am aware of has adequately incorporated some of the mechanisms which might make size structure an important determinant of distribution, in particular (*a*) the extent to which small or labour-intensive firms in one sector deal disproportionately with small or labour-intensive firms in other sectors; and (*b*) the extent to which small firms imply not only a more equal distribution of capital and returns to capital than larger firms but also a more equal distribution of savings, with the corresponding impact on the future distribution of capital income. To incorporate the first mechanism in a general equilibrium model requires input–output data by firm size (not available thus far to my knowledge), and the second requires more subtle data on capital accumulation than we seem to have. Until such mechanisms are satisfactorily incorporated, such modelling exercises will not by themselves resolve the issue.

The effort of Meller and Marfan for Chile was a first step (1981). For each branch of manufacturing these authors disaggregated the intermediate-transactions matrix and the final-demand matrix into large and small establishments, thus giving some indication of the differences in linkages assuming small and large establishments in a given branch were characterized by the same input coefficients. But a complete analysis would require that all matrices include disaggregation by size so that any tendency for small firms in one sector to purchase from small (or otherwise atypical) firms in another sector would be picked up.

36. Tyler estimated the direct and indirect labour requirements to produce Brazil's manufactured exports at 1.4% of the labour force in 1971; the sector's expansion over 1964–71 accounted for 5.7% of the increase in the labour force (1976, p. 175).
37. Apart from the lack of data on this point there is the problem that input–output tables, used to estimate the indirect employment creation of exports, also fail to distinguish size categories within the sectors designated in the table. If, as may be the case, large manufacturing firms are linked to large, above-average capital-intensity firms in other sectors, the indirect employment generated by exports may also be overestimated in figures like those cited above from Tyler for Brazil. Probably such an overestimate would not exceed 25% for direct and indirect employment combined. One may also wonder whether and when the average figures of an input–output matrix provide a good feel for the marginal figures with which policy is typically concerned. It may even be that when capital-intensive firms shift into exports part of the domestic market they give up is picked up by smaller firms, a process which appears to have occurred in the case of agricultural machinery in Colombia (Escandon 1981).
38. By 1976, an estimated 34% of employment was created directly or indirectly by the export sector (Kuo *et al.* 1981, p. 128).
39. Pre-1964 distribution figures are not comparable to the series beginning in that year. Still the sharp fall between available 1953 figures and those for 1964

40. E.g. a belief that heavy industry was essential because of the externalities it generates or the independence it helps to provide vis-à-vis the rest of the world.
41. Levy 1988*b*, pp. 3–4. Note that some observers attribute the lack of flexibility on the part of Korean businesses in part to the heavy involvement of the public sector in the economy and the corresponding passivity of business.
42. E.g. using the data presented in Cortes *et al.* (1987), Table 1. 1, p.18.
43. I owe this observation to Kyu-Uck Lee.
44. Scitovsky notes that the economics literature has to a surprising degree ignored the role of the middleman, both as a promoter and necessary condition for trade and as a possibly important recipient of income generated in trade. Even when export items are produced in a labour-intensive way, the final distribution of trade-related income may not be egalitarian if the trader's share is large and trader incomes are high, as appears often historically to have been the case.
45. Bias against new firms overlaps considerably with that against small firms but is not synonymous; nor are its effects synonymous. Ease of entry at all size ranges helps to maintain good levels of competition. Here, as in so many other respects, Taiwan stands out as a paragon. The country had a vigorous policy of aiding people with entrepreneurial inclinations and know-how but insufficient capital (Scitovsky 1985, p. 224), and the access to foreign exchange must have helped. Entry was also facilitated, probably, by the small size of most already-existing firms, and by the country's high personal savings rate.
46. Administrative rationing is also likely to discriminate against firms wishing to achieve entry into an industry, even if they *are* capable of quickly attaining substantial size. Since they have no record of previous imports, and since they often do start small, administrative inertia may work against them.
47. The relative vulnerability of smaller and larger firms is a complicated issue. One starts with the known fact that the mortality rate is higher among small firms, but this may not be as significant as it might appear since a case could be made that some small firms simply have no potential and are appropriately weeded out in the competition process. Many small firms show a lot of resilience and flexibility to expand and contract quickly. Still, this observed flexibility may largely reflect a sort of vulnerability which leaves them little choice but to adjust quickly or perish.
48. Wade's (1988) discussion of 'The Rise of East Asian Trading States—How They Managed Their Trade' shows how much ambiguity and attendant difference of opinion holds in the cases of Japan, Korea, and Taiwan.
49. Evidence for India and several other countries is reviewed in Little *et al.* (1987), Ch. 14.
50. Even here, however, measurement and identification problems are difficult and only modest confidence can be placed in most results available to date.
51. An important recent survey presents some evidence. See Liedholm and Mead (1987, p. 95).
52. A point made in the context of trade-related categories by Wade (1988).
53. Note however that whereas the difference in access to capital tends to be

exogenous to the relative performance of large and small firms, that in wage costs may more likely be partly endogenous, with wage costs rising to some extent in response to an existing surplus or potential surplus. In that case, the two differentials might not have the offsetting effect mentioned.
54. Recognizing that other distortions, in particular those in the labour market, favour smaller firms and that the net effect of the various distortions is not obvious.
55. Cf. the multifaceted programmes to promote exports in Korea and Taiwan.
56. It is well known that it is much harder to predict the distributional impact of trade when there are three or more factors than when there are only two. If unskilled labour were, in the extreme, unusable in the production of exports, this would in some countries automatically assure that trade would worsen income distribution by raising the demand for the higher income factors. If, however, labour were uniformly or nearly uniformly well skilled, the model might be closer to the two-factor one and the positive distributional outcome would probably result.

4

Market Structure and Trade in Developing Countries

Norman Lee

1. INTRODUCTION

Over the last decade the research interests of trade and industrial economists[1] have moved closer together. Previously, trade theorists were mainly concerned with highly competitive market structures. Now they also have major interests in the trade implications of imperfect market structures, and are turning to the industrial economics literature for guidance on these. For their part, industrial economists typically assumed closed economies in their market analysis. Now they pay increasing attention to the overseas dimension of market behaviour and to examining the competitive process in its international setting. These developments have progressed much further in industrialized country analysis than in that of the developing countries, especially at the empirical level. Empirical studies based on the 'new' trade theories are as yet few in number in developing countries, as are industrial market analyses of good quality. The high level of interest in studies of transnational corporations which may link industrial and trade analyses only partly compensates for this.

This chapter has been prepared from the standpoint of an industrial economist exploring the relationship between market structure and overseas trade (particularly intra-industry trade) in developing countries. The traditional paradigm used by most industrial economists in their work has been the market structure–conduct–performance (S–C–P) model. In keeping with this paradigm, the natural thing to attempt is to 'stretch' the S–C–P model to incorporate an international trade dimension. Hence, for example, the types and extent of intra-industry trade are assumed to depend, *inter alia*, upon the structural characteristics of the markets in which such trade takes place.

However, industrial economics is itself passing through a phase of major reappraisal and reconstruction. This is not confined to the closed-economy assumption mentioned above—more fundamentally it is directed at the appropriateness of the traditional S–C–P model itself.[2] The sources of criticism are quite diverse including, for example, Austrian theory (Ferguson 1988), contestable markets (Baumol *et al*. 1982), transactions costs (Demsetz 1988), game and strategic-behaviour theory (Morris *et al*. 1986; Jacquemin

1987), and their conclusions do not all point in the same direction for reform. Of the new approaches, the use of game and strategic behaviour theory to model imperfect market behaviour is of particular significance to this review because this body of theory has also been used in developing and empirically testing 'new' trade theory.[3]

The issue yet to be decided is whether these diverse new insights can be satisfactorily incorporated within a stretched and amended S–C–P model or whether they will eventually require its replacement. The present state of knowledge, particularly at the empirical level in the developing country context, is insufficient to reach a safe conclusion. Therefore, the less radical presumption (that the S–C–P model will survive in *some* form) has been retained for the purpose of organizing this chapter.

The discussion proceeds as follows. Section 2 examines the role of market structure in industrial analysis, covering both the traditional S–C–P model and the critique of this. Section 3 reviews the definitional and measurement issues relating to the market structure variables most commonly in use. Section 4 reviews the structure–performance studies which have already been undertaken in developing countries. Section 5 examines how the international trade dimension might be systematically incorporated into an updated version of the S–C–P model. Section 6 draws together a number of conclusions which may be helpful in guiding future work.

2. MARKET STRUCTURE AND INDUSTRIAL ANALYSIS

The traditional view is that certain exogenous characteristics of a market (dimensions of market structure) condition the behaviour of firms within that market (market conduct) which in turn determines the outcomes of the competitive process within that market (market performance). Hence, structure determines conduct which, in turn, determines performance or, in its simplest form, structure determines performance in each market.

Different writers have incorporated different structure, conduct, and performance variables within their models.[4] The four most commonly identified structure variables have been:

1. seller concentration (number and size distribution of sellers in the market);
2. buyer concentration (number and size distribution of buyers in the market);
3. entry barriers (the degree of ease or difficulty with which new entrants may come into the market); and
4. product differentiation (the extent to which differentiated products are sold within the market).

Seller concentration and entry barriers have been the two most frequently used variables in S–C–P studies. This is partly a reflection of measurement problems with the other two variables but also of some hesitancy, in the case of product differentiation, as to whether it should be treated as an exogenous structure variable. The most commonly used performance indicator has been profits but some studies have also used X-efficiency and total factor productivity indicators. Both research and development and advertising intensity variables are frequently included in S–C–P studies but their role varies—as determinants of structure, as expressions of conduct, and as indicators of performance. Overseas trade, as already mentioned, has received much less attention—either as a determinant of market structure, or in analysing market conduct and performance.

The origins of the S–C–P paradigm lie in the USA and, not surprisingly, it reflects the thinking and institutional conditions of that country. Its academic roots can be traced back through Bain and Hason to Chamberlin, that is, a common point of intellectual origin with some elements of new trade theory (Devine *et al.* 1985, ch. 1: Grether 1970). It is most appropriate, at least in its original form, to an economy with a relatively small foreign-trade sector, where private enterprise is the dominant organizational form and where government activity is primarily confined to correcting market imperfections. The paradigm has been adopted, some would argue too readily (Caves 1985), by other Anglo-Saxon industrial economists. It has not achieved the same prominence in continental Europe (de Jong 1986). Its use in developing countries has been uneven but generally much less than in industrialized ones (see Kirkpatrick *et al.* 1984, ch. 3, and Section 4 below) —the main reasons have been the generally less developed state of industrial economic analysis in developing countries, lack of appropriate data to apply the S–C–P model, and the view that, in its North American form, it is less appropriate to the developing country situation.

However, even within the Anglo-Saxon world, as previously indicated, the traditional form of the S–C–P model is being reappraised. The principal areas of concern are summarized below.

1. Once outside the large-numbers case (that is, low seller concentration) the deterministic nature of the model breaks down. It is no longer safe to assume that conduct (and, hence, performance) is 'controlled' by structure. The more powerful sellers have some discretion as to how they behave— hence choice of objectives and forms of tactical behaviour (sometimes called 'strategic' behaviour) become relevant. Objectives may differ between small and large, privately owned and publicly owned, domestic and multinational firms. The forms of tactical behaviour which may be adopted are as extensive as the oligopolist theorists choose to explore. Frequently, these are derived from fairly stylized behavioural assumptions, for example Cournot-

type behaviour. The modelling of this tactical behaviour lies at the heart of a number of the new developments in industrial economics.

2. In the small-numbers case, discretionary behaviour cannot necessarily be confined within limits predetermined by market structure. Some enterprises may be sufficiently powerful to change market structure. Advertising, research and development, merger activities etc. can change seller concentration, entry barriers, the degree of product differentiation, etc. Similarly, if profit margins are high enough, new entrants will materialize and market structure and conduct will change as a result. In brief, the relationships between structure, conduct, and performance are not unidirectional. As the strategic behaviour models suggest, the forms of tactical behaviour adopted help to shape the market structure within which the future competitive behaviour takes place.

3. The structural variables which are typically included within the S–C–P model are themselves the product of more fundamental determinants and such variables may therefore be more appropriately treated as endogenous variables. The two, most frequently mentioned, fundamental variables are market demand characteristics and production technology. These influence the nature and degree of product differentiation, seller concentration (via economies of scale), and entry barriers (via economies of scale and the nature of sunk costs). However, not even these two are entirely exogenous in nature, since they may be quite profoundly influenced by the R & D and advertising activities of the relevant enterprises. Chance factors, as incorporated into stochastic growth models, also have their part to play in 'determining' market structures.

4. The markets to which the model is expected to apply are often ill-defined. In one respect, they are defined too broadly because each contains a range of different products rather than of differentiated products. In another respect, they are frequently defined too narrowly by neglecting the international aspect of market structures. (This is part of the wider 'trade issue' with which this chapter is concerned.)

5. Profit is an ambiguous performance indicator and may need to be replaced by more appropriate welfare measures. In particular, high profits may not reflect the exercise of market power any more than low profits indicate no adverse effects from market power.

6. The mode of analysis used often assumes that the market is in equilibrium at the point in time to which the model is being applied. In reality, the competitive process which is being modelled is of a dynamic nature whose outcomes are only revealed over a period of time.

Taken together these comments imply that if the S–C–P model is to be retained it may need to be extensively modified. The resulting form may be more complex and therefore require more and better-quality data for its application. These are likely to be very demanding requirements in the developing country context. However, before this is pursued further the problems associated with the definition and measurement of the existing principal structural variables in the S–C–P model are reviewed.

3. DEFINITION AND MEASUREMENT OF MARKET STRUCTURE VARIABLES

As shown below, each market structure variable can be defined and measured in many different ways. However, the preferred definition for each can be identified only when its role in the chosen model has been determined. It is then a matter of finding an empirical measure which most closely approximates to this, abandoning the search or developing the model in an alternative way if none exists.

Of fundamental importance is the market definition to be used, since this directly influences the values of seller and buyer concentration, entry barriers, and product differentiation which are obtained. The limits of the market can be defined unambiguously only for a perfectly competitive market. In an imperfect market cases of product differentiation (same market) should be distinguished from those of different products (different markets) but, even at the theoretical level, the boundary line between these is arbitrary. In practice, the market boundaries of product range and geographic scope have been mainly dictated by the data sources used. Principal among these has been the Census of Production, according to which sales, employment, etc. are aggregated according to a country's standard industrial classification system (SIC). The SIC is constructed with production rather than market considerations in mind (ignoring imports and possible exports) and defines industry boundaries at different levels of aggregation. Table 1 contains two extracts from the UN Standard Industrial Classification, relating to the manufacture of motor vehicles and the spinning, weaving, and finishing of textiles (United Nations 1971a). It is apparent from this illustration that even at the four-digit level a number of products are included in the same category which are not differentiated products sold within the same market. In reality many market structure studies are undertaken at a considerably more aggregate level than this.

Census of Production data are often subject to other limitations, especially the exclusion of data relating to small-size establishments. Surveys suggest that the informal sector containing these establishments may, depending upon the precise definition used and the country to which it is applied, account for 5–25 per cent of total manufacturing output and 20–95 per cent of total manufacturing employment in developing countries (Kirkpatrick *et al.* 1984, pp. 49–52). Their exclusion is therefore potentially

Table 1. UN standard industrial classification: two four-digit categories

3843 Manufacture of motor vehicles

The manufacture, assembly, rebuilding and major alteration of complete motor vehicles such as passenger automobiles, commercial cars and buses, lorries and truck trailers, universal carriers, special purpose motor vehicles (ambulances, taxicabs, etc.); trailer and pick-up coaches; vehicle-drawn caravans; motorized sleighs; specialized manufacture of motor-vehicle parts and accessories such as engines, brakes, clutches, axles, gears, transmissions, wheels and frames. This group does not include the manufacture of tyres and tubes (group 3551); automobile glass (group 3620); electrical equipment (appropriate group of major groups 383) or agricultural, road building and industrial tractors, and fork-lift and industrial trucks (appropriate group of major group 382).

3211 Spinning, weaving and finishing textiles

Preparing fibres for spinning, such as ginning, retting, scutching, scouring, carding, combing, carbonizing and throwing; spinning; weaving; bleaching and dyeing; printing and finishing of yarns and fabrics. Manufacture of narrow fabrics and other small wares; braid and other primary textiles. Yarn, fabric and jute mills. Asbestos spinning and weaving is classified in group 3699 (manufacture of non-metallic mineral products not elsewhere classified).

Source: United Nations (1971*a*).

important in underestimating the size of industrial markets and in overestimating the level of seller concentration within them. On the other hand, if the informal sector produces different goods from the formal sector and sells in different markets, its exclusion is of less significance.

Of all the dimensions of market structure, seller concentration is the one which has been most extensively analysed. The most common measure used has been the seller concentration ratio (SCR). Technically this is a production concentration ratio if imports and exports are ignored. SCR typically measures the percentage of sales, value added, employment, or capital employed of the x largest sellers (producers) in the market (industry). The value of x usually lies between 3 and 7 but can vary considerably outside these limits. Each enterprise (firm) should be treated as a separate seller for this purpose but in studies where enterprise data are not available, each establishment is often treated as a separate seller.

The main limitation of the SCR is that it selects one point on the cumulative sales curve as the critical determinant of conduct and performance in a market. By implication, the variation in size between sellers and the total number of sellers in the market is considered to be irrelevant.

More sophisticated measures which take these two factors into account are the Herfindahl index and the Entropy index. However they require more information for their calculation. A number of studies have suggested that the correlation between the different seller concentration measures is fairly high, so that for certain purposes (and especially given other limitations in the data) the choice between them may not be a critical consideration (see, for example, Vanlommel *et al.* 1977; Lee, K. U. 1988).

By comparison with seller concentration, buyer concentration has received much less attention in empirical studies. Low buyer concentration may be assumed for most final goods markets but this is an unsafe conclusion in the case of intermediate products. The basic problem is lack of data which has been partially overcome in some studies by the combined use of Census of Production and input–output data (Scherer 1980, ch. 10). However, these combined sources of data are unlikely to be available for most LDCs.

The second most researched dimension of market structure is the entry barrier. This traditionally refers to the degree of ease or difficulty with which new firms may enter a market. More recently emphasis has also been placed on the ease with which firms may leave the market, in the so-called theory of contestable markets.[5] It is argued that, in a market with no entry barrier (perfect contestability), the threat of potential competition causes existing sellers, even where there is high seller concentration, to behave as they would in a competitive market situation. Where, however, entry barriers are high, they serve to protect and preserve the exercise of any monopoly power already existing within the market.

A variety of different methods has been used to assess the height of entry barriers. First, there are those dependent on subjective judgement—either of management in existing firms who are surveyed for their own assessments of entry barriers or of researchers taking into consideration the technology, raw material availability, consumer buying practices, legal environment, etc., operative in the market in question (Bain 1956). Secondly, there are attempts to measure the significance of particular components of the entry barrier, for example the presence of economies of scale, accumulated goodwill for the products of existing sellers, and levels of protection against overseas competition.

There is a very substantial literature on the definition and measurement of economies of scale (Devine *et al.* 1985, ch. 2; Scherer 1980, ch. 4; Shepherd, W. G. 1985, chs. 9 and 10). These may relate to the individual establishment (technical economies), the individual firm (also including marketing, financial, and R & D economies), or groups of establishments or firms (external economies), economies of scope (associated with multi-product production), or dynamic economies (for example learning effects during long production runs). Most empirical work has been undertaken on the first type of scale effect, using engineering data, statistical cost analysis, or survivor techniques, but data on other types are growing. Overall, data (especially relevant to developing country conditions) are very incomplete. This leads to the use of crude proxy measures, notably average plant size.

Scale economies can influence both entry barriers and seller concentration levels—hence there are dangers in including both scale economies and concentration measures as market structure variables. Accumulated goodwill (buyer loyalty) is typically measured by a proxy variable of advertising intensity (for example the advertising/sales ratio). This is sometimes used as a proxy for the degree of product differentiation within the market and therefore also requires careful use and interpretation.

Both the concept of product differentiation as a dimension of market structure and the measurement of the degree of product differentiation in a market present difficulties. The basic qualities of the product and the character of the demand for it affect the potential for product differentiation but it is also affected by the marketing strategies (that is, market conduct) adopted by existing sellers within the market. Attempts to measure the degree of product differentiation have sometimes been based on the use of physical indicators, for example the number of brands or close substitutes sold in the market. This usually requires fairly careful and detailed market investigations. It inevitably involves making rather arbitrary judgements and, crucially, the correct interpretation of the resulting physical measures is not at all clear. More meaningful economic indicators might be based on cross-price elasticities of demand which provide the most appropriate measures of substitutability between products, but such measures are rarely available. As previously mentioned, advertising intensity is frequently used as a proxy measure for the degree of product differentiation. However, there is a range of different factors which affect advertising intensity and, though market-specific characteristics are important among these, it is less clear that these relate only to the degree of product differentiation.

This brief survey of definitional and measurement issues has been confined to the main structural variables traditionally used in structure–performance studies. Similar kinds of issues would arise if the survey were extended to include the definition and measurement of market conduct and market performance indicators (Devine *et al.* 1985, ch. 8). The conclusions to be drawn, however, are not dissimilar from those reached at the end of the previous section—the need for a carefully formulated model of the competitive process for the market(s) being investigated, precise definition of the variables to be included so that they may be most appropriately measured, and considerable effort to obtain sufficiently appropriate and reliable data for the purpose.

A number of the variables which appear in intra-industry trade models (see Section 5) are those used in the S–C–P models and which have been reviewed above—for example, product differentiation, economies of scale, seller concentration, advertising/sales ratios. Similar conclusions about the need for care in model formulation, variable definition, and in securing appropriate data also apply in these cases.

4. MARKET STRUCTURE AND PERFORMANCE IN DEVELOPING COUNTRIES

The main findings of over twenty studies of market structure–performance in LDCs are summarized in Tables 2 and 3 below and update an earlier review (Kirkpatrick *et al.* 1984, ch. 3). The geographic distribution of these studies (for example the relatively large number of Indian studies) reflects the influence of the Anglo-American interest in industrial economics and in the linkage of market structure analyses to the policy issue of monopoly power. The studies were undertaken at different points of time over a twenty-year period, during which the S–C–P model has been progressively developed and refined, and this should be taken into account when evaluating them. Further, the data base on markets in developing countries is much more deficient than that in industrialized countries and this must have restricted the kinds of investigation which could be undertaken.

Seller concentration (Table 2)

The main characteristics of the seller concentration measures in the above studies are:

1. Data relate to industries rather than markets and adjustments for overseas trade are rare, although a number of studies include separate trade variables when explaining performance; industrial categories are broadly defined in most cases.
2. Data relating to small establishments and/or enterprises are typically excluded.
3. Time-series data are only available in a small proportion of studies.
4. Concentration measures are frequently based on establishments rather than firms, most commonly using either sales or employment data.
5. The four-establishment or four-firm concentration ratio is most often used; Herfindahl and Entropy indices are used but much less frequently.

Because of variations in the measures used, and uncertainty about the underlying quality of the data, the following conclusions are tentative and are confined to domestic concentration levels (that is, ignoring overseas trade).

Table 2. Selected studies of industrial or market concentration in LDCs

Country	Study	Data (Year)	Number of industries	Concentration measure	Treatment of imports and exports
Barbados	Whitehall (1986)	1980	24	3-firm sales concentration ratio	Export concentration ratio and level of protection are separate variables
India	Bain (1966)	(a) 1956 (b) 1960–1	16 16	Number of largest plants accounting for 50% of total employment in industry. % of output or capacity of industry controlled by 1–4 largest firms	None
India	Gupta (1968)	1958	29	4-plant employment concentration ratio	None
India	Sawhney and Sawhney (1973)	1958	25	8-plant employment concentration ratio	None
India	Walgreen (1971)	1958	29	4-plant employment concentration ratio	None
India	Ghosh (1975)	1948, 1953 1958, 1963 1968	22	4- and 8-firm asset concentration ratios (also estimates Gini ratios and Herfindahl measures)	None

MARKET STRUCTURE IN DEVELOPING COUNTRIES

Country	Study	Years	N	Concentration measure	Notes
India	Sandesara (1979)	1951, 1960, 1970		4-factory employment ratio; 20-factory employment ratio; Herfindahl and Entropy measures	
India	Katrak (1980)	1963	55	4-plant asset concentration ratio	Treated as separate variables in structure-performance regression analysis
India	Siddharthan and Dasgupta (1983)	1975–8	30	4-firm seller concentration ratio	Exports/sales ratio treated as separate variable
India	Goldar (1986)	1960, 1970	17–19	20-factory employment ratio	Import substitution is a separate variable
Pakistan	White (1974b)	1967–8	23[a] 59[b]	4-firm output or capacity concentration ratio	Import protection level treated as a separate variable
Pakistan	Amjad (1977)	1968	25[b]	4-firm output or sales concentration ratio	Imports treated as a separate variable
Pakistan	Sharwani (1976)	1967, 1968, 1970, 1973	27	2-firm sales concentration ratio	Imports treated as a separate variable
Malaysia	Gan and Tham (1977)	1968–71	42	8-plant output concentration ratios	Import protection level treated as a separate variable
Malaysia	Gan (1978)	1968–71	42	4- and 8-plant output concentration ratios	Ratios adjusted for imports
Malaysia	Lall (1979)	1972	46	4-plant employment concentration ratios	None

Table 2. (Cont'd.)

Country	Study	Data (Year)	Number of industries	Concentration measure	Treatment of imports and exports
Philippines	Sicat and Villarroel (1974)	1960	18	Large number of different measures used based on fixed assets, employment and value-added plant data	None
Philippines	Lindsey (1977)	1970	18	3-plant employment and value added	Imports treated as a separate variable
Korea (S.)	Nam (1975)	1966–9	234	4- and 8-firm output and employment concentration ratios	Deliberately ignores imports because very small in this period
Korea (S.)	Lee, J. (1986)	1970 (3 years ave.)	51	4-firm seller concentration ratio	Effective protection treated as a separate variable
Korea (S.)	Lee, K. U. (1988)	(a) 1977 and 1985 (b) 1970–1985, Various years	(a) 214 (1977) and 425 (1985) — 5 digit (b) 1,492 (1970) and 2,516 (1985) — 7 digit	(a) 3-firm output concentration ratio (b) 1-, 2-, 3-firm output concentration ratios	None. Export ratios calculated separate

Taiwan	Chou (1986)	1976	124	Herfindahl sales index	Import and export variables handled separately
Kenya	House (1973)	1963	31	3-establishment employment concentration ratios, adjusted for exports and imports	Concentration measure adjusted for exports and imports
Kenya	House (1976)	25	As above	As above	
Brazil	Newfarmer and Mueller (1975)	1968	302	4-plant output concentration ratio	None
Brazil	Evans (1977)	1961, 1965 1967, 1968	1	4-, 8-, 20-, 50-firm output concentration ratios	None
Chile	de Melo and Urata (1986)	1967, 1976	41	Herfindahl sales index, based on plant data	Export and import variables handled separately
Argentina Chile Colombia Costa Rica Ecuador Mexico Paraguay Peru Uruguay Venezuela	Mueller (1978)	Various years, 1963–8	18	Entropy index based on plant employment ratio	None
Peru	Tello (1988)	Various years, 1971–85	19 (2 digit) 86 (4 digit)	4-, 10- and 20- establishment output concentration ratios.	None

[a] All Pakistan.
[b] W. Pakistan.

1. The level of seller concentration in individual markets is generally higher in developing countries than in industrialized ones.

2. Developing countries with small domestic markets tend to have higher seller concentration levels than those with large domestic markets.

3. The ranking of markets according to level or seller concentration tends to be broadly similar in different countries, that is (*a*) relatively high in: tobacco, basic metals, certain chemicals, paper, cement, artificial fibres and certain foodstuffs and beverages: and (*b*) relatively low in: wood products, furniture, clothing, cotton textiles, certain foodstuffs and beverages, small-scale engineering products.

This pattern is probably related to differences in economies of scale between different industries but the relationship is far from being an exact one.

The above conclusions point to the prevalence of oligopolistic markets in the formal sector in developing countries and the consequential importance of discretionary (for example strategic) behaviour by leading firms (see Section 2 above). This highlights the potential importance to any explanation of market behaviour of the pattern of business ownership in developing countries. This has been surveyed elsewhere (Kirkpatrick *et al*. 1984, ch. 3) and only the main features are summarized here:

1. The important role of transnational corporations (TNCs) in many developing-country markets. A number of studies have analysed both the individual market share of TNCs and the structural characteristics of the markets in which they operate as well as the forms of market conduct in which they engage (Lall 1980, ch. 2; Dunning 1981, ch. 7; Newfarmer 1985*a*; Jenkins 1987, ch. 3).

2. The importance of large public enterprises (PEs) and joint ventures in manufacturing and other sectors in a range of LDCs (Kirkpatrick *et al*. 1984, Tables 3.3 and 3.4).

3. The importance of large, indigenous economic groups, especially where TNCs and PEs are less prominent (Kirkpatrick *et al*. 1984, pp. 56–9, 129–39).

Many of these large enterprises undertake a range of industrial activities and operate in a number of different markets in which both their market share and the market seller concentration level are high. A number of important questions arise to which, as yet, there are very incomplete answers. For example:

1. Does the possession of business interests in many different markets enable large-scale enterprises to exercise greater economic power than if their operation were confined to a single market?

2. Who controls the policies and operations of these enterprises and in what ways does that control affect their objectives and resulting conduct and performance?

3. Do different kinds of large-scale enterprise—private domestic, public enterprise, foreign-owned, joint-venture—behave in discernably different ways, and does this result in different patterns of resource allocation?

There is a tendency, in more recent studies, to use both market-structure variables and leading-firm characteristics variables to explain performance and this would seem to be particularly appropriate in the developing-country situation (Newfarmer and Mueller 1975; Shepherd W. G. 1985; Blomstrom 1986a). Of the different types of large-scale enterprise, most is known about TNCs since a substantial amount of theoretical and empirical work has been undertaken on their characteristics, conduct, and performance in the developing country context. This has not yet been integrated, in a sufficiently systematic manner, into either the industrial economics or trade literature though it is obviously relevant to both—for example, in the case or studies of the impact of TNCs on market structure, the determinants of direct foreign investment or of the impact of technology transfer, product cycles, international sourcing, etc. (Kirkpatrick *et al.* 1984, ch. 4). Much less is known about the conduct and performance of large indigenous economic groups, public enterprises, and joint ventures in LDCs despite their potential importance.

Market Performance (Table 3)

As in industrialized countries, the main focus of market structure–performance studies in developing countries has been in explaining profit performance (the ambiguous nature of which as a welfare indicator has already been highlighted). The main features of these studies have been:

1. Variability in the measures of profit used; data are often only recorded for a single year or a small number of years.
2. The majority of the studies (particularly the earlier ones) only use a small number of variables to explain profit levels. Seller concentration is virtually always included—other variables, incorporated with varying frequency, include trade measures, capital intensity, economies of scale, advertising intensity, capital utilization, and enterprise characteristics.

There is great variation in the detailed form of the S–C–P model used and in the quality of data employed in testing it. Only very provisional conclusions can be drawn (especially as a large proportion of the observed profit variation often remains unexplained) which are:

1. The majority of studies find a statistically significant positive relationship between seller concentration levels and profit margins (two Indian studies establish an inverted-U-shape correlation). Certain of the most

Table 3. Studies of the relationship between industrial/market concentration and profitability in LDCs

Study	Country	Profit measure	Explanatory variables	Concentration–profitability relationship
Whitehall (1986)	Barbados	Gross price–cost margin (1980)	Concentration ratio, number of sellers, capital/output ratio, advertising dummy variable, industry growth rate, export concentration ratio, input/output ratio, level of protection	Not statistically significant
Gupta (1968)	India	One-year profit rate (definition not given)	Three measures of entry barriers and concentration ratio	Positive but not statistically significant (test of significance not defined)
Sawhney and Sawhney (1973)	India	Gross and net price–cost margins averaged over 5 years	Concentration ratio, capital/output ratio, ratio of capacity utilization.	Positive and significant at 5% level or better. Non-linear formulation gives better results
Walgreen (1971)	India	Same as Gupta	Concentration ratio and economies of scale variable	Average profit rate higher in industries where concentration ratio >50% than where ratio is <50%, but difference is not statistically significant
Katrak (1980)	India	Gross price–cost margin (1963)	Concentration ratio, capital intensity, import competition, export orientation, tariffs	Statistically significant; non-linear formulation gives better results

MARKET STRUCTURE IN DEVELOPING COUNTRIES

Siddharthan and Dasgupta (1983)	India	Profit after tax as % of net worth	Concentration ratio, growth of sales, advertising intensity, R & D intensity, ave. size of firms in industry, exports/sales ratio, labour skill variable	Concentration not statistically significant (but correlated with firm size variable)
White (1974b)	Pakistan	Pre-tax profit on net worth by industry (2 years)	Concentration ratio, import restriction and capacity utilization variables	Positive; dummy variable dividing the concentration ratio at 33.3% is significant at 5% level
Amjad (1977)	Pakistan (W.)	Net price–cost margin (1965–7, single years and average for period)	Concentration ratio, capital/output ratio, foreign competition variables, capacity utilization	Positive and consistently significant at 5% level or better
Sharwani (1976)	Pakistan	Two alternative measures of rate of return on capital (data for 4 years)	Concentration ratio, presence of TNC, presence of govt. regulated firm, import penetration, capacity utilization	Positive and significant at 5% level or better
Gan (1978)	Malaysia	Gross price–cost margins (average 1968–71)	Concentration ratios, capital/output ratios	Positive and significant correlation at 10% or better in case of both 4-plant concentration ratio (CR4) and 8-plant concentration ratio (CR8) (continuous and discontinuous versions). Threshold levels are CR4: 55%, CR8: 85%

Table 3. (Cont'd.)

Study	Country	Profit measure	Explanatory variables	Concentration–profitability relationship
Gan and Tham (1977)	Malaysia	Gross price–cost margin (average 1968–71)	Concentration ratio, economies of scale, absolute capital requirement, advertising/sales ratio, effective tariff protection, presence of foreign-owned enterprise, growth of market demand, administrative controls, capital/output ratio, export/output ratio	Positive and significant correlation at 10% level dependent upon other explanatory variable included
Lindsey (1977)	Philippines	Gross price–cost margin (1970)	Value-added concentration ratio is only variable	Positive and significant at 5% level
Nam (1975)	Korea (S.)	Net profit/gross capital ratio, net profit/net sales ratio, 1967–8 (single years and average for period)	Concentration ratio is only variable	Higher profits and greater under-utilization of capacity among industries with seller concentration ratio above 70% (no significance test reported)
Lee, J. (1986)	Korea (S.)	Pre-tax profit as % of total capital (also technical efficiency)	Concentration ratio, effective protection, relative economies of scale, credit variable, relative capital intensity, minimum efficient scale, growth rate of industry	Not statistically significant

Study	Country	Dependent variable	Model/variables	Results
Chou (1986)	Taiwan	Price–cost margin	Simultaneous 4-equation model, incorporating a larger number of variables, including trade variables	Positive, statistically significant relationship
House (1973)	Kenya	Gross and net price–cost margin (1963)	Concentration index, capital/output ratio, proportion of industry's output exported	Positive and significant at 5% level or better where 'hybrid' concentration index is used (both 'continuous' relationship and 'distinct break' when index exceeds 40%)
House (1976)	Kenya	Gross and net price–cost margin (1967)	Similar variables as in (1973)	Similar results to those in House (1973): 'hybrid' concentration measure positive and significant at 20% level or better
De Melo and Urata (1986)	Chile	Price–cost margin	2-equation model incorporating a number of variables, including trade variables	Positive, statistically significant relationships in certain equations
Newfarmer and Mueller (1975)	Brazil	As below (1972)	As below	Where market share exceeds 25%, broad earnings ratio is three times greater than where share is less than 10%
Newfarmer and Mueller (1975)	Mexico	'Broad earnings' (inc. technology fees) of US manufacturing affiliates as % of their equity (1972)	Market share of affiliate (NB. Seller concentration ratio for industry not used)	Where market share exceeds 50%, broad earnings ratio is two-thirds higher than where share is less than 10%

Table 3. (Cont'd.)

Study	Country	Profit measure	Explanatory variables	Concentration–profitability relationship
Connor and Mueller (1982)	Brazil	Two measures, 'simple' profits and 'broad' profits, as % of stockholder equity for TNC affiliates (1972)	4-firm concentration ratio, relative market share of affiliate, advertising/sales ratio, financial leverage, industry growth rate, firm size, trade intensity, % affiliate stock owned by parent TNC	Both the concentration ratio and the relative market share of the affiliate have a positive and significant correlation with profit levels at the 5% level
Connor and Mueller (1982)	Mexico	As above	As above	As above

recent studies fail to find a statistically significant relationship and it is not clear whether this is due to the quality of data used, the incorporation of other variables (for example scale economies) which may be correlated with concentration levels, or other factors.

2. Typically profit margins are negatively correlated with import penetration and positively correlated with import protection variables. Few studies have incorporated export variables, but both negative and positive relationships with profit margins have been established. However, a number of writers have expressed caution in the interpretation of the relationship between profitability and trade variables (Katrak 1980; Chou 1986; Nakao 1986) and it is clear that this is one of the aspects of the S–C–P model that requires more detailed investigation.

3. Capital/output ratios usually have a statistically significant positive association with gross (but less frequently with net) price cost margins. In general (though with exceptions, for example Gan and Tham 1977; Connor and Mueller 1982) studies in developing countries have not been particularly successful in determining the influence of non-trade entry barriers on profit. This may arise from the particular formulation of the S–C–P model (for example correlation between measures of seller concentration and entry barriers) or the quality of data used.

4. The types of firms operating within the market have been investigated in a small number of studies (Sharwani 1976; Gan and Tham 1977; Chou 1986) and have been found to have a significant association with profit margins—positive in the case of TNCs, negative or positive in the case of PEs (depending on the particular government financial policy for the PEs concerned).

Relationships between market structure and other aspects of performance have been investigated to a much more limited extent. High seller concentration and import protection are associated with lower productive efficiency in a study of Pakistan industries, although import protection appears to have been the stronger influence (Kemal 1978). Goldar (1986) found, in the case of Indian manufacturing, a significant negative relationship between total factor productivity (TFP) and import substitution but a positive relationship with seller concentration (which might be reflecting an effect of economies of scale). Blomstrom (1986b) reached similar conclusions in the case of Mexican manufacturing industry.

In summary, domestic seller concentration levels tend to be higher in developing countries than in industrialized ones and, in many of the studies reviewed, are positively correlated with profit margins. However, the fundamental relationships and lines of causality are almost certainly more complex than a simple interpretation of the S–C–P model might imply. Trade variables and the characteristics of market leaders loom important and interact with the concentration variable to influence conduct and performance. The underlying determinants of the traditional structure variables (economies of scale, advertising, and R & D activities) have not yet been properly investigated. Similarly, the analysis of performance indicators, even the profit indicator, is still in its infancy. Much remains to be done to achieve a real understanding of S–C–P relationships in developing-country markets.

5. INTERNATIONAL TRADE AND THE S–C–P MODEL

The task of improving the S–C–P model is a formidable one and the purpose of this section is limited to exploring briefly one aspect—the incorporation of a foreign-trade dimension.[6] One approach to this is to take the individual elements of the model (including refinements and modifications suggested by more recent work in industrial economics) and systematically work through the implications of incorporating a foreign dimension into each. *Inter alia*, this involves reviewing the following— definition of markets, definition and measurement of market structure variables, determinants of market structure variables, market conduct including the conduct of leading firms, market performance, and the relationships between them. Some of the implications of doing this, and the issues they raise, are examined below.

Market Definition

The simplest way in which to modify the closed domestic economy assumption is to adjust the data for each domestic market to take account of imports and exports. This is probably the most common approach although it is complicated by the fact that trade and production statistics may use different classification systems.[7] However, this implicitly assumes that all markets for a given product set can be defined as separate national markets (that is, there are no international or regional markets). It also implies that there are no interdependencies between markets (for example conduct in market B being influenced by structure in market A because leading firms in A sell in both markets). If there are such interdependencies, as seems likely to be the case, the S–C–P model has to move into multi-market analysis. This may imply, for example, that a particular category of intra-industry trade is affected by the market characteristics of all the countries participating in that trade. Only limited attention has yet been given to this issue which could raise some severe difficulties for empirical work (see Harris 1984; Newfarmer 1985*b*; and Nakao 1986).

Market Structure

Most attention has been given to how foreign trade may affect seller concentration and, through this, profit performance. The simplest approach, in the case of imports, is to treat these as adding to the competitive fringe in the domestic market—hence they are assumed to lower seller concentration and reduce profit margins. However, the situation may be more complex than this (see, for example, the series of articles in Caves 1980; Kumar 1985):

1. The impact of imports on performance depends upon the existing concentration level among domestic producers.
2. Importers may also be major sellers in the domestic market.
3. Business links may exist between domestic producers and importers.
4. Increased imports may lead to increased domestic concentration (see de Melo and Urata 1986).

Similarly, in the simple case, exporters are assumed to be the major domestic producers and correcting for exports may thus lower the measure of seller concentration in the home market. However even if this is the case, the likely effect on profit margins is ambiguous. The ability to tap new markets and to exploit economies of scale can increase profit margins; dependence on highly competitive international markets can have the opposite effect (Caves 1986).

Levels of import protection (and of export support) can be important dimensions of entry barriers in any open-economy S–C–P analysis. Less obviously, the existence of potential competition from importers may reduce the market significance of entry barriers facing domestic entrants—potential international competition may be more important than potential domestic competition in securing contestability. Redefining the scope of the market to include importers will also tend to increase the recorded degree of product differentiation.

In summary, the treatment of a number of the market structure measures needs to change, not always in easily predictable ways, when foreign-trade data are incorporated into their calculation.

Market Conduct

The competitive strategies of firms operating within the redefined 'small-numbers' market case have also to be provided with an international dimension. This might be achieved in two ways.

The first is to draw upon recent developments in game theory and strategic behaviour analysis to derive competitive strategies (see, for example, Morris et al. 1986) which may then be extended to include foreign-trade conduct. Indeed, as previously indicated, small-number, competitive strategy, models which incorporate a foreign-trade dimension have been developed, over recent years, within the new trade theory literature. (An overview of this literature is provided in Greenaway and Milner 1986, ch. 3, and Greenaway and Milner 1987. For specific recent examples, also see Helpman and Krugman 1985; Greenaway and Tharakan 1986; Krugman 1986). What urgently needs to be established is the extent to which the different conduct patterns and market outcomes that have been identified through theoretical analysis approximate to those observable in real market structures. Unfortunately, this kind of empirical work is not yet well developed, especially in the developing country context where lack of appropriate data is a real problem. This is now receiving increasing attention (Feenstra 1987; Baldwin, Chapter 9 this volume). For example the use of simulation models, which require less data, is discussed elsewhere in this volume (Chapter 10). However, further experience is needed with these different approaches before confident conclusions can be drawn on their usefulness.

The second approach, which could be complementary to the previous one, is to draw upon the potentially rich source of theorizing and empirical evidence about the international activities of TNCs. This body of work has already been reported in the previous section and could shed considerable light on the competitive strategies of international corporations. One difficulty is that a good deal of previous research work relating to TNC conduct has not been sufficiently focused on the particular issues of central concern in this chapter. For example, Helleiner's comment, made a number of years ago, bears repeating: 'A further research question is whether non-market international decision making is likely to, or actually does, generate different outcomes from those of the market . . . whether they are similar, to put it no more strongly, is a matter for empirical investigation; and such investigation has scarcely even begun' (Helleiner 1981, p. 91).

TNC studies should also shed more light on how firm conduct modifies market structure. Blomström (1986b) reviews the earlier literature on the impact of TNCs on seller concentration and summarizes the findings of a recent study relating to Mexico. However, well-researched case-studies and econometric evidence on this topic are still in short supply. P. L. Shepherd (1985) illustrates, in his study of the international cigarette industry, the kind of TNC research, within an S–C–P framework, that might be usefully developed.

Market Behaviour and Performance

Both market outcomes and performance indicators could be broadened, beyond consideration of profits, X-efficiency, total factor productivity, etc.

to include foreign-trade outcomes and performance in markets of specified structural and conduct characteristics. However, as indicated earlier, the appropriateness of whichever performance measures are to be chosen needs to be carefully established in the first instance. Given this, and the underdeveloped nature of the preceding stages of the open-economy S–C–P model (and the data requirements which it may generate), immediate expectations need to be suitably modest. Two potential applications of this broadened approach might be: (a) in helping to explain the foreign trade performance of manufacturing industries in individual economies (Pickering and Sheldon 1984); and (b) in helping to explain intra-industry trade between countries with given market structure and conduct characteristics. It is the second of these that is of greater concern here.

A number of econometric studies have been undertaken which attempt to explain intra-industry trade in terms of a range of factors, which include market structure and conduct variables. Eleven[8] of these were the subject of a comparative review by Greenaway and Milner (1986, ch. 9) but others also exist, for example Koo and Martin (1984) and Balassa (1986b). The sample is dominated by studies in industrialized countries, but this is not atypical. Collectively they incorporate a number of the kind of structure or conduct variables used in industrial economic analysis—seller concentration, scale economies, advertising/sales ratios, R & D intensity, firm characteristics. However, the number of studies in which any one of these variables has been used is often quite small—for example seller concentration only appears in two of the eleven studies surveyed by Greenaway and Milner (1986). (It also appears in the studies by Koo and Martin 1984; and Balassa 1986b.) Also, data problems often mean that the actual models used for empirical testing differ considerably from the theoretical models derived for intra-industry trade analysis. Quite possibly, such a collection of studies could provide a useful focus for a more detailed critique of the current state of knowledge on the market structure determinants of intra-industry trade. The following questions should be considered:

1. How far is it meaningful to isolate this particular outcome (intra industry trade) of the international competitive process for analysis? Clegg (1987), for example, considers it more appropriate to analyse trade, foreign investment, and licensing as a combined means by which TNCs simultaneously compete in international markets.

2. Are seller concentration and other market structure variables determinants of intra-industry trade or are both jointly determined by a common set of more basic factors? ('[E]mpirical investigations of the determinants of the structure of international trade need to be joined with the analysis of market structures, in recognition that the pattern and extent of international trade and the organisation of domestic production are jointly determined by more fundamental structural characteristics'—Caves 1985, p. 386.)

3. What is the precise nature of the assumed relationship between intra-industry trade and each market structure variable (for example seller concentration) and/or each underlying determinant (for example economies of scale)? In particular, what is the assumed nature of the tactical behaviour which underlies this relationship and what is its justification? The prevailing view reflected in this sample of studies is that both seller concentration and economies of scale are negatively correlated with the extent of product differentiation and with the volume of intra-industry trade. This is broadly supported by the majority of the relatively small number of econometric studies which have included one or other of these variables. However, other interpretations of these relationships have been presented and different findings have been obtained. The implied view that these two variables influence trading outcomes only through their impact on product differentiation is a fairly narrow one.

4. How can such models help in identifying the welfare implications of particular intra-industry trade flows and of the policy measures to correct for adverse welfare effects where these arise? S–C–P analyses reveal that performance indicators (for example changes in profit levels, in intra-industry trade levels, etc.) are often difficult to interpret (even where the policy objective is known and agreed) unless the process by which change has occurred, and the other consequences which accompany it, are also known.

6. CONCLUSIONS

At a broad level of analysis it is relatively easy to establish that imperfect market structures and, in particular, relatively high levels of domestic seller concentration, are widespread in many developing countries. Similarly, though less clearly established, these appear to correlate with particular features of market performance—notably higher profit margins and/or greater X-inefficiency—although the lines of causality may be complex and are not yet fully understood.

Intra-industry trade is, in theory, explainable in part by the existence of imperfect markets. Therefore, one might expect developing countries' intra-industry trade also to be explainable in part by their market structures and market conduct and those of their trading partners. If so, industrial economists may have a contribution to make in illuminating the intra-industry trade phenomenon. Alternatively it might be that imperfect markets are a *sine qua non* for intra-industry trade but that the relationship between differences in such trade and differences in market structures is, at best, tenuous. If so, the industrial economist's contribution could be relatively limited. We are not yet in a position to determine which of these two views is nearer the truth.

However, the thrust of the argument here is that there are good reasons, in any case, for incorporating an international dimension into industrial economic analysis. This may be undertaken within an extended and modified S–C–P model or it may be attempted in other ways. The former approach seems to be preferable in present circumstances—at least until alternative approaches, which involve the complete abandonment of the S–C–P model, have been more thoroughly tried and tested. The incorporation of intra-industry trade into the S–C–P model is one element in its improvement but it is not the only one. In particular, more effective treatment of the rivalrous conduct of large sellers within the market is also needed. If such changes as these can be made, the resulting model should be more useful for both developing-country industrial and trade analysis than its predecessor which was too closely conditioned by USA market circumstances.

If a more precise, empirical understanding is to be achieved of the relationships between developing-country market structures and international trade (particularly intra-industry trade), the following difficulties will have to be overcome: (*a*) the boundaries of the required analysis (for example the geographic scope of the investigation, the outcomes to be explained) are not yet well defined; (*b*) the underlying relationships which link market structure, conduct, and performance in an international setting are complex and insufficiently identified; and (*c*) data requirements are potentially substantial and may be difficult to satisfy.

These three difficulties are linked. Initial progress on the first two through further analytical work should help in defining preliminary data needs and priorities. However, further progress beyond this point is likely to require greater practical insight through empirical investigation of the competitive process at work in a small number of carefully specified case-studies.

Each of these case-studies should relate to a single international industry or sub-industry in which a significant amount of South–South or South–North trade is taking place (preferably between a relatively small number of trading nations to keep the initial case-studies within manageable limits—more complex international industries could be examined later).

A number of global industry studies have been completed[9] and it might be thought that these could provide a model for the case-studies which are now proposed. However, a number of them lack a sufficiently clear analytical structure and are therefore of limited use for present purposes. Some more recent studies are better from this point of view (see, for example, Newfarmer 1985*a*, especially ch. 2, and the other case-studies relating to Latin America) and could provide some useful guidance.

A broadly similar analytical framework should be formulated at an early stage for each chosen industry but in the expectation that it would need to be modified in detail as the study proceeds. It should have the following features:

1. The principal focus of the analysis should be the international competitive process in the chosen industry and its welfare impacts (intra-industry trade is only one of the aspects of that process and it should not have an intellectual wall built around it).

2. The market characteristics (structures, etc.) of all the trading countries engaged in the chosen industry should be taken into consideration.

3. The structural characteristics of those markets should not be treated as fixed (that is, their underlying determinants should also be identified).

4. The principal forms of market conduct (that is, tactical/strategic behaviour) of leading enterprises (not only TNCs) should be incorporated.

5. Each study should analyse data over a sufficient time-period to enable the dynamic nature of the competitive process to be properly examined and understood.

A high priority should be given to the quality of data collection and analysis. Indiscriminate and excessive data gathering should be avoided. Equally, the shortage of readily available data should not dominate the choice of models nor be used to justify their inadequate testing.

All of this points to an eclectic research approach, drawing upon different skills—theoretical and analytical, model construction and econometric estimation, historical and qualitative. It is suggestive of team research using a range of skills drawn from each of the nations engaged in trade within the chosen industry.

REFERENCES

AMJAD, R. (1977), 'Profitability and Industrial Concentration in Pakistan' *Journal of Development Studies* 33/3, pp. 181–98.

BAIN, J. S. (1956), *Barriers To New Competition* (Harvard University Press, Cambridge, Mass.).

—— (1966), *International Differences in Industrial Structure* (Yale University Press, Newhaven, Conn.).

BALASSA, B. (1986a), 'Intra-Industry Trade Among Exporters of Manufactured Goods', in D. Greenaway and P. K. M. Tharakon (eds.), *Imperfect Competition and International Trade: The Policy Aspects of Intra-Industry Trade* (Wheatsheaf, Brighton).

—— (1986b), 'The Determinants of Intra-Industry Specialization in US Trade', *Oxford Economic Papers*, 38, pp. 220–33.

BALDWIN, R. F. (1988), *Trade Policy Issues and Empirical Analysis* (University of Chicago Press, Chicago).

BAUMOL, W., and WILLIG, R. (1986), 'Contestability: Developments since the Book', *Oxford Economic Papers* 38 (Nov. suppl.), pp. 9–36.
—— PANZAR, J., and WILLIG, R. (1982), *Contestable Markets and the Theory of Industrial Structure* (Harcourt Brace Jovanovich, San Diego, Calif).
BERGSTRAND, J. H. (1983), 'Measurement and Determinants of Intra-Industry International Trade', in P. K. M. Tharakan (ed.), *Intra-Industry Trade: Empirical and Methodological Aspects* (North-Holland, Amsterdam).
BLOMSTRÖM, M. (1986a), 'Foreign Investment and Productive Efficiency: The Case of Mexico', *Journal of Industrial Economics* 35/1, pp. 97–110.
—— (1986b), 'Multinationals and Market Structure in Mexico', *World Development*, 14/4, pp. 523–30.
CAVES, R. E. (1980), 'International Trade and Industrial Organisation, Introduction', *Journal of Industrial Economics*, 29/2, pp. 113–8.
—— (1981), 'Intra-Industry Trade and Market Structure in the Industrial Countries', *Oxford Economic Papers*, 33, pp. 203–23.
—— (1985), 'International Trade and Industrial Organisation: Problems, Solved and Unsolved', *European Economic Review*, 28, pp. 377–95.
—— (1986), 'Exporting Behaviour and Market Structure: Evidence from the United States', in de Jong and Shepherd (1986).
—— PORTER, M. E., and SPENCE, D. (1980), *Competition in an Open Economy* (Harvard University Press, Cambridge, Mass.).
CHOU, T. C. (1986), 'Concentration, Profitability and Trade in a Simultaneous Equation Analysis: The Case of Taiwan', *Journal of Industrial Economics*, 34/4, pp. 429–41.
CLARKE, R. (1985), *Industrial Economics* (Blackwell, Oxford).
CLEGG, J. (1987), *Multinational Enterprise and World Competition* (Macmillan, London).
CONNOR, J. M., and W. F. MUELLER (1982), 'Market Structure and Performance of US Multinationals in Brazil and Mexico', *Journal of Development Studies*, 18/3, pp. 329–53.
DE JONG, H. W. (1986), 'European Industrial Organisation: Entrepreneurial Economics in an Organisational Setting', in de Jong and Shepherd, (1986).
—— and SHEPHERD, W. G. (eds.) (1986), *Mainstreams in Industrial Organisation*, bks. 1 and 2 (Kluwer, Dordrecht).
DE MELO, J., and URATA, S. (1986), 'The Influence of Increased Foreign Competition on Industrial Concentration and Profitability', *International Journal of Industrial Organisation*, 4, pp. 287–304.
DEMSETZ, H. (1988), *Ownership, Control and the Firm*, 1 (Blackwell, Oxford).
DEVINE, P. J., LEE, N., JONES, R., and TYSON, W. J. (1985), *An Introduction to Industrial Economics*, 4th ed. (Allen & Unwin, London).
DUNNING, J. (1981), *International Production and the Multinational Enterprise* (Allen & Unwin, London).
EVANS, P. B., (1977), 'Direct Investment and Industrial Concentration', *Journal of Development Studies*, 13/4, pp. 373–86.
FEENSTRA, R. (ed.) (1987), *Empirical Methods for International Trade* (MIT Press, Cambridge, Mass.).

FERGUSON, P. R., (1988), *Industrial Economics: Issues and Approaches* (Macmillan, London).
FINGER, J. M., and DE ROSA, D. A. (1979), 'Trade Overlap, Comparative Advantage and Protection', in H. Giersch, ed., 1979, *On The Economics of Intra-Industry Trade* (Mohr, Tübingen).
GAN, W. B. (1978), 'The Relationship Between Market Concentration and Profitability in Malaysian Manufacturing Industries', *Malayan Economic Review*, 23/1, pp. 1-13.
—— and THAM, S. Y. (1977), 'Market Structure and Price-Cost Margins in Malaysian Manufacturing Industries', *Developing Economies*, 15/3, pp. 280-92.
GHOSH, A. (1975), 'Concentration and Growth of Indian Industries, 1948-68', *Journal of Industrial Economics*, 23/3, pp. 203-22.
GOLDAR, B. (1986), 'Import Substitution, Industrial Concentration and Productivity Growth in Indian Manufacturing', *Oxford Bulletin of Economics and Statistics*, 48/2, pp. 143-64.
GREENAWAY, D., and MILNER, C. (1984), 'A Cross-Section Analysis of Intra-Industry Trade in the UK', *European Economic Review*, 25, pp. 319-44.
—— (1986), *The Economics of Intra-Industry Trade* (Blackwell, Oxford).
—— (1987), 'Intra-Industry Trade: Current Perspectives and Unresolved Issues', *Weltwirtschaftliches Archiv.* 123, pp. 39-56.
—— and THARAKAN, P. K. H. (eds.) (1986), *Imperfect Competition and International Trade: The Policy Aspects of Intra-Industry Trade* (Wheatsheaf, Brighton).
GRETHER, E. T. (1970), 'Industrial Organisation: Retrospect and Prospect', *American Economic Review*, 82, pp. 83-9.
GUPTA, V. E. (1968), 'Cost-Functions, Concentration and Barriers to Entry in Twenty-Nine Manufacturing Industries in India', *Journal of Industrial Economics*, 26/1, pp. 57-72.
HARRIS, R. (1984), 'Applied General Equilibrium Analysis of Small Open Economies with Scale Economies and Imperfect Competition', *American Economic Review*, 74, pp. 1016-32.
HELLEINER, G. K. (1981), *Intra-Firm Trade and the Developing Countries* (Macmillan, London).
HELPMAN, E., and KRUGMAN, P. R. (1985), *Market Structure and Foreign Trade: Increasing Returns, Imperfect Competition, and the International Economy* (Wheatsheaf, Brighton).
HOUSE, W. J. (1973), 'Market Structure and Industry Performance: The Case of Kenya', *Oxford Economic Papers*, 25/3, pp. 405-19.
—— (1976), 'Market Structure and Industry Performance: The Case of Kenya Revisited', *Journal of Economic Studies*, 3/2, pp. 117-32.
JACQUEMIN, A. (1987), *The New Industrial Organisation: Market Forces and Strategic Behaviour* (MIT Press, Cambridge, Mass.).
JENKINS, R. (1987), *Transnational Corporations and Uneven Development* (Methuen, London).
KATRAK, H. (1980), 'Industrial Structure, Foreign Trade and Price-Cost Margins in Indian Manufacturing Industries', *Journal of Development Studies*, 17/1, pp. 62-79.
KEMAL, A. R. (1978), 'An Analysis of Industrial Efficiency in Pakistan, 1959/60-

1969/70', Ph.D. Thesis, University of Manchester, Manchester.

KIRKPATRICK, C. H., LEE, N., and NIXSON, F. I. (1984), *Industrial Structure and Policy in Less Developed Countries* (Allen & Unwin, London).

KOO, A. Y. C., and Martin, S. (1984), 'Market Structure and US Trade Flows', *International Journal of Industrial Organisation*, 2, pp. 173-97.

KRUGMAN, P. R. (ed.) (1986), *Strategic Trade Policy and the New Industrial Economics* (MIT Press, Cambridge, Mass.).

KUMAR, M. S. (1985), 'International Trade and Industrial Concentration', *Oxford Economic Papers*, 37, pp. 125-33.

LALL, S. (1979), 'Multinationals and Market Structure in an Open Developing Economy: The Case of Malaysia', *Weltwirtschaftliches Archiv*, 115 (June), pp. 325-50; repr. in Lall (1980), pp. 65-90.

—— (1980), *The Multinational Corporation: Nine Essays* (Macmillan, London).

LEE, J. (1986), 'Market Performance in an Open Developing Economy: Technical and Allocative Efficiencies of Korean Industries', *Journal of Industrial Economics*, 35/1, pp. 81-96.

LEE, K. U. (1988), *International Trade and Industrial Organisation: the Korean Experience*. Paper presented to WIDER Conference: New Trade Theories and Industrialization in the Developing Countries, Helsinki.

LINDSEY, C. W. (1977), 'Market Concentration in Philippine Manufacturing, 1970', *Philippine Economic Journal*, 16/3, pp. 289-312.

LOERTSCHER, R., and WOLTER, F. (1980), 'Determinants of Intra-Industry Trade: Among Countries and Across Industries', *Weltwirtschaftliches Archiv*, 116, pp. 281-93.

LUNDBERG, L. (1982), 'Intra-Industry Trade: The Case of Sweden', *Weltwirtschaftliches Archiv*, 118, pp. 302-16.

MORRIS, D. J., SINCLAIR, P. J. N., SLATER, M. D. E., and VICKERS, J. S. (eds.) (1986), 'Strategic Behaviour in Industrial Competition', *Oxford Economic Papers*, 38 (Nov. suppl.).

MUELLER, P. (1977), *The Pattern of Industrial Concentration in Latin America* (NBER, Santiago).

—— (1978), 'The Pattern of Industrial Concentration in Latin America', *Journal of Industrial Economics*, 27/1, pp. 41-7.

NAKAO, T. (1986), 'Industrial Organisation in an International Framework', in de Jong and Shepherd, (1986).

NAM, W. H. (1975), 'The Determinants of Industrial Concentration: The Case of Korea', *Malayan Economic Review*, 20/1, pp. 37-48.

NEWFARMER, R. S. (ed.) (1985*a*), *Profits, Progress and Poverty: Case Studies of International Industries in Latin America* (University of Notre Dame Press, Notre Dame, Ind.).

—— (1985*b*), 'International Industrial Organisation and Development: A Survey', in Newfarmer, (1985*a*), pp. 13-62.

—— and MARSH, L. C. (1981), 'Foreign Ownership, Market Structure and Industrial Performance: Brazil's Electrical Industry', *Journal of Development Economics*, 8, pp. 47-75.

—— and MUELLER, W. F. (1975), *Multinational Corporations in Brazil and Mexico: Structural Sources of Economic and Non-Economic Power* (US Senate Subcommittee

on Multinational Corporations, Washington, DC).
PAGOULATOS, E., and SORENSEN, R. (1975), 'Two-way International Trade: An Econometric Analysis', *Weltwirtschaftliches Archiv*, 111, pp. 454–65.
PICKERING, J. F., and SHELDON, I. M. (1984), 'International Trade Performance and Concentration in British Industry', *Applied Economics*, 16, pp. 421–42.
REID, G. (1987), *Theories of Industrial Organisation* (Blackwell, Oxford).
SANDESARA, J. C. (1979), 'Size of the Factory and Concentration in the Factory Sector in India, 1951–1970', *Indian Economic Journal*, 27/2, pp. 1–34.
SAWHNEY, P. K., and SAWHNEY, B. L. (1973), 'Capacity-Utilisation, Concentration and Price-Cost Margins: Results of Indian Industries', *Journal of Industrial Economics*, 21/2, pp. 145–53.
SCHERER, F. M. (1980), *Industrial Market Structure and Economic Performance*, 2nd edn. (Houghton Mifflin, Boston, Mass.).
SCHMALENSEE, R. (1988), 'Industrial Economics: An Overview', *Economic Journal*, 98/392, pp. 643–81.
SCHWARTZ, M. (1986), 'The Nature and Scope of Contestability Theory', *Oxford Economic Papers*, 38 (Nov. suppl.), pp. 37–57.
SHARWANI, K. (1976), 'Some New Evidence on Concentration and Profitability in Pakistan's Large-Scale Manufacturing Industries', *Pakistan Development Review*, 27/1, pp. 272–89.
SHEPHERD, P. L. (1985), 'Transnational Corporations and the International Cigarette Industry', in Newfarmer (1985*a*), pp. 63–112.
SHEPHERD, W. G. (1985), *The Economics of Industrial Organisation*, 2nd edn. (Prentice-Hall, Englewood Cliffs, NJ).
SICAT G. P., and VILLAROEL, A. M. (1974), 'Industrial Concentration in the Philippines', *Philippine Economic Journal*, 13/2, pp. 85–129.
SIDDHARTHAN, N. S., and DASGUPTA, A. K. (1983), 'Entry Barriers, Exports and Inter-Industry Differences in Profitability', *Developing Economies*, 21, pp. 14–23.
SILVER, M. S. (1985), 'United Republic of Tanzania: Overall Concentration, Regional Concentration and the Growth of the Parastatal Sector in the Manufacturing Industry', *Industry and Development*, 15, pp. 19–36.
STIGLITZ, J. E., and MATHEWSON, G. F. (eds.) (1986), *New Developments in the Analysis of Market Structure* (MIT Press, Cambridge, Mass.).
TELLO, M. D. (1988), 'Industrial Organisation Characteristics and Commercial Policy in Peruvian Manufacturing Industries 1971–1985'. Paper presented to WIDER Conference: New Trade Theories and Industrialization in the Developing Countries, Helsinki.
THARAKAN, P. K. M. (1984), 'Intra-Industry Trade between the Industrial Countries and the Developing World', *European Economic Review*, 26, pp. 213–27.
TOH, K. (1982), 'A Cross-Section Analysis of Intra-Industry Trade in US Manufacturing Industries', *Weltwirtschaftliches Archiv*, 118, pp. 281–300.
UNITED NATIONS (1971*a*), *Indexes to the International Standard Industrial Classification of all Economic Activities*, Ser. M, No. 4, rev. 2 (United Nations, New York).
—— (1981), *Commodity Indexes for the Standard International Trade Classification*, Ser. M, No. 38, rev. 2, i and ii (United Nations, New York).

—— (1971b), *Classification of Commodities by Industrial Origin*, Ser. M, No. 43, rev. 1 (United Nations, New York).

VANLOMMEL, E., DE BRABANDER, B, and LIEBAERS, D. (1977), 'Industrial Concentration in Belgium: Empirical Comparison of Alternative Sector Concentration Measures', *Journal of Industrial Economics*, 26, pp. 1–20.

WALGREEN, J. A. (1971), 'Cost Functions, Concentration and Barriers to Entry in Twenty-Nine Manufacturing Industries in India: A Comment and Reinterpretation', *Journal of Industrial Economics*, 20/1 pp. 90–95.

WHITE L. J. (1974a), 'Industrial Organisation and International Trade: Some Theoretical Considerations', *American Economic Review*, 64, pp. 1013–20.

—— (1974b), *Industrial Concentration and Economic Power in Pakistan* (Princeton University Press, Princeton, NJ).

WHITEHALL, P. (1986), 'Profit Variation in the Barbados Manufacturing Sector', *Social and Economic Studies*, 35/4 pp. 67–91.

NOTES

1. For the purposes of this chapter the terms 'industrial economics' and 'industrial organization' are treated as synonymous.
2. A number of recent books, symposia, and journal reviews have been devoted to different aspects of this issue. See e.g. Caves (1980), de Jong and Shepherd (1986), Morris *et al.* (1986), Stiglitz and Mathewson (1986), Jacquemin (1987), Reid (1987), and Schmalensee (1988).
3. See e.g. Helpman and Krugman (1985), Greenaway and Tharakan (1986), Krugman (1986), Feenstra (1987), and Baldwin, Ch. 9, this volume.
4. The literature on the S–C–P model is vast. A number of industrial economics texts survey the relevant literature e.g. Clarke (1985), Devine *et al.* (1985), Scherer (1980), Shepherd, W. G. (1985).
5. A substantial literature now exists on contestable markets, the tone of some of which suggests it may have been both oversold and over-criticized. See e.g. Baumol *et al.* (1982), Baumol and Willig (1986), and Schwartz (1986).
6. The literature on particular aspects of this subject is considerable but relatively few studies have explored the topic as a whole, from an industrial economics standpoint. Those in the latter category include White (1974a), Caves *et al.* (1980), Caves (1985), and Newfarmer (1985b).
7. E.g. in the UN classification, trade data are generally classified more finely and somewhat differently from industrial production data (United Nations 1971a, 1981). As far as is possible, trade categories are grouped according to their most appropriate industrial category in United Nations (1971b).
8. These are: Pagoulatos and Sorenson (1975), Finger and de Rosa (1979), Loertscher and Wolter (1980), Caves (1981), Lundberg (1982), Toh (1982), Bergstrand (1983), Greenaway and Milner (1984), and Tharakan (1984), and Balassa—two studies—(1986a; 1986b).
9. See e.g. the studies of the textile, natural gas, steel, and electronic industries in the Unwin Hyman 'World Industry' series and of the defence, construction and high technology industries in the Routledge 'International Industry' series.

5

Externalities, Development, and Trade*

Frances Stewart and Ejaz Ghani

> [I]f one man starts a new idea, it is taken up by others and combined with suggestions of their own; and thus it becomes the source of further new ideas. And presently subsidiary trades grow up in the neighbourhood, supply it with implements and materials.
>
> A. Marshall, *Principles of Economics*

> Here is not just another exception to the doctrine of free trade. What is involved is the problem of a structural change in the pattern of specialisation which may be all too important in the early stages of economic development.
>
> P. Bardhan, 'External Economies, Economic Development and the Theory of Protection'

1. INTRODUCTION AND PRELIMINARY DEFINITIONS

Externalities occur where market prices, and therefore transactions between economic agents that are based upon them, do not fully incorporate all the benefits and costs associated with these transactions. Externalities thus constitute market failures. Their presence means that the unregulated price system does not result in a social optimum, and consequently provides a prima-facie reason for government intervention.[1]

Pigou defined an externality as occurring in a situation where 'one person, A, in the course of rendering some service, for which payment is made, to a second person B, incidentally also renders services or disservices to other persons (not producers of like services) of such a sort that payment cannot be exacted from the benefited parties or compensation enforced on behalf of the injured parties' (Pigou, 1938, ch. 9, p. 183).

Linkages describe *all* transactions between economic agents, whether through the market or outside it, fully or partially priced. Consequently, externalities are a subset of linkages. The linkage approach provides useful insights: the conceptualization of linkages, and in particular the breakdown into different *types* of linkage, suggests a similar classification of externalities;

---

* We are grateful to participants at the WIDER meeting 'New Trade Theories and Industrialization in Developing Countries', Aug. 1988, for useful comments on an earlier draft.

while the empirical work on linkages, although evidently capturing a much larger range of transactions than externalities alone, points to the areas where externalities may be found, since the existence of linkages is generally a precondition for the existence of externalities.[2] 'Spill-overs' is a rather loosely defined concept, which is sometimes used to mean the same as linkages, sometimes externalities. We will not be using the term.

This chapter is concerned with categorizing externalities, and assessing their relevance to trade policy. Section 2 presents a typology of externalities, making reference to some empirical work to help elucidate the nature and significance of the different types of externality. Section 3 presents a case-study where externalities have played a major role in securing rapid growth—the development of the electronics industry in California. Section 4 briefly considers some problems in measuring externalities. Section 5 concludes with an analysis of some implications for industrial and trade policies.

2. A TYPOLOGY OF EXTERNALITIES

Let us start with a more formal version of the definition: externalities exist where the utility function of a consumer or the production function of a producer is affected not only by their market activities but also by the activities of other economic agents (producers or consumers).

Formally if u_1 represents the utility function of the ith consumer, and $x_1, x_2, x_3 \ldots$ purchases of goods and services by this consumer,

$$u_1 = f(x_1, x_2, x_3 \ldots z_1, z_2 \ldots), \qquad (1)$$

where z_1, z_2 are the activities of others (consumers and producers) which directly affect consumer welfare. These may take the form of non-market effects, for example consumer satisfaction depending on the behaviour of the Joneses, or of effects mediated through the market, where the behaviour of other units affects the conditions (price, availability, qualities) of their own consumption bundle.

In parallel, the profit function of the ith producer, p_i, may be a function both of its own purchases of inputs and expenditures on factors, $y_1, y_2, y_3 \ldots$ and of the activities of other economic agents, $z_1, z_2 \ldots$, that is

$$p_1 = f(y_1, y_2, y_3 \ldots z_1, z_2 \ldots). \qquad (2)$$

As in the case of consumption, the externalities, $z_1, z_2 \ldots$ take the form both of non-market effects, for example smoke nuisance for laundries, and market effects.

Externalities can be categorized in a number of (cross-cutting) ways, which are useful for understanding their origin, estimating their significance, and more generally for designing policy. The following categorization will be considered:

1. Externalities categorized by the nature of the interacting agents.
2. Externalities categorized by the numbers of agents involved.
3. Externalities categorized by location of recipient.
4. Externalities categorized into 'real' and 'pecuniary'.

2.1 The Nature of the Interacting Agents

The major distinction here is between producers (p) and consumers (c). External effects may in principle go in four ways (Scitovsky 1954):

p–p, from producers to other producers
p–c, from producers to consumers
c–c, from consumers to other consumers
c–p, from consumers to producers.

It is easy to devise examples of each of the first three types, and, as we shall see, each is very relevant to trade policies. The last category is less easy to fill with examples,[3] although consumer groups which exercise non-market influence over producers are an example of this type of interaction. This is less common in developing countries. In the discussion below we shall focus on producer externalities. Consumer externalities—which are of considerable importance, and are frequently neglected—raise rather different issues and are better treated separately.

2.2 The Number of Interacting Agents

Externalities caused by any one agent may affect one other agent, a few others, or many others. Equally, one agent may be affected by externalities caused by one other, a few others, or many other agents.

The externalities caused by one agent may be of very minor significance for any one other agent (so minor as to be negligible), but the aggregate effects on a number of agents may be significant. One agent may be affected to an insignificant extent by externalities associated with any one other agent, but the added-up external effects of a large number of other agents may again be significant.

We shall define the different types of interaction as shown in Table 1. The distinction between the various types is of importance in determining the relevant type of policy approach. For example, one–one interactions might be expected to be dealt with by individual negotiations between the agents (see Coase 1960) but this is less likely as the number involved increases, whether on a one–many or many–many basis. Large one–one interactions may lead to integration of the agent into a single unit.

Table 1. Types of interaction of externalities

Externalities, defined as	Definition	Example
One → one* (or one → few)	The externalities of one agent significantly affect one other agent, or a few other agents	Factory smoke → laundry/laundries
One → many individually	The externalities caused by one agent significantly affect each of many other agents	Bhopal, Chernobyl
One → many collectively	The externalities caused by one agent significantly affect many other agents, when the effects are added up	Radiation effects of nuclear power stations
Many individually → many individually	The externalities caused by many agents individually have significant effects on the activities of many agents, individually	Same as one → one, but multiplied up, by number of agents
Many individually → many collectively	The externalities caused by many individual agents have significant effects on the activities of many agents collectively	Same as one → many collectively, but multiplied up by number of agents
Many collectively → many individually	The externalities of many agents collectively have significant effects on many individual agents	Farming/desertification Ozone destruction
Many collectively → many collectively	The externalities of many agents added together have significant effects on many other agents when added together	Car pollution Training

* No distinction is made here between one and a few agents. For completeness these types could be distinguished but the important distinction, for policy purposes, is between one (or a few) and many.

2.3 Location of Agents

The *location* of agents here includes *spatial* location and *industrial* location. Space can be divided up in a variety of ways—by nation, by region, urban or rural, etc. Externalities may occur among agents within the same sub-division, or across divisions, that is, externalities may occur between agents close together in the same town (as with smoke and laundries) or rural area (bees and orchards), and they can also occur across the various subdivisions (from rural to urban), or across national boundaries. The spatial dimension of the externalities is relevant because policies are normally focused on a spatial subdivision; for example concern may be with regional development, or rural development, or national development, but is rarely with 'world' development where the spatial dimension can be ignored. The only relevant externalities are those that occur between agents in the subdivision of space which is the concern of policy. As far as international trade is concerned, this means that the relevant externalities are domestic, and externalities that occur across national boundaries can generally be ignored. We therefore need to add a spatial dimension to the initial definition, including only $z_1^d, z_2^d \ldots$ (equations (1) and (2)) and excluding z_1^f, z_2^f, where superscript d represents externalities between domestic agents, and superscript f refers to externalities that affect foreign agents.

The spatial dimension of externalities is also relevant to the formulation of appropriate policies. For example if externalities occur mainly between agents in the same area policies to subsidize production in that area (for example favourable tax treatment, or provision of infrastructure) can be used to help realize the externalities. This is not possible where the agents affected by the externalities are spatially dispersed.

Another dimension is *industrial* location. Externalities can occur within an industry or between industries. In the latter case they can be clustered among a few industries or widely distributed across industries. Where externalities are confined to a single industry (or a cluster of a few well-defined industries), selective industrial promotion may be justified, whereas if the externalities are distributed across many industries the promotion would be required across all these industries.

2.4 Pecuniary/Real

The distinction between pecuniary and technological externalities was first drawn by Viner (1931), and developed by Meade (1952) and Scitovsky (1954).

The definition of externalities adopted earlier includes both real and pecuniary externalities. Real (or technological) externalities affect a firm's production function (or a consumer's utility function) while pecuniary externalities affect the price vector.[4]

Scitovsky and others (for example Corden 1974) have suggested that real externalities are—with the important exception of human skill formation—*relatively insignificant* in developing countries, with the implication that they can and should be ignored. In contrast, Scitovsky, Rosenstein-Rodan, and others argued that pecuniary externalities are of significant magnitude, justifying economic planning and other interventions. However, before making any judgement on this issue, and to get a more precise idea of what we are looking for in empirical work, we need further to unpackage the two types of externality.

Real externalities
Real externalities involve changes in the environment affecting the firm, resulting from the activities of other firms. Meade (1952) defined such externalities as being a property of the production function, and as occurring whenever the output of a firm, 'depends not only on the factors of production utilised by this firm but also on the output and factor use of another firm or firms'. The examples given by Meade and others of real externalities are of a one–one (or one–few), p–p, and static nature. This is the case both in the laundry–factory and the bee-keeper–orchard example. Other examples could be found, but it seems reasonable to agree with Meade and Scitovsky that these are not likely to be of widespread significance.

However, departing from the one–one, p–p, static type, greatly extends the prevalence of real externalities.

One class of externalities which is being given increasing attention is that coming under the broad heading of 'environmental' effects (see James 1981, and the Bruntland Report for many examples and references). These environmental externalities generally involve unpriced (negative) effects of producers' decisions, and may lead to enormous environmental degradation (for example desertification), and even to changes in the world's climate (for example destruction of the rain forest). In other cases, their effects are confined to localized health hazards (increasing cancers or bronchial problems) of a chronic or prolonged nature, or sudden local disasters to the environment and health (Bhopal, Chernobyl, Mexican oil disaster). No one could claim that these effects are insignificant. In some cases, the effects are due to the activities of a great number of agents, with the effects being spread among a great number of producers or consumers (for example those resulting from farming practices in the Sahel, or car pollution). These are p–c, p–p-type externalities, of the one–many, many–many variety. These real externalities are difficult to handle because they are often difficult to identify, measure, and evaluate. The most appropriate policy interventions are normally specific to the particular case, though some general principles can be drawn up. Since the policy implications for the most part concern government regulations, taxes, and subsidies and not trade policy (apart from their use as a protective device), these environmental externalities will not be considered further here.

Another class of real externalities is that related to economic growth: there are three types in this class—changing attitudes and motivation, skill formation, and changing knowledge about technologies and markets. Because these are all of fundamental importance to sustained economic growth, we describe them as *dynamic* externalities.

Attitudes and motives. One of the fundamental changes that occurs in the transition to modern growth is the change in attitudes from one of following well-established traditions in technologies and markets to one of accumulation, continuous technological change, and extension of markets. All sorts of factors are responsible for this change, including education and cultural change, as well as various 'push' factors (for example the impossibility of surviving without change because of population pressure). The spread of modern ideas, modern technologies, and modern products through trade and improved communications is a major influence on attitudes. These influences are a form of externality—that is for any agent they depend on developments resulting from the actions of many *other* agents, in adopting new technologies, selling new products, etc. Work on agricultural–industrial linkages has shown that the growth of nearby industry has positive effects on agricultural productivity, which is in part a result of these demonstration-type effects on attitudes (see Tang 1958; Nicholls 1969; Katzman 1974; and summary in Ranis *et al.* 1990).

These attitudinal changes have been looked at most closely for the agriculture–industry linkage, but they can also be expected to apply within industry. These externalities are of a p–p, p–c, and c–c-type and mostly many collectively–many collectively.

Human capital formation. This is the one area which is generally acknowledged to be an important source of real externality (see Scitovsky 1954; Corden 1974).

Human capital formation is not only a matter of formal training, but also informal learning on the job, and consists not only of acquisition of a body of knowledge and know-how but also of attitudes to work. Where the human capital transfer relates to technological change, it is discussed further below.

For the most part this externality is of a p–p, many collectively–many individually type—that is the training activities of large numbers of agents collectively materially affect the production conditions of large numbers of agents individually. Some aspects of this human capital formation are industry-wide, that is, apply to all industries, and some are industry-specific (the skills only being helpful in a particular industry).

Policy prescriptions derived from this well-acknowledged market failure include special training subsidies, and generalized support for industrialization.

Technology change and technology transfer. Many aspects of technology transfer leading to technological upgrading occur through interactions between firms that are partially or wholly outside the market. Such interactions occur in the following forms:

(a) Movement of labour from one firm to another bringing knowledge of new or improved technologies/products. Bell (1986) records the significance of labour movement as a source of technological upgrading: 'Hiring more-or-less ready-made resources for change seems to have been significant in the accumulation of technological capability reported in some plant studies' (p. 109). One example was the Ducilo Rayon plant where technical change was associated with peaks in expenditure on technicians and engineering staff (Katz 1980). Hiring was also found to be an important source of technological change for several machinery producers in Brazil and Argentina (Da Cruz 1980; Da Cruz and Da Silva 1981; Castana *et al.* 1981).

A study of a capital goods firm in South Korea identified a jump in technological capabilities associated with the joining of a new individual to the firm with a higher-calibre technical capability. Similar evidence was found in all twenty firms in South Korea shown to have made a technical transition, where those who played a central role in upgrading technology 'gained experience of producing related but more sophisticated products elsewhere' (Kim 1981).

Diffusion of knowledge through labour mobility is not confined to high-technology industries. Bagachwa (1988) found that 35 per cent of the proprietors of small maize-mills in Tanzania had previously served apprenticeships in other milling firms.

The externality associated with movement of labour could be classified under the 'human capital' label. It is distinguished here because it is related to technological change, and because it is not so much due to formal training as to on-the-job experience with more advanced technologies; and therefore cannot be appropriately dealt with by providing training subsidies.

This type of externality is of greatest significance *within* an industry. It may be one–one, one–many, or many–many.

(b) Technology transfer through trade journals, meetings, etc. Technology diffusion among firms within an industry has been shown to occur through trade journals and meetings of people from different firms. This has been most thoroughly documented by Saxonhouse (1971) in connection with the early history of the Japanese textile industry, where there was a well-developed system for exchange of information, including both local and foreign technology. 'The pages of the monthly trade journal were filled with discussions of attempted innovations on the part of Japanese firms, reports from correspondents on practices in foreign industries, discussions on the appropriateness of the practices for Japan' (p. 46).[5]

There is well-known disagreement about how to treat technology change in economic theory, and precisely how to measure its contribution to growth (Kaldor 1957; Balogh and Streeten 1963; Denison 1967; Solow 1970; Scott 1986). But all are agreed that technology change has accounted for the bulk of growth of productivity among the now-developed countries.

Similar conclusions apply to contemporary developing countries, although here it is to a greater extent a question of importing new or improved methods from abroad, adapting them to local conditions, diffusing them, learning to operate them more efficiently, and upgrading them over time (see Katz 1980; Westphal 1981; Fransman and King 1984; Pack and Westphal 1986; Lall 1987). Some of these developments occur within a single firm, and some through market transactions, but many result from non-market interactions between firms, that is, constitute externalities. These externalities occur within and between industries. Interactions leading to diffusion of best-practice techniques and upgrading of existing technologies may occur largely within an industry. But induced innovations also occur as a result of interactions between suppliers and users across industries, although these are frequently not industry-wide but are concentrated in clusters. While, as noted above, each of these types of externality may be one–one, one–many, or many–many, it seems that the existence of quite a large number of independent firms (suppliers and producers) is likely to be specially conducive to such technology change, because it increases the range of experience and contacts, and also the degree of competition which is likely to encourage such change.

(c) *Technology innovation induced by interaction between innovations and requirements in complementary activities.* Interactions between suppliers of inputs (capital goods and materials and parts) and purchasers have been shown to be a very important source of innovation and diffusion in nineteenth-century experience in Europe, the US, Japan, and in some contemporary developing countries (see Landes 1969; Saxonhouse 1971; Rosenberg 1976; Bell 1986; and Ranis and Saxonhouse 1987).

After examining American technological development in the nineteenth century, Rosenberg (1982) concludes that:

Inventions hardly ever happen in isolation. Time and again in the history of American technology, it has happened that the productivity of a given invention has turned on the question of the availability of complementary technologies ... technologies depend upon one another and interact with one another in ways that are not apparent to the casual observer, and often not the specialist. . . . The growing productivity of industrial economies is the complex outcome of large numbers of interlocking, mutually reinforcing technologies, the individual components of which *are of very limited consequences in themselves.* (pp. 56, 57, 58, 59; my italics)

Some of these interactions are captured *within* an industry, but many are captured in industries other than where the innovation is made. Rosenberg gives examples in electricity and aluminum, the development of commercial fertilizers and chemicals (see also Landes 1969, on textiles).

In his review of technical change in infant industries, Bell (1986) finds that: 'technical change will often involve detailed interaction between product-centred change and cost-reducing change... not only within firms but also between them. Hence *technical change may generate significant external economies; while productivity growth may depend on external costs*— those involved in the technical change efforts of other firms' (p. 29; my italics).

These externalities take the form of interactions between machine-users and producers, and between suppliers of other inputs and producers (Bell 1986, p. 92). In the latter case subcontracting from large to small firms has often involved a significant element of technology transfer (see Paine 1971; and Watanabe 1978, on Japan and Taiwan; Lall 1980, on India). Machinery user-producer interaction leading to improved technologies has been documented for textiles in Japan and India (Saxonhouse 1971; Ranis 1973) and nineteenth-century Britain (Rosenberg 1976), as well as for agricultural tools in the Punjab. Component suppliers have been shown to be an important source of technological transfer in Argentinian machinery production (Cortes 1978), and machine tools in Japan and Taiwan (Fransman, 1986). For Korea, interaction between purchasers of exports and suppliers led to technology-upgrading (Pursell and Rhee 1978).

The rate of technical change appears to be strongly related to these technology interactions between firms. Since they are externalities, they are not automatically generated in sufficient quantities by the market mechanism. It is argued (for example Bell 1986) that they may be rather limited in some developing countries, as for example in Thailand's modern industry, according to Bell and Scott-Kemmis (1987). Amsden (1977) notes non-diffusion in Taiwan from the modern sector, using foreign technology, to local machine-tool firms.

Interaction leading to technology change is likely to be greater: (*a*) the greater are *local* linkages, that is, if foreign firms supply capital goods and parts *local* technological externalities will be limited; and (*b*) the greater is firm specialization: 'specialised producers typically provide a substantial push behind the process of change. Their efforts to market their goods and services induce change in other firms' (Bell 1986, p. 92). This specialization is in turn related to the size of the market. It is a form of pecuniary externality arising with growth which leads to a real externality.

The type of externality involving this technology interaction of firms in the process of technical change occurs both within and across industries. It occurs among *clusters* of technologies which may be located in different industries but are all *linked* to the production of related products. As with the labour mobility type it may be one–one, one–many, many–many.

Summary of findings on 'real' externalities. In contrast to the conventional view that the real externalities are relatively insignificant except for manpower training, this chapter has suggested that they are widely prevalent and potentially of substantial magnitude in two broad areas: (*a*) environmental effects, where the externalities are generally negative in direction; (*b*) technology change, where the externalities are mostly positive.

Pecuniary externalities
Pecuniary externalities occur where the activities of one firm affect the *terms of trade* of other firms, that is, the price or characteristics of their inputs, or the markets for their output:

$$\text{i.e. they occur where} \quad |\mathbf{p}| = f(y_1, y_2 \ldots z_1, z_2), \tag{3}$$

where $|\mathbf{p}|$ is the firm's price vector.

However, the activities of some agents affect the prices faced by others all the time in the normal working of a competitive economy, and appear to be satisfactorily mediated through the market, without calling for government intervention, for example with changes of taste. For this reason Mishan (1971) and others suggested that the concept of pecuniary externalities was misplaced. This conclusion is correct where there is perfect competition and no indivisibilities throughout the economy. However, in certain cases where indivisibilities are present, pecuniary externalities can give rise to market failures which may justify government interventions. Two cases illustrate this:

(1) Suppose two firms are 'linked', that is, each supplies inputs to the other, both are large enough for their prices to influence the market price, and both are subject to economies of scale. Then it might be that investments in both firms would be profitable (privately and socially) but in one alone would not be. Consequently, some intervention would be justified. This one–one case is illustrated in Figure 1.[6]

(2) Suppose a competitive industry is linked to some other industry subject to indivisibilities (internal or external). Expansion of the first industry increases the market of the second, whose costs fall because of indivisibilities thereby improving the terms of trade of the first industry, justifying the initial expansion. Consequently, expansion of the competitive industry is both privately and socially justified. This could be a many–many or one–many example.

In neither of these examples would the market alone lead to an optimal solution. They are not examples of internal economies of scale or of real externalities *alone*. It is the combination of internal economies of scale or external economies with linked activities that gives rise to pecuniary externalities meriting policy intervention. In these cases the Mishan–Newbery conclusion that the market can and does deal satisfactorily with all cases of pecuniary externality is incorrect.

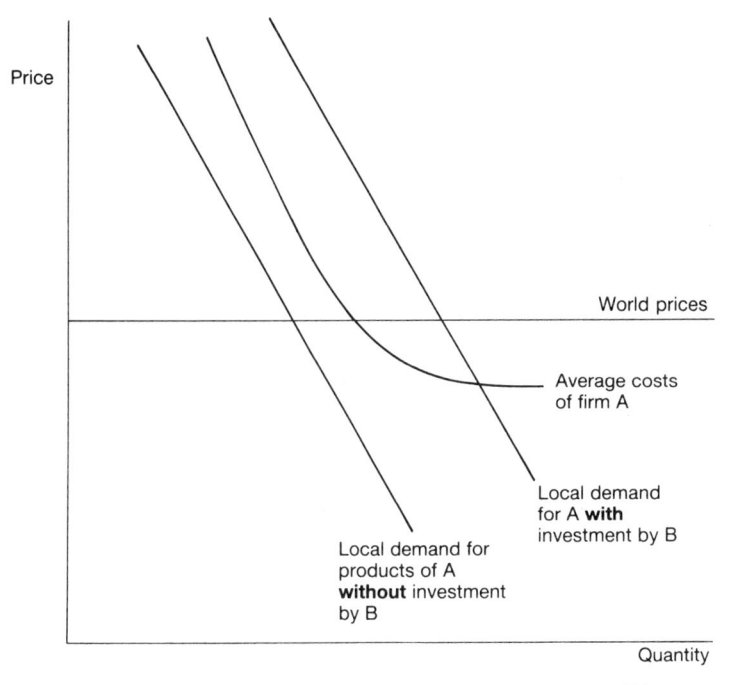

FIG. 1. Market demand in the presence of pecuniary externalities

However, in each case of pecuniary externality, policy intervention is only justified in the presence of indivisibilities, learning economies, or real externalities in one or other of some linked industries. From a policy perspective, then, it is normally sufficient to deal with these cases of market failure directly.[7] Consequently, the policy prescriptions to be discussed in Section 6 will be concerned with real externalities. The interaction of real and pecuniary externalities can be very important in causing (or preventing) a dynamic growth path, as is shown in the two case-studies below. It is therefore of relevance to identify the conditions which give rise to pecuniary externalities.

Since pecuniary externalities occur where firms' activities affect the relevant prices of inputs or output, they can only occur if local prices (and/or product characteristics) are affected by local activities and would not exist if world prices ruled locally. In practice, barriers to trade, both natural (transport costs and other transaction costs) and artificial (trade restrictions) lead to divergences between local and world prices. The high level of such barriers in most developing countries creates the potential for pecuniary externalities. As these barriers are reduced, with falling transaction costs and reduced trade restrictions, pecuniary externalities will diminish in importance, which is one reason why pecuniary externalities can be expected to be greater in developing countries than at later stages of development. Formally, if world prices w are given by

$$l_i \geq w_i + t_i + b_i, \qquad (4)$$

where l_i represents local prices of the ith commodity, t_i transaction costs, and b_i the monetary value of trade barriers, then the potential size of pecuniary externalities is $t_i + b_i$.[8]

It is worth stressing that the size of indivisibilities necessary to create such externalities is relative to the size of the market. The smaller the market the greater the likelihood of such externalities. Pecuniary externalities, therefore, may be particularly relevant to less developed economies with small markets, and to regional planning.

Pecuniary externalities may involve a change in the characteristics of goods available, related to local needs. Adaptation of product characteristics requires sufficient local demand to justify the overhead expenses of research, development, and adaptation, and, of course, will not occur at all with no local production. Examples of local adaptation of product characteristics are given in Ranis (1973), Van Ginneken and Baron (1984), Stewart (1977), and James and Stewart (1981).

Pecuniary externalities may occur through reorganization of production and increased firm specialization. The division of labour is limited by the extent of the market: as the market expands, and new specialization develops, this often takes the form of specialist firms emerging to perform functions that were previously performed in-house. The capital goods industry developed in this way, as did firms specializing in particular types of capital goods (Landes 1969; Rosenberg 1976). New types of specialist firms are continuously emerging in a growing economy. This tendency is reinforced by and also reinforces technical change. In modern economies specialist firms abound, for example for specialized legal services, computer services, repair and maintenance, etc. At an early stage of development, developing countries have few such firms and have to rely on in-house capabilities or imported services, which are generally subject to long delays and have inadequate knowledge of local circumstances. Some specialist services may emerge in response to a general expansion of the production base; other more specialized services depend on the emergence of a *particular* industry.

Pecuniary externalities can interact with real externalities: thus pecuniary externalities may lead to increased production, which in turn results in learning, increased technological capability, and technological adaptation, all of which are strongly associated with real externalities.

3. CASE-STUDY: THE SEMICONDUCTOR INDUSTRY IN THE UNITED STATES

The Silicon Valley in the Santa Clara county, where the semiconductor industry is based, was a 'peaceful agricultural valley' in the 1940s (Saxenian 1985). In the 1950s a few firms moved to the county to take advantage of the science park set up by Stanford University. By 1970 the region had gained international fame with the highest concentration of high-technology enterprises.

The history of Silicon Valley presents an example of an industry whose development depended on, and which in turn generated, substantial and significant externalities both within the industry and within the rest of the economy. The clustering of firms in the Silicon Valley was induced by the diffusion of research and development knowledge that stemmed from the university and independent research institutes in the region. The rapid development of the semiconductor industry induced substantial growth in a number of related industries, including telecommunications equipment, computer products, consumer products, industrial process control equipment, scientific instruments, and defence systems. The expansion of related industries has in turn generated additional demand for semiconductor devices. A dynamic process developed resulting in successive rounds of innovations and applications in both semiconductor and related industries. It has also created dozens of new industries; from software industry, data processing, and robotics to videograms.

3.1 Public Policy

Government support was vital in nurturing the nascent silicon industry in the early 1960s. Prior to the Second World War, the American electronics industry was less developed than the British or the German. But today Europe lags behind America in this industry. This development has been attributed to the catalytic role of the government in the US (Malerba 1985; Saxenian 1985). American defence and space programmes provided the market and the funds for the industry.

The main areas where public policies played an important role are public procurement, research and development, and some direct investment assistance. One of the most improtant factors was public procurement which offered a market in the early 1960s, when a commercial market for the semiconductor products did not exist. In 1962, government procurement constituted 100 per cent of the total value of US integrated-circuit sales. This share fell gradually to 10 per cent of the market by 1978, while the industrial and computer market had increased to 75 per cent, as the industry matured.

Public procurement was important in the initial phases because it stimulated innovations in the industry by reducing the market uncertainty associated with the introduction of innovative products and R & D efforts. Secondly, it helped firms to acquire volume on which scale and learning economies depend.

3.2 Externalities in the Semiconductor Industry

The development of the industry exhibited very substantial dynamic externalities, both real and pecuniary, with interaction between the two.

In the first place, the presence of considerable amounts of highly trained manpower from universities and government research laboratories provided the human capital essential for this high-technology industry. Rapid technology change in the industry both led to and was partly caused by technology transfer between firms in the industry, often mediated outside the market (for example by transfer of people, and through the products themselves). Technological change in one product frequently induced technology change elsewhere (via the cumulative process)—a process which took place both within firms and also between them.

The very high rate of technology change, and the greatly increased volume of production, led to rapidly falling costs. This cost reduction formed a pecuniary externality for user-industries, which also benefited from the changing products available and were in turn stimulated to change their own processes and products in response. Thus we observe the dynamic process shown in Figure 2.

The following section provides some evidence on this dynamic process.

(a) Silicon Valley benefited from a large supply of scientific and engineering manpower coming out of the universities and research laboratories in the area. The rising supply of engineers made it easier for small firms in the area to recruit, whereas large firms, for example IBM, could recruit nationally and internationally.

(b) An important characteristic was the very high mobility of skilled engineers and scientists (Markusen et al. 1986), which formed a major source of real externalities. A large number of highly skilled engineers and scientists trained and paid by government research centres set up their own firms. Defence spending accounted for 48 per cent of aeronautical engineers, 23 per cent of physicists, 21 per cent of electrical engineers, and 19 per cent of all mathematicians (Rutzik 1970). Although many of the projects they worked on were 'classified', the scientific processes they used, were not. Research concepts, originating in publicly financed research institutions, landed in private commercial firms.

The existence of publicly funded research programmes in Silicon Valley also attracted a number of new firms which benefited from the intellectual

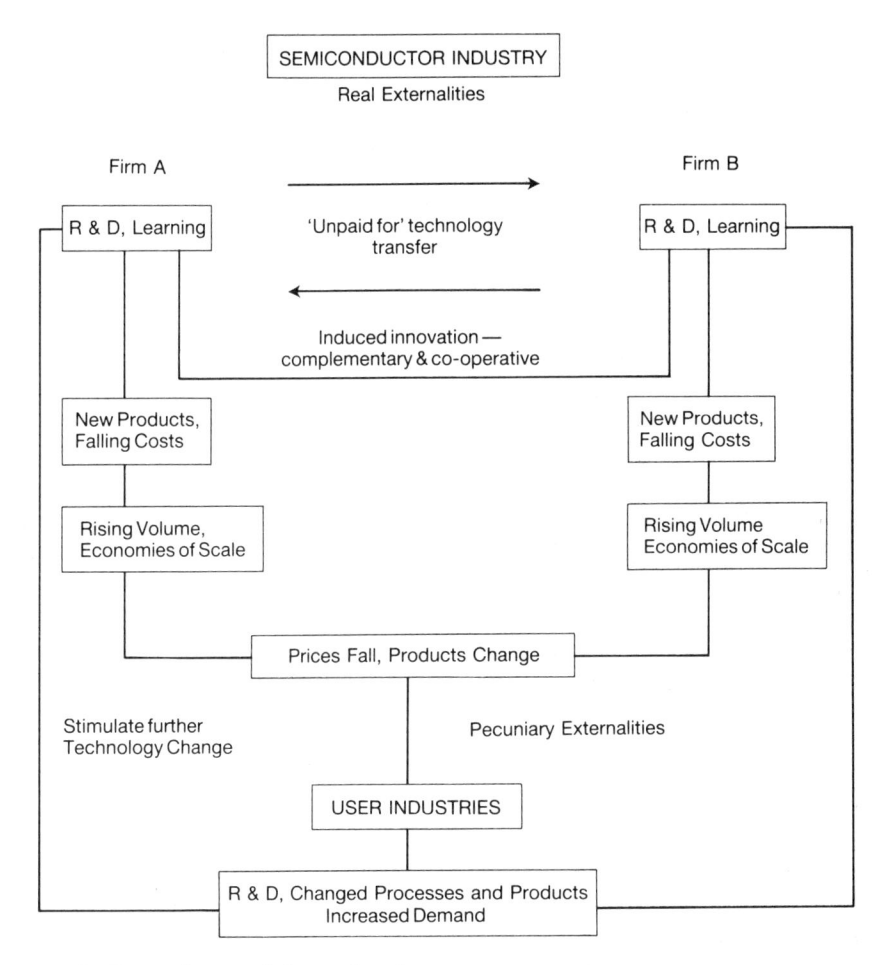

```
                    SEMICONDUCTOR INDUSTRY
                        Real Externalities

   Firm A                                              Firm B
┌─────────────┐      'Unpaid for' technology      ┌─────────────┐
│ R & D,      │ ───────────────────────────────→  │ R & D,      │
│ Learning    │                                   │ Learning    │
│             │       Induced innovation —        │             │
│             │ ←────  complementary & co-operative│             │
├─────────────┤                                   ├─────────────┤
│ New Products,│                                  │ New Products,│
│ Falling Costs│                                  │ Falling Costs│
├─────────────┤                                   ├─────────────┤
│ Rising Volume,│                                 │ Rising Volume│
│ Economies of │                                  │ Economies of │
│ Scale        │                                  │ Scale        │
└──────┬───────┘                                  └──────┬───────┘
       └────────── Prices Fall, Products Change ─────────┘

   Stimulate further          Pecuniary Externalities
   Technology Change
                         ┌──────────────────┐
                         │ USER INDUSTRIES  │
                         └──────────────────┘
                         │ R & D, Changed Processes and Products │
                         │        Increased Demand               │
```

FIG. 2. Dynamic growth in semiconductors

external economies and could recruit from the available pool of experienced and skilled labour.

'Spin-offs' were a more enterprising form of mobility, where skilled people left their initial employer, both public and private, to set up their own firms. W. Shockley, one of the three original inventors of the transistor, left Bell Laboratories to establish the first semiconductor firms. In 1957, eight of Shockley's scientists in turn broke off to start their own firms. Intel, which introduced the first microprocessor in 1971, was a spin-off of skilled personnel from Fairchild. Many of the thirty new firms that emerged in the semiconductor industry, in the period 1966–72, were a direct consequence of spin-off of skilled engineers who had worked at Bell Laboratories and Fairchild Semiconductors.

(c) In a high-technology industry, a new product does not embody the entirety of a new technology. Understanding how the technology was developed, the know-how, its uses, and the potential for further modifications extends beyond the market into the 'network or community of people who developed the technology and who help to apply it' (Borrus et al. 1987, p. 93).

The substantial degree of connectedness between firms, due to the Stanford science park, and 'complementary facilities', including university research, encouraged the diffusion of technological information among firms. The flow of information between firms, the firms and Stanford University, and the research institutions was, in turn, important in the further technological development in the semiconductor industry. As noted by one commentator: 'there was an unusually high degree of interaction between employees of rival firms in the Santa Clara county... much information, brainstorming and gossip were exchanged... at the local "watering holes". Stanford's education and seminar programmes... further encouraged this interchange' (Saxenian 1985, p. 30).

The presence of patents and licensing internalizes some potential externalities. However, given the shortness of the product cycle in the semiconductor industry, patents were circumvented with ease through 'inventing around' (Taylor and Silberston 1973; Levin 1982). Two special historical circumstances, Bell's liberal patent-licensing for the transistor, and Fairchild's and Texas Instruments's claims on integrated-circuit patents, led to wide availability of key patents and subsequent patents did not effectively protect inventions (Malerba 1985).

(d) The semiconductor industry has linkages in both input industries (backward linkages) and user industries (forward linkages). In both innovations have fed on each other, creating a cumulative cycle of innovation, extended markets, and falling prices. The importance of linkages has sometimes been questioned on the grounds of low transportation costs, especially given that silicon chips are relatively light and can be easily transported. However, in a survey the majority of the firms emphasized the importance of local input linkages (Oakey 1985). Given rapid technical change, it is important that the input supplier can respond rapidly to meet new requirements.

A variety of local input firms established themselves to produce the photomasks, testing jigs, chemicals, silicon, and special production equipment essential to manufacturing semiconductors. Providing all these inputs and services in-house would have been relatively expensive for small firms. Even the larger firms benefited from taking advantage of the lower costs due to learning economies and economies of scale in producing inputs and services for a large number of firms.

The software industry was a direct offshoot of the semiconductor industry. The industry's sales were $20bn in the 1970s, increasing substantially in the 1980s. It is estimated that nearly 4,000 to 4,500 firms exist in the software industry (Hall *et al.* 1985, p. 45). The majority of the software products and services come from small firms, many of which are spin-offs from other firms.

Over the past thirty years, the rise of the semiconductor industry has been associated with very major changes in a number of other industries. Semiconductor devices are used by a wide range of final markets: industrial, military, commercial, and consumer.

The transistor, the integrated circuit, and the microprocessors constitute the basic components of most electronic final products. Innovations in the semiconductor industry thus led to innovations in electronics final products. Since electronic final products have also become important inputs in many other sectors, product and process innovations in the semiconductor industry set in motion waves of innovations in many industries.

The wide range of end-users benefited both from real externalities in the form of new products and technology transfer, and also pecuniary externalities, arising from the rapid fall in prices associated with the high rate of learning in the industry, and economies of scale as volumes increased.

Price and pecuniary externalities
It is impossible to distinguish and quantify the relative impact of learning economies, economies of scale, and technological development in contributing to the fall in semiconductor prices. All three were important. There is considerable evidence to suggest that learning economies and accumulation of experience played an important role in the semiconductor industry (Finan and LaMond 1987).

The net effect of research and development, learning economies, and rising scale (Finan and LaMond 1987) was a rapid fall in prices, as exhibited in Table 1, which shows the fall in average price per unit of transistors and integrated circuits.

For example, in the case of linear integrated circuits the price fell from $30 in 1964 to $1.08 in 1972. The decline in the costs of semiconductor devices opened a multitude of possibilities for applications, and profitable investments in many sectors, playing a crucial role in stimulating demand for semiconductor products by end-users. The extent of pecuniary externalities which arose from falling prices is indicated by the increase in usage of semiconductor products by other industries. Pecuniary externalities mostly occurred across industries.

Table 1. Average price per unit of transistors and integrated circuits
(in current $US)

	Transistors		Integrated Circuits	
Year	Geranium	Silicon	Digital	Linear
1960	1.70	11.27	—	—
1961	1.14	7.48	—	—
1962	0.82	4.39	—	—
1963	0.69	2.65	—	—
1964	0.57	1.46	17.35	30.00
1965	0.50	0.86	7.28	28.83
1966	0.45	0.64	4.34	13.39
1967	0.43	0.58	2.98	6.18
1968	0.41	0.44	2.17	3.35
1969	0.37	0.37	1.58	2.22
1970	0.41	0.38	1.42	1.86
1971	0.46	0.33	1.22	1.48
1972	0.52	0.27	1.01	1.08

Source: OECD (1985) and *Electronic Market Data Book*, pp. 106-7.

3.3 Conclusion

This brief survey of the dramatic developments in the Silicon Valley indicates the very substantial extent of externalities, within the industry and between industries. Strong US government support for the industry through government procurement, training, and government R & D laboratories permitted the realization of these externalities. Although some of these externalities occurred between industries, support for the semiconductor industry alone was sufficient for their realization. However, it is not possible to say whether government intervention in this case was 'optimal'. Much more information would be required on many areas—some intrinsically 'unknowable', including the potential of other nationally supported industries, what would have happened with more (or less) government support in this industry, and the effects of alternative forms of industry support. Externalities in the semiconductor industry have been realized in different ways in other countries. For example in Japan there was an implicit 'buy Japanese' policy among major companies which ensured a high-volume market. In South Korea, networking among companies producing and using chips in the same group guaranteed significant market size for producers. The varied experience demonstrates that the incidence of externalities and the kind of government intervention that is appropriate varies according to firm structure and industrial organization.

4. MEASUREMENT OF EXTERNALITIES

If policy internalities are to be justified on the basis of externalities it is necessary to have some idea of potential orders of magnitude involved, in principle, *ex ante*, that is before decisions are made. A subsidy or tariff should not exceed the value of the externalities if it is directed solely to correct the market failure caused by the existence of externalities.

By their nature externalities do not have direct market value (since by definition they are not priced and traded). Therefore, unavoidably they are difficult to measure, and can be estimated only by indirect means.

The discussion that follows focuses on the measurement of dynamic production externalities, dividing them into the three categories put forward in Section 2, viz. attitudes and motives, human capital formation, and technology transfer.

1. The first—attitudes and motives—tends to be a discontinuous change that occurs in the early stage of industrialization. It can have a very large effect on rates of capital accumulation and productivity change. A switch in capital accumulation from 5 per cent to 10–15 per cent of national income is not uncommon, with a doubling or more in rates of productivity growth. Once these rates have been achieved—as in most contemporary LDCs—this type of externality loses significance, except in isolated areas.

2. The value of human capital formation is approximated by the change in earnings associated with different levels of education/training.[9] Numerous estimates have been made of the returns to formal education (see summary in World Bank 1980); although less attention has been paid to the returns to training, estimates for skill differentials should indicate the value placed on training, assuming equilibrium in non-segmented labour markets. Differentials in wages between the skilled and unskilled of 2 or more are typical in developing countries (see for example Chowdhury and Bhuiyan (1985) for some evidence for Bangladesh). To the extent that individuals receive additional earnings for training, they have an incentive to pay for this training themselves, but where wages are at subsistence there is no scope for this. Imperfect foresight and imperfect capital markets prevent workers from borrowing to finance their training.

3. Technology change and technology transfer. This is the most important source of dynamic externalities and also the most difficult to estimate. As shown in Section 2 it is composed of a variety of elements, including movement of labour transferring technology from one firm to another, technology transfer through networking of various kinds, and technology innovation induced by interaction between firms.

The technology transfer via labour transfer element could be measured by the additional wages that firms are prepared to pay for workers moving from one firm to another. Figures for 'transfer' wages, or more generally of how wages change as particular industrial experience accumulates, would provide an estimate of the value of technology transferred in this way, aggregated (and discounted) over the remaining working life of the worker (see Baldwin, Chapter 9 this volume). There is no obvious way of making a direct estimate of the value of technology transfer through networking (magazines, useful meetings, and so on). However, the potential maximum value of such transfer is suggested by the difference in total factor productivity of the best-practice technology in an industry and the average. The dispersion represents how much technology a firm might acquire by efficient networking, that is, the maximum value of the externalities to be acquired. This measure would also include the technology which might be acquired by human transfer, so this estimate should not be added to the previous estimate to avoid double-counting. Another measure of the externality potential would be given by profit differences between the most profitable and average firms. Much information has been collected on disparities in productivity within industries (see for example Tyler 1979; Tyler and Lee 1979; Page 1980; Pitt and Lee 1981). In most cases these productivity differences persist over time, suggesting either that the potential externalities are not realized, and/or that they are realized but the leading firms are improving their own performance over time, and thus opening up new opportunities for the exploitation of externalities. The former explanation is more likely in industries whose productivity is changing little over time; the latter in industries exhibiting rapid productivity gains. In the latter type of industry, the potential size of externalities, accumulated over time, tends to be much greater than in the more static industries.

The third type of dynamic externality—induced technical change caused by interactions between input and user industries—is most difficult to measure. A necessary but not sufficient condition for it to occur is the existence of significant linkages between industries. It is easy to find examples where this type of interaction has occurred (see for example Rosenberg 1976, 1982; and the semiconductor study), but difficult to estimate the extent to which technological change is due to the change in the linked industry as against innovative activity in the industry itself, which would have occurred anyway. Possible indicators of the existence of interactive technology change include (*a*) a high degree of linked activities, (*b*) technology change in each of the two or more linked industries, and (*c*) a large element of *product* change (as against process change) in the linked industries. Where all three occur, the existence of such externalities is indicated, but this does not provide an estimate of their value. An upper estimate would be given by an estimate of the increase in the factor productivity (weighting for product changes) associated with technical changes that qualify under the three indicators. This would represent an upper estimate because other changes—not related to these externalities—may also have contributed to the technical changes.

To conclude, identifying and estimating individual elements does not permit precise estimation of externalities, but it does allow broad indications of the range of externalities in particular industries. While externalities can create a strong case for government action, it does not, of course, follow that *any* government intervention is justified by externalities. As is well known many government actions have proved costly, including, for example, Anglo-French support for Concorde. Careful assessment of costs as well as benefits is needed.

5. CONCLUSIONS AND IMPLICATIONS FOR POLICY

The existence of externalities of significant magnitude creates a prima-facie case for departures from non-interventionist industrial or trade policies, since without intervention it seems likely that the externalities will not be taken into account in resource allocation. Consequently, there would be a tendency for under-investment in areas subject to a high degree of external economies relative to those with fewer external economies. Developing countries may have a dynamic comparative advantage in an industry subject to dynamic externalities—but be uncompetitive according to static comparative advantage. Consequently temporary intervention (by subsidy, tariff, quota, or other means) would appear to be justified to enable dynamic comparative advantage to be realized, as in Figure 3.

While this simple depiction applies most directly to real externalities, it also extends to cases of pecuniary externalities where these interact

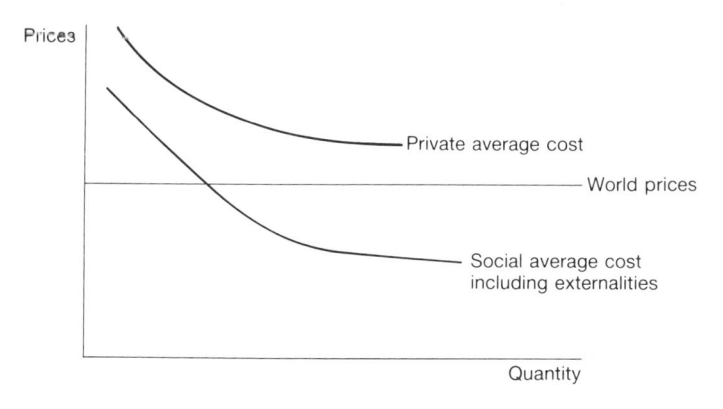

FIG. 3. Costs and externalities

with economies of scale, learning economies, or real externalities so that industrial expansion causes social costs to fall, as occurred in the US semiconductor industry. However, in the policy analysis that follows we shall focus on real externalities, since pecuniary externalities can normally be dealt with as an aspect of policies towards economies of scale, learning economies, or real externalities.

Current recommendations on trade and industrial policy fall broadly into three categories: first, a free-trade approach, according to which a country's investment, production, and trade patterns should be left to market forces, which are assumed to reflect its current comparative advantage. The second category are recommendations of policies intended to give *mild* support for industrialization. The version favoured by most economic advisers is to provide a small general subsidy to industrialization (for example 5 per cent), together with some government expenditure on industrial infrastructure. An alternative is to provide the same generalized support for import substitution, by the use of a low uniform tariff (see for example Balassa 1975; Little 1982; Corden 1984). The third category has been described as the 'strategist's' approach (by Pack and Westphal 1986), involving a strong *selective* support for particular industries. Again the promotion may take the form of subsidies to production or exports, or of import restrictions (or both). The practice is intended to be temporary.

One of the main differences in hypotheses between the proponents of the different approaches concerns the existence, size, and nature of externalities, since it is the extent and nature of market failures (of which externalities are an important, but not the only, component) which justify departures from the free-trade position and which suggest the most appropriate design for policy interventions. However, the precise implications of the existence of externalities for industrial and/or trade policies depends on the nature of the externalities and of the economy in which they occur.

The first issue is the pervasiveness of industries subject to externalities: if every part of the economy were subject to similar external economies, there would be no case for special support of any sector, since one cannot protect everything. However, although externalities of some sort are pervasive, they are likely to be much stronger in some industries and sectors than others, because of the nature of dynamic externalities. As shown earlier, the prime source of real dynamic externalities—which are the most important beneficial ones—lies in technological change and the (unpriced) ways in which this technical change is transmitted from one firm to another, both within and between industries. It follows that externalities will be more pervasive in industries subject to considerable technical change as in the case of the semiconductor industry. Industries with broadly stable or slowly changing technologies will not experience the same level of externalities. The extent of technical change in an industry may differ according to the stage of development of the country, that is, more industrialized countries may have reached the stable plateau (of slowly changing technology) while in other countries, the industry is experiencing rapid technical change as it catches up to the frontier country.

From a policy perspective, special support would be justified for those industries going through a dynamic phase. In Figure 4, if the trajectory shown depicts the typical technical change of an industry, then special support would be justified in the BC stage.

The second issue concerns the spatial location of externalities: if external economies created by an industry were transmitted world-wide, then each industry could benefit from externalities created by any other industry irrespective of where the industry was located. Therefore there would be no case for special promotion of home industries. The evidence suggests that some externalities do cross boundaries, through general communications and international trade. These provide a justification for a pro-trade set of policies. But the majority of dynamic externalities described earlier are nation-specific, and some of them are specific to a particular region (for example Silicon Valley). Krugman has argued that even where the externalities are nation-specific no intervention is justified where factor prices are unaffected and where the externalities are industry-specific (see Helpman and Krugman 1985; Krugman 1986). But his model is a full-employment model where real wages are determined in the constant-returns sector which is shared by both trading partners. In this model, a rise in productivity throughout the economy can happen only if either (a) a nation specializes entirely in external economy industries; or (b) the external economies arising from one industry benefit the whole economy raising productivity everywhere. In contrast, developing countries which succeed in raising productivity in the externality-creating sector may increase the size of the modern sector (through absorbing surplus labour) and thereby raise real incomes for the economy as a whole. The recent efforts of Taiwan, S. Korea, and Singapore in their post-labour surplus phase can be seen as a

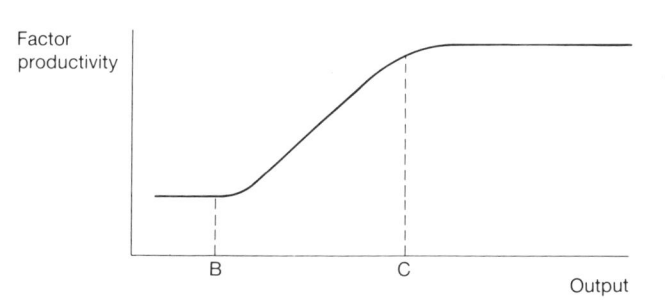

FIG. 4. An industry-learning trajectory

gradual effort to shift the whole economy into technologically dynamic increasing returns sectors (that is, to fulfil condition (*a*)) though the policy has to start with one industry at a time.

The third question is the industrial location of externalities: as noted earlier, externalities can be concentrated industrially as to source and also as to beneficiary, but they may be dispersed in either or both senses. Assume they are all nation-specific. Where they are concentrated as to source, there is a case for selective promotion of the source industry, irrespective of whether it is also the beneficiary or the sole beneficiary as with the semiconductor industry. Where other industries are the main beneficiaries it is the recipient industries which may acquire international competitiveness as a result of the policy, not the promoted industry. (Examples would be the competitiveness acquired by user industries in the US as a result of the development of the semiconductor industry, or competitiveness or other advantages, such as appropriate technology, that user industries might gain as a result of promotion of capital goods industries.) In all cases where linked industries are the main beneficiaries care is needed to establish that the externalities are nation-specific and could not equally (or better) be acquired by importing. An example of the latter might be India's protection of its capital goods industry, which has probably led to lower technology transfers to user industries than those they would have received through imported capital goods (as well as involving them in worse terms of trade).

Where the externalities are concentrated as to source, and nation-specific as to beneficiary, then selective industrial promotion is justified. But if the source of externalities is spread widely among industries, but not outside industry, then the type of intervention justified is non-discriminatory industrial promotion.

In practice, the industrial location of externalities depends upon the nature of the externalities. Some, like engendering work habits and learning some management techniques, are likely to be pervasive. These may be particularly common in the early stages of industrialization. Others, like the dynamic externalities associated with technical change, are likely to be focused on particular types of technology and industry, where the rate of frontier technology is changing fast. These externalities will generally be concentrated on a single industry or a few closely linked industries.

A popular criticism of selective policies is that it is difficult (some say impossible) to 'pick winners'—indeed this is used as a decisive criticism of the approach in much discussion by orthodox economists (for example Krugman 1983; Schultz 1983; Council of Economic Advisors 1984). The empirical counter-argument is the undoubted success of Japan and later S. Korea apparently in doing precisely that (Pack and Westphal 1986; Chung 1988; Enos and Park 1988).

But the phrase 'pick winners' is incorrect: what is at stake is *not* for the most part picking winners, but *creating winners*. Assume that *every* industry is subject to the same significant external economies, real and pecuniary, static and dynamic. Assume that with a 'non-intervention' policy, very limited industrialization would occur and these externalities would not be realized. Neither across-the-board import-substitution policy of the type commonly adopted, nor a generalized low subsidy to industrialization of the type commonly recommended, might be sufficient in this situation to realize enough of the external economies to secure socially competitive production. Sufficient externalities would only be realized if some industries were heavily promoted while the rest were not. With this model—where it is assumed that all industries are subject to the same externalities—it is not a question of picking winners—any industry could be a winner—it is a matter of choosing a *few* industries (and *not* promoting all industries) and then creating winners.[10]

In practice, it may not be true that such externalities are likely to be equal irrespective of industry, and, more importantly, a country's comparative advantage (static and dynamic) after allowing for externalities, learning effects, etc. is likely to differ between industries, according to its own history and stage of development. Consequently, it is not realistic to argue that it does not matter what you pick as long as you pick something (as with Buridan's donkey). In reality, the situation is somewhere between picking winners and creating winners. But given industry-specific dynamic economies (internal as well as external), the policy of low generalized support for industry (or across-the-board import substitution) could prove to be worse than a random policy of selective promotion.

To summarize, the prima-facie case for intervention in the presence of externalities in a developing country has justification where the externalities are nation-specific, and are concentrated on particular parts of the economy. The externalities must be sufficient to ensure eventual competitiveness in the industry in question or in user industries, and the eventual gains must be sufficient to outweigh the temporary costs (the Mill–Bastable test). Selective promotion is justified where the source of externalities is concentrated on one or a few industries. The evidence of rapid and uneven technical change suggests that these conditions are quite often met—but empirical investigation is needed to ensure they are, or losses can ensue. As shown earlier, even *ex post* empirical evidence is problematic. It is even more difficult to estimate the significance of externalities before the industrial development occurs, but some orders of magnitude are needed to take well-founded decisions on industrial promotion.

Type of intervention
Suppose a case for intervention has been established. This leaves open the question of the type of intervention, or indeed whether the market

will not bring about its own solution without government intervention.

Much of the literature on externalities has been concerned with this issue. Three categories of solution have been proposed: (1) integration; (2) negotiations and bargaining between the agents leading to voluntary co-ordination and/or the creation of property rights; and (3) government interventions.

(1) *Integration.* This solution may occur where the externalities are large in relation to other costs, and where they are of a one–one type. Some pecuniary externalities fit this model. But this solution is not suitable for one–many or many–many-type externalities, since too many agents are involved for integration. As noted earlier, many of the dynamic externalities are of the many–many type (for example those associated with mobility of skilled workers; technology diffusion, etc.). Most of the externalities in the semiconductor case were many–many types.

(2) *Bargaining and the creation of property rights.* Coase—who saw defects in the 'traditional' solution of taxes/subsidies—suggested that negotiated solutions might be brought about by the agents themselves, without outside interventions. The potential gains (losses) would induce those benefiting (suffering) from the externalities to bribe those imposing them to generate (limit) the externalities, thereby creating property rights, or a market, in the externalities. However, this will happen only if the benefits exceed the transaction costs. Where this occurs the externalities are effectively internalized. A similar solution is voluntary co-ordination among agents. Direct bargaining (or co-ordination) is likely to occur only where there are very few agents and/or very large benefits/costs to each agent, because of the increasing transaction costs arising with greater numbers.

In the many–many case too many agents are involved and the gains for each individually are likely to be too small to warrant the transactions costs. There can also be enforcement problems where many agents are involved. For dynamic externalities there is the further problem that the potential gains may not be known and/or uncertain—not a promising scene for bargaining and property rights (for example where they involve stimulation of technical change).

Property rights could be extended to cover some aspects of real externalities of the many–many type, with legal changes. For example, if firms 'owned' workers and sold them to other firms (like footballers or baseball players), this would internalize the training/learning externality. But there could be objections to this on grounds of civil liberties! In Japan internalization has been achieved by the system of lifelong employment. The patent system could be extended (again on the Japanese model of 'utility' patents) to extend markets over technology transfer. But this has enforcement costs, limits the diffusion of technology, and will never fully 'marketize' all the ways in which technology is diffused.

(3) *Government intervention*. It thus appears that for a large proportion of the dynamic externalities described in this chapter, the market cannot provide an adequate solution on its own, and direct government intervention is needed. This applies to most dynamic externalities, where many agents are involved. Government interventions can take a variety of forms. These include facilitating and perhaps partially financing co-ordination among agents (for example the MITI in Japan organized joint research among major companies); providing subsidies in various forms (for example investment subsidies or tax relief; support for R & D, education, hiring); government procurement (which was the most powerful policy used in the US semiconductor industry); and trade measures, including tariffs, quotas, and export subsidies.

In this area, as in others, the more directly the intervention deals with the situation which justifies it, the better. This means subsidies to the externality-creating source (for example for R & D) are preferable to more indirect measures. In view of this, direct trade measures are rather clumsy instruments compared with many other policy instruments. However, in a second-best world, where there are limited funds for subsidies, protection may be appropriate. The protection should be directed to those industries experiencing an actual (or potential) phase of high externalities. In this phase, high levels of protection could be justified on a temporary basis. It should be temporary, not only because the realization of externalities and economies of scale should normally make protection unnecessary after a specified time, but also because the industry will be denied externalities coming from abroad during protection.

REFERENCES

AMSDEN, A. (1977), 'The Division of Labour is Limited by the Type of Market: The Case of the Taiwanese Machine Tool Industry', *World Development*, 5/3, pp. 217–34.

BAGACHWA, M. D. (1988), Ph.D. thesis, University of Dar-es-Salaam, Tanzania.

BALASSA, B. (1975), 'Reforming the System of Incentives in Developing Countries', *World Development*, 3, pp. 365–82.

BALDWIN, R., and KRUGMAN, P. (1988), 'Industrial Policy and International Competition in Wide-Bodied Aircraft', in R. Baldwin (ed.), *Trade Policy Issues and Empirical Analysis* (Chicago University Press, Chicago).

BALOGH, T., and STREETEN, P. P. (1963), 'The Coefficient of Ignorance', *Oxford Bulletin of Economics and Statistics*, 25/2, pp. 99–107.

BARDHAN, P. (1978), 'External Economies, Economic Development, and the Theory of Production', in S. P. Singh (ed.), *Underdevelopment and Developing Economies* (OUP, Oxford), pp. 452–68.

BECKER, G. (1975), *Human Capital* (Columbia University Press, New York).
BELL, M. (1986), 'Technical Change in Infant Industries: A Review of Empirical Evidence' (World Bank, Washington, DC), mimeo.
——and SCOTT-KEMMIS, D. (1987), 'Transfers of Technology and the Accumulation of Technological Capability in Thailand' (World Bank, Washington, DC), mimeo.
BHADURI, A. (1973), 'On the Formation of Usurious Interest Rates in Backward Agriculture', *Cambridge Journal of Economics*, Dec.
BORRUS, M. L., TYSON, D'ANOREA, and ZYSMAN, J. (1987), 'Creating Advantage: How Government Policies Shape International Trade in the Semiconductor Industry', in P. R. Krugman (ed.), *Strategic Trade Policy and the New International Economics* (MIT Press, Cambridge, Mass.).
BRUNTLAND REPORT (1987), *Our Common Future* (OUP, Oxford).
CASTANA, A., KATZ, J., and NAVAJAS, F. (1981), *Etapas Historicas y Conductas Technologicas en una Planta Argentina de Maquinas Herraminenta*, IDB/ECLA/UNDP/IDRC Research Programme on Scientific and Technological Dependence in Latin America, Working Paper 38 (ECLA, Buenos Aires).
CHUNG, I-Y. (1988), 'Infant Industry Protection and Industrialisation: The Case of Korea', M.Sc. Essay, Oxford, mimeo.
COASE, R. H. (1960), 'The Problem of Social Cost', *Journal of Law and Economics*, 3, pp. 1–44.
COOPER, C., and SERCOVICH, F. (1970), 'The Channels and Mechanisms for the Transfer of Technology from Developed to Developing Countries', UNCTAD TD/D/AC, 11/5.
CORDEN, W. M. (1974), *Trade Policy and Economic Welfare* (Clarendon Press, Oxford).
COUNCIL OF ECONOMIC ADVISORS (1984), *Economic Report to the President* (GPO, Washington, DC).
CRAWFORD, J. G. (1969), 'India', in R.T. Shand (ed.), *Agricultural Development in Asia* (Australian National University, Canberra), pp. 53–102.
DA CRUZ, H. N. (1980), *Mudanca Tecnologia no Seta Metal Mecanico: Um Estudo de Caso de Maquinas para Processar Gerais*, IDB/ECLA/UNDP/IDRC Research Programme on Scientific and Technological Dependence in Latin America (ECLA, Buenos Aires), mimeo.
——and DA SILVA, M. E. (1981), *Mudanca Tecnologia Setor Metal Mecanico: Relatocio Parcia, Part II*, IDB/ECLA/UNDP/IDRC Research Programme on Scientific and Technological Dependence in Latin America (Fundacão Instituto de Perquisa Economicas, São Paulo), mimeo.
DENISON, E. (1967), *Why Growth Rates Differ* (Brookings Institution, Washington, DC).
DHAWAN, B. D. (1982), *Development of the Tubewell Irrigation* (Agricole, New Delhi).
DIEBOLD, J. (1983), 'The Information Technology Industries: A Case Study of High Technology Trade', in W. R. Cline (ed.), *Trade Policy in the 1980s* (Institute for International Economics, Washington, DC), pp. 639–72.
ENOS, J. L., and PARK, W. H. (1988), *The Adoption and Diffusion of Imported Technology: The Case of Korea* (Croom Helm, New York).

FINAN, W. F., and LaMOND, A. M. (1987), 'Sustaining US Competitiveness in Microelectronics: The Challenge to US Policy', in B. R. Scott and G. C. Lodge (eds.), *US Competitiveness in the World Economy* (Harvard Business School Press, Boston, Mass.).

FRANSMAN, M. (1986), 'International Competitiveness, International Diffusion of Technology and the State: A Case Study from Taiwan and Japan', *World Development*, 14/12, pp. 1375–96.

—— and KING, K. (eds.) (1984), *Technological Capability in the Third World* (Macmillan, London).

HALL, P., and MARKUSEN, A. (eds.) (1985), *Silicon Landscapes* (Allen & Unwin, London).

—— OSBORN, R., and WACHSMAN, B. (1985), 'The American Computer Software Industry: Economic Development Prospects', in Hall and Markusen (1985).

HELPMAN, E., and KRUGMAN, P. (1985), *Market Structure and Foreign Trade* (MIT Press, Cambridge, Mass.).

HENDRIX, W. E. (1981), 'Availability of Capital and Production Innovations on Low-Income Farms', *Journal of Farm Economics*, Feb.

JAMES, J. (1981), 'Growth, Technology and the Environment in Less Developed Countries: A Survey', in P. Streeten and R. Jolly (eds.), *Recent Issues in World Development* (Pergamon, Oxford).

—— and STEWART, F. (1981), 'New Products: A Discussion of the Welfare Effects of the Introduction of New Products in Developing Countries', *Oxford Economic Papers*, 33/1.

KALDOR, N. (1957), 'A Model of Economic Growth', *Economic Journal*, 67/268, pp. 591–624.

KATZ, J. (1980), 'Domestic Technology Generation in LDCs: A Review of Research Findings', IDB/ECLA/UNDP/IDRC Research Programme on Scientific and Technological Dependence in Latin America, Working Paper 35 (ECLA, Buenos Aires).

KATZMAN, M. (1974), 'The Von Thunen Paradigm, the Industrial-Urban Hypothesis and the Spatial Structure of Agriculture', *American Journal of Agricultural Economics*, 56/4, pp. 638–46.

KIM, L. (1981), 'Technological Innovation in Korea's Capital Goods Sector: A Micro Analysis', mimeo.

KRUGMAN, P. (1983), 'Targeted Industrial Policies: Theory and Evidence', in *Industrial Change and Public Policy* (Federal Reserve Bank of Kansas City).

—— (1986), 'Strategic Sectors and International Competition', in R. Stern (ed.), *US Trade Policies in a Changing World Economy* (MIT Press, Cambridge, Mass.), pp. 207–34.

LALL, S. (1980), 'Vertical Inter-Firm Linkages in LDCs: An Empirical Study', *Oxford Bulletin of Economics and Statistics*, 42/3, pp. 203–26.

—— (1987), *Learning to Industrialize* (Macmillan, London).

LANCASTER, K. (1979), *Variety, Equity and Efficiency* (Blackwell, Oxford).

LANDES, D. S. (1969), *The Unbound Prometheus* (CUP, Cambridge).

LITTLE, I. M. D. (1982), *Economic Development: Theory, Policy and International Relations* (Basic Books, New York).

MALERBA, F. (1985), *The Semiconductor Business* (Frances Pinter, London).

MARKUSEN, A., HALL, P., and GLASMEIER, A. (1986), *High Tech America* (Allen & Unwin, London).
MARSHALL, A. (1920), *Principles of Economics* (Macmillan, London).
MEADE, J. E. (1952), 'External Economies and Diseconomies in a Competitive Situation', *Economic Journal*, 62, pp. 54–67.
MISHAN, E. J. (1971), 'The Postwar Literature on Externalities', *Journal of Economic Literature*, 9, pp. 1–28.
NEWBERY, D. M. G. (1980), 'Externalities: The Theory of Environmental Policy', in G. A. Hughes and G. M. Heal (eds.), *Public Policy and the Tax System* (Allen & Unwin, London), pp. 106–49.
NICHOLLS, W. (1969), 'The Transformation of Agriculture in a Presently Semi-Industrialized Country: The Case of Brazil', in E. Thorbecke (ed.), *The Role of Agriculture in Economic Development* (National Bureau of Economic Research, New York), pp. 311–78.
OAKEY, R. (1985), 'High Technology Industry and Agglomeration Economies', in Hall and Markusen (1985).
OECD (1985), *The Semiconductor Industry: Trade Related Issues* (Organization for Economic Co-operation and Development, Paris).
PACK, H., and WESTPHAL, L. (1986), 'Industrial Strategy and Technological Change', *Journal of Development Economics*, 27, pp. 87–128.
PAGE, J. M. (1980), 'Technical Efficiency of Economic Performance: Some Evidence from Ghana', *Oxford Economic Papers*, 32/2, pp. 319–39.
PAINE, S. (1971), 'Lessons for LDCs from Japan's Experience with Labour Commitment and Subcontracting in the Manufacturing Sector', *Oxford Bulletin of Economics and Statistics*, 33, pp. 115–34.
PIGOU, A. C. (1938), *Economics of Welfare* (Macmillan, London).
PITT, M. M., and LEE, L. (1981), 'The Measurement of Sources of Technical Inefficiency in the Indonesian Weaving Industry', *Journal of Development Economics*, 9, pp. 43–64.
RANIS, G. (1973), 'Industrial Sector Labour Absorption', *Economic Development and Cultural Change*, 21/3, pp. 387–408.
—— and SAXONHOUSE, G. (1987), in K. Ohkawa and G. Ranis (eds.), *Japan and the Developing Countries* (Blackwell, London).
—— STEWART, F., and ANGELES-REYES, E. (1990), *Linkages in Developing Countries: A Philippine Case Study* (International Center for Economic Growth, San Francisco).
RHEE, Y. W., ROSS-LARSON, B., PURSELL, G. (1984), *Korea's Competitive Edge: Managing the Entry into World Markets* (Johns Hopkins Press, Baltimore).
ROSENBERG, N. (1976), *Perspectives on Technology* (CUP, Cambridge).
—— (1982), *Inside the Black Box: Technology and Economics* (CUP, Cambridge).
ROSENSTEIN-RODAN, P. N. (1943), 'Problems of Industrialisation of Eastern- and South-Eastern Europe', *Economic Journal*, 53/210, pp. 202–11.
SAXENIAN, A. (1985), 'The Genesis of Silicon Valley', in Hall and Markusen (1985).
SAXONHOUSE, G. R. (1971), 'Productivity Change in the Japanese Cotton Spinning Industry 1891–1935', Ph.D. thesis, Yale University, New Haven, Conn.
SCHULTZ, C. (1983), 'Industrial Policy: A Dissent', *Brookings Review*, 2/1, pp. 3–12.

SCITOVSKY, T. (1954), 'Two Concepts of External Economies', *Journal of Political Economy*, 62/2, pp. 143–57.
SCOTT, M. F. G. (1986), 'Explaining Economic Growth', Keynes Lecture in Economics (British Academy, London).
SHAND, R. T. (ed.) (1986), *Off-Farm Employment in the Development of Rural Asia*, (Australian National University, Canberra).
SOLOW, R. (1970), *Growth Theory* (Clarendon Press, London).
STEWART, F. (1977), *Technology and Underdevelopment* (Macmillan, London).
STIGLITZ, J. E., and WEISS (1981) 'Credit Rationing in Markets with Imperfect Information', *American Economic Review*, 71/3, pp. 393–410.
TANG, A. (1958), *Economic Development in the Southern Piedmont* (University of North Carolina, Chapel Hill, NC).
TYLER, W. G. (1979), 'Technical Efficiency in Production in a Developing Country: An Empirical Examination of the Brazilian Plantation and Steel Industries', *Oxford Economic Papers*, 31/3, pp. 477–95.
—— and LEE, L. F. (1979), 'On Estimating Stochastic Frontier Production Functions of Average Efficiency: an Empirical Analysis with Colombian Micro Data', *Review of Economics and Statistics*, 61, pp. 435–8.
VAN GINNEKEN, W., and BARON, C. (eds.) (1984), *Appropriate Products, Employment and Technology* (Macmillan, London).
VINER, J. (1931), 'Cost Curves and Supply Curves', *Zeitschrift für Nationalokonomie*, 3, pp. 23–46, repr. in American Economic Association (1953), *Readings in Price Theory* (Allen & Unwin, London).
WATANABE, A. (1978), *International Subcontracting: A Tool of Technology Transfer* (Asian Productivity Organization, Tokyo).
WESTPHAL, L. E. (1981), 'Empirical Justification for Infant Industry Protection', World Bank Staff Working Paper 469 (World Bank, Washington, DC).

NOTES

1. There are of course other reasons why the market system may not lead to a social optimum, e.g. unsatisfactory income distribution.
2. However, negative externalities could be present where there are *no* linkages, since the negative effect might be e.g. to eliminate local supplies of inputs.
3. Scitovsky used the example of the influence of an inventor on producers, but we would interpret this as p–p type.
4. Technological externalities are here termed 'real' because of the many other uses of 'technological'.
5. See also Cooper and Sercovich, 1970 for some documentation on this form of technology transfer between countries.
6. This is the type of case noted by Rosenstein-Rodan (1943), and Scitovsky (1954), both of whom believed it has wide empirical application.
7. See e.g. Pack and Westphal (1986) on policies towards learning economies and economies of scale.
8. The same approach can be used to identify pecuniary externalities within a

particular region, but in this case w_i should be interpreted as prices in the economic centre of the country, t_i the transactions costs of trade with the centre, while b_i would usually be zero.

9. To the extent that private returns to education reflect screening or credentialism, these will exaggerate the social returns.

10. Suppose a student asks advice on whether she should be a doctor or a lawyer. Assume in fact she would be equally good at either if she undertakes the required training. Should the adviser recommend doing a little training for both because it is difficult to pick a winner?

6

Closing the Productivity Gap: Does Trade Liberalization Really Help?*

Dani Rodrik

1. INTRODUCTION

The import-substitution strategy's fall into disrepute among academics, and increasingly among policy-makers, has been greatly assisted by the discovery that most infant industries spawned by the strategy have failed to mature. It has become increasingly clear that indiscriminate protection of nascent industries yields few productivity gains, and that the benefits of the strategy are unlikely to offset its costs in terms of resource misallocation. For this and other reasons, 'outward-orientation' has now become the new orthodoxy. The new strategy's siren song has many refrains, but one which is particularly appealing is the promise of improved technical efficiency once protective trade barriers are lifted. With trade liberalization set into motion, policy-makers are told, protected firms will have no choice but to modernize their techniques and cut their costs in order to compete with foreign producers. What is at stake is no longer some Harberger triangles, but hefty rectangles of unexploited technological opportunities.

The relationship between trade policy and technical efficiency is an old theme in economics, but one that has been overshadowed by the emphasis on the Ricardian doctrine of comparative costs. The traditional case for comparative advantage and free trade is one that stresses *allocative* efficiency, that is, the allocation of domestic resources into sectors where they are most productive; it is mostly silent on *technical* efficiency. Interestingly, the original case for the gains from trade—as articulated by Adam Smith—relied on overall gains in productivity deriving from an expanded division of labour within a larger market.[1] This rationale for trade—based on scale economies—was hidden from the view of academic economists by the intellectual appeal of the Ricardian outlook, and has only recently been resuscitated in the works of the 'new' trade theorists.[2] But unlike the

---

* I am grateful to Amy Kim for research assistance, and to the Japanese Corporate Associates Program at the Kennedy School, Harvard University, for partial financial support. Conference participants Albert Berry, Patrick Conway, Gene Grossman, Gerry Helleiner, and Jaime de Melo provided helpful comments on an earlier draft.

Ricardian perspective, the new one lacks a clean model: except for the limiting case where they are 'external' to firms, scale economies must go hand in hand with *imperfect* competition. The range of possible outcomes of trade policy then becomes limited only by the analyst's imagination.

The hopes for trade liberalization are by no means based only on the exploitation of scale economies. Protection typically leads to the monopolization of the domestic market by a few producers. A common presumption is that the resulting market structures will not be conducive to improvements in productivity and technical efficiency.

Liberalization, it is argued, would reverse the incentives.[3] Here we bump against one of the oldest concerns of the literature on industrial organization: the relationship between market structure and innovation. The ease with which pro-liberalizers make their case is belied by the continuing debates in this literature about the nature of the relationship.[4] The Schumpeterian perspective would disagree strongly with the view that competition is conducive to either innovation or cost-reducing investments.

My objective in this chapter is to clarify some of the conceptual issues in the debate over the relationship between trade policy and technical efficiency. After a brief review of the arguments and the evidence in the next section, I will devote most of my analysis to a set of highly stylized models that shed light on different aspects of the debate. I will argue that much current discussion has served only to muddy the waters by inadequately distinguishing between trade policy proper and other (mostly macro-) policies deployed in support of outward orientation. Once attention is focused on trade policy, it becomes extremely difficult to sustain the case that liberalization, as a general rule, must have a positive impact on technical efficiency. The models considered here demonstrate the fundamentally ambiguous nature of the relationship.

2. THE ARGUMENTS AND THE EVIDENCE

The available evidence suggests that increases in productivity have played an important role in the economic growth of the developing countries. But the contribution of productivity change relative to the growth of factor inputs has been typically not as high as in developed countries. On average, the increase in total factor productivity (TFP) accounts for about half of the growth in value added in developed economies; the comparable figure for developing countries is around a third (see Table 1).

Is there any reason to believe that choices with respect to trade strategy will have systematic effects on the level of technical efficiency and its change over time? The straightforward answer is 'No'. The theory of trade policy is

Table 1. The comparative role of total factor productivity (TFP)

	Growth of value added (%)	TFP growth (%)	TFP share (%)	factor inputs growth (%)	factor inputs share (%)
Average for developing countries	6.3	2.0	31.0	4.3	69.0
Average for developed countries	5.4	2.7	49.0	2.7	51.0

Source: Chenery *et al.* (1986), Table 2.2.

generally silent on the effects of liberalization on the *rate of growth* of output or productivity. Different but equally plausible models can produce diametrically opposite conclusions on this score.[5] The conventional benefits of liberalization are once-and-for-all gains, and although such gains can accumulate over time, they do not necessarily put the economy on a superior path of technological development.[6]

To be sure, there is no shortage of arguments regarding how trade policy *can* affect domestic productivity. There is an abundance of channels through which this can happen: differential sectoral rates of product innovation or productivity enhancements, relative factor prices, overall market stability, and so on. The above comments refer to the lack of any *general* theoretical presumptions; particular stories do abound. Among such stories, three deserve special mention as the ones that come closest to satisfying minimum standards of logical coherence, and it is on these that I will focus in this section.

X-efficiency. The first set of arguments revolve around X-efficiency. While the particular rendition differs, the general theme here is that protection makes it more likely that domestic entrepreneurs will succumb to the 'quiet life' of the monopolist. Why work hard to improve productivity and cut costs if foreign competition presents little threat? In its simplest form, this argument relies on satisficing, rather than optimizing, behaviour on the part of entrepreneurs, and requires further that domestic competition be not severe enough of a threat to keep them on their toes. With optimizing behaviour, it cannot be shown in general that protection weakens the pursuit of higher productivity. In fact, as I will argue in the following section, the normal case would be quite the opposite: for an individual firm, the larger market share provided by trade restrictions increases at the margin the benefits of cost improvements, and is likely to spur, not retard, technological effort. If entrepreneurs satisfice instead, the presumed negative effect can indeed occur. But the working hypothesis of satisficing behaviour would require liberalizers to sacrifice too many other beliefs held even more firmly: for example how many of them would be likely to reject the notion that devaluation spurs exports, as they must if entrepreneurs are indeed prone to satisficing?

A more satisfactory theoretical explanation for this hypothesis is provided by the possibility that liberalization may influence entrepreneurs' choice between labour and leisure. Suppose that reducing X-inefficiency requires constant effort and diligence, which cuts into leisure. Protection increases the rents to entrepreneurs, who take some of their increased income in the form of leisure. As overall effort declines, technical efficiency settles on a lower path. Liberalization would then reverse the process. The definitive analysis of this question can be found in Corden (1974, pp. 224–31),[7] who carefully dissects the argument and shows its fragility. Notice that this line of reasoning is valid only when income effects outweigh substitution effects, that is, when the labour supply curve of entrepreneurs is backward-bending; as indicated in the preceding paragraph, the substitution effect is likely to go in the other direction. In addition, this argument has some disconcerting implications when viewed in general equilibrium terms: liberalization increases the incomes of exporters, who, by the same reasoning, would be prone to relax on their technological efforts. I suspect that this contradicts a widely held belief to the contrary.[8]

Macroeconomic instability. The second major line of reasoning relies on the evidence that inward-oriented regimes are prone to foreign exchange bottlenecks and stop-go macroeconomic cycles. The instability in the macroeconomic environment and the consequent tendency for output periodically to fall below the full-capacity level are certainly inimical to growth in measured productivity. There is evidence that instability in import levels, for whatever reason, can constrain savings, investment, and growth (see Helleiner 1986; Leff and Sato 1987). In addition, the overvaluation of the domestic currency and shortages of imported inputs discourage domestic firms from attempting to reap the benefits of scale via foreign markets. While these arguments have an important kernel of truth, they say practically nothing about the role of *trade* policy *per se*. Conceptually, any level of trade protection is compatible with macroeconomic stability, realistic exchange rates, and the like. The view that protection leads to chronic current-account deficits mixes up macroeconomics with microeconomics. Indonesia, for example, has had a very restrictive trade regime in combination with exchange rate and macro-policies that are quite unobjectionable.[9] Similarly, Korea and Taiwan achieved macroeconomic stability in the 1960s without any sizeable trade liberalization.[10]

Current terminology ('outward orientation', 'export promotion strategy') has the glaring shortcoming that it lumps together macroeconomic policies with trade policies. Worse still, the combination is sometimes referred to as the 'trade regime', with devaluation-cum-stabilization episodes referred to as 'trade liberalization'.[11] While this terminology may be useful for a descriptive categorization of country experiences—exceptions notwithstanding, restrictive trade regimes do tend to go hand in hand with macroeconomic instability—it confuses things for prescriptive purposes. When inferior technological performance is due to mismanagement of macroeconomic policy, countries should be told to change their exchange rate and fiscal policies; the inclusion of trade liberalization in the policy package—sometimes as the lead policy initiative—gives the upper hand to ideology over economics.

Increasing returns to scale. The third line of argument is based on economies of scale. More open trade regimes, it is argued, are conducive to lower overall costs since domestic firms can achieve larger levels of output by participating in world markets. In a broad general equilibrium sense, this is of course true. Small, open economies are likely to specialize in a narrow range of products which they can produce and export at sufficient scale to be competitive. In more practical terms, as long as trade liberalization leads to an expansion (on average) of firms and sectors with increasing returns to scale (IRS), the conventional resource allocation benefits are magnified by enhanced overall productivity. But getting from here to there could be problematic. If IRS activities are predominantly located among import-competing (that is, protected) sectors, as they indeed tend to be,[12] we cannot take for granted that liberalization will work to expand such activities. Whether scale effects add to or subtract from the resource allocation gains depends on a variety of factors (see the discussion in Rodrik 1988) with no clear-cut presumption either way.

A variant of this argument is based on partial equilibrium reasoning about the adverse effects of protection in markets where entry by new firms is relatively unrestricted. Protection increases profitability and attracts new entrants. One possible outcome is the coexistence of too many firms, producing too many varieties of products. With IRS, each producer operates at far below efficient scale, but can do so because protection shields it from foreign competition. The hope for liberalization is that the ensuing shake-up of the industry will lead to a more rational structure of production, with fewer firms operating at larger levels of output and hence at higher levels of productivity. Note that the argument relies crucially on the assumption of frictionless entry to and exit from the industry. This assumption has a poor empirical basis in most developing countries.

In addition, the argument is silent about what stops incumbents from taking advantage of exports, if there are indeed substantial economies of scale to be reaped by expanding output. Unlike what is commonly claimed, it cannot be domestic protection *per se* that turns these firms away from foreign markets. It is telling that all significant cases of export boom in manufactures—Korea and Taiwan in the 1960s, Brazil in the late 1960s and the 1970s, Turkey in the 1980s—took place well before any significant trade liberalization had been attempted.[13] The Chilean trade liberalization, on the other hand, appears to have fostered exports of primary or primary-related products with little scope for IRS.

In Section 5 below, I will discuss some of these arguments further and show why trade restrictions do not affect adversely the export incentives of protected firms. What is true is that with sufficiently restrictive levels of protection, trade policy may end up fostering an industry which is unable to compete abroad at any level of output. This, then, is an argument against 'excessive' protection, rather than protection *per se*. The benefits from liberalization in this instance will derive predominantly from the contraction of industries with no underlying comparative advantage in the conventional sense, and not from an overall expansion of production runs and associated increases in overall productivity.

To summarize, I conclude that the first of these arguments (about X-efficiency) is rather contrived, the second (about macro-stability) is largely irrelevant to trade policy, and the third (about IRS) is potentially important but incomplete. I will return to the more important of these arguments below. What about the empirical evidence?

Examining whether any broad cross-sectional correlations emerge between trade regimes and TFP growth has proved to be a tempting exercise. A survey by Howard Pack (1990) suggests that the evidence from such studies is quite inconclusive: 'to date there is no clear cut confirmation of the hypothesis that countries with an external orientation benefit from greater growth in technical efficiency in the component sectors of manufacturing' (p. 38). Bhagwati, a proponent of outward orientation, has also concluded recently that there is little empirical or theoretical support for favouring export promotion over import substitution on grounds of scale economies, technical efficiency, or innovation (1988, pp. 39–40). In any case, the evidence surveyed by Pack and Bhagwati does not directly bear on the issues at hand, since none of the studies discriminates between trade policy and macro-policy choices.[14] As argued above, causality cannot be attributed to trade policy proper if what one understands from 'trade regimes' is the entire complex of trade and payments policies. To conclude, then, there is no convincing empirical evidence that less protectionist trade policies do better in terms of technical efficiency.

I now move on to a series of stylized models that investigate the relationship between trade policy and productivity. In light of the discussion above, my objective will be to make points in the context of simple models rather than to demonstrate the validity of a single general proposition.

3. PROTECTION AND TECHNOLOGICAL CATCH-UP

I start with a case which shows the opposite of the orthodox argument. I consider a firm which invests in technological development[15] to cut its costs, and ask: how will the rate of increase of productivity depend on the level of trade protection afforded to the firm? Once the backward-bending entrepreneurial effort curve is ruled out, the answer is surprisingly general. The larger is the firm's market share, the greater is its investment in productivity-enhancing technology. As long as protection increases the firm's market share, then, trade restrictions improve the level of technical efficiency.

Let the firm have a monopoly at home. The case of domestic oligopoly will be considered in the next section. Its maximized flow profits can be written as

$$\pi(c, m) = \max_q \{qp(q, m) - cq\}, \quad (1)$$

where c denotes the firm's (constant) marginal cost, q its output, $p(\cdot)$ the inverse demand function it faces at home, and m the quantity of imports allowed in. Import liberalization in this context will refer to increases in m. For the moment, I ignore the possibility that the firm may want to export. Let the foreign level of marginal costs be c^*, with $c > c^*$ initially. The firm can reduce its costs (all the way down to c^*) by investing resources in technology and overall tinkering. I model this by letting the firm choose the rate at which domestic costs decline, and denote this rate β. Then at any point in time, the cost level is given by:

$$c(t) = \begin{bmatrix} c_0 - \beta t, & t < T, \\ c^*, & t \geq T. \end{bmatrix} \quad (2)$$

Here T denotes the time that elapses before the domestic firm fully catches up with foreign technology, and c_0 represents the initial level of domestic costs. This implies $\beta = (1/T)(c_0 - c^*)$, or:

$$c(t) = c_0 - (t/T)(c_0 - c^*), \quad \text{for} \quad t \leq T. \quad (3)$$

The present discounted value of expenditures made on technological effort increases with β, and can be written simply as $\phi(\beta)$, with $\phi' > 0$ and $\phi'' > 0$.

What is of interest is the length of time it takes for the firm to catch up with foreign technology. Since both $c(t)$ and β can be written as a function of T, the firm's objective function can also be stated as a function of T alone:

$$V(T) = \int_0^T \exp(-\rho t) \pi(c(t), m) \, dt + \int_T^\infty \exp(-\rho t) \pi(c^*, m) \, dt - \phi(\beta), \quad (4)$$

where ρ is the firm's discount factor. After simplifying, the first-order condition becomes:

$$V'(T) = \int_0^T \exp(-\rho t)\, t\pi_c(c(t), m)\, dt + \phi'(\beta) = 0. \tag{5}$$

This sets the marginal cost of technological effort equal to the discounted sum of its benefits over the catch-up period. Notice that equation (1) implies $\pi_c = -q$, so that the benefits of effort are directly proportional to the scale of domestic output. As long as $\phi'(\cdot)$ is finite and strictly positive, and assuming the second-order condition is satisfied, the catch-up is completed within the open interval $(0, \infty)$.

To gauge the effects of trade policy, we can perform comparative statics with respect to m. Differentiating (5) yields:

$$dT/dm = -[V''(\cdot)]^{-1}\left\{\int_0^T \exp(-\rho t)\, t\pi_{cm}(\cdot)\, dt\right\}. \tag{6}$$

Since the second-order condition requires $V''(\cdot)$ to be negative, the sign of this expression depends solely on π_{cm}. But from equation (1), $\pi_{cm} = -\partial q/\partial m$ so that π_{cm} is *positive* as long as import liberalization (an increase in imports) reduces the output of the domestic firm. Since this is the regular case, we can conclude that $dT/dm > 0$; a more liberal trade regime slows down the rate of increase of domestic productivity and delays technological catch-up. The economic mechanism at work here is simple. The larger the scale of output, the greater the benefits to the firm from a given reduction in costs. Since import liberalization shrinks the domestic firm's sales, it reduces the incentive to invest in technological effort.

The above ignored two possibilities: (*a*) the domestic firm may export, and (*b*) it may eventually overtake foreign competitors in productivity. We can incorporate both possibilities in the above framework by changing the formulation of technical progress at home. Suppose that the domestic firm can set its own target for the eventual level of productivity it reaches, $\bar{c}$. This target could lie above or below the foreign level of productivity, c^*. Its costs at any point in time are now written as follows:

$$c(t) = \bar{c} + (c_0 - \bar{c})\exp(-\beta t). \tag{7}$$

The firm's flow profit function is as in equation (1) when it decides not to export. When it does export, its flow profits are also a function of the foreign level of costs, c^*, so can be written generally as $\tilde{\pi}(c, c^*, m)$. As before, $\tilde{\pi}_c = -\tilde{q}$, the level of total output (domestic sales and exports combined). The point in time at which the firm becomes an exporter is determined endogenously. Let $\tilde{c}$ denote the level of productivity at which the firm just breaks even in world markets; $\tilde{c}$ is defined implicitly by the relation $\tilde{\pi}(\tilde{c}, c^*, m) - \pi(\tilde{c}, m) = 0$. When costs are lower than $\tilde{c}$, the firm's profits from foreign sales add on to existing profits in the domestic market. I will only look at the case where it pays to export eventually, that is, where the firm's target level of costs ($\bar{c}$) is lower than $\tilde{c}$. As long as $\bar{c} < \tilde{c}$, there exists a finite length of time, T, after which the firm services both the domestic and the foreign markets. T is determined as follows: since $\tilde{c} = \bar{c} + (c_0 - \bar{c}) \exp(-\beta T)$ from equation (7),

$$T = (1/\beta)[\ln(c_0 - \bar{c}) - \ln(\tilde{c} - \bar{c})]. \tag{8}$$

The firm's objective function can now be stated as a function of the target level of productivity alone:

$$V(\bar{c}) = \int_0^T \exp(-\rho t) \pi(c(t), m) \, dt$$

$$+ \int_0^T \exp(-\rho t) \tilde{\pi}(c(t), c^*, m) \, dt - \phi(\bar{c}), \tag{9}$$

with $c(t)$ and T defined as in equations (7) and (8). The first-order condition can be simplified to:

$$\int_0^\infty \exp(-\rho t) \pi_c (1 - \exp(-\beta t)) \, dt$$

$$+ \int_0^\infty \exp(-\rho t)[\tilde{\pi}_c - \pi_c](1 - \exp(-\beta t)) \, dt - \phi' = 0. \tag{10}$$

The marginal benefits of innovation are now larger as they are spread over a larger scale of output: $-[\tilde{\pi}_c - \pi_c]$ represents the net increase in output that is made possible through exports. Hence the carrot of future exports adds to the incentive to enhance productivity.

Once again, we can investigate the effects of import liberalization on the rate of technical progress. Differentiation of equation (10) yields:

$$d\bar{c}/dm = -(V'')^{-1} \left\{ \int_0^T \exp(-\rho t) \pi_{cm} (1 - \exp(-\beta t) \, dt \right.$$

$$\left. + \int_T^\infty \exp(-\rho t) \tilde{\pi}_{cm} (1 - \exp(-\beta t)) \, dt \right\}, \tag{11}$$

where I have made use of the fact that $[\tilde{\pi}_c(\tilde{c}) - \pi_c(\tilde{c})] = 0$. V'' is negative from the second-order condition, so the sign of this expression depends on the signs of π_{cm} and $\tilde{\pi}_{cm}$. As long as increased foreign competition reduces the total output of the domestic firm, $d\bar{c}/dm > 0$, and liberalization is inimical to technical progress. The explanation is as before: while the export potential is now an added inducement for cutting costs, a policy that reduces the scale of domestic output diminishes the incentives to catch up with foreign technology.

Finally, let us consider briefly the question of temporary versus permanent protection. Suppose the government commits itself to a path of trade policy such that trade is liberalized after a certain point in time, τ. How does this affect the behaviour of the firm?

Ignoring with no loss of generality the role of exports, let the profit functions of the firm be written as $\pi(c,m)$ and $\pi(c,m')$, corresponding to pre- and post-liberalization periods. Liberalization implies $m' > m$. The firm maximizes its objective function:

$$V(\bar{c}) = \int_0^\tau \exp(-\rho t)\pi(c(t), m)\,dt$$
$$+ \int_\tau^\infty \exp(-\rho t)\pi(c(t), m')\,dt - \phi(\bar{c}). \quad (12)$$

The first-order condition is:

$$\int_0^\tau \exp(-\rho t)\pi_c(1 - \exp(-\beta t))\,dt$$
$$+ \int_\tau^\infty \exp(-\rho t)\pi_c(1 - \exp(-\beta t))\,dt - \phi' = 0. \quad (13)$$

We investigate what happens when the liberalization is brought forward in time (that is, τ is reduced). The comparative statics yield:

$$d\bar{c}/d\tau = -(V'')^{-1}[\exp(-\rho\tau)(1 - \exp(-\beta\tau))]\{\pi_c(c(\tau), m)$$
$$- \pi_c(c(\tau), m')\}. \quad (14)$$

Since the level of domestic output is smaller when imports are liberalized ($\pi_c(c(\tau), m) - \pi_c(c(\tau), m') < 0$), we have $d\bar{c}/d\tau < 0$. Shortening the period over which temporary protection is granted reduces the firm's technological effort. This contradicts once again the conventional wisdom regarding the productivity-boosting effects of temporary, rather than permanent, protection.[16]

In sum, simple partial equilibrium models of technological catch-up point in the direction diametrically opposed to arguments made by liberalizers. Note that all that is needed for our result to withstand general scrutiny is that the costs of technological effort be independent of (or decreasing with) overall scale of output. This produces a complementarity between production and technological investment, as the benefits of the latter are greater the larger is the former. While models of the sort analysed here need not be taken too seriously as an actual description of the process of innovation in developing countries, they cast doubt on the productivity-enhancing effects of trade liberalization.

An important *caveat* to this line of reasoning has to do with the partial equilibrium nature of the analysis. Protection enhances the profitability of firms in import-competing sectors, but acts as a tax on firms in exporting sectors. Unless there are under-utilized resources, protection cannot expand output in import-competing and exporting sectors simultaneously. Consequently, productivity gains in the former have to be weighed against forgone productivity improvements in the latter. An important implication, therefore, is that the analysis above cannot be used as a justification for indiscriminate, across-the-board protection. A related *caveat* is that in the absence of some knowledge regarding the externalities involved in technological effort, we cannot judge a faster technological catch-up induced by protection to be necessarily welfare-improving.[17] At best, then, there is a case for selective protection of industries where (*a*) the catch-up potential is largest, and (*b*) there exist positive spill-overs to the rest of the economy.[18]

4. THE ROLE OF OLIGOPOLY

The framework utilized above abstracted from interactions among competing firms in the domestic market. The new trade theory has stressed such interactions as an important determinant of the effects of policy. Accordingly, I now concentrate on the implications of an oligopolistic market structure at home. The question to be analysed is the same as before: how does protection influence the level of technical efficiency of firms?

The model that follows illustrates a rather simple and intuitive story. In an oligopolistic industry, incumbents could increase profits, in the absence of perfect collusion, if they could all somehow commit themselves to lower sales. In practice, centrifugal forces tend to prove too strong, and firms waste some of their profits by 'excessive' competition. Now, one way that firms could credibly commit themselves to less aggressive behaviour is by choosing outdated or costly technology. By maintaining costs artificially high, they could facilitate collusion.

How does protection affect all this? As the level of protection increases, the profits forgone by excessive competition increase as well, so that the potential pay-offs to a strategy of high costs rise. Therefore, as long as firms' strategic behaviour is conducive to an increase in costs, protection serves to inflate costs even further. Notice that this argument is entirely different from any stated so far; the adverse effect on costs is purely the consequence of the nature of oligopolistic interactions among incumbent firms. For the liberalizers, this is of course good news. The bad news is that the argument is extremely brittle. As is common in models of oligopoly, it is easy to reverse the result by assuming a different mode of behaviour on the part of firms.

To formalize the argument, let us consider a two-stage game being played by a pair of duopolists. In the first period, each firm undertakes a certain amount of investment in technological effort, denoted by k_i and k_j respectively, taking as given the decisions of its rival. In the second, the firms compete in the domestic market. At the beginning of the second period, k_i and k_j are predetermined, and the profit function of firm i looks as follows:

$$\pi^i(q_i, q_j, k_i) = p^i(q_i, q_j)q_i - c^i(q_i, k_i), \tag{15}$$

where $p^i(\cdot)$ is the inverse demand function faced by firm i, and $c_k^i < 0$. Firm j's profit function is symmetric. For the moment I have suppressed imports; trade policy will be discussed below in terms of changes in the form of the inverse demand function faced by the firms. The first-order condition is:

$$\pi_i^i + v^i \pi_j^i = 0, \tag{16}$$

where a subscript denotes a partial derivative with respect to the relevant argument, and v^i is firm i's conjecture regarding how firm j will respond to changes in the former's output (see Dixit 1986). Equation (16) and its analogue for firm j define a pair of best-response functions $q_i(q_j, k_i)$ and $q_j(q_i, k_j)$, and an equilibrium which is a function only of the predetermined investment levels k_i and k_j. Therefore, the second-period equilibrium can be expressed as $q_i = q_i^*(k_i, k_j)$ and $q_j = q_j^*(k_j, k_i)$.

In the first period, firms are fully cognizant of the effects of their investment decisions on the subsequent game, so choose k_i and k_j accordingly. Letting $\phi(\cdot)$ stand for the cost of investment ($\phi' > 0$, $\phi'' > 0$), the problem for firm i is:

$$\max_{k_i} \tilde{\pi}^i(k_i, k_j) = \pi^i(q_i^*(k_i, k_j), q_j^*(k_j, k_i), k_i) - \phi(k_i). \tag{17}$$

If the firm takes its rival's decision as given, the first-order condition for k_i is:

$$\pi_i^i(dq_i^*/dk_i) + \pi_j^i(dq_j^*/dk_i) + \pi_k^i - \phi' = 0. \tag{18}$$

Notice that firm j's output is sensitive to changes in k_i only in so far as the latter affects firm i's output. So we can write $dq_j^*/dk_i = (dq_j/dq_i)dq_i^*/dk_i$. Let us define r^j as the slope of firm j's best-response function, that is, $r^j = (dq_j/dq_i)$. Then $dq_j^*/dk_i = r^j(dq_i^*/dk_i)$. Now making use of equation (16), we can rewrite equation (18) as follows:

$$(r^j - v^i)\pi_j^i(dq_i^*/dk_i) + (\pi_k^i - \phi') = 0. \tag{19}$$

The second term in parentheses here captures the conventional trade-off between the costs and benefits of technological effort. In the absence of oligopolistic interactions, this would be the only determinant of the level of investment in technological development. The first term, on the other hand, captures the strategic role of the choice of technology, and it is on this that I will now concentrate.

Under standard assumptions, a decrease in marginal costs will make a firm produce more ($dq_i^*/dk_i > 0$) and an increase in the rival's output will hurt profits ($\pi_j^i < 0$), so that the sign of the strategic effect depends solely on the sign of $(r^j - v^i)$.[19] This term is the difference between the actual slope of j's best-response function and the conjecture entertained by i, and is a familiar one in models of oligopoly. When firms behave too 'aggressively' in the second period, v^i will be negative and large, so that $(r^j - v^i) > 0$. This is the presumption when firms compete in Bertrand fashion (setting prices and taking the price of the rival as given), for example. In this instance, the strategic effect makes a *negative* contribution to the first-order condition in equation (19); the optimal level of k_i will now be *lower* than would have been the case in the absence of a strategic motive. Intuitively, it is in the interest of the firm to increase its costs as this blunts some of its aggressiveness in the second period. And the same is true for its rival. The profits to the firms from a consequently greater degree of collusion can outweigh the losses in productivity. But from a social viewpoint, the costs of oligopoly are now exacerbated by technical inefficiency.

So far, this is standard material.[20] The only new wrinkle comes with the role of trade policy. How does trade liberalization affect the technological choice in this framework? First, and most obviously, it affects the base level of output on which cost savings are distributed. This is the effect discussed in the previous section. As shown earlier, trade liberalization will reduce the incentive to increase productivity on this account as long as domestic output is reduced. This is captured in the present framework by a reduction in π_k^i.[21]

Secondly, and this is the key point, liberalization reduces the excess profits available in the home market, and therefore may be expected to de-emphasize the strategic motive for under-investment in technology. The algebra here gets quite complicated, but the point is simple enough. As can be seen from equation (19), the incentive to inflate costs is proportional to π_j^i, which equals $q_i(\partial p i/\partial q_j)$ (see equation (15)). In symmetric equilibrium ($q_i = q_j$), $q_i(\partial p^i/\partial q_j)$ can also be written as p^i/ε, where ε is the price elasticity of demand facing each firm. As the domestic market is opened, we expect p^i to decrease and ε to increase (in absolute value). On both accounts, the strategic disincentive for technological effort becomes smaller. In the limit of free trade, ε goes to negative infinity, so that the strategic disincentive disappears altogether.

This line of reasoning provides one possible rationale why the oligopolistic market structures created by protection may create a bias against technological effort. But, as stated at the outset, this argument is not particularly robust. It relies on the possibility that firms compete 'too aggressively', which in the present framework is captured by $(r^j - v^i) > 0$. If instead, firms have 'consistent' conjectures $(r^j - v^i = 0)$, the strategic motive disappears and the considerations discussed above no longer come into play. Moreover, when firms behave in Cournot (quantity-setting) fashion, $v^i = 0$, and a negatively sloped reaction function $(r^j < 0)$ implies that the strategic incentive will work to *enhance* productivity.[22] With Cournot behaviour in the second period, there will be *over*-investment in technology as each firm would like to pre-commit itself to a larger scale of output. Trade liberalization will now be doubly inimical to technological performance.

5. THE ROLE OF ECONOMIES OF SCALE

One of the most appealing arguments for trade liberalization is the one that has been mentioned at the beginning of the chapter: liberalization may foster the rationalization of industry structure by forcing inefficient firms out. The maintained hypothesis here is that protection tends to crowd in too many firms producing at too low levels of output.

The industry-rationalization argument relies crucially on two features of the industry concerned: (*a*) economies of scale, and (*b*) free entry and exit. In the presence of these two, there is indeed a very good case for trade liberalization on the grounds of productivity. The argument goes as follows. With free entry, the domestic price has to equal the average cost of the representative firm since incumbents cannot make excess profits. With IRS, average costs are a declining function of firm-level output. Therefore, any policy which tends to increase the domestic price (for example protection) will also increase the average cost level in the industry. The mechanism that enables this is the entry of additional firms, which squeezes the output of the incumbents and forces them up their average cost curves. Conversely, liberalization reduces the domestic price and leads some of the incumbents to leave the industry. The remaining firms have to produce at sufficiently greater scale for the reduced level of average costs to match the lower domestic price.

Notice that this industry-rationalization argument is based on partial equilibrium reasoning. Once the likely changes in relative factor prices are taken into account, the force of the argument can be blunted somewhat. The reason is that these factor price changes are likely to dampen (or reverse) the increase in firm-level output as prices fall. Consider the following likely scenario for developing countries. Suppose that the fixed costs of production (the basis for IRS) consist primarily of capital costs. Then, if trade liberalization reduces capital costs relative to wages sufficiently—as the Stolper–Samuelson theorem would predict for developing countries— average costs at unchanged output levels could fall so much that restoring the equality between price and average cost may require a *reduction* in the scale of production of the typical firm. The consequence, paradoxically, may be derationalization (see Brown and Stern 1988), with free entry contributing to higher rather than lower costs.

Barring these general equilibrium complications, the cost savings from industry rationalization can greatly magnify the traditional gains from liberalization (Harris 1984). In an earlier paper, I carried out some simple partial equilibrium simulations for three Turkish industries to assess the likely welfare effect of partial quota liberalization under various scenarios of market conduct (Rodrik 1988). The existence of IRS was assumed in each case, and modelled by incorporating some fixed costs of production. Table 2 summarizes the relevant results for the case of Cournot conjectures. The numbers highlight the crucial role of free exit, when such exists. In all cases, the industry rationalization promoted by exit adds a considerable boost to the overall welfare effect, turning a negative outcome into a positive one in one instance.

In the presence of free entry and exit, a rather similar outcome could obtain even when IRS is not particularly important, as long as firms differ in their levels of productivity. There is evidence that such differences may be quite important in some developing countries and in some industries (Page 1984). Large differences in productivity are of course sustainable only with trade protection. Under free entry, the domestic price equals the average cost of the marginal firm. With liberalization, the least efficient firms have to exit until the new marginal firm is defined by the level of productivity which equates its average cost with the (lower) domestic price.

Table 2. Effects of partial trade liberalization with scale economies, Turkey, c.1980

	Autos	Tyres	Electrical appliances
Welfare effects[a] with:			
fixed number of firms	2.6	0.6	−0.5
free exit	5.2	4.1	1.2

[a] Increase in welfare, measured as a share of base consumption, arising from a 10% quota liberalization.

Source: Rodrik (1988), Tables 5, 6, and 7.

Just as in the IRS case, the average level of productivity rises with liberalization.

Enthusiasm for such arguments, however, has to be tempered by realism about market circumstances in developing countries. In practice, frictionless entry and exit are likely to be the exception rather than the rule. Exit is particularly problematic, as it implies a well-developed secondary market in capital equipment: if firms cannot dismantle and sell their operations—in other words, if capital is sunk—the productivity benefits of liberalization can be easily cancelled. Firms will not exit until prices fall below average *variable* cost, and may not even do so then if they are cross-subsidized by affiliates in other sectors. On the other side of the ledger, depreciation of machinery and equipment may provide a natural form of exit over time. Market obstacles aside, governments typically impose complex licensing and investment regulations which restrict entry into protected sectors. The 'too many incumbents' story is a caricature to begin with. There is as yet no convincing empirical evidence for developing countries that shows liberalization to be conducive to industry rationalization.[23]

With free entry downplayed, we are left with a more suspect argument: it is frequently asserted that it is the high profitability of the domestic market itself which discourages firms from reaping the benefits of scale via exports. In this view, protection serves to discourage exports from the protected sector, and hence works against reaping scale economies. But this argument makes sense only when firms behave myopically.

To see why, consider a single firm operating in a protected home market and whose technology exhibits IRS. Let IRS be modelled by a cost function of the form $C(q) = F + cq$, where F is a fixed cost and c is the (constant) marginal cost. Suppose that the firm has an overall capacity constraint, Q. Denoting exports (if any) and domestic sales as q_x and q_d, respectively, the firm's problem is to maximize its profits subject to the capacity constraint and non-negativity requirements on sales. The associated Lagrangian is:

$$\mathscr{L} = p(q_d, m)q_d + p^* q_x - F - c(q_d + q_x) + \lambda(Q - q_d - q_x) + \mu_d q_d + \mu_x q_x, \tag{20}$$

where p^* is the (exogenous) world price, λ is the Lagrange multiplier for the capacity constraint, and μ_d and μ_x are the respective multipliers for the non-negativity constraints. The first-order condition for exports is:

$$p^* - c - \lambda + \mu_x = 0. \tag{21}$$

We can now distinguish two cases. In the first, $p^* < c$ so exports would not even cover marginal costs. Then $\mu_x > 0$ and $q_x = 0$. But when $p^* \geq c$, exports are worth while ($\mu_x = 0$), so that the firm increases its export sales all the way until the capacity constraint is hit and $\lambda > 0$.[24]

Notice that the firm's export incentives are not adversely affected by circumstances in the domestic market, and in particular by the extent of trade protection. If anything, trade protection is *conducive* to exports in the following sense: protection allows the firm to make some excess profits at home which can be used to cover its fixed costs; exports then become attractive even if the world price is *below* the firm's average cost (case two above). Protection allows some exports in a sector where, in the absence of protection, there may not have been any domestic production to begin with.

When we relax the assumption of constant marginal costs, the case for protection becomes even stronger. Suppose that IRS takes the form of decreasing marginal costs. Now protection allows the home firm to increase its domestic sales, and therefore to reduce its marginal cost. With a lower marginal cost, the firm can become more competitive in world markets, and therefore increase its exports as well. This is Krugman's (1984) model of 'import protection as export promotion'. The sheltered home market provides the domestic firm with the cost savings needed to compete with larger rivals in world markets. Notice that this is a vision diametrically opposed to the one where free entry crowds in too many firms operating at high cost. Which story one believes in depends on one's prior views regarding the ease of entry and exit and the effectiveness of entry restrictions imposed by governments.

6. CONCLUDING REMARKS

My objective in this chapter was to identify some of the arguments commonly made regarding the trade–productivity nexus, and to hold them to the analytical light. I have argued that many of these arguments lack coherence. While we cannot expect prolonged high levels of trade protection to be socially costless on many grounds, we are far from having any systematic theories which link trade policy to technical efficiency *per se*. In particular, we do not have any good reason to expect that trade liberalization will generally be helpful to overall technological performance.

The usual call for more empirical evidence is perhaps more appropriate in this instance than in any other. As more countries experiment with trade reform, the universe of empirical studies should broaden. The challenge, however, is to escape the identification problem which has plagued all previous studies. In practice, the arguments for following sensible macro-economic policies—realistic exchange rates and moderate fiscal deficits, in particular—are too often confused for arguments on behalf of trade liberalization. Partly as a result, countries that reform their trade policies often do so in the context of macro-stabilization programmes. When stabilization alleviates the foreign exchange bottleneck and capacity utilization increases, industry typically experiences an increase in its measured productivity level. It becomes tempting to credit the improved productivity performance to trade policy.

Until more evidence becomes available, then, a healthy scepticism is in order. In the meantime, if truth-in-advertising were to apply to policy advice, each prescription for trade liberalization would be accompanied with a disclaimer: 'Warning! Trade liberalization cannot be shown to enhance technical efficiency; nor has it been empirically demonstrated to do so.'

REFERENCES

BALASSA, BELA (1988), 'Interest of Developing Countries in the Uruguay Round', *World Economy*, 11 (Mar.), pp. 39–54.

BHAGWATI, JAGDISH (1978), *Foreign Trade Regimes and Economic Development: Anatomy and Consequences of Exchange Control Regimes* (Ballinger, Cambridge, Mass.).

—— (1988), 'Export-Promoting Trade Strategy: Issues and Evidence', *World Bank Research Observer*, 3 (Jan.), pp. 27–57.

BROWN, DRUSILLA, and STERN, ROBERT (1988), 'Computation Analysis of the US–Canada Free Trade Agreement: The Role of Product Differentiation and Market Structure', paper presented to the Universities Research Conference on Trade Policies for International Competitiveness, 30 Apr., Cambridge, Mass.

BULOW, JEREMY I. D., GEANAKOPLOS, JOHN D., and KLEMPERER, PAUL D. (1985), 'Multimarket Oligopoly: Strategic Substitutes and Complements', *Journal of Political Economy*, 93, pp. 488–511.

CHENERY, HOLLIS, ROBINSON, SHERMAN, and SYRQUIN, MOSHE (1986), *Industrialization and Growth: A Comparative Study* (OUP, New York).

CONDON, TIMOTHY, and DE MELO, JAIME (1986), 'Industrial Organization Implications of QR Trade Regimes: Evidence and Welfare Costs' (World Bank, Washington, DC), mimeo.

CORDEN, W. MAX (1974), *Trade Policy and Economic Welfare* (OUP, Oxford).

DIXIT, AVINASH (1986) 'Comparative Statics for Oligopoly', *International Economic Review*, 27, pp. 107–22.

DORNBUSCH, RUDIGER, and PARK, YUNG CHUL (1987), 'Korean Growth Policies', *Brookings Papers on Economic Activity*, 2, pp. 389–454.

EATON, JOHN, and GROSSMAN, GENE (1986), 'Optimal Trade and Industrial Policy Under Oligopoly', *Quarterly Journal of Economics*, 101, pp. 383–406.

EDWARDS, SEBASTIAN, and EDWARDS, ALEJANDRA COX (1987), *Monetarism and Liberalization: The Chilean Experiment* (Ballinger, Cambridge, Mass.).

HARRIS, RICHARD (1984), 'Applied General Equilibrium Analysis of Small Open Economies with Scale Economies and Imperfect Competition', *American Economic Review*, 74, pp. 1016–33.

HELLEINER, G. K. (1986), 'Outward Orientation, Import Instability and African Economic Growth: An Empirical Investigation', in Sanjaya Lall and Frances

Stewart (eds.), *Theory and Reality in Development: Essays in Honour of Paul Streeten* (St Martin's Press, New York).

HELPMAN, ELHANAN, and KRUGMAN, PAUL (1985), *Market Structure and Foreign Trade: Increasing Returns, Imperfect Competition, and the International Economy* (MIT Press, Cambridge, Mass.).

KAMIEN, MORTON I., and SCHWARTZ, NANCY L. (1982), *Market Structure and Innovation* (CUP, Cambridge).

KRUEGER, ANNE O., and TUNCER, BARAN (1982), 'An Empirical Test of the Infant Industry Argument', *American Economic Review*, 72, pp. 1142–52.

KRUGMAN, PAUL (1984), 'Import Protection as Export Promotion', in H. Kierzkowski (ed.), *Monopolistic Competition and International Trade* (OUP, Oxford).

LEFF, NATHANIEL H., and SATO, KAZUO (1987), 'The Prospects for Higher Domestic Savings Rates in Latin America', *Journal of Policy Modeling*, 9/4.

MELO, JAIME DE, and URATA, SHUJIRO (1986), 'The Influence of Increased Foreign Competition on Industrial Concentration and Profitability', *International Journal of Industrial Organization*, 4, pp. 287–304.

NISHIMIZU, MIEKO, and ROBINSON, SHERMAN (1984), 'Trade Policies and Productivity Change in Semi-Industrialized Countries', *Journal of Development Economics*, 16, pp. 177–206.

PACK, HOWARD (1990), 'Industrialization and Trade', in Hollis Chenery and T. N. Srinivasan (eds.), *Handbook of Development Economics*, i, pp. 333–80.

PAGE, JOHN M. (1984), 'Firm Size and Technical Efficiency: Application of Production Frontiers to Indian Survey Data', *Journal of Development Economics*, 16, pp. 129–52.

PAPAGEORGIU, DEMETRIS, MICHAELY, MICHAEL, and CHOKSI, ARMEANE (1986), 'The Phasing of a Trade Liberalization Policy: Preliminary Evidence' (World Bank, Washington, DC), mimeo.

RODRIK, DANI (1988), 'Imperfect Competition, Scale Economies, and Trade Policy in Developing Countries', in Robert E. Baldwin (ed.), *Trade Policy Issues and Empirical Analysis* (University of Chicago Press, Chicago.).

SACHS, JEFFREY D. (1987), 'Trade and Exchange Rate Policies in Growth-Oriented Adjustment Programs', in Vittorio Corbo, Morris Goldstein, and Mohsin Khan (eds.), *Growth-Oriented Adjustment Programs* (IMF and World Bank, Washington, DC), pp. 291–325.

SELTEN, REINHARD (1986), 'Elementary Theory of Slack-Ridden Imperfect Competition', in J. E. Stiglitz and G. F. Mathewson (eds.), *New Developments in the Analysis of Market Structure* (MIT Press, Cambridge, Mass.).

SMITH, ADAM (1937) [1776], *An Inquiry into the Nature and Causes of the Wealth of Nations* (Modern Library, New York).

TAYLOR, LANCE (1988), 'Economic Openness—Problems to the Century's End', WIDER Working Paper 41 (Apr.).

WESTPHAL, L. E. (1982), 'Fostering Technological Mastery by Means of Selective Industry Promotion', in M. Syrquin and S. Teitel (eds.), *Trade, Stability, Technology and Equity in Latin America* (Academic Press, New York).

WOO, WING THYE, and NASUTION, ANWAR (1988), 'Indonesian Economic Policies and Their Relation to External Debt Management', in Jeffrey Sachs (ed.), *Developing Country Debt* (University of Chicago Press, Chicago).

World Bank (1987), *World Development Report, 1987* (OUP, Washington, DC).

NOTES

1. 'By means of [foreign trade], the narrowness of the home market does not hinder the division of labour in any particular branch of art or manufacture from being carried to the highest perfection. By opening a more extensive market for whatever part of the produce of their labour may exceed the home consumption, it encourages them to improve its productive powers' (Smith (1937 [1776]), bk IV, ch. 1, p. 415).
2. See Helpman and Krugman (1985) for an integrated treatment of trade theory with increasing returns to scale.
3. A representative statement is from Balassa (1988, p. 45): 'It has often been observed that [monopolies and oligopolies] prefer a "quiet life" to innovative activity, which entails risk and uncertainty. In turn, the carrot and stick of competition gives inducement for technological change. For one thing, in creating competition for domestic products in home markets, imports provide incentives for firms to improve their operations. For another thing, in response to competition in foreign markets, exporting firms try to keep up with modern technology in order to maintain or improve their market position.'
4. For an excellent analytical survey, see Kamien and Schwartz (1982).
5. See e.g. Taylor (1988).
6. The language in the World Bank's *World Development Report, 1987* (focusing on trade and industrialization) reflects an all too obvious tension between the desire to make a positive case for liberalization on productivity grounds and the need to acknowledge that the theoretical and empirical support for such a case is weak (pp. 90–2).
7. I am grateful to Howard Pack for pointing me in Corden's direction.
8. Corden points out, rightly, that the welfare consequences of liberalization are not necessarily magnified by these X-efficiency effects even when entrepreneurial labour supply is backward-bending. The reason is that the additional leisure taken by entrepreneurs is part of social welfare as well. Rescuing the argument then requires some additional hypotheses regarding externalities and the like. See also Selten (1986) for a model of imperfect competition in which 'slack' is assumed to increase with profits.
9. For a fascinating recent account see Woo and Nasution (1988).
10. See Sachs (1987) which stresses the distinction and its importance for the design of macro-stabilization policies.
11. See e.g. Papageorgiou, *et al.* (1986) which summarizes the findings of a multi-country study.
12. See the evidence presented in Rodrik (1988, Table 4).
13. The experience of these countries strongly suggests that a realistic exchange-rate policy and a generous programme of export subsidies, rather than trade liberalization *per se*, are the key ingredients for successful export performance.
14. The leading studies are Bhagwati (1978, chp. 5), Krueger and Tuncer (1982), Nishimuzu and Robinson (1984), and Chenery *et al.* (1986, chp. 6).

15. This discussion abstracts from the possibility that factor market distortions may influence choice of technique. Clearly, when factor prices are distorted certain types of technological 'advance' could be privately beneficial yet socially harmful. I am focusing on movements from one isoquant to another rather than along a given isoquant.
16. This is a bit sensitive to the way temporary protection is viewed, however. If entrepreneurs anticipate protection to be removed once a certain level of productivity is reached they may find it in their interest to delay that outcome, provided of course that at that level of productivity protection does not become superfluous.
17. In fact, when no such externalities exist, trade protection can be shown to lead to welfare losses regardless of its effect on technological performance.
18. See Westphal (1982) for an interpretation of Korean technological development in terms of selective promotion of infant industries. On Korea, see also Dornbusch and Park (1987), pp. 402–6.
19. See Dixit (1986) for more on this.
20. See in particular Bulow *et al.* (1985) and Dixit (1986).
21. Note that $\pi_k^i = -c_k^i$. A reduction in domestic output therefore reduces π_k^i as long as c_{kq}^i is negative, i.e. as long as increased investment in technology lowers the marginal cost of production.
22. See Eaton and Grossman (1986) for a systematic discussion on the importance of conjectures.
23. Chile experienced a radical trade liberalization in the second half of the 1970s, so would be a natural testing-ground for this hypothesis. In their book on Chile, Edwards and Edwards (1987, pp. 118–21) discuss some suggestive but indirect evidence on productivity improvements. In a paper bearing more directly on this issue, de Melo and Urata (1986) report substantial exit and increase in concentration ratios in Chilean industry between the bench-mark years of 1967 and 1979. However, it appears that their tabulation for 1979 excludes nearly half of the existing firms on the ground that these did not cover average costs (Condon and de Melo 1986, Table 1). This of course presupposes the conclusion. The problem is the uncertainty as to the eventual exit and/or consolidation of these loss-making enterprises.
24. This assumes that the firm finds it profitable to produce in the home market.

7

Marketing Manufactured Exports from Developing Countries: Learning Sequences and Public Support*

Donald B. Keesing and Sanjaya Lall

1. EXPORT MARKETING AND TRADE THEORIES

Much of trade theory is concerned with what determines comparative advantage in the production of traded commodities. In almost all of this theory, once an enterprise or industry has achieved 'competitiveness' in the sense of being able to produce and deliver goods at (or below) ruling prices in world markets, the marketing of those goods is not regarded as a problem.

In the real world, by contrast, profits associated with manufacturing depend on information flows, getting orders from buyers and customers, and the design, packaging, distribution, 'selling', and servicing of the products. Thus marketing and the acquisition and transmission of relevant information are essential and rewarding activities even in exporting products manufactured to the orders of buyers who undertake subsequent distribution and marketing.

Trade theories pay almost no attention to the information requirements, information flows, and marketing efforts involved in exporting. Neoclassical explanations of comparative advantage, based on idealized assumptions of perfect competition, treat the pattern of trade as being determined by relative 'endowments' of labour and capital (physical and human). Later explanations, less rigorously modelled but more empirically based, draw on technological differences between countries characterized by imperfect markets and accord an important role to economies of scale.

The development of theories of intra-industry trade belongs to this second tradition. While accepting the existence of trade based on differences in 'endowments', it looks to 'market imperfections' such as economies of scale in production, technological leads and lags, learning from experience, product differentiation, or linkages between industries (for example between traded goods and non-traded inputs) for explanations of why particular products *within* industry groups are competitively manufactured

---

* The views and interpretations put forward are those of the authors and not of the World Bank or the Oxford University Institute of Economics and Statistics.

in particular locations. One outcome is that national economic characteristics do not fully determine trade patterns (Gray 1988).

What are now being called the 'new trade theories' combine the explanations of comparative advantage given by intra-industry trade theorists with recent developments in industrial organization theory, involving principally modelling of non-competitive games (Dixit 1984; Brander 1986; Krugman 1986*a*, 1986*b*). Such modelling has been given an empirical basis by applying it to specific industries, where the players are leading exporting firms in different countries, as well as the governments of these countries.

Most of the applications have been taken from highly industrialized countries, but as Krugman (1986*a*) points out, there may be a greater role for the new theories in explaining the trade patterns and illuminating the policy choices of developing countries than developed ones. Scale economies, not least in infrastructure, loom large in poorer countries, while productivity gains by cumulative learning are likely to be particularly significant for them, along with externalities of various kinds. Besides, the very existence of developing countries with low incomes implies massive 'market imperfections'.

In all these theories and others (even product cycle theories), however, there is as yet no explicit recognition of marketing and information flows, or the learning they involve. Economic theory has increasingly tried to incorporate information-related issues, and a business literature does exist on marketing, but these issues are not yet comfortably incorporated into trade theory.

The need for marketing and transmission of information can be seen as arising from 'market imperfections', since in a neoclassical model sales and information flows are costless and instantaneous. Information gaps, costs of acquiring information, and costs of finding buyers and selling goods are complications outside the model, even though a large share of a country's gross national product (GNP) (and even its GNP from manufacturing) comes from marketing and distribution, information flows, and information activities.

In practice, exports depend on buyer and seller finding each other and a lot of information being transferred between them (and to supporting export participants). The buyer-importer in turn depends on a further distribution chain in which he is a seller looking for customers. Putting these realities into trade theory, even in simple partial equilibrium models, could perhaps throw light on what actually happens.

For that matter, none of the old and new trade theories properly recognizes other leading problems of exporting manufactured goods from developing countries, such as obtaining access to competitively priced inputs, services, and infrastructure. The complexity of learning to export, the information required, and the vulnerability of exports to inappropriate government controls or policies are implicitly played down as a result.

A major problem associated with the marketing of manufactured exports from developing countries is that products made in a developing country for export to a developed one are generally quite different from the analogous products made for the domestic market. This is partly because of the huge contrasts between the poorly supplied, shortage-ridden, overly protected 'suppliers' markets of most developing economies and the extreme 'buyers' markets for exports to industrial market economies. Another challenging reality is the rapidly changing designs and specifications of most consumer goods in demand in these richer economies.

As a result of these systematic product differences and changing product specifications, information must be collected and supplied, order by order, on what is needed. Moreover, to produce what is sought, various technical problems have to be overcome, even by ostensibly competitive suppliers, before reaching the standards of finish, styling, quality, reliability, and packaging needed for export markets. Often instruction on these points is part of the crucial information transmitted to suppliers. While the latter are still inexperienced, either buyers or someone must teach them details of input procurements, quality control, inspection, packing, shipping, documents required, sizes and size assortments, and much else different from what is done in production for the local market.

The area related to marketing is rife with such phenomena as learning by experience, acquisition of foreign knowledge, externalities, and scale economies. Thus it should prove a fruitful region for the extension of new trade theories. More realistic models are much needed, however, since the usual theories are practically unserviceable as a basis for understanding the problems involved in expanding manufactured exports.

2. SOME STYLIZED RESEARCH FINDINGS

Marketing and information links, and associated learning processes in exports of consumer goods made by local firms in developing economies for industrial market economies, were one leading focus of a research project[1] sponsored by the World Bank and directed by one of the present authors (Keesing). The project included visits by consultants to five East Asian economies (South Korea, Hong Kong, Thailand, the Philippines, and Taiwan) and analysis by a consultant with experience in five South American economies (Argentina, Brazil, Colombia, Peru, and Uruguay).[2] Related research at the World Bank around the same time looked at marketing and related aspects of Korean exports and at the case of clothing exports from Colombia.[3]

The largest share of manufactured exports from developing economies, including a majority of the exports from East Asia, is accounted for by products—typically finished consumer goods, though some are intermediate goods—manufactured by locally owned firms to the orders of buyers from industrial countries in what are typically frequently changed designs and specifications.

Producing what is sought calls in each case for a vector of inputs meeting exacting quality requirements and specifications, since such exports are only saleable as complete packages meeting all buyer specifications (for example packaging, labels, printed instructions, exterior printing, and packing materials, as well as colours and raw materials and finishes and technical specifications). The costs of importing an incomplete or defective package and correcting the defects in a further stage of manufacturing are prohibitive. As a result, not being able to get one input, even if it only accounts for a tiny share of the cost of production, turns out to be a disaster that can knock a country out of a large export business.

In consequence, a country's trade arrangements providing easy access to imported inputs and a free-trade regime for exporters (and preferably their local suppliers as well) are critical for manufactured exports. Favourable prices and exchange rates are not an acceptable substitute. Moreover, no amount of marketing or informational assistance or subsidies to exporters can overcome defects of the policy regime in this regard. Nor can exporters attract orders through their own marketing efforts except in products for which the policy regime allows them access to suitable inputs at competitive costs.

Export manufacturers must also meet demanding price, quality, and delivery standards. For many orders, not only dependable and punctual delivery but also rapid delivery and a readiness to meet reorders are required. This depends on rapid access to suitable inputs as well as quick response capabilities on the part of suppliers, both difficult to achieve in a developing-country setting.

Only a small and shrinking share of manufactured exports from developing economies these days are standardized intermediate goods. An even smaller proportion are products made to local specifications in the developing country, and exported unchanged to other (usually neighbouring) developing countries or in barter trade to socialist countries. Some exports of standardized or local products are often feasible from local production, even in a developing country with badly flawed policies, typically as a 'vent for surplus' at prices that only cover marginal costs. However, markets for these goods tend to be small and stagnant compared to the fast-growing markets for made-to-order manufactured goods.

Other manufactured exports from developing economies, made under different arrangements, also cannot succeed in the face of problems of access to inputs or long delays caused by government controls. This is generally true of manufactured exports made by local firms to their own designs and distributed in richer countries through their own distributors.

(These are typically large firms making products involving standardized or slow-changing designs.) It is also true of products—in practice predominantly integrated circuits and other electronic products, but also others—made by subsidiaries of multinational corporations.[4] It tends to be true only to a lesser extent of capital goods, which are exported more often than not to other, less industrialized developing countries.

When consumer goods exports are made to buyers' orders by local firms, buyers' help or that of similarly knowledgeable consultants is generally indispensable at first, in showing these new exporters what is required and how to put together the entire package exactly as required, even though by local standards the exporters are already capable manufacturers. More and more learning by the manufacturers is essential to meet changing orders after that. If results are satisfactory, the know-how acquired becomes the basis for growing export earnings. This learning associated with successful exporting also spills over to other exporters and becomes the basis for export success by more and more firms at an economy-wide level.

Among the skills gained that are attractive to buyers are knowing exactly what is required in exporting to different countries and how to carry out all the usual steps without help, even in such matters as styling, labelling, documentation, and size assortments. Thus the firm learns how to put the whole export package together reliably with only a minimum of instructions and assistance. Many entrepreneurs acquire the ability to study a sample of a product, a fashion design, or set of diagrams and quickly translate it into a suitable production process using the means at hand; some become expert at making 'knock-off' copies overnight. More than a few firms learn to make high-priced products of excellent quality, using expensive materials and demanding designs. Some firms become expert in quality control for large volumes of output.

Most exporting firms also become expert in marketing their skills to buyers. Some acquire a particularly thorough knowledge of their potential customers, and learn how to obtain and schedule orders from them so as regularly to command premium prices. (Quality retailers buying directly are often ready to pay better prices than importer-wholesalers or some other retailers if they can be sure of reliable quality, timely fulfilment of reorders, and only a minimal need for supervision and inspection; but their orders tend to be small by comparison.)

3. LIGHT THROWN ON POLICY REQUIREMENTS AND HISTORICAL PATTERNS OF MANUFACTURED EXPORTS

The recent history of manufactured exports from developing economies, starting when Hong Kong began exporting consumer goods to the UK, on a significant scale around 1950, can be seen in light of these findings as a story of the build-up of information links as well as entrepreneurial, managerial, and technical skills. This was aided by improving communications and based on learning by manufacturers, buyers, intermediaries, and final customers. It took place within a framework of improving access to imported inputs, at first in Hong Kong as a free port and then in South Korea and elsewhere, as other developing economies learned ways of facilitating imported inputs despite their own protection and exchange controls.

These stylized facts also help to explain why policies have had to be adjusted on so many fronts to attain a sustained expansion of manufactured exports. Creation of a free-trade regime for exporters and their suppliers allowing them swift, easy access to imported inputs has turned out to be crucial. Other challenges have also had to be met relating to infrastructure and port facilities, a disciplined and suitable labour force ready to be used flexibly and work hard for realistic pay, and suitable financial and credit institutions offering both pre-shipment credit for working capital and term-loans for investments. Export expansion has also depended on suitable industrial and investment policies, for example, arrangements for approving investments expeditiously, helping investors obtain suitable sites and infrastructure, and channelling investments into needs of exports including especially industries making inputs competitive with imported inputs. Systematic incentives and assistance have been provided for improvements in industrial technology, productivity, and quality control, as well as access to capital goods at prices near world trade prices. *All this is additional to the suitable management of exchange rates, macroeconomic policies, and incentives for exporting compared to production for the domestic market.*

The difficulty of achieving and maintaining a free-trade regime for imported inputs within a sovereign economy with its own tariffs and import restrictions and currency and monetary and fiscal policies is one of the main reasons why as much as 55 per cent of the developing economies' manufactured exports come today from three economies—Taiwan (the leading exporter), the Republic of Korea, and Hong Kong—and over 7 per cent from Singapore. The remaining 45 per cent is also concentrated, with the People's Republic of China and Mexico the other leading suppliers.[5] Their shares have been increasing; the first four expanded the US dollar value of their exports by 37 per cent in 1987 over 1986 to a combined total of over $US155 billion, and China and Mexico achieved comparably high growth rates.[6] The first four achieved about a tenfold increase in their share of world manufactured exports in the fourteen years from 1973 to 1987 after spectacular earlier export growth. They are the only developing economies offering quick, easy duty-free access to imported inputs in any location, while China and Mexico are among those offering this within some regions.

4. LEARNING SEQUENCES IN MARKETING MANUFACTURED EXPORTS

The usual starting-point for manufactured exports is a local policy environment that has only recently become favourable for exports of the product, and a local manufacturer who is already well established in the domestic market and has low costs by world standards. If he decides to export, he can probably do so to another developing country by lining up marketing representatives or distributors there, but to export to a major industrial market economy he has so much to learn that he usually must rely on a buyer who knows what the market requires and will supply the design and take the risks and costs of holding inventory and distributing the product. Even firms knowledgeable enough in the local market to have their own chains of retail outlets selling their own designs almost always rely on foreign buyers' orders in getting into major industrial-country markets.

Usually, it is the initial buyer who seeks out the manufacturer and convinces him to export while bringing him under contract as a supplier. The first buyers in an industry are typically importer-wholesalers in narrow product lines, partly specialized in finding new sources of supply and teaching them what is required and how to make it in exchange for very low prices for the product. In East Asia, however, the first buyer may be instead a Japanese general trading company dealing in a wide variety of products (and exporting this one to the West, playing a role much like that of an importer-wholesaler) and also offering credit to the manufacturer (which most buyers will not do). Other trading and intermediary firms also sometimes play this first-buyer role; in Latin America, buyers for groups of department stores have been known to launch new export industries.

These first orders are generally given for products with only slow-changing designs, so that long and uncertain delivery times, to be expected at first, are not disastrous.

Typically the first buyers teach the export manufacturers how to set up each stage of the production process and improve management methods to accomplish what is needed. This is a risky business for the buyers, and they prefer to work with producers who already know more than most beginners, are motivated and quick to learn, and have access to credit (and to equipment they may have to add) to expand and improve their production. This is also a risky business for the manufacturers, who may lose money and do badly in these unaccustomed tasks, or encounter insurmountable obstacles in the policy environment. If things go badly they may not be paid at all.

The manufacturing firm, by learning to make the first order and then a succession of others for the first buyer or buyers, becomes familiar with the stringent quality requirements of export markets, with some product designs, and with the production adjustments, steps, and management tasks involved. Over time, the manufacturing firm gradually acquires enough know-how to make its capabilities as a supplier potentially attractive to other buyers.

In consumer goods later buyers are usually importer-wholesalers or retailers. The former tend to place large orders but may bargain hard to squeeze the price down, and are often quick to desert the manufacturer over a few cents in price or to move on to other sources of supply or other types of merchandise. Retailers buy directly for different types of stores, some of which are extremely concerned about quality, styling, and punctual delivery, and tend to offer higher prices in exchange. Buyers also include manufacturers or erstwhile manufacturers or designers from industrial countries who still design their own products and market them under their own brand names, but subcontract some or all actual production. Like many retailers they tend to be concerned to achieve reliable quality and stable relationships. The retailers can afford to pay extra since by direct buying they cut out one or more layers of middlemen, though they also give up middleman services in overseeing production and quality control and holding inventory.

Some consumer goods, by contrast, come through a whole chain of middlemen. They may include trading companies from developing economies, or distributors or agents working for the manufacturer, as well as more than one wholesaler.

Learning on the part of the management of the local manufacturing firm on how to 'sell' itself accelerates as the enterprise begins to deal with new buyers. Most buyers, before placing an order, come to visit the enterprise, inspect its showroom and samples of products already made, study its plant in operation, and talk with the management about its experience and know-how. They also check with other sources on the firm's reputation and experience, performance, credit standing, financial position, and the like. Local entrepreneurs in turn learn to find out quickly about the buyers, and become educated on different kinds of buyers. They also learn how to take the initiative in finding and approaching suitable ones, taking with them samples of their previous output.

These local entrepreneurs are soon required to formulate a business strategy as to which buyers and orders to accept and to seek, and to adopt rules on the minimum size of orders the firm will accept, while drawing up flexible marketing plans.

Most buyers prefer to deal with an export manufacturer who already knows a lot about what is needed and how to manufacture to order. When their orders are not especially large, as in most orders by quality retailers, they are willing to pay extra to avoid having to become involved more than minimally in the manufacturers' production problems. However, practically all buyers are prepared to help an experienced enterprise make new and difficult orders, and most provide useful information and advice in their routine visits for quality control and to inspect the product. Some offer much useful instruction as part of large orders or a stable buying relationship. The lessons they impart are often transferable to exports of other unrelated as well as related products.

An important point that leaps out of the evidence is that for firms exporting from developing countries, *marketing in the sense of finding or attracting customers and persuading them to place orders or buy output is almost inseparable in practice from building up the firm's supply capabilities. In getting orders, firms sell the whole package of their capabilities and knowledge together with their readiness to learn more and invest further in their exports.* Familiarity with the latest technology, designs, styling, the customer's own markets, or other aspects of the business may be selling points, but what is marketed is above all the firm's ability to meet all the buyer's requirements. Thus improving supply capabilities is central, and is virtually inseparable from developing skills in communicating to customers what the firm can do for them.

Successful exporters supplement learning from buyers by taking the initiative to learn about trends and significant details in product designs, manufacturing technology, management, training, distribution, retailing, and other aspects of the business. They travel abroad, talk with experts, hire people with experience, and use whatever other means may be available, including consultants and information services. This becomes a selling point in winning export orders. During travel abroad they visit current and potential buyers, so that acquisition of relevant information and technical skills is combined with purposeful efforts to market their supply capabilities.

This accumulation of skills is also the foundation for building up the exporter's own distribution channels abroad. Design know-how for the target market and overall familiarity with that market are critical in this. As the enterprise gains skills and know-how, relationships in which the buyer supplies the design, holds inventory, and distributes the product give way systematically (in some industries and markets, but not in others) to relationships in which the manufacturing firm develops its own designs and begins to distribute its exports through its own marketing representatives and distributors in the importing countries.

The designs, like those of many buyers who supply designs, may show little originality; and the brand names used may be obscure or bought from defunct firms or belong to the customers. Marketing agents and distributors may not be specialized but rather work for a shifting set of manufacturers on commission. The firm may not produce to inventory, but only to orders obtained for it. Thus the manufacturing firm may remain only a tiny rival of larger enterprises that dominate the market. As it gains size and experience and becomes ambitious, however, the firm may begin producing for inventory, build up its own distribution subsidiaries, line up after-sales service suppliers as necessary, and take the risks of marketing and distributing the product at the next stages within the importing economy. This implies considerable confidence in its designs and knowledge of the market and involves increased financial outlays and risks.

Products in which manufacturers from developing economies frequently line up their own marketing agents or distributors are typically ones in which designs change infrequently except as a marketing tactic by the manufacturers with well-known brand names, and products are standardized in one or very few designs over long production runs. Scale economies are thus important. It is typically only large exporting firms that rely on their own distributors or agents in the largest markets. Lesser manufacturers may continue to rely heavily on large buyers, but try to line up their own distribution in lesser markets to increase their volume of orders.

In some other industries, however, including most types of garments or apparel, which are the easiest consumer goods for developing countries to break into, manufacturers, even in developed countries, almost always produce to buyers' orders. In some other industries such as shoes this is also the dominant pattern. Experienced manufacturers from developing economies do begin to take an active part in the design decision, and may offer their own designs, but only rarely do they become involved in post-shipment marketing and distribution. As a rule these are products with fast-changing fashions in which production can be readily adapted to a succession of new designs, while economies of scale at the plant level are modest. Thus competition is intense in production and, based on *different* skills and accumulated know-how and personal connections, in subsequent distribution. Indeed, scale economies tend to be substantial in importing, wholesaling, and retailing, although people with much experience can be found running virtual one-person companies.

Examples of products in which distribution by some firms was found to take place through representatives, distributors, or distribution subsidiaries were television sets, radios, electric fans, furniture, and towels. In each, production to buyers' orders was also found.

At the time of the research (around 1979 and 1980) no developing-economy brand or product line was being advertised to households or individual consumers in the largest industrial countries such as the United

States. Since then, Korean electronics brand-names have been widely advertised, and an even greater push has been made in establishing Hyundai cars from Korea as a leading imported brand, with its own dealers and servicing.

One lesson that emerges from this research is that as a rule, manufactured exports from developing countries are a 'co-operation game' in which the buyers help the manufacturers learn all sorts of business skills required, and the two pool their skills and insights to obtain their overlapping goals. However, because of the perils of the local policy and cost environment as well as the weakness of the local manufacturers in the earliest stages, often they have to give up their joint efforts after losses.

Another striking finding is the enormity of the contrast between fledgeling exporters and the entrepreneurs and managers of experienced export enterprises, busily travelling abroad and developing strategies for further export expansion. Imitators and people with experience in related businesses have an easier time than the earliest exporters. Consequently developing economies with favourable policies and experience attract hordes of buyers—some with local offices manned by locally hired employees—and soon diversify their manufactured exports, moving on from success to greater success.

Elsewhere, glaring failures and policy obstacles tend to cut off the learning and evoke lasting buyer mistrust of an economy as a source of supply, leading to a slow or negative growth of manufactured exports.

In their extent, these externalities and learning phenomena and the possibilities for acquisition of technology and valuable information and advice practically free—in exchange for exports at low prices—are almost certainly without parallel in the economic activities open to a developing economy. This may help to explain the extraordinary returns that some developing economies have achieved by giving high priority and much energy to the needs of manufactured exports. The rapid and sustained growth of this business world-wide, decade after decade, suggests that *it is not too late for other developing economies to follow their example.*

The benefits come at a national level not only from the exports themselves or rather what they can pay for, but also from trying to become internationally competitive across the whole spectrum of activities crucial to these exports. Probably no other goal in development calls for and leads to such rapid advances in modernization and competitiveness. This research suggests that the transformation takes place in the know-how of the entrepreneurs and higher-level personnel of the local firms involved, as much as in any other dimension of change. It also suggests that this learning is practically inherent in exporting manufactured products made by local firms to industrial countries, as long as exports are not stymied by serious policy mistakes.

5. PUBLIC SUPPORT TO EXPORT MARKETING

Related research has been undertaken this year at the World Bank by one of the authors (Keesing) and a consultant (Andrew Singer) on how to provide cost-effective public support in developing economies to export marketing, particularly for manufactured goods. This research seeks above all to learn how best to proceed in assistance to developing countries that have thus far attained intermediate degrees of success in exporting manufactured goods, with policies that are improving but are only in transition toward being fully satisfactory for these exports. The research also includes in-depth studies of experience and what has been done by the trade development organizations of four East Asian success stories—Korea, Hong Kong, Singapore, and Taiwan;[7] an examination of the contrasts and trends in institutional arrangements in this area in developed market economies; and interviews with experts of international (and other) organizations that advise developing countries in this field.

The need to improve assistance in this area has arisen as an important concern in World Bank lending operations and advice to developing countries, and in the countries themselves. Many borrower countries in recent years have made improvements in their policies, and then when exports failed to pick up, or as part of the technical assistance accompanying policy-based lending or project-lending, have asked for help with their institutional support and export-promotion efforts. Yet good advice in this area is hard to find, and many efforts to provide technical assistance have turned out to have little or no effect.

Indeed, many developing countries have for many years maintained official trade or export-promotion organizations (TPOs) in the public sector—generally in the government itself—offering information services, promotional support, and assorted other assistance to export marketing free of charge to exporters. Often such an organization is also responsible for other export-related functions ranging from policy advice, or trying to represent exporters' needs to the government and the government to exporters, to administering regulatory controls on exports.

In the eyes of international experts, local businessmen, and other knowledgeable observers, most of these public-sector organizations are ineffective in expanding exports. Yet their counterparts in some leading export-oriented economies in East Asia are regarded as a resounding success, and some business experts give them credit for important contributions in expanding exports rapidly in a favourable situation. Probably most effective of all have been the China External Trade Development Council, started in Taiwan in 1970, and on a more limited front of activities dictated by Hong Kong's *laissez-faire* policies, Hong Kong's Trade Development Council, launched in 1966.

One of the issues under study is whether a permanent, public-sector TPO is the appropriate organizational form for channelling foreign assistance and government funds into support for export marketing, before a country has achieved suitable policies for manufactured exports. Hong Kong and Taiwan already had fully satisfactory policies and had attained experience and success in manufactured exports for many years before their TPOs were started, as had Singapore before it started its Trade Development Board in 1983. Thus, much of what they did may not be appropriate or cost-effective in support of much smaller exports at a much earlier stage in export development.

In sharp contrast, in other developing economies TPOs have been started at an early stage in the country's policy evolution from inward-looking, import-substitution policies toward export-oriented policies. This has come about primarily because of an abundance of aid funds and technical assistance in this area, as well as fashions in favour of early 'institution building' in it. Neither the countries nor the donors have focused this aid on export expansion targets or results, but rather on a collection of functions that include provision of information related to trade and organizing subsidized participation by local firms in trade fairs and missions, even where these prove ineffective in promoting exports. In some cases, 'promotion' has been embraced as a low-cost substitute for policy reforms in favour of exports and as a convenient source of travel opportunities and publicity for prominent public officials. Most of the resulting support services and promotional activities are premature or hardly relevant for most industries, given policy obstacles to exports and the dearth of marketable export experience and capabilities.

One hypothesis being weighed, supported by experience in some recent aid projects in India and elsewhere, is that in countries with mixed and transitional policies, it is better to organize assistance to export marketing and related aspects of export expansion in a time-bound, three-to-five-year project focused on a small number of promising export products, attaching the project to a well-managed financial institution or other fairly independent organization or giving it a separate management of its own. This time-horizon is enough to help particular industries to solve most of their specific problems, and learn a lot about how to expand their exports, provided the policy environment is already favourable for them.

The design of assistance at the enterprise or narrow industry level can usefully be closely related to the learning sequences of exporters. Helping firms in their export marketing cannot be entirely separated from providing them assistance and advice on how to improve their supply capabilities. This includes, for example, teaching them techniques and skills they need in order to make the products exactly as required for demanding markets; or showing them how to adjust production for changing designs, or how to improve their technology and management and equipment and quality control methods, reduce their costs, shorten their delivery times, overcome their technical problems, strengthen their local suppliers, and so on.

Thus, the heart of an effective support programme seems to be consultancy assistance (complemented by training or design assistance or whatever else may be most needed) aimed at *improving the export supply capabilities* of promising enterprises with significant capacity and motivation to export, and then helping them learn *how to market these capabilities*. Export consultants familiar with the business and the market can potentially teach the enterprises so that they become attractive to early buyers or to buyers beyond the early ones. As part of giving them expert advice in marketing, they may even be assisted in setting up their own distribution overseas to supplement orders they may receive.

The essence of this assistance is that it is carried on at a very small scale and budget, in selected enterprises and products, but is thoroughly expert and oriented to the enterprises' immediate challenges and requirements. What is learned can then be expected to spread to imitators and firms as yet unborn.

There may be problems in achieving such enterprise-oriented assistance in countries where existing TPOs want to control or benefit from the project. However, some of the organizations that supply technical assistance to developing countries in this field have begun to change their recommendations and technical assistance in the direction of a more enterprise-oriented approach and greater attention to the supply-side problems of exporters.

One policy instrument that appears promising is a fund providing grants sharing up to half of the costs of well-designed programmes of export marketing by firms themselves, involving new products or markets or quantum changes in the way exports are marketed in demanding markets. Such a fund is given out by Singapore's Trade Development Board, and others have been included in World Bank projects in India and Indonesia. This allows firms to choose what they want advice on and also to choose service suppliers, not least from the private sector.

A plurality of private or independent sources of support services, information, and consultancy assistance to both exporters and buyers, from people with a business outlook and relevant experience, appears important to complement and supplement buyers' efforts. Service firms will generally charge customers directly or indirectly for the information and advice they provide, but this is not necessarily negative—much of this information can be supplied cheaply by the service firms as a by-product or added attraction of their main line of business, yet may be valuable for an exporter.

Charging exporters at least part of the costs of services and advice provided them, beyond a brief introductory period of free services to motivate them and give them a sample of what they can get, may be a good idea even for public or publicly subsidized support services, since it will help sort out the firms for whom the assistance is potentially valuable and help motivate them to pay attention and learn, while demand will help guide choices on what services to provide. TPOs in industrial countries are increasingly trying to cover part of their costs by charging for services.

Associations of manufacturers, traders, or exporters and/or chambers of commerce and industry can usefully be fostered and perhaps assisted with subsidies to play significant roles in providing to their member firms training, information, support services, and assistance in exporting.

A wide range of business and financial firms—engineering and management consultants, business publishers, accountants, banks, shipping agents, product inspection and testing firms, credit-checking firms, trade-facilitation firms, and many others—deserve to be fostered while offering advice, services, and information to exporters and buyers. It appears particularly desirable to have among these firms branches of foreign or multinational enterprises, making use of information and analyses and on-line data bases produced abroad. Trading firms acting as intermediaries can be another useful source of services and advice.

6. HOW TO ACCELERATE EXPORT EXPANSION: FURTHER INSIGHTS

The research findings on learning sequences in export marketing at the enterprise level and the findings up to now on public-sector support to export marketing together suggest that the central requirements for accelerating the expansion of manufactured exports, along with suitable policies, are first, to give an initial boost to—and thereafter accelerate—the learning process of the private participants involved, and secondly, to make available and affordable high-quality services to help firms in areas where they are weak.

What appears most needed is ready access and frequent exposure to service suppliers and consultants with much business experience and expertise in their specialties, at affordable costs. This would ideally involve a combination of instruction, advice, and field extension services responsive to each firm's particular needs, allocated mainly to the promising exporters and promising export industries with production capacity. This implies allocation based on willingness to pay, supplemented selectively by a grant or subsidy element, allocated on the basis of other criteria relating to export prospects, management quality, or the quality of the proposal.

If such assistance can be offered together with appropriate policy reforms, decentralized private actions can be counted on to bring about a sustained, rapid expansion of manufactured exports in countries with sufficient basic production capabilities.

Making policies attractive has to include creating a favourable environment for private enterprise and desirable foreign investments. The policy environment must allow foreigners not only to come as visiting buyers, but also to set up their own buying-offices or joint venture companies or hire local firms as their agents. Just as important is allowing them to set up service companies ranging from banks to consultant firms, accountants, testing and inspection firms, business publishers, and branches of trading companies.

Thus the findings of both research studies support the freeing of trade-related services from protection and barriers against foreign entry and investment. By letting foreigners in, a country can quickly provide services of world quality to supplement and reinforce buyer instructions and advice. Barriers to trade and investment in services will tend to raise the price, reduce the quality, and reduce competition in trade-related services.

Trade-related services can be regarded as infant industries generating positive externalities and hence potentially deserving subsidies or equivalent assistance in their early years. Subsidies if used should almost certainly be extended to foreign service firms. All service firms, regardless of ownership, will generally have to rely primarily on foreigners (including former buyers) as expert consultants, until local nationals have sufficient experience. Well-qualified local firms are sure to be created over time as spin-offs from foreign service firms and buying-offices, which ordinarily are attracted by labour-cost differences to hire and train mainly local nationals.

Public-sector subsidies could be channelled into these services by means such as government support to services by associations, matching grants to exporting firms allowed to pick their own service suppliers, tax exemptions and tax holidays, and financial support to jointly public and private or quasi-public organizations while requiring these organizations to cover part of their costs by charging for services. Meanwhile, ineffective existing organizations funded by the public sector ought to be disbanded. Everything they do can potentially be done better by private service suppliers.

REFERENCES

BRANDER, J. A. (1986), 'Rationales for Strategic Trade and Industrial Policy', in P. Krugman (ed.), *Strategic Trade Policy and the New International Economics* (MIT Press, Cambridge, Mass.).

DIXIT, A. (1984), 'International Trade Policies for Oligopolistic Industries', *Eco-*

nomic Journal, 94, Suppl. pp. 1–16.

GRAY, H. P. (1988), 'Intra-Industry Trade: An "Untidy" Phenomenon', *Weltwirtschaftliches Archiv*, 124/2, pp. 211–29.

HELLEINER, G. K. (1978), 'Market Structure and Buyer Characteristics in Canadian Imports of Manufactures from Low-Wage Countries', *Canadian Journal of Economics*, 2, pp. 324–33.

—— (1981), *Intra-Firm Trade and the Developing Countries*, (St Martin's Press, New York).

HONE, A. (1974), 'Multinational Corporations and Multinational Buying Groups: Their Impact on the Growth of Asia's Exports of Manufactures—Myths and Realities', *World Development*, 2, pp. 145–9.

KEESING, D. B. (1983), 'Linking Up to Distant Markets: South to North Exports of "Manufactured Consumer Goods"', *American Economic Review: Papers and Proceedings*, 73, pp. 338–42.

—— (1988), 'The Four Successful Exceptions: Official Export Promotion and Support for Export Marketing in Korea, Hong Kong, Singapore, and Taiwan, China', UNDP-World Bank Trade Expansion Program, Occasional Paper 2.

KRUGMAN, P. (1986a), 'New Trade Theory and the Less-Developed Countries', Paper presented for 'Debt, Stabilization and Development', conference in memory of C. Diaz-Alejandro, Helsinki.

—— (1986b), 'Introduction: New Thinking about Trade Policy', in Krugman (ed.), *Strategic Trade Policy and the New International Economics* (MIT Press, Cambridge, Mass.).

MORAWETZ, D. (1981), *Why the Emperor's New Clothes Are Not Made in Colombia* (OUP, for the World Bank, New York).

RHEE, Y. W., ROSS-LARSON, B., and PURSELL, G. (1984), *Korea's Competitive Edge: Managing the Entry into World Markets* (Johns Hopkins University Press, for the World Bank, Baltimore).

SHARPSTON, M. (1972), 'International Subcontracting', *Oxford Economic Papers*, 24, pp. 94–135.

WATANABE, S. (1972), 'International Subcontracting, Employment and Skill Promotion', *International Labour Review*, 104, pp. 425–50.

WESTPHAL, L. E., RHEE Y. W., and PURSELL, G. (1981). 'Korean Industrial Competence: Where It Came From', Staff Working Paper 469, July (World Bank, Washington, DC).

WORTZEL, L. H., and WORTZEL, H. V. (1980), 'Export Marketing Strategies for NIC and LDC-Based Firms', *Colombia Journal of World Business*, 16 (Spring), pp. 51–60.

NOTES

1. RPO 671-69, 'Key Institutions and the Expansion of Manufactured Exports'.
2. The East Asian interviews were by Lawrence H. and Heidi V. Wortzel; the analysis of South American experience was by Camilo Jaramillo. Some of these findings have been published by Keesing (1983) but the rest have remained

unpublished. Wortzel and Wortzel (1980) have put forward some of their own interpretations. The research on this subject was carried out between 1978 and 1982.
3. Some of the findings in Korea have been published in Westphal *et al.* (1981) and Rhee *et al.* (1984) but others remain unpublished. Morawetz (1981) presents his findings on Colombia. Other relevant literature on this subject is far from abundant. Sharpston (1972), Watanabe (1972), Hone (1974), and Helleiner (1978) are among the other papers that have dealt with marketing aspects of manufactured exports involving local firms.
4. As Helleiner (1981) shows, watches, cameras, and passenger cars are other items in which shares of multinationals appear particularly high.
5. This is based on actual or estimated 1987 exports for what the UN and GATT call developing market economies, plus China.
6. Based on national statistics. The total includes over $US27 billion in re-exports from Hong Kong and Singapore in 1987, up from $US18 billion in 1986.
7. See Keesing (1988).

PART II

Case-studies: Countries and Industries

8
Foreign Direct Investment and Patterns of Industrialization and Trade in Developing Countries: The Brazilian Experience*

Winston Fritsch and Gustavo H. B. Franco

THE last two or three decades have witnessed marked changes in the global organization of industry with far-reaching effects for the evolving patterns of integration of developing countries into the world economy. The long-run process of world-wide industrial redeployment has been intensified and accompanied by remarkable growth of manufactured exports from a small group of rapidly (or newly) industrializing developing countries (NICs). In parallel, the post-war period also witnessed the world-wide spread of multinational corporations (MNCs). By the late 1970s shares of domestic industrial production accounted for by MNC affiliates in Western countries—developed and developing—reached between a third and a quarter on average.[1] These developments are by no means independent. The importance of MNCs' participation in manufactured exports from NICs and of intra-firm trade more generally have been observed by many authors.[2] Both seem to be on the increase under the influence of the trading opportunities opened by the processes of global vertical integration and world-wide sourcing, in which MNCs have been playing the leading role. In this context, it seems clear that strategic planning by globally minded MNCs operating in global oligopolistic structures is bound to be a crucial determinant of developing countries' trading patterns in manufactures.

The precise consequences of these developments have not yet been fully analysed or understood.[3] In particular, it is not at all clear whether their influence on resource allocation and patterns of specialization would be consistent with that which traditional comparative advantage theory would suggest. In this respect, according to one authority, 'rather than thinking of the micro level problems of world trade in terms of *international* trade,

---

* The authors would like to thank especially M. Blomström and G. K. Helleiner as well as M. Agosin, M. Casson, D. Keesing, S. Lall, and F. Stewart for comments and suggestions made during the presentation of an earlier draft of this chapter. We thank also Diva Façanha and Mario Carvalho, jun. for kindly allowing access to special Cacex listings and Cesar C. A. de Matos and Marvelo Monteiro for research assistance. The usual caveats strongly apply.

i.e. as trade between nations, it is time—in the global village—to begin to think of them in terms of *global industrial organization*'.[4]

To probe further into the relationship between incoming foreign direct investment (FDI) and trade orientation in developing countries may constitute a partial but important step in this direction as this may shed light on common aspects of two hitherto unconnected areas of international economics. On the one hand, given the importance of FDI in manufacturing in the NICs, it may add to a better understanding of the relationship between industrialization and trade orientation in developing countries. Indeed, current orthodoxy in the normative analysis of industrialization and trade patterns, by placing exclusive emphasis on the determining influence of domestic policies[5] has lost sight of the importance of exogenous developments affecting the behaviour of international corporations in shaping observed manufactured-export performance in developing countries. On the other hand, the discussion of a typology of incoming FDI patterns in the relatively more industrialized areas of the South—stressing their relation with the different post-war 'waves' or 'vintages' of international direct-investment flows with markedly changing characteristics as to trade orientation—may provide an interesting counterpoint to the large and growing literature on patterns of outgoing direct investment from developed countries.

The chapter is organized in three sections. Section 1 addresses the possible relationships between the character of incoming FDI and host countries' tradability; and it explores the exogenous influence of FDI upon host countries' trade orientation during the process of industrialization. It is observed that historically distinct FDI 'waves' have had very different characteristics as regards trade propensities, and these are relevant to explain well-known differences in tradability between NICs. Section 2 explores the Brazilian experiences in some detail with the purpose of observing the importance of such exogenous influences on the growth and diversification of manufactured exports observed from the 1970s on. Section 3 summarizes the main conclusions and draws attention to global developments affecting international firms as a crucial element in shaping host countries' industrial and trade policies.

1. MNCS AND PATTERNS OF TRADE AND INDUSTRIALIZATION IN DEVELOPING COUNTRIES

To the extent that foreign direct investment represents an addition to a country's capital stock, it affects resource allocation in several ways.[6] The presence of MNC affiliates may affect capital accumulation[7], industrial structure, and performance,[8] and, among many other structural characteristics of the host economy, her trade propensities. Thus, it is natural to assume that MNCs do influence, at least to some extent, the observed patterns of industrialization and trade orientation in host countries. This should be especially important, for example, in the larger Latin American economies in which the presence of foreign capital is very significant: in Brazil broadly defined MNCs accounted for 27.5 per cent of total industrial production in 1980;[9] in Mexico this share was 27.2 per cent for the same year.[10] These numbers are not far from OECD standards.[11]

Of course trade and industrialization patterns are affected by many influences, endogenous and exogenous to the host country. 'Outward orientation' is certainly affected by the host country's trade policies and structural features, as extensively argued in the relevant literature. However, although such endogenous elements should in principle act on established affiliates in the same way as on domestic firms of equal attributes, the 'outward orientation' of MNC affiliates may differ from that of domestic firms in so far as globally minded MNCs respond to a much broader environment than the one shaping the decisions of domestic firms.

1.1 MNCs, Domestic Firms, and 'Outwardness'

The significance of such exogenous influences over a country's overall outward orientation, and the influence of foreign subsidiaries over the economy's *ex ante* 'outward orientation' could be gauged if MNC affiliates' trade orientation is different from that of its host countries' domestic firms. Several studies have searched for differences in trade orientation between MNC affiliates and domestic firms, and their results show some consistent patterns. In general, studies focusing upon Latin American countries in the 1960s and early 1970s have found the export propensity of MNC affiliates to be very low. Yaitsos reports that majority-owned US MNC affiliates exported only 6.2 per cent of their sales on average for Latin America in 1966[12] and an ECLA study, using a much larger sample for 1965, found a similar ratio (7 per cent).[13] It was also generally found that export propensities of foreign subsidiaries were lower or at most statistically no different from the ones for domestic firms, though these early studies often did not control for other factors affecting trade orientation. A study of Mexico found MNC affiliates' sales abroad to be 2.8 per cent of total sales in 1970, just slightly above the 2.6 per cent found for domestic firms.[14] Jenkins (1979, pp. 93–4) considered a sample of 658 exporting firms responsible for 77 per cent of Mexican exports of manufactures in 1974, and found that locally owned firms exported 19.5 per cent of their total sales on average, while foreign subsidiaries registered only 12.6 per cent. Using a pooled sample of 500 Brazilian manufacturing firms for 1971–7 Naetke and Newfarmer (1985) found no significant differences in export propensities between foreign and domestic firms operating in Brazil when controlling for factors like capital intensity, size, and concentration.[15] In sum, it was generally found that MNC affiliates were heavily oriented towards domestic markets in Latin America up to at least the 1960s and early 1970s.

In recent years this situation has significantly changed. A recent study of Brazil, considering a sample of 20,107 firms in 1980, 3,903 of which were exporters, has established unambiguously that 'foreign ownership has a strong, independent effect on both export performance and import propensities of individual firms' when controlling for factors like size, skill and advertising intensity, and vertical integration.[16] Another study shows that the probability of exporting is at least three times as big for foreign firms as for domestic ones.[17]

This growing outward orientation of MNC affiliates in the leading Latin American economies can be illustrated with the help of Table 1 showing export propensities of majority-owned US MNC affiliates located in different regions.

The table shows a very clear upward trend in export propensities by majority-owned US MNC affiliates located in Latin America. At the same time a sharp contrast is readily observed in the export orientation of US MNC affiliates established in Latin America, on the one extreme, and in East Asia, on the other. In East Asia it appears that MNC affiliates were 'born' markedly outward orientated. To a significant extent these huge differences in export propensity between the two areas can be explained by aspects of host countries' trade policy—especially export targeting and

Table 1. US MOFAs[a] in manufacturing: propensities to export (%)

Countries	1966	1977	1982	1986
All countries	18.6	30.8	33.9	38.3
Developed	20.4	33.1	36.6	39.3
Canada	16.1	29.9	34.5	n.a.
Europe	25.8	37.7	41.2	n.a.
Underdeveloped	8.4	18.1	22.0	32.6
Latin America	6.2	9.7	11.9	20.1
Brazil	3.0	8.7	12.4	17.4
Mexico	3.2	10.4	10.8	34.8
Asian NICs[b]	—	81.2	76.2	76.0

[a] Majority-owned foreign affiliates.
[b] Hong Kong, Korea, Singapore, and Taiwan.
Source: Adapted from Blomström (1987), p. 20 and (1988), Tables A1, B1, and C1.

the early creation of export-processing zones in East Asia[18]—which shaped the sectoral composition of foreign investment. Greater export orientation in Latin America in recent years would seem to explain their pattern of change in the late 1970s and 1980s.

What is interesting to consider, however, is whether MNCs' export orientation reinforced overall inward orientation in the earlier stages of industrialization in Latin America and its growing 'outwardness' in recent years. In order to perform a preliminary test of these propositions one should note first that an economy's overall openness is jointly determined by the 'openness', or export ratios, of foreign subsidiaries and of domestic firms. Next, it is possible to decompose an economy's (or the manufacturing sector's) openness into the foreign and the domestic component to see how each contributes to the overall trade orientation. One cannot compare, however, the most usual measure of openness—the exports to GDP ratio—with the ratios of Table 1 because the former has value added in the denominator and the latter have gross sales. It is possible, however, to 'correct' the ratios of Table 1 to turn them into exports to value-added ratios and to make comparisons possible. This correction is easily grasped from the following decomposition of an economy's export ratio for manufacturing:

$$(X/Y)_m = (X_{mn}/S_{mn}) \cdot \beta \cdot \Omega + (X_n/S_n) \cdot \beta \cdot (1 - \Omega), \qquad (1)$$

where $(X/Y)_m$ stands for the overall export to value-added ratio in manufacturing, which is written as a weighted average of 'corrected' ratios of sales abroad to total sales for domestic firms (X_n/S_n), and for foreign subsidiaries (X_{mn}/S_{mn}). The 'correction' is made by multiplying the latter ratios by β, defined as the ratio of the average value of production to value added in manufacturing, or $(S/Y)_m$. The weights are given by Ω, the sales of foreign affiliates as a proportion of total sales in manufacturing (S_{mn}/S).

Table 2 reports export to value-added ratios for manufacturing, namely $(X/Y)_m$, and for majority-owned US MNC affiliates (given by $(X_{mn}/S_{mn} \cdot \beta)$ for 1970 and 1983.

The ratios in Table 2 confirm the conjecture that foreign subsidiaries reinforce openness in Asia. Except in Hong Kong, foreign subsidiaries are much more outward oriented than the average for the manufacturing sector, both in 1970 and in 1983.[19] Note also that the ratios of exports to value added for foreign affiliates are very high for the Asian countries listed, in contrast to Brazil and Mexico. Table 3 illustrates the contrasting patterns of industrialization and trade between the two regions: Brazil and Mexico alone are responsible for about a third of MVA generated in LDCs while the three Asian countries listed account for only a 7 per cent share in 1980. In contrast, these three Asian countries are responsible for 42 per cent of exports of manufactures from LDCs in 1980, while Brazil and

Table 2. Exports of manufactures as a proportion of value added in manufacturing (MVA) for MNC affiliates and overall manufacturing

Country	1970		1983	
	Manuf. Exp. MVA	(Manuf. Exp.)$_{mn}$ (MVA)$_{mn}$	Manuf. Exp. MVA	(Manuf. Exp.)$_{mn}$ (MVA)$_{mn}$
Hong Kong	2.520	2.310	3.200	2.337
Korea	0.358	2.014	0.747	1.928
Singapore	0.686	3.542	1.570	3.480
Taiwan	0.507	2.099	0.961	1.823
Brazil	0.037	0.065	0.148	0.290
Mexico	0.110	0.084	0.071	0.260

Source and Methodology: (X_m/Y_m) computed from the formula $(X_m/Y_m) = (X/Y) * (X_m/Y) (Y_m/Y)$, where X denotes exports, Y value added, and the subscript denotes manufacturing. These ratios were obtained from CEPAL (1984), James et al. (1987), and IBGE (1987). 'Correction' factors (see text) are gross value of manufacturing output to value-added ratios, obtained from UNIDO (1987) for all countries (using 1970 and 1980) except Brazil, the figures for which were taken from IBGE (1987). Export to sales ratios were obtained from Table 1.

Mexico together account for only 9.1 per cent. This evidence is very much consistent with the high exports to value-added ratios in Asia reported in Table 2, although, of course, it does not explain why this ratio is higher for MNC affiliates.

It is also interesting to observe from Table 2 that foreign subsidiaries become slightly less outward oriented from 1970 to 1983 in Korea and Taiwan, a period of some FDI in import-substituting activities, especially in Korea.[20] Foreign subsidiaries are very clearly inward oriented in Latin American countries in 1970, and in the Mexican case even more inward oriented than the average for the economy. By 1983, MNC affiliates had become much more outward oriented than the national average both in Brazil and Mexico, suggesting that the influence of foreign subsidiaries was important to raise these economies' openness. In fact, as observed in Table 1, the outward-oriented drive of US MOFAs in Latin America was extraordinary, especially after 1982. In Mexico the share of foreign firms in non-oil exports rose from 27 per cent in 1981 to 55 per cent in 1987.[21] Higher openness is also very clear in overall manufacturing in Brazil, suggesting that domestic firms were also becoming more trade oriented. This was not the case in Mexico where 'Dutch disease' caused by the oil boom seems to have hit domestic firms, especially up to 1982, thus

Table 3. Shares of total LDC manufacturing value added (MVA) and exports of manufactures from LDCs, selected countries

Country	% of MVA in LDCs		% of Mnf. Exps. from LDCs	
	1970	1980	1970	1980
Brazil	17.5	22.7	3.8	7.4
Mexico	11.4	10.9	4.0	1.7
TOTAL	28.9	33.6	7.8	9.1
Singapore	0.7	1.0	4.4	9.0
Korea	2.0	4.5	6.6	15.6
Hong Kong	1.5	1.5	23.9	17.8
TOTAL	4.2	7.0	34.9	42.4

Source: MVA data from national accounts and manufactured exports defined as SITC categories 5 to 8 less 68. Adapted from Naygar (1983, p. 16).

modifying the trend towards greater outward orientation in foreign subsidiaries.

1.2 FDI as an Exogenous Determinant of Trade and Industrialization Patterns in LDCs[22]

One should be careful at this point not to jump to the conclusion that these countries' outward (or inward) orientation was, to some extent, *determined* by the character, or the trade orientation of MNC affiliates located therein. One should have in mind first the limitations of the exercise built around Table 2. It says nothing on the influence of foreign subsidiaries over the economy's export ratio in manufacturing which depends on the weight, Ω, and the share of MNC affiliates' industrial production in total domestic output.[23] Moreover, since trade orientation is affected by factors like firm size and the sectoral distribution of domestic value added, none of which is unrelated to the presence of MNCs,[24] these influences should be controlled for before any firm conclusions are reached.

It is also important to observe that foreign subsidiaries are perhaps more sensitive to incentives than domestic firms, as MNCs possess a superior flexibility to respond to changes in the policy environment within which they operate in specific host countries. Besides, more often than not, export-promotion policies are biased towards MNCs: targeting exports has become one of the more common performance requirements applied by host countries.[25] These factors could surely explain to some degree the 'over-reaction' to incentives (and disincentives) displayed in Table 2.

Finally, we have been considering that foreign subsidiaries affect a country's trade propensity directly, without 'displacement effects' on domestic firms' investments and exports. The presence of these effects might be very important, as shown by Hufbauer and Adler (1968), for example, who observe that the net balance-of-payments effect of the establishment of foreign subsidiaries might be drastically changed if displacement effects are allowed. On the other hand, such effects might not be especially important in countries in the process of industrialization, where most often FDI comes to occupy new sectors.

With those *caveats* in mind it remains to explore the extent to which wholly exogenous elements in the character of FDI directed to different nations at different periods contributed to the shape of the regional differences in MNC affiliates' trade propensities observed above. In this connection it is interesting to explore whether the differences in export propensities observed in Table 1 could be explained by the fact that they refer to different 'vintages' of foreign investment. In addressing this issue it is crucial to observe that the first major wave of international direct investment in the 1950s and 1960s, dominated by US and European firms ('the American Challenge' and the 'European Responses'),[26] has had its determinants neatly described along Hymer–Kindleberger lines, or along the lines of the more recent 'eclectic theory':[27] firms in possession of a 'unique asset', unexploitable by means of exporting from the parent country (thus the need to jump trade barriers in Latin America and in Europe), or by means of licensing (such markets were too thin), choose to establish affiliates in locations in which some attractiveness is provided by market size and growth prospects, labour costs, government incentives, and other possible locational advantages. This 'Hymerian' wave of US FDI was *predominantly geared to domestic markets*, as the very low export propensities of foreign subsidiaries in Latin America up to the 1970s illustrate. The very same is true for US MNC affiliates established elsewhere in the 1950s, including those in Canada and EEC countries. For US firms in the EEC in 1957, for example, the propensity to export to countries outside the Common Market was only 15 per cent.[28]

This 'inward' orientation of US FDI in its 'Hymerian' phase in the 1950s and 1960s can also been seen in the investment and trade sequences characteristic of the original product cycle model: in the first stage exports to host countries are reduced as local production is started and grows to the point where it occupies the whole market in the host country. At this point, however, as the affiliate 'matures', or it overcomes its initial competitive disadvantage related to production in a new location, it can become an exporter.[29] As production moves to the host country the MNC parent country's exports are displaced.[30] Foreign investment works as a substitute for exports, and one very clear implication of this fact is that

US FDI occurs in industries in which US comparative advantage is strong, that is, industries with high R & D intensity, as shown in Gruber *et al.*'s (1967) classic study.

This 'US Model' of FDI geared at domestic markets, has been described as 'anti-trade oriented' by the authors describing the Japanese early pattern of multinationalization, which was basically a strategy for relocating exports made uncompetitive by real wage increases and natural resource shortages in Japan.[31] The contrast as regards trade propensities in these two types or vintages of foreign direct investment has been extensively explored by the proponents of the 'Japanese Model' of foreign investment.[32] Differently from the US pattern, early Japanese FDI involved a strategy of adjustment to rising factor prices carried out essentially by marginal firms in relatively technologically unsophisticated and unconcentrated sectors. These firms chose to cross the country rather than the industry frontier, helped to a not inconsiderable extent by incentives granted by the government and large trading companies.[33] The output of the migrating firms was basically aimed at the home-country market; hence the crucial difference in trade propensities.

It would be natural, therefore, to infer that the specific trade orientation embodied in the different waves of incoming foreign investment would influence very significantly the outward orientation of the industrialization drive in host developing countries. Surprisingly, however, these possible relations between the pace and character of structural transformation in the semi-industrialized areas in the South and the changing nature of industrial countries' outgoing FDI have never been explored. The fact that the larger Latin American economies experienced an important industrialization drive during the 'Hymerian' phase, while the Asian NICs had their 'take-offs' in terms of production of relatively sophisticated goods a little later, at a time when foreign investment was already more 'outward-oriented', may help to explain the differences in industrial sectors' tradability—and, especially that of their internationalized segments—between the two areas observed in Tables 1 and 2.

An interesting point to explore further is that there appears to be a 'natural' increase in outward orientation for investments made during the 'Hymerian' phase, as one easily grasps from Vernon's (1979) revision of his original product cycle theory. As subsidiaries' networks are extended and the degree of internationalization is advanced, established MNCs start to develop a different outlook; this leads to rationalization of activities and sourcing on a global scale with ample consequences as regards trade orientation of individual affiliates. It is natural to expect, in this connection, intra-firm trade to grow significantly, which is indeed observed in the 1960s and 1970s. Moreover, the growing internationalization of multinational groups is at the root of the intensification of the long-run process of world-wide industrial redeployment. An important part of the transfer of industrial capacity to the South corresponds to the relocation of industrial (exporting) capacity within multinational groups.[34] These transfers have implied important changes in patterns of trade and industrialization in NICs, among which are the increasing share of MNCs in manufactured exports from some NICs, especially in Latin America.[35]

If one considers that this 'maturing' of the product cycle orientated investments occurs more or less simultaneously with the multinationalization of Japanese firms along lines suggested by the Kojima model, one is able to understand the marked increase in the trade orientation of foreign subsidiaries in Latin America suggested by Table 1. Not only are newcomers, especially the Japanese, more export orientated, but previously established affiliates are now involved in parent firms' world-wide sourcing and, consequently, also become more trade orientated. Of course, these exogenous influences should not be the only reason why Latin American countries become more export orientated in the 1970s; many other domestic influences are relevant, as the analysis of the Brazilian experience in the next section will reveal. Yet the notion that trade orientation is also determined by exogenous factors relating to the nature of FDI is very much consistent with observed patterns.

Finally, one further *caveat* should be offered before ending this section, namely that such broad characterizations of FDI vintages as 'Japanese' and 'Hymerian' should be seen as no more than caricatures or approximations; actual patterns are much more complex. There are, for instance, US investments in Mexico and in Asia that follow a 'Japanese' pattern, while Japanese investments in the US that are *quid pro quos* for trade restraints are pretty much 'Hymerian'. Besides, there are other nationalities of FDI, some with very specific characteristics, and other stereotypes.[36] A recent study focusing upon German, British, and Swedish, as well as American and Japanese FDI concludes that 'country specific factors dominate in the determination of international production'.[37]

2. FDI AND PATTERNS OF INDUSTRIALIZATION AND TRADE IN BRAZIL

After three decades of rapid industrialization based on import substitution, Brazilian industrialization turned outwards in the late 1960s: manufactured exports grew at very high rates from then on, and especially so after the first oil shock. High export growth rates were not confined to natural-resource-based or labour-intensive industries; export performance was also exceptionally good in sectors receiving newer 'vintages' or more 'outward-oriented' FDI, and in several of the more technology- or capital-intensive sectors set up through import substitution and intensive FDI penetration during the formative years of Brazilian heavy industry.[38]

Given Brazil's resource endowments it would not be difficult to explain the high export growth rates in resource-based or labour-intensive industries on the basis of traditional comparative advantage, once the excessively export-repressing trade and exchange-rate policies in force since the late 1940s were put to an end. To reconcile the exceptional performance of technology- and capital-intensive sectors with conventional trade theory is more difficult. To what extent is export diversification towards these sectors the result of greater outward orientation in the more recent waves of direct investment, as suggested in the previous section, the operation of learning processes accompanying the maturation of already established foreign firms, and/or domestic policies?

2.1 The Changing Character of FDI in Brazilian Industrialization: An Overview

The building of a modern and vertically integrated industrial sector was the main feature of the process of rapid growth and structural transformation experienced by the Brazilian economy in the post-war years. Two distinct phases, distinguished by their implied degree of outward orientation, can easily be identified in this process. The first was characterized by the response to incentives to domestic production, created by foreign-exchange shortages from the late 1940s, and corresponds to the classic import-substitution industrialization (ISI) pattern.[39] During this period FDI sought protected sectors with a view to exploiting a large and rapidly growing domestic market,[40] and made a decisive contribution to import substitution and growth, especially in modern segments of consumer durables, mechanical and electrical equipment, and a number of basic inputs and capital goods industries. This first wave of FDI in Brazil in the post-war period was characteristically Hymerian. In view of trade barriers and impediments or disincentives to licensing, US firms, and some time later their European competitors, chose to exploit their 'unique assets' by the establishment of subsidiaries in Brazil. This 'inward-oriented' internalization of oligopolistic structures geared to domestic markets of host countries was typical of the heyday of import-substituting industrialization in Brazil in the 1950s, after many decades of 'spontaneous' substitution in non-durable consumer goods.[41]

Two later investment spurts followed a sharp recession in the early 1960s and the reorientation of the economy towards greater integration into the world economy: first, the so-called Brazilian Economic Miracle of 1967–73, and, later, the investment projects under the PND II (the

Second National Development Plan) launched in 1974. In the former, emphasis was given to large government projects in basic chemicals and capital goods, and in the latter, the need to adjust to the oil crisis added energy and intermediate goods to these priorities. The period of the Economic Miracle witnessed significant modifications in the relative weights of state, domestic, and foreign firms in Brazilian manufacturing. Large state enterprises strengthened and consolidated their dominance in steel, oil refining, and some segments of petrochemicals. Foreign firms advanced in all non-traditional sectors, with the exception of mechanical equipment and those occupied by state-owned conglomerates, and thus more or less maintained their share in total capital in manufacturing at around 50 per cent. Again, a significant correlation was found between best-growth performance and the presence of MNC affiliates across sectors.[42]

It is significant, though, that the presence of US firms was substantially reduced relative to firms of European and Japanese origins during the 1970s; the rapid development of chemicals, mechanical equipment, and branches of precision mechanics and instruments, was undertaken predominantly by smaller firms of non-US origin. Since, according to Newfarmer and Marsh (1981), European and Japanese 'late-comers', were much more outward orientated than American firms (even considering that US firms had also become significantly more export orientated during the 1970s) this change in the geographical origin of foreign capital in Brazil had important implications for the overall outward orientation of foreign firms in Brazil.

After the first oil shock, the government strongly favoured the formation of joint ventures, often with state participation, to undertake the investment projects defined in the PND II. Brazilian experience with joint ventures with state participation had been positive—in steel and

Table 4. Shares of domestic, foreign, and state-owned firms in domestic and foreign markets in manufacturing in Brazil, 1980 (% of total sales in each market)

Type of firm	Number of firms	Domestic sales	Exports	Total sales
Domestic private	48 615	59.5	54.2	59.0
Foreign[a]	1 089	27.5	38.3	28.5
State-owned	65	13.0	7.5	12.5
Total	49 769	100.0	100.0	100.0

[a] Foreign firms are defined as those in which non-residents hold more than 10% of voting capital and state presence is insignificant.

Source: Willmore (1987a, p. 163).

in the petrochemical industry[43]—and it was presumed that they had the advantages of preventing full foreign control, increasing export market access, and facilitating technology transfer. These years witnessed an important rise in 'spontaneous' partnerships between private domestic and foreign firms. Although the spread of joint ventures was not extensive in the early years of PND II,[44] by the late 1970s and early 1980s they were becoming much more common. Over 1,500 joint ventures were in operation in the Brazilian economy in 1984.[45]

The maturation of investments associated with import-substitution projects implemented up to the early 1960s generated a reasonably integrated manufacturing sector, with well-defined 'leaders' in several industries. Brazilian manufacturing enjoyed a system of inter-industrial links with great complementarities between firms with different patterns of ownership. Market leadership patterns were not significantly altered during the boom of the early 1970s; nor were ownership patterns in different branches of manufacturing.[46]

Table 4 provides an overall picture of the weight of foreign firms in Brazilian industry. Although foreign firms do not control an abnormally high share of industrial output in Brazil,[47] they are dominant in some sectors—for example transport equipment (68 per sent of sales), rubber products (tyres) (63 per cent), pharmaceuticals (71 per cent), and tobacco (73 per cent)—and they share leadership positions in several others. In sixty-seven of the 174 sectors there is not a single foreign firm—defined as those with over 10 per cent of non-residents' participation[48]—among the leading four. Foreign firms' participation in exports is significant, the more so if one considers only the larger firms; in the largest 100 foreign firms— defined as in Table 4—foreign firms are responsible for 49.2 per cent of exports.[49]

2.2 FDI and Changing Comparative Advantage in Brazilian Industry

An outstanding feature of Brazilian industrialization has been its impact on the country's volume and commodity pattern of trade in manufactures. After a long period of contracting imports as a proportion of GDP and export stagnation, manufactured imports and exports began to grow again by the late 1960s, as mentioned above. With the first oil shock, however, the situation changed significantly. On the one hand, investments geared to the PND II had an important impact on industrial-sector tradability, producing an uncommon combination of a further deepening of import substitution with, this time, sound export performance in the same sectors in which import substitution was taking place.[50] Many consider the investments of this period as the key to the structural transformation that permitted the Brazilian economy to effect the dramatic adjustment of

Table 5. Brazilian manufactured-export indicators, 1970–1983

Product grouping[a]	World market share (%)		Average growth rate (%) 1970–2 to 1981–3[b]
	1970–2	1981–3	
SITC 5	0.22	0.80	31.4
SITC 6 (less 68)	0.46	1.26	24.7
SITC 7	0.15	0.74	33.5
SITC 8	0.24	0.69	28.4
Total	0.26	0.86	29.0

[a] SITC groups defined as: chemicals (group 5), manufactures classified according to materials less non-ferrous metals (group 6 less 68), machinery and transport equipment (group 7), and miscellaneous manufactures (group 8).
[b] Of current US dollar values.
Source: Gonçalves (1987, Table 1, elaborated from UNCTAD trade data-base).

1982–4, when a current account deficit of nearly 8 per cent of GDP was turned into a small surplus. On the other hand, there were important improvements in competitiveness and outward orientation in several established sectors not benefiting from government encouragement under the Plan. Indeed, overall export performance was exceptional, the more so as one notes that the economy had not been entirely freed from anti-export biases.[51] As can be seen in Table 5, from the early 1970s to the early 1980s, Brazil substantially increased her share in world markets for manufactures in all SITC groupings and average yearly growth rates of exports aproached 30 per cent.

This exceptional performance reflected to a large extent increased competitiveness, as opposed to external demand. Constant market-share analysis shows that competitiveness—that is, the unexplained residual—accounts for two-thirds of the total observed growth of manufactured exports, the other third being accounted for by growth in world trade; changes in composition and on the direction of trade had negligible impact.[52] The relative importance of the competitiveness component, which compares very favourably to estimates made for other developing-country exporters of manufactures, and shows no significant difference from that estimated for South Korea,[53] the best performer among Asian NICs, reflects increased diversification, and to some extent, the upgrading of Brazilian manufactured exports.

To what extent can this changing pattern of comparative advantage be primarily attributed to the behaviour of the subset of foreign firms in the manufacturing sector? The available evidence regarding the influence of foreign ownership and export orientation in the Brazilian manufacturing sector can be seen in Table 4, in which it is shown that foreign firms were responsible for no less than 38.3 per cent of total sales abroad in 1980. Moreover, two out of three of these firms are exporters, against less than half of the national firms in the sample. As already mentioned in Section 1.1, foreign ownership was recently found to be a strong and independent influence on export propensity—when controlling for concentration, size, and other firm and market characteristics—a result that studies for earlier periods in Brazil have failed to produce.

The recent change in foreign firms' trade orientation in Brazil was not restricted to export performance. The last decade also witnessed an important reduction in multinationals' import propensities,[54] which was an important contributory factor to the impressive swing in their trade balance to a sizeable surplus in the 1980s, as seen in Table 6.

This amazing improvement in the trade performance of foreign firms can certainly be credited largely to the reduction in the anti-trade bias of Brazilian trade and exchange-rate policies from the late 1960s. Large international firms possessing inherent competitive advantages in international markets (for example marketing channels) and superior managerial flexibility are generally believed to react strongly to changes in the trade policy environment.[55] Moreover, there is circumstantial evidence that, following the first oil shock, the usual export requirements associated with access to subsidies were complemented by informal but effective import-limitation targets imposed with special zeal on international firms by the import-licensing authorities.

The main concern of this section is, however, to probe further into the

Table 6. Trade balance of foreign firms[a] in Brazil, 1978–1985

Year	Exports	Imports	Trade balance
1978	2 918	2 949	−31
1979	3 773	3 482	291
1980	5 719	3 921	1 978
1981	7 141	3 567	3 574
1982	5 670	2 874	2 796
1983	5 824	2 342	3 481
1984	7 197	2 414	4 783
1985	7 123	2 305	4 818

[a] Defined as majority foreign-owned.
Source: BNDES (1988, Table B, p. 8).

Table 7. Foreign firms'[a] shares in exports of selected commodity groups[b] in Brazil, 1974–1985 (% of total exports of each group)

	1974	1977	1980	1983	1984	1985
Basic products	11	14	16	15	15	15
Manufactures						
Equipment and Instruments	67	64	62	62	67	63
Other	17	23	22	17	18	18
TOTAL	17	22	25	22	23	23

[a] Foreign firms defined as those with over 25% foreign direct control.
[b] Groups defined according to the Brazilian Commodity Nomenclature: basic products (sections I to V), manufactures (sections VI to XXI), equipment and instruments (sections XVI, XVII, and XVIII).
Source: CACEX, processed by the authors.

determinants of the growing comparative advantage of Brazil in technologically sophisticated and/or capital-intensive sectors, some of which were typical horror stories of highly protected 'infants' during the classic import-substitution phase. In the voluminous literature addressing the issue of the determinants of the growth of manufacturing exports in Brazil one does not find strong evidence of the influence of the change in crucial elements of the policy regime—such as exchange rates and export subsidies—on the performance of these sectors.[56] A suggestive explanation for high growth rates on the lines of 'import protection as export promotion'[57] has been provided by Teitel and Thoumi who argue that given Brazil's large markets, ISI was 'a preamble to the export phase' and that the 'new manufactured exports of the 1970s were not in fact, an exclusive consequence of export incentives but a "natural" result of the maturation of the process of industrial growth, helped by the substantial expansion of world trade verified during the period'.[58] This interpretation introduced important considerations of dynamic efficiency gains which must have a central place in any explanation of this phenomenon. However, it underemphasizes one of its crucial features, namely the substantial concentration of *foreign* firms among exporters in more technologically sophisticated branches of manufacturing, as can be seen by inspection of Table 7. Thus, in explaining the changing trade orientation of technologically sophisticated sectors in Brazil one must not only move away from traditional trade theories based on simple notions of comparative advantage determined by relative factor endowments, but also deal with the fact that the improving export performance came from a subset of predominantly foreign firms.

Table 8. Mean values of sectoral indicators of manufactured-export performance

Product grouping	Tech.-intensive sector	Non-tech.-intensive sector
Overall RCA index	0.52	1.21
RCA index for foreign firms	1.28	0.52
Share of foreign firms in output (%)	52.2	16.5

Source: Adapted from Gonçalves (1987, Table 4).

That the comparative advantage of foreign firms may diverge from that of the host country has been noted in the FDI literature.[59] Indeed, this seems to be the case in Brazil where no significant rank correlation was found between revealed sectoral comparative advantage (RCA) indices[60] (for twenty-eight sectors at the two-digit level of the ISIC classification) and the RCA indices for only the foreign firms operating in those sectors. While for the aggregate (all firms) data Brazilian RCA is generally higher in less technology-intensive sectors, it tends to be otherwise when only foreign firms' RCA indices are calculated.[61] Table 8 shows that Brazil has a high RCA in traditional sectors but that the foreign firms operating in the country have, relative to domestic firms, a higher RCA in technologically sophisticated goods, where they also hold a larger share of domestic production.

What seems to have occurred in Brazil is that, after the ISI crystallized in a stable ownership structure in which foreign firms were leaders in several technologically sophisticated domestic oligopolies, Brazil's comparative advantage in these sectors changed with the changing 'outward orientation' of the Brazilian part of these firms. Thus, the roots of the growing comparative advantage which accompanied the 'maturation' of these now dynamic foreign-owned exporters in Brazil may lie in the global developments affecting the trade orientation of multinational firms as a world-wide phenomenon, as outlined in Section 2. Indeed the extent of intra-firm trade in these technologically intensive sectors is disproportionally high as compared to that of traditional sectors.[62] When specific characteristics of the process of FDI penetration in Brazilian industry are taken into account, however, there are grounds for believing that the influence of these general trends upon the export propensities of foreign firms might have been strongly reinforced by the usual processes of learning and dynamic efficiency gains operating in already established subsidiaries.

Learning and efficiency gains in already established foreign-owned firms could a priori be explained on the lines suggested by the vast literature on technical progress in semi-industrialized economies, according to which a crucial role is played by minor innovations implicit in the process of adaptation of exogenously developed technologies to smaller market sizes, different input (including skill) specifications, and different demand characteristics.[63] Although in the study of these learning and adaptation phenomena special emphasis has been given to the experience of indigenous firms, a strong case could clearly be made that it should also be observed in the case of foreign firms whose entry into the country had its origins—as in the vast majority of the cases in the Brazilian and Latin American industrialization experience, as discussed in the previous section—in import-substitution projects of the Hymer–Kindleberger type.

Recall that, according to the latter view of the determinants of FDI, the competitive advantage of foreign firms stems from the possession of some firm-specific 'unique asset'—the market for which is thin or nonexistent—which more than offsets the inherent informational disadvantages of doing business in a strange environment.[64] The very existence of these latter learning and communication costs must give rise to substantial X-efficiency gains as the subsidiary survives and matures. That is to say that, implicit in this explanation of the FDI process, and especially so for those investments geared to domestic markets, there is the notion that survivors should benefit from a learning curve. Indeed, on the basis of existing evidence as to the very limited extent of technological search by multinational corporations before investment in developing countries,[65] a case could be made that there has typically been ample room for efficiency-improving technological adaptation by their foreign subsidiaries. In the Brazilian case, this potential for improvement could be even greater than that available to local firms as existing evidence suggests substantially greater prior technological search by the latter.[66]

The influence of changing trade policy should not, however, be dismissed in explaining these 'distortions' of Brazil's traditional patterns of comparative advantage through dynamic efficiency gains. Low technological search before entry is not, of course, unrelated to the degree of protection from foreign competition—among other temporary favours—granted to import-substituting investors in countries such as Brazil. Consequently, subsequent reductions in the 'inward orientation' of the host country's trade policies—together with the natural phasing out of other *ad hoc* locational incentives—could play an important role in inducing efficiency-enhancing adaptation over time. If that is accepted, the greater neutrality of incentives in Brazilian trade and exchange-rate policies from the late 1960s onwards following a wave of low search cost import-substituting projects undertaken by foreign firms, should also have contributed to spur these firms to move faster down their learning curves.[67]

3. SUMMARY AND SOME POLICY CONCLUSIONS

This chapter has stressed the importance of exogenous influences—related to the strategic reactions of international firms in industrial countries to global developments and their impact upon the trade orientation of international direct investment flows—in explaining the export propensity of the manufacturing sector in semi-industrialized developing countries. It has offered two main conclusions: first, that such exogenous elements can, to a large extent, explain the wide divergence in export propensities existing between foreign firms located in the semi-industrialized economies of Latin America and East Asia as well as their observed change over time; secondly, that exogenous influences accounting for differences in 'outward orientation' between foreign entrants of old and new vintages in Brazilian industry, should be taken into consideration—together with the operation of learning processes in established subsidiaries and a more trade-orientated policy environment—in explaining the country's manufactured-export diversification towards technologically sophisticated goods, in which foreign firms played a leading role.

Recognizing that global trends have a central influence on the organization of cross-border transactions of international firms has important implications for the design of effective trade and industrial policies in open developing economies. Although analysis of the complex interdependence of domestic measures and the motivations of multinational firms in determining observed outcomes goes beyond the scope of this study, it should be clear that policies are not likely to be effective if they go against the strategic decisions of these firms, that is, if they do not conform with prevailing global trends shaping those decisions. This seems increasingly true as these firms have adapted to the economic and technological shocks of the 1970s and early 1980s by learning to respond faster to environmental volatility, so that, as suggested by Dunning, 'in the formation and development of their industrial, technological and trading strategies, governments must *explicitly* recognise the role of MNEs in fashioning cross-border trade'.[68]

A corollary of this assertion is that the quality of active trade and industrial policies in the semi-industrialized periphery depends upon the policy authority's ability to predict global trends affecting the strategic behaviour of internationally orientated firms and thus the nature of future North–South FDI flows.[69] This is by no means reassuring, as complex and far-reaching structural trends—such as the process of industrial restructuring in OECD countries, the intensification of industrial redeployment in the NICs, and acceleration in the rate of innovation in industrial applications of electronics and biotechnology—persist, while the potential for global macroeconomic imbalance and consequent instability have, if anything, increased.

REFERENCES

ARESKOUG, K. (1976), 'Private Foreign Investment and Capital Formation in Developing Countries', *Economic Development and Cultural Change*, 24/3, pp. 539–48.
BAER, W., DA FONSECA, M. A. R., and GUIHOTO, J. J. M. (1987), 'Structural Change in Brazil's Industrial Economy, 1960–1980', *World Development*, 15/2, pp. 275–86.
BALASSA, B. (1986), *Toward Renewed Economic Growth in Latin America* (Colegio de Mexico, Mexico City; Institute for International Economics, Washington, DC).
BANDERA, V. N., and WHITE, J. T. (1968), 'US Direct Investment and Domestic Markets in Europe', *Economia Internazionalle*, 21.
BATISTA, J. C. (1986), 'Brazil's Second National Development Plan and its Growth cum Debt Strategy', *Instituto de Economia Industrial* (UFRJ, Rio de Janeiro).
BAUMANN NEVES, R. (1985), *Exportaçoes e Crescimento Industrial no Brasil* (IPEA-INPES, Rio de Janeiro).
BERGSMAN, J. (1970), *Brazil: Industrialization and Trade Policies* (OUP for OECD, London).
BERGSTEN, C. F., HORST, T., and MORAN, T. (1978), *American Multinationals and American Interests* (Brookings Institution, Washington, DC).
BLOMSTRÖM, M. (1987), 'Transnational Corporations as Instruments for the Exports of Developing Countries' (UNCTC, New York).
—— (1988), 'Transnational Corporations and International Trade' (National Bureau of Economic Research, New York).
—— KRAVIS, I. B., and LIPSEY, R. E. (1988), 'Multinational Firms and Manufactured Exports from Developing Countries' (National Bureau of Economic Research, New York).
BNDES (1988), *O Capital Estrangeiro na Industria Brasileira: atualidade e perspectivas* (Estudios BNDES-DEEST, 10, Rio de Janeiro).
CAVES, R. E. (1982), *Multinational Enterprise and Economic Analysis* (CUP, Cambridge).
CEPAL (1971), *Estudio Economico de America Latina, 1970*, pt. 4 (New York).
—— (1983), *Dos Estudios sobre Empresas Transnacionales en Brasil* (Estudios e Informes de la CEPAL, 31, Santiago).
—— (1984), *Anuario Estadistico de America Latina e el Caribe* (CEPAL, Santiago).
—— (1985), *Market Structure, Firm Size and Brazilian Exports* (Estudios e Informes de la CEPAL, 44, Santiago).
CLEGG, J. (1987), *Multinational Enterprise and World Competition, A Comparative Study of the USA, Japan, the UK, Sweden and West Germany* (Macmillan, London).
COHEN, B. J. (1975), *Multinational Firms and Asian Exports* (Yale University Press, New Haven, Conn.).

DOELLINGER, VON, C., and CAVALCANTI, L. C. (1975), *Empresas Multinacionais na Industria Brasileira* (IPEA-INPES, Rio de Janeiro).
DUNNING, J. H. (1979), 'Explaining Changing Patterns of International Production: In Defense of an Eclectic Theory', *Oxford Bulletin of Economics and Statistics*, 41, pp. 269-95.
—— (1988), 'International Business, the Recession and Economic Restructuring', in N. Hood and J. E. Vahlne (eds.), *Strategies in Global Competition* (Croom Helm, London).
FAJNZYLBER, F. (1971), *Estratégia Industrial e Empresas Internacionais: posiçao relative de América Latina e do Brasil* (IPEA-INPES, Rio de Janeiro).
FINEP (1977), *Estrutura Industrial e Empreasa Lideres* (FINEP, Rio de Janeiro).
FISHLOW, A. (1972), 'Origens e Consequências da Substituiçao de Importaçoes no Brasil', *Estudos Econômicos*, 2, pp. 7-76.
FRANCO, G. H. B. (1988) 'Capital Investment in Brazil: Its Role in Adjustment and Emerging Issues', in P. Coffey and L. A. Correa do Lago (eds.), *Brazil and the EEC* (Pinter Publishers, London).
FRITSCH, W., and FRANCO, G. H. B. (1988), 'Brazilian External Adjustment in the 1990s: the Role of Foreign Direct Investment', presented in the conference Beyond the Debt Crisis: Latin American Growth Strategies for the 1990s, Caracas, 28-30 June.
GONÇALVES, R. (1987), 'Competitividade Internacional, Vantagem Comparative e Empresas Multinacionals: a caso des exportaçoes brasileiras de manufaturados', *Pesquisa e Planeiamento Econômico*, 17, pp. 411-36.
GORDON, L., and GROMMERS, E.L. (1962), *United States Manufacturing Investment in Brazil* (Graduate School of Business Administration, Harvard University, Boston, Mass.).
GRUBER, W., MENTA, D., and VERNON, R. (1967), 'The R & D Factor in International Trade and International Investment of the US', *Journal of Political Economy*, 75, pp. 20-37.
GUIMARAES, E. A., MALAN, P., and AVAUJO, J. T. jun., (1982), 'Changing International Investment Strategies: The "New Forms" of Foreign Investment in Brazil' (PIEA-INPES, Rio de Janeiro).
HELLEINER, G. K. (1973), 'Manufactured Exports from Less Developed Countries and Multinational Firms', *Economic Journal*, 83/329, pp. 21-47.
—— (1988), 'Direct Foreign Investment and Manufacturing for Export in Developing Countries: A Review of the Issues', in Sidney Dell (ed.), *Policies for Development* (Macmillan, London), pp. 125-53.
—— (1990), 'Transnational Corporations, Direct Foreign Investment, and Economic Development', in H. Chenery and T. N. Srinivasan (eds.), *Handbook of Development Economics* (North-Holland, Amsterdam).
—— and LAVERGNE, R. (1979), 'Intra-Firm Trade and Industrial Exports to the US', *Oxford Bulletin of Economics and Statistics* 41/4, pp. 297-312.
HILL, H., and JOHNS, B. (1985), 'The Role of Direct Foreign Investment in Developing East Asian Countries', *Weltwirtschaftliches Archiv*, 121/2, pp. 355-81.
HORTA, M. H. (1985), 'Fontes de Crescimento das Exportaçoes Brasileiras na Década de Setenta', *Pesquisa e Planeiamento Econômico*, 13.

HUFBAUER, G. C., and ADLER, F. M. (1968), *Overseas Manufacturing Investment and the Balance of Payments* (US Treasury, Washington, DC).
HYMER, S. H. (1976), *The International Operations of National Firms: A Study of Direct Foreign Investment* (MIT Press, Cambridge, Mass.).
—— and ROWTHORN, R. (1970), 'Multinational Corporations and International Oligopoly: The Non-American Challenge', in C. P. Kindleberger (ed.), *The International Corporations, A Symposium* (MIT Press, Cambridge, Mass.).
IBGE (1987), *Estatisticas Historicas do Brasil* (IBGE, Rio de Janeiro).
JAMES, W. E., NAYA, S., and MEIER, G. M. (1987), *Asian Development, Economic Success and Policy Lessons* (International Center for Economic Growth, San Francisco).
JENKINS, R. (1979), 'The Export Performance of Multinational Corporations in Mexican Industry', *Journal of Development Studies*, 15/2, pp. 89–107.
JO, S. H. (1976), 'The Impact of Multinational Firms in Employment and Incomes: The Case Study of South Korea' (International Labour Office, Geneva).
—— (1988), 'Foreign Direct Investment and Industrial Growth in South Korea' (OECD Development Centre, Paris).
KATZ, J. (1984), 'Domestic Technological Innovations and Dynamic Comparative Advantage: Further Reflections on a Comparative Case Study Program', *Journal of Development Economics*, 16/1–2, pp. 13–38.
KINDLEBERGER, C. P. (1969), *American Business Abroad* (Yale University Press, New Haven, Conn.).
KNICKERBOCKER, F. T. (1973), *Oligopolistic Reactions and the Multinational Enterprise* (Harvard University Press, Cambridge, Mass.).
KOJIMA, K. (1973), 'A Macroeconomic Approach to Foreign Direct Investment', *Hitotsubashi Journal of Economics*, 14/1, pp. 1–21.
—— (1975), 'International Trade and Foreign Investment: Substitutes or Complements', *Hitotsubashi Journal of Economics*, 16/1, pp. 1–12.
KOO, B. Y. (1985), 'Korea', in J. H. Dunning (ed.), *Multinational Enterprises, Economic Structure and International Competitiveness* (Wiley & Sons, Chichester), pp. 281–308.
KRUGMAN, P. R. (1984), 'Import Protection as Export Promotion: International Competition in the Presence of Oligopoly and Economies of Scale', in H. Kierzkonski (ed.), *Monopolistic Competition and International Trade* (Clarendon Press, Oxford).
LALL, S. (1978), 'Transnational Corporations, Domestic Enterprises and Industrial Structure in Host LDCs', *Oxford Economic Papers*, 30/2, pp. 217–48.
—— and STREETEN, P. (1977), *Foreign Investment, Transnationals and Developing Countries* (Westview Press, Boulder, Col.).
LEVY, B. (1988), 'The Determinants of Manufacturing Ownership in Less Developed Countries', *Journal of Development Economics*, 28/2, pp. 217–32.
LIPSEY, R., and KRAVIS, I. (1987), 'The Competitiveness and Comparative Advantage of US Multinationals, 1957–84', *Banca Nazionale del Lavoro Quarterly Review*, 161.
MASCOLO, J. L., and BRAGA, H. (1985), 'Caracteristicas Tecnologicas do Setor Industrial Exportador', *Pesquisa e Planeiamento Econômico*, 15.
MASON, R. H. (1973), 'Some Observations on the Choice of Technology by Multi-

national Firms in Developing Countries', *Review of Economics and Statistics*.
MORLEY, S., and SMITH, G. (1971), 'Import Substitution and Foreign Investment in Brazil', *Oxford Economic Papers*, 23/1, pp. 120–35.
—— 'The Effects of Changes in the Distribution of Income on Labor, Foreign Investment and Growth in Brazil', in A. Stepan (ed.), *Authoritarian Brazil* (Yale University Press, New Haven, Conn.).
—— (1977), 'Limited Search and the Technological Choices of Multinational Firms in Brazil', *Quarterly Journal of Economics*, 91/2, pp. 263–88.
NAETKE, P., and NEWFARMER, R. S. (1985), 'Transnational Corporations, Trade Propensities and Transfer Pricing', in *Transnational Corporations and International Trade: Selected Issues* (UNCTC, New York).
NAYGAR, D. (1978), 'Transnational Corporations and Manufactured Exports from Poor Countries', *Economic Journal*, 88/349, pp. 59–84.
—— (1983), 'International Relocation of Production and Industrialization in LDCs', *Economic and Political Weekly*, 18/31, PE13–PE26.
NEWFARMER, R., and MARSH, L. (1981), *Industrial Interdependence and Development: A Study of International Linkages and Industrial Performance in Brazil* (University of Notre Dame Press, Notre Dame, Ind.).
—— and MUELLER, W. (1985), *Multinational Corporations in Brazil and Mexico: Structural Sources of Economic and Non-Economic Power* (US Senate, Washington, DC.).
NUNES, W. P. (1988), 'Foreign Direct Investment and Industrial Development in Mexico' (OECD Development Centre, Paris).
OECD (1987), *Recent Trends in International Direct Investment* (Committee on International Investment and MNEs, OECD, Paris).
OZAWA, T. (1975), 'Peculiarities of Japan's Multinationalism: Facts and Theories', *Banca Nazionale del Lavoro Quarterly Review*, 115.
—— (1979), 'International Investment and Industrial Structure: New Theoretical Implications from the Japanese Experience', *Oxford Economic Papers*, 31/1, pp. 72–92.
—— PUTIENNIK, M., and NAGARAJA RAO, K. (1976), 'Japanese Direct Investment in Brazil', *Columbia Journal of World Business*, 11/3, pp. 107–16.
PHELPS, D. M. (1936), *The Migration of Industry to South America* (McGraw-Hill, New York).
PINTO, M. B. P. (1984), 'Efeitos Alocativos de Politica de Promoçao de Exportaçoes: uma reavaliaçao', *Pesquisa e Planeiamento Econômico*, 14.
REUBER, G., CROOKELL, H., EMERSON, M., and GALLAIS-HAMONNE, G. (1973), *Private Foreign Investment in Development* (OUP, London).
SAFARIAN, A. E. (1983), 'Trade-Related Investment Issues', in W. R. Cline (ed.), *Trade Policy in the 1980s* (Institute for International Economics, Washington, DC), pp. 611–38.
SEKIGUSHI, S. (1979), *Japanese Direct Foreign Investment* (Atlantic Institute of International Affairs, Macmillan, London).
SEPULVEDA, B., and CHUMANCERO, A. (1973), *La Inversion Estrangeira en México*, (Fondo de Cultura Economica, Mexico).
SUAREZ, M. A. (1983), 'A Evoluçao de Industria Petroquimica Brasileire e o Modelo Tripartite de Empresa', *Revista de Economia Politica*, 3.

TEITEL, S. (1984), 'Technology Creation in Semi-Industrial Economies', *Journal of Development Economics*, 16/1–2, pp. 39–62.
—— and THOUMI, F. (1986), 'From Import Substitution to Exports: The Manufacturing Exports Experience of Argentina and Brazil', *Economic Development and Cultural Change*, 34/3, pp. 455–90.
TYLER, W. (1976), *Manufactured Export Expansion and Industrialization in Brazil* (Mohr, Tübingen).
—— (1983), 'The Anti-Export Bias in Commercial Policies and Export Performance: Some Evidence from the Recent Brazilian Experience', *Weltwirtschaftliches Archiv*, 119/1, pp. 97–108.
UNCTAD (1987), *Trade and Development Report* (United Nations, Geneva).
UNCTC (1983), *Transnational Corporations in World Development* (United Nations, New York).
UNIDO (1987), *Industry and Development, Global Report 1987* (United Nations, Vienna).
VERNON, R. (1966), 'International Investment and International Trade in the Product Cycle', *Quarterly Journal of Economics*, 80/1, pp. 190–207.
—— (1979), 'The Product Cycle Hypothesis in a New International Environment', *Oxford Bulletin of Economics and Statistics*, 41/4, pp. 255–68.
WILLMORE, L. (1985), 'Estudo Comparativo do Desempenho des Empresas Estrangeiras e Multinacionais no Brasil', *Pesquisa e Planeiamento Econômico*, 15.
—— (1987a), 'Controle Estrangeiro e Concentraçao na Industria Brasileira', *Pesquisa e Planeiamento Econômico*, 17.
—— (1987b), 'Transnationals and Foreign Trade', *Anais XV° Encontro de ANPEC*, Salvador.
WORLD BANK (1983), *Politica Industrial e Exportaçao de Manufaturados do Brasil* (Fundaçao Getulio Vargas, Rio de Janeiro).
YOSHINO, M. Y. (1974), 'The Multinational Spread of Japanese Manufacturing Investment Since World War II', *Business History Review*, 48/3, pp. 357–81.
ZONINSEIN, J. (1986), 'Politica Industrial, Joint Ventures e Exportaçoes', *Instituto de Economia Industrial* (UFRJ, Rio de Janeiro).

NOTES

1. UNCTC (1983), pp. 136, 350–1.
2. See e.g. the contributions of Helleiner (1973) and Naygar (1978).
3. Indeed, as noted in a recent survey on international investment, 'current modes of thinking and analysis have not yet absorbed the full implications of the fact that a large proportion of various international economic transactions takes place within transnational corporations', cf. UNCTC (1983), p. 6.
4. Helleiner (1984), p. 4, emphasis in the original.
5. See e.g. Balassa (1986).
6. By and large the very extensive literature on the costs and benefits of FDI is addressed to assessing the net effects of such changes in resource allocation. See e.g. Lall and Streeten (1977).

7. Positively or negatively depending e.g. on whether it displaces or supplements domestic savings; see Areskoug (1976).
8. As extensively discussed in Lall (1978).
9. Cf. Willmore (1987a), p. 163 which considers a sample of 55,730 firms responsible for about 95% of domestic industrial production. A 'foreign' firm is defined as having a foreign share of at least 10% of total capital. For other samples, usually covering the largest 500 or 1,000 firms, the foreign share is much larger, as e.g. in one study, in which this share for 1977 was estimated at 44%, cf. UNCTC (1983), p. 136.
10. According to figures from the Industrial Census for 1980, considering as foreign firms those with at least a 15% foreign ownership share. Cf. Nunes (1988), p. 38.
11. See UNCTC (1983), p. 350.
12. Falling to 5.4% in 1972. See Jenkins (1979), p. 90.
13. CEPAL (1971), p. 335. Indications are that export propensity was even lower for Mexican MNC affiliates: a study for 1966–7 found that sales abroad represented between 3% and 5% of total sales (Sepulveda and Chumacero, 1973, p. 77).
14. Fajnzylber and Tarrago, see Jenkins (1979), p. 93.
15. Similar comparisons were performed by Lall and Streeten (1977), pp. 133–5, for a sample of LDCs—Kenya, Jamaica, India, Iran, Colombia, and Malaysia. They found that transnationality had no impact on export propensities.
16. Willmore (1987b). Similar findings are reported by Willmore (1985).
17. CEPAL (1985).
18. While majority-owned US investments in Latin America are quite diversified, in Asia they are heavily concentrated on light electrical equipment. See Blomström (1987), p. 22.
19. Evidence related to the comparison between the trade orientation of affiliates and of domestic firms in larger East Asian economies tends to indicate that MNCs are more outward oriented than domestic firms, at least during the early 1970s: Cohen (1975) has shown e.g. that foreign subsidiaries exported a higher proportion of sales than domestic firms in Korea, and the same proportion in Taiwan. These findings were confirmed by Jo (1976) for Korea, in which foreign subsidiaries were reported to be 'substantially more export oriented than local firms'. See Jenkins (1979, p. 91). This notion has been challenged by Koo (1985), however.
20. See Koo (1985, p. 293) and Jo (1988, p. 30 *passim*).
21. Nunes (1988), p. 269.
22. Some of the main issues of this subsection have been outlined in Fritsch and Franco (1988).
23. There are cases of very high values for Ω, as for Singapore (83% in 1978), very low values as e.g. in Korea (11% in 1975), and intermediate values as in Brazil (27.5% in 1980) and Mexico (27.2% in 1980). These values are obtained from a variety of methods and samples, using different concepts of the foreign firm, and for this reason should not be used with the ratios of Table 1, which refer to majority-owned US MNC affiliates. This inconsistency turns out to be important for purposes of calculation since there are sharp differences as

regards, e.g. trade orientation of foreign subsidiaries of different nationalities. In Singapore e.g. the export propensity of Japanese firms was only 37.1% (in 1973), while for US firms it was 93.2% (in 1977), cf. Hill and Johns (1985, p. 367). If we perform, even in this precarious form, the computation of equation (1) to find the 'openness' of domestic firms, assuming all foreign firms behave like US MOFAs and the Ωs have not changed over time, the result is hardly surprising: in 1970 domestically owned Korean firms are not much more trade orientated than Mexican ones (15.4 against 12.0%). From 1970 to 1983 the aggressive export-promotion policies in Korea increased domestic firms' trade orientation to 60.1%. A very significant 'opening' is also observed for Brazil (2.65 to 9.3%). In Mexico a significant 'closure' is observed.
24. The importance of firm size as a determinant of ownership patterns, in particular that larger size is positively related to the extent of foreign ownership, has been asserted recently by Levy (1988).
25. See Safarian (1983).
26. European firms belong in this wave of foreign investment to the extent that they went multinational by means of a process described as 'oligopolistic response' by Knickerbocker (1973). The 'European Response' to the 'American Challenge' bore, however, very much the same characteristics as the latter, cf. Hymer and Rowthorn (1970).
27. Dunning (1979)
28. Bandera and White (1968), p. 119.
29. Vernon (1966).
30. As forcefully argued e.g. by Bergsten et al. (1978, p. 97).
31. Yoshino (1974) and Sekigushi (1979).
32. The pioneer contribution is Kojima (1973). See, however, Kojima (1975) and Ozawa (1975, 1979) for an extended discussion.
33. The fact that these firms chose FDI instead of establishing themselves in the expanding sectors at home has also to do with more favourable factor endowments abroad and the 'thin' technological gap between them and host countries' industries and not with the existence of firm-specific factors which usually explain FDI within oligopolistic structures. Cf. Ozawa (1979, p. 80 ff).
34. See e.g. Lipsey and Kravis (1987).
35. Blomström et al. (1988, p. 11).
36. See e.g. Vernon's 'global scanners' (1979).
37. Clegg (1987, p. 8).
38. As shown by Morley and Smith (1971).
39. Rigorously, classic ISI started from the collapse of the international economy in the early 1930s. Except for a brief exceptional period in the immediate aftermath of the war, it is fair to say that foreign-exchange shortages had been endemic since. An account can be found e.g. in the classic study of Bergsman (1970) and also Fishlow (1972).
40. This emerges from surveys such as Gordon and Grommers (1962) on US investments and also from Ozawa et al. (1976) on Japanese investments.
41. This pattern of direct investment can actually be traced, albeit on a far less important scale, to the inter-war years. On this see Phelps (1936).

42. Von Doellinger and Cavalcanti (1975, pp. 56–7) report a Spearman rank correlation of 0.60 between sectoral growth rates in manufacturing for 1967–73 and the share of foreign capital in each sector.
43. The outstanding early example is the Usiminas steel plant organized as a joint venture of the Brazilian government and Japanese associates in 1957. For the more extensive experience in petrochemicals see Guimaraes *et al.* (1982) and Suarez (1983).
44. For a general discussion of the extent to which the incentives for joint ventures were applied see Guimaraes *et al.* (1982, p. 75).
45. Zoninsein (1986, p. 17).
46. On patterns of competition in Brazilian industry during this period see Morley and Smith (1973) and FINEP (1977).
47. The sample of Table 4 is responsible for nearly 95% of Brazilian industrial production, cf. Willmore (1987*a*, p. 162).
48. Note that the share of production accounted for by foreign firms would fall to only 23.2% in case just those with over 50% non-resident's participation were considered.
49. Willmore (1987*a*, p. 167).
50. See Batista (1986) and Franco (1988).
51. Tyler (1983, pp. 97–108) observed anti-export biases in 51 out of 58 industrial sectors in 1977.
52. This analysis was carried out at a three-digit level of the SITC classification and considers 11 trading regions (Tyler (1976) and Horta (1985)).
53. See Gonçalves (1987, pp. 418–20).
54. See CEPAL (1983).
55. Changes in both exports and imports in more recent years should also be attributed to the collapse of domestic demand, especially for capital goods following the debt crisis.
56. See e.g. Tyler (1983), World Bank (1983), Baumann Neves (1985), Teitel and Thoumi (1986), and also Pinto (1984).
57. A phrase coined in Krugman (1984).
58. Teitel and Thoumi (1986, p. 163).
59. As shown e.g. in Lipsey and Kravis (1987).
60. Defined for each industrial sector as the ratio between the share of that sector in the country's total manufactured exports to that sector's share in world manufactured exports.
61. See Gonçalves (1987, p. 422ff). Technology-intensive sectors are mechanical equipment, transport material, rubber, chemicals, pharmaceuticals, cosmetics, and plastics. Non-technology-intensive sectors are non-metallic minerals, metallurgy, iron and steel, wood products, furniture, paper, leather, textiles, clothing, and footwear. The RCA index for foreign firms is calculated for each sector as the ratio between manufactured exports from that sector as a proportion of total manufactured exports by foreign firms and the share of that sector in total world exports of manufactures.
62. The proportion of US imports coming from American subsidiaries in Brazil in 1979 was 9.2% for textiles, 0.5% for footwear, 95.3% for electrical equipment, and 59.9% for non-electrical equipment (Helleiner and Lavergne, 1979).

63. On this see e.g. Teitel (1984) and Katz (1984).
64. Cf. Kindleberger (1969) and Hymer (1976). The existence of these disadvantages is by no means a hypothesis peculiar to this particular strain of theory but a widely recognized element in the so-called 'industrial organization' approach to the theory of FDI. See e.g. Caves (1982).
65. Of the sample of 77 foreign-investment projects in developing countries surveyed in Reuber *et al.* (1973) not less than 50 claimed not to have made any initial adaptation to local conitions.
66. On this see Morley and Smith (1977). For similar evidence for Mexico and the Philippines see Mason (1973).
67. Whether this has in fact induced greater adaptation efforts by foreign firms is an empirical question. The weak evidence available, based on the estimation of CES production functions for 10 Brazilian manufacturing sectors, suggests however, that foreign firms displayed greater capacity for technological adaptation to changing factor prices than domestic firms in the 1970s. See Mascolo and Braga (1985).
68. Dunning (1988, p. 100), emphasis in the original.
69. For an illustrative discussion of how a continuing dollar depreciation against the currencies of the leading surplus countries would increase the locational advantages of the semi-industrialized Latin American countries, see Fritsch and Franco (1988).

9

High-Technology Exports and Strategic Trade Policy in Developing Countries: The Case of Brazilian Aircraft

Richard Baldwin

IN the 1980s several developing countries have challenged the traditional stages of industrialization by jumping straight into the production and export of high-technology goods. With the help of a variety of policies, countries such as Brazil and Korea have managed to export products such as semiconductors and aircraft which traditionally have been considered the preserve of the most highly industrialized economies. Until recently, neoclassical economics could definitely condemn such targeting policies on purely theoretical grounds. As the argument goes, since prices reflect tastes, technology, and scarcity, the free market allocates resources optimally. Targeting merely misallocates resources by distorting price signals.

Recent developments in trade theory—collectively known as strategic trade policy—have removed the definitiveness from this condemnation. As it turns out there do exist situations where targeting makes perfect economic sense (for example Krugman 1981; Brander and Spencer 1983, 1985; and Venables 1985 and Krugman 1986). Industries marked by imperfect competition and significant scale economies may offer firms pure economic profits (rents) that will be divided among home and foreign producers. In such situations trade policy can take on a strategic role. Since governments have tools (for example subsidies) which firms do not, intervention can help firms commit to strategies that would not otherwise be credible. This commitment, in turn, can tilt the international playing-field in favour of the home firm, allowing the home firm to grab a larger share of world markets and profits. Under certain conditions, a subsidy or tariff can shift enough additional rents to the home country actually to pay for itself, making the home country as a whole better off.

However, here we must make an important distinction; theory tells us that trade policies *may* increase home welfare, not that they must; and certainly not that government-chosen policies are *likely* to do so. On the contrary, if strategic trade policies work at all, they typically work because the rent gains to politically well-organized corporations and unions outweigh the losses to dispersed consumers or taxpayers. Political economy theory would therefore lead us to expect that governments would systematically choose the wrong trade policies. Clearly then theory alone is incapable of telling us whether any given targeting policy constitutes a successful strategic trade policy, or rather is simply a redistribution of income from taxpayers and consumers to politically powerful groups.

This chapter exposits empirical and theoretical methods of determining whether any given trade policy is welfare-improving or not. As an example of the empirical methodology discussed (the so-called calibration methodology), we evaluate empirically one of Brazil's high-tech targeting efforts—the EMB-120, an aircraft sold to commuter airlines mostly in the US. At first glance, the market for this commuter aircraft seems to match the original strategic trade policy situation almost exactly. There are only three serious competitors in the market (one Brazilian, one Swedish, and one Canadian). Their products are close substitutes, and are almost exclusively sold in third markets (so that domestic consumers are unaffected). Production technology is marked by large economies of scale, both static and dynamic. However the prima-facie evidence suggests that profit-shifting cannot justify the EMB-120. Production difficulties led to delays in introducing the plane; as a result it seems unlikely that the project will break even, much less earn above normal profits.

None the less, it is an industry with the possibility of significant spillovers. Yet the spill-overs are probably not of the most obvious type. There seems to be little correlation between success in one generation of commuter aircraft and success in another. The problems of the Brasilia (also called the EMB-120) arose despite the enormous success its manufacturer (Embraer) had with its 19-seater, the Bandeirante. Moreover, the Swedish plane is selling extremely well and is likely to turn a profit despite the fact that its manufacturer (SAAB) has never produced a commercial aircraft before.

On the other hand, the employees of Embraer involved in the Brasilia project probably are more productive than they would be in alternative jobs. Indeed in the case of the US, Katz and Summers (1988) found that employees of the aircraft industry enjoy a 20 per cent wage premium even after controlling for differences in observed measures of workers' skill and union effects. They go on to argue that such inter-industry wage differentials may justify strategic trade policy, even when profit-shifting does not. It is likely that such effects are operating in Brazil as well and we will argue that this type of spill-over may justify the project.

Another type of spill-over that we shall be concerned with here is human capital formation. The dynamic economies of scale in aircraft production are of the learning-by-doing type (Spencer 1981). Specifically, the learning is done by the production workers and engineers whose experience long outlasts the particular project. We argue that in such instances, simple cost-benefit analysis based on flows (profits, consumer surplus, and subsidies) can go seriously wrong, since in fact some of the subsidy gets capitalized in the form of worker experience.

In Section 1 we outline the logic of the two types of strategic trade policy which are relevant to the market in which the EMB-120 competes, and discuss theoretical and empirical criteria for evaluating targeting policies. In Section 2 we discuss the market in which the EMB-120 competes, present a model of the competition in that industry, and calibrate and simulate the model. This enables us to derive an estimate of the size of the implicit subsidy Embraer has received. Section 3 introduces a criterion for judging the dynamic spill-overs into human capital. The final section presents the conclusions.

1. THEORETICAL AND EMPIRICAL EVALUATION OF STRATEGIC TRADE POLICIES

There are several important theoretical considerations that can help us evaluate the advisability of any particular targeting policy. These points were first made by Gene Grossman, Jonathon Eaton, Avinash Dixit, and others (Krugman 1986 contains references and summaries by the authors of their own work in the field). The synthesis in Baldwin (1988c) is the basis for the reasoning in this section.

In order to facilitate our evaluation of strategic trade policy, it will be useful first carefully to work through the logic of such policies. There are basically two types of strategic trade policy: profit-shifting policies and strategic infant-industry policies. In both types, the key is that the domestic government possesses tools which the domestic firms do not and which can tilt the international 'playing-field' in favour of the domestic firm.

A. Profit-Shifting Policies

The Classic Example—'Battle-of-the-Sexes' in Large Commercial Jets
We first work with an extreme example from the industrialized countries: the market for 150-seat commercial jet aircraft. This market is about as far as one can get from the traditional trade-model assumptions of perfect competition and static, constant returns to scale. The production of a new jet aircraft is marked by massive R & D costs as well as dynamic scale economies. An enormous initial expenditure on R & D costs ($1–2 billion to design and test the airframe) is followed by a steep learning curve at the firm level (learning-by-doing reduces the time and expense of assembling the planes).

The sunk R & D costs and dynamic scale economies combine to ensure that only a small number of firms can profitably exist in the 150-seat market segment. Indeed there are currently only three potential producers in the Western world (Airbus Industrie, Boeing, and McDonnell-Douglas), and

	McDONNELL-DOUGLAS			
	Produce		Not Produce	
Produce	AB −$1bn.	MD −$1bn.	AB $5bn.	MD 0
Not Produce	AB 0	MD $5bn.	AB 0	MD 0

FIG. 1. Airbus versus McDonnell-Douglas in the 150-seat jet market

industry experts forecast that the market can only profitably support two of them. However, exactly because of the barriers to entry, the two firms that do produce the plane will earn above normal profits (or rents). That is, the returns realized on the resources used to make the jets will be higher than they would earn in alternative uses. Since Boeing is the industry leader, it was generally assumed that it would be one of the two. The focal point of the international competition was between Airbus and McDonnell-Douglas.

As a matter of history, Airbus won the competition. In 1985 McDonnell-Douglas stopped development work on its potential entrant, the MD3300. As of 1987, Airbus is the only manufacturer to be actually delivering a new 150-seater (the A320). Boeing is working on an advanced-technology competitor (based on a revolutionary unducted-fan engine) which it plans to introduce in the 1990s. Be that as it may, what we wish to do here is to delineate how the participation of the Airbus consortium governments (France, Germany, UK, and Spain) might have acted as a strategic deterrent, aiding Airbus's victory.

Leaving Boeing aside, the 150-seat market could profitably support only the US firm or the European firm. Clearly then there are four possible outcomes. These are depicted in Figure 1. Each cell represents one of the possible outcomes, and lists the profits each firm would realize if that outcome occurred. If both produced, both would lose money (upper left cell). If neither produced, a profitable opportunity would go unexploited (lower right cell). If Airbus produced but McDonnell-Douglas did not, Airbus would earn $5 billion in rents (this figure is a rough estimate based on a study by the US Office of Competitive Assessment; as long as the actual figure is greater than zero the analysis would go through) while McDonnell-Douglas gets nothing (upper right cell). Conversely, if McDonnell-Douglas produced and Airbus did not, Airbus would earn zero profits while McDonnell-Douglas got the $5 billion (lower left cell). Clearly the profit of each firm depends not only on its own actions, but also the action of its opponent. Game theorists call this type of strategic interaction the 'battle-of-the-sexes'.

With the outcomes and their respective pay-offs displayed in Figure 1, we are ready to examine the decision of Airbus (AB). Suppose that for some reason, AB was absolutely convinced that McDonnell-Douglas (MD) would produce regardless of AB's own decision. Under this supposition, if AB goes ahead with production it will lose $1 billion. If it does not produce it will not make any profits, but at least it will not lose money. Plainly, it is in AB's best interest not to produce, if it believes MD will. Of course if AB is convinced that MD will not produce, AB will.

Likewise if AB can somehow convince MD that it will produce the A320 whether or not MD also produces the MD3300 then the only rational thing for MD to do is to cede the market. If AB will definitely be in the market, then MD's going ahead with production would simply be throwing away the stockholders' money ($1 billion of it, to be specific).

What this analysis shows is that there are two stable equilibria. The first (upper right cell) is where the A320 is sold, but the MD3300 is not. To see that this is a stable outcome, note that if MD believes AB will produce, it would withdraw. And of course if MD withdraws, AB will actually produce. Thus neither firm would want to change its decision when the outcome occurred. Each firm is optimizing taking as given the action of the other firm. In game theory this is referred to as a Nash equilibrium. Congruently the lower left cell is also a stable outcome. Here AB does not produce since MD does, and MD produces since AB does not.

Which equilibrium occurs depends on which firm can convince the other that it will actually produce. MD can announce that it will produce irrespective of AB's decision. It may even initiate some research to back up its claim. However when AB is trying to decide whether to believe this announcement, it will examine MD's profits in all cases. Since MD is ultimately responsible to its investors, its threat to produce even if AB also produces is not believable. A company like MD cannot credibly commit itself to an action that will lose it money. MD's announcement is like a child's threat to hold its breath until it turns blue—disturbing but not believable.

Likewise if AB were a private company, it could not really convince MD that it would produce 'no matter what'. However, with four governments backing it up, AB's decision to produce the A320 (regardless of MD's actions) was taken as credible. The governments loaned AB money to pay for the R & D and start-up costs. The loans are to be paid back according to the success of the A320. Essentially the governments are investors who were willing to suffer the negative rate of return which would have occurred if MD had entered the market. Certainly the governments might have backed out if the losses were great enough. While it is unreasonable to assume that governments can credibly commit themselves to *any* action, their ability to commit is certainly greater than that of firms. Recall that the UK and France were the governments that went ahead with Concorde despite almost certain losses.

By now it should be evident that government intervention can affect the strategic interaction among firms. Governments have tools at their disposal (taxes, tariffs, subsidies, laws, etc.) that firms do not. These tools can help a domestic firm commit to a decision that would not be credible in absence of the government intervention. In a strategic game between home and foreign firms, this commitment can give an edge to the home firm—an edge which can result in home firms grabbing a larger share of the rents.

There is nothing new about the conclusion that a subsidy can give home firms larger market shares and profits. What is new about 'strategic' trade policies is that this may actually improve the overall welfare of the home country.

If the A320 and the MD3300 are roughly similar planes (they are) and the two firms are roughly equally efficient producers (they are), then the price of 150-seat planes would be roughly the same, regardless of who the producer is. Consumers world-wide would therefore be roughly indifferent as to the outcome of the game. However in one case the US gets the abnormally high profits, while in the other the rents go to Europe. The only thing we have left out is the cost of the subsidy. From a European perspective, any subsidy to Airbus is simply the left hand taking from the right. Airbus's workers and shareholders are, after all, Europeans. As a matter of fact, many industry analysts actually expect the government loans to be fully repaid, so the right hand will be taking it back. Thus taking into account European consumers, taxpayers, and profit-earners the targeting policy seems actually to have improved overall European welfare.

In the context of developing countries, the issue of a government's credibility looms larger than in the Europe–US example discussed above. For instance in the extreme case where an LDC government's policies were completely incredible, strategic trade policy would not be possible; in this case the government possesses no tools that the firm itself does not. To deal with this we could view the pay-offs in Figure 1 as expected pay-offs. That is, both the local and foreign firm would choose based on their expectations of what will actually happen. Thus McDonnell-Douglas might place 50 per cent probability on the outcome that if they produce Airbus will also produce, and 50 per cent probability on the outcome that if they produce the European government will back down. This implies that the expected value of McDonnell-Douglas producing is $2 billion (that is, $0.5(-1) + 0.5(5)$).

Credibility considerations might lead to a modification of the standard strategic trade policy conclusions. For instance, suppose a country is considering a project that is, by traditional criteria, slightly welfare-worsening. If the government gains credibility in the eyes of future potential competitors by actually undertaking the project, then this reputation-building aspect of undertaking a welfare-worsening project needs to be appended to the plus column of our cost-benefit analysis. The value of the reputation-building effect stems from the fact that the announcements of a more credible government will be more likely to deter foreign entry in the next generation of planes, or in other industries.

This is sometimes referred to as the 'mad dog' strategy since it is essentially an attempt to convince future potential competitors that the government is 'mad' enough to do things that do not appear to be in its self-interest. However, if such mad dog tactics are to work for a government that is known to be genuinely interested in welfare, then it must be that the very playing of the tactic provides additional information to competitors about the nature of the home government. In the case at hand, undertaking a money-losing airplane may work by convincing opponents that the Brazilian government views aircraft production as a national priority in itself. That is, it might convince an American firm that is considering entering the next generation that the Brazilian government gives very heavy weight in its objective function to the very fact that Brazil is producing airplanes. To examine such reputation effects formally, it is necessary to use a repeated-game framework rather than the one-shot game we analyse in this chapter.

This example from the developed countries spotlights the logic of how government-backed commitments can shift the outcome of strategic interaction between international competitors in favour of the home country. However, the decisions and outcomes are not so stark in most industries, especially in industries LDCs are likely to enter. In most industries government policies alter the outcome in a more continuous manner. It is important to study such a case, not only to increase the applicability of the analysis, but also to make more detailed statements about exactly when a strategic trade policy is likely to improve domestic welfare. The welfare evaluation of strategic trade policy was straightforward in the 'battle-of-the-sexes' case. As we shall see, it is not so in general.

Here we study an example which more closely resembles the Brazilian and Mexican targeting policies in the computer industries. Consider a home firm and foreign firm (say IBM) that are selling in the home market (say Brazil). Just to keep things simple suppose that the home firm does not export. With only two firms, the market will surely be marked by strategic interactions. The quantity the home firm will want to sell depends upon the level of imports. And conversely, the level of imports chosen by the foreign firm will depend upon the sales level chosen by the home firm.

Which price and market shares would result in such a situation? This is not an easy question. Home sales depend upon what the home firm conjectures foreign sales (imports) will be. But this conjecture depends on what the home firm thinks the foreign firm thinks about home sales, which depends upon what the foreign firm thinks the home firm thinks about foreign sales. This cycle can continue *ad infinitum*. In 1897 Cournot cut this Gordian knot by asserting that in the end the firms would settle down to the stable point where each was acting optimally taking as given the sales of the other firm.

Since we wish to quantify the effects of government intervention, it is useful to work out this idea in a more quantitative framework. Figure 2 facilitates the analysis. The home firm chooses output to maximize profits, taking as given that the level of imports is M^0. Graphically this is as if the home firm faced the home demand curve shifted inward by the quantity of imports. This schedule is referred to as the residual demand curve, RD^0. Corresponding to the residual demand curve is a marginal revenue curve,

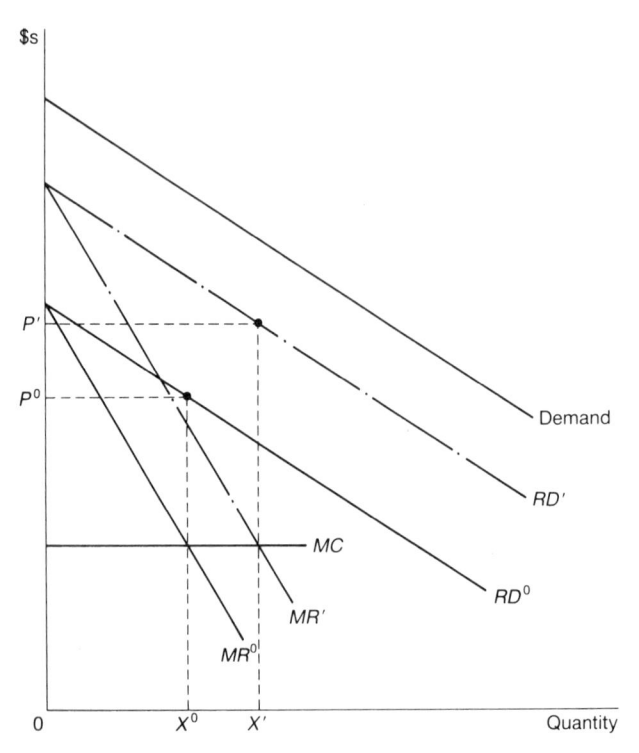

FIG. 2. The problem of a single home firm facing a single foreign firm

MR^0. As usual the profit-maximizing output choice of the home firm is given by the intersection of marginal revenue and marginal costs (X^0 in Figure 2). The price will be P^0 since that is the price at which the total sales (M^0 plus X^0) clear the market. Now suppose for some reason the foreign firm is induced to sell less to the home market (specifically, M'). Clearly there will be more home demand left over for the home firm, so the home firm will face a higher residual demand curve, RD', and a higher marginal revenue curve, MR'. Consequently the home firm will expand its output to X', partially offsetting the fall in imports. The market price will rise to P.

To clean up the diagram, we redraw the problem in Figure 3 but instead of including the marginal revenue and marginal cost curves, we simply draw in the locus of prices and home sales that correspond to the various levels of imports. We refer to this schedule as the pseudo-supply curve of the home firm. It is important to note that this schedule does not indicate that home sales are a function of price. Rather it is the plot of the optimal home sales and resulting prices which would be observed under various import levels.

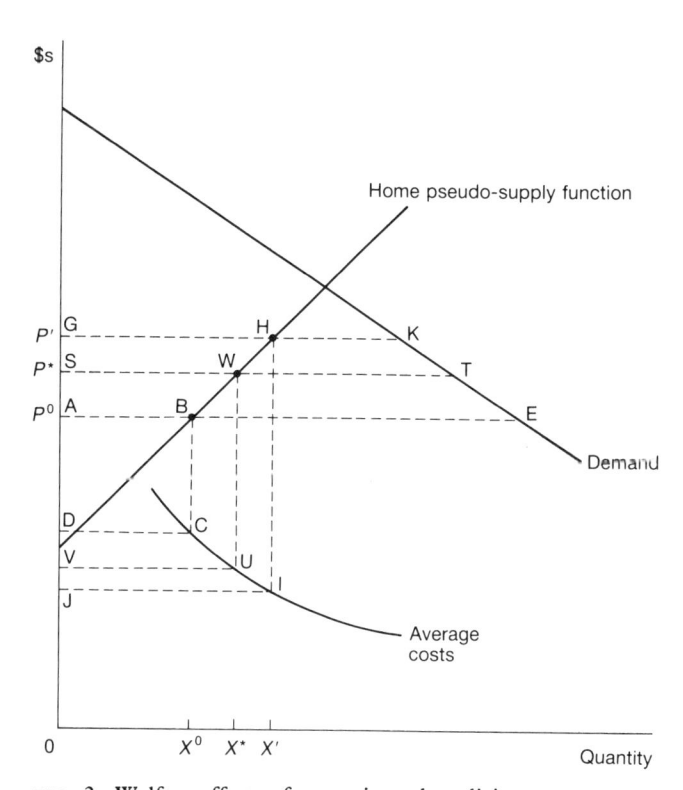

FIG. 3. Welfare effects of strategic trade policies

(P^0, X^0) and (P', X') are two points on the pseudo-supply curve. The import levels are given by the horizontal distance between the home pseudo-supply curve and the demand curve, that is, $M = Q - X$. Clearly the lower are imports the higher will be the home firm's profits. If imports are M^0 (equal to horizontal distance BE), then home profits would be ABCD. If instead imports were only M' (equal to HK), the home firm would find it optimal to sell more, would get a higher price and face lower average costs too. Thus home profits would be GHIJ.

In order to determine what the actual level of production, imports, and price will be, we need to examine the strategic interaction between the home and foreign firm.

Figure 2 shows how to calculate the best response (that is, the profit-maximizing production) of the home firm to any arbitrary level of foreign firm's sales, M. We graph the optimal X's as a function of M in Figure 4, and refer to the graph as the home best-response function. Of course (X^0, M^0) and (X', M') are two points on the home best-response function. A symmetric exercise could be performed for the foreign firm. That is we could ask: What is the profit-maximizing level of foreign sales given any level of home sales, X? Without explicitly working this problem out (it involves a straightforward repetition of the Figure 3 exercise, keeping X constant and finding the optimal M), we graph the profit-maximizing choices of M for any given level of X in Figure 4. We label this the foreign best-

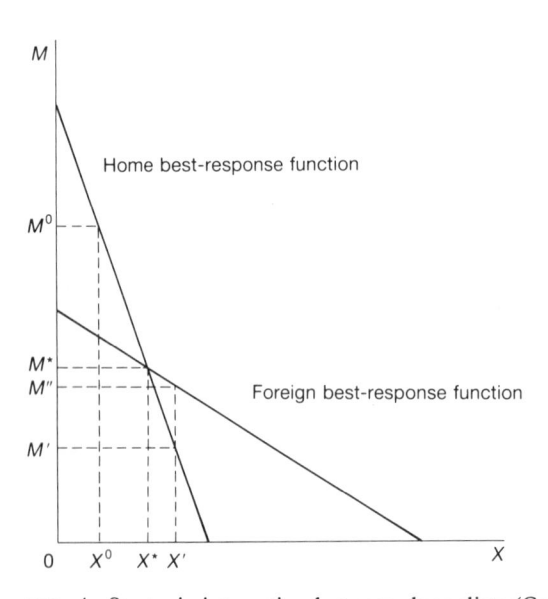

FIG. 4. Strategic interaction between duopolists (Cournot–Nash solution)

response function. It is downward-sloping because the less the home firm sells, the more the foreign firm will want to sell.

The intersection of the two best-response functions is a Nash equilibrium. At this point each firm is selling the profit-maximizing quantity, taking as given the sales of the other firm. That is, given that the foreign firm is producing M^*, the best response of the home firm is X^*. And given that the home firm is selling X^*, the foreign firm would find that its best response would be to produce M^*. Let us suppose that Cournot was right so that X^* and M^* are the home and foreign sales that would actually take place. This outcome can be represented in Figure 3 as X^*, Q^* (recall $Q^* = X^* + M^*$) and P^*.

As we saw above, home-firm profits would be higher if somehow it could get the foreign firm to sell only M' instead of M^*. Indeed let us imagine that the home firm announced that it would produce X' irrespective of the foreign firm sales. If the foreign firm believed this announcement, Figure 4 shows us that its best response would be to reduce its sales from M^* to M''. But in fact the foreign firm should not believe the announcement. The foreign firm would realize that if it continued selling M^*, the best thing for the home firm would be to sell only X^*—not the threatened X'. In other words, the foreign firm could deduce that the home firm's announcement was just a bluff.

What this shows is that in the duopoly case (just as in the aircraft example) there are outcomes that would be advantageous to the home firm which it can never reach due to its inability credibly to commit itself to certain actions. This is where trade policies take on a strategic dimension. While the home firm may not be able to force down imports to M' through its own actions, the home government certainly can through any number of trade policies. To be concrete, we shall concern ourselves with a quota which reduces imports to M'. To focus on the new aspects of strategic trade policy we assign the quota rents to the foreign firms.

We have already seen what effect the quota would have on home-firm profits. Again, there is absolutely nothing new in the result that a quota can boost the domestic firm's profits. What is different is that the quota may actually raise total domestic welfare as measured by the sum of consumer surplus and profits.

To see this, note that the quota raises the home price to P' from P^*, reducing consumer surplus by GKTS in Figure 3. Part of this consumer loss (GHWS) is directly offset by higher profits, so the question of whether the country gains on the whole from the quota boils down to the question of whether HKTW is larger than WHIJVU. It is our intent here to identify characteristics of industries in which such strategic protection will be more likely to benefit the home country.

Figure 3 is useful in organizing our discussion of criteria for theoretically evaluating strategic trade policies. The first requirement for the quota to be welfare-enhancing is that there actually are some above-normal profits to be had in the industry. In Figure 3 this was obviously the case since even without the policy, the price, P^0, was greater than average costs. If on the contrary the industry was so competitive that price was always driven to average costs, then there would be no rents to offset the consumer welfare loss. For example it might be the case that the American SST project was deterred in part by the commitment of the British and French governments to produce the Concorde. However since the market was not big enough for even a monopolist to cover costs, this targeting was a failure. The policy was successful in increasing Concorde's market share, but the larger market share corresponded to larger losses, not larger profits.

The second requirement is that the policy must actually succeed in reducing foreign sales. While a quota accomplishes this directly, other trade policies may not. For example the first jet launched by Airbus was the medium-range, wide-bodied A300. Despite the fact that the A300 was in the market first, Boeing went ahead to produce a close competitor, the 767. Here the subsidy failed to deter entry and as a result the A300 is likely to lose money (Baldwin and Krugman 1988). More recently, the US imposed a 100 per cent tariff against Toshiba lap-top computers. Since this market is marked by imperfect competition, the tariff failed to have the standard effect on the price of Toshiba's product. Indeed, the US retail price of the machines did not increase at all (at least not in New York City). Plainly if a trade policy fails to reduce imports (as it may in certain market structures) then there cannot possibly be strategic gains (although in the case of the tariff there would at least be the additional tariff revenue).

Thirdly, the home producer must not be too inefficient compared to the foreigners. Figure 3 shows an average-cost curve which is significantly lower than the price. If instead home average costs were high in relation to the price the potential for profit increase would be low. That is, WHIJVU would be small. To interpret this requirement, notice that if home average cost is high relative to the price, it must be that the home country has a strong comparative disadvantage in the good. We can therefore say that the third requirement for the quota to be beneficial is that the home country's comparative disadvantage is not too great.

Similarly the steeper is the average-cost curve the larger will be the UVJI area, and the more likely it is that the policy will be a success. A steep average-cost curve indicates large economies of scale (due either to large fixed costs or falling marginal costs). Moreover large economies of scale provide large entry barriers and so make it more likely that the industry is marked by significant rents. Thus the larger are the economies of scale, the more likely it is that the policy will improve welfare.

Next it is important that the home marginal costs do not rise in response to the policy. Certainly it is conceivable that unions would raise wage demands in response to the firm's higher profits. (It is commonly asserted that this occurred in the US steel industry.) In Figure 3 this would correspond to an upward shift of the pseudo-supply curve and a shift up of the average-cost curve. Both of these would tend to negate any gains from the policy.

Lastly, note that the size of HKTW depends on how large the initial import share was. If before the policy most of the demand was met by imports then very little of the price-induced consumer loss would be directly offset by home-firm profit gains (that is, GHWS would be small compared to GKTS). This would make it more unlikely that the strategic profit gain (WHIJVU) would offset HKTW. Moreover if the home firm is only supplying a small part of the market, then the cost savings, VUIJ, will likewise be small.

Before moving on to the next type of strategic trade policy, we note that Figure 3 can be used to show how *foreign* targeting can be harmful to the domestic economy. To take a common example, suppose that we are initially at the Nash equilibrium (X^*, M^*, P^*) and the foreign government provides an export subsidy to the foreign firm. With this backing the foreign firm can credibly increase its output, forcing the home firm to reduce its output. Just as a reduction in imports might improve overall home welfare, this subsidy-induced increase in import penetration might harm overall home welfare. Foreign targeting can be a beggar-thy-neighbour policy.

B. *Strategic Infant-Industry Protection*

The second type of strategic trade policies are strategic infant-industry policies. The traditional infant-industry argument asserts that providing temporary protection to a new industry may be good policy. As the argument goes, the protection provides a wall behind which the industry can gain experience, increasing its efficiency to the point where it is competitive with foreign firms even in the absence of the protection. This rather plausible-sounding argument has a fundamental flaw if capital markets are perfect. If firms have access to good capital markets, then they should themselves be willing to undergo a period of losses, provided that they expect to become profitable after an initial learning phase. Essentially the losses during the learning phase are simply a form of R & D investment. If the capital market is working well, firms should have no trouble financing even very large, very long start-up phases (witness the financing of the Chunnel and the telephone grid in the US). At least for industrialized countries, the general conclusion is that this counter-argument is correct and infant-industry arguments for protection are merely self-serving rationalizations. Introducing the possibility of strategic interactions, however, may change this conclusion. This point was first made by Krugman (1984) and Venables (1985).

Of course in most developing nations the capital market would be more accurately modelled as non-existent rather than as perfect. The traditional infant-industry argument thus is valid in those countries. None the less, the logic of strategic infant-industry protection is important to LDCs in two ways. It provides a possible motivation for subsidizing or protecting industries (such as Brazilian aircraft) that already have achieved world-class export performance. Also if this logic gains increasing acceptance in the industrialized countries, LDCs may face industrialized countries undertaking such policies, serving to increase the difficulty of LDCs breaking into high-tech sectors.

Again we illustrate the point with an example from the developed countries. One of the most prominent examples of a strategic infant-industry policy is the alleged Japanese targeting of the memory-chip segment of the semiconductor industry. According to many sources, the six large Japanese electronics firms agreed to an implicit 'buy Japanese' policy for dynamic random-access memory chips. This allegation has never been proven but the fact that Japan signed the 1986 Semiconductor Accord (admittedly under duress) has been interpreted as an admission of the policy's existence.

Since the production of random-access memory chips (RAMs) is marked by a very steep learning curve (cumulative production experience increases chip yield and thereby lowers marginal costs), the effect of this market-access restriction (MAR) was dramatic. The closing of the Japanese market (about a third of the world market) to US producers meant that each US firm sold fewer chips and each Japanese firm sold more chips than they would have without the MAR. Thus the MAR pushed the Japanese firms down their learning curves and the US firms up theirs. This shift in the relative marginal costs not only enabled the Japanese firms to gain a larger share of their home market, but also allowed them to grab larger market shares in the US and the rest of the world. Here import protection constituted export promotion.

To see this a little more carefully, we turn to Figure 5. This figure shows a learning curve for a typical Japanese RAM producer. The curve is downward-sloped since as production experience accumulates, marginal costs fall. For the sake of illustration, assume that the firm is planning to produce 50 million chips. Ignoring fixed costs and discounting, the total cost of making these 50 million chips is the sum of the marginal costs of making each one. Graphically, this corresponds to the area under the learning curve up to 50 million. Now we ask: What is the true cost of one more chip? The answer is simply the marginal cost of producing the last

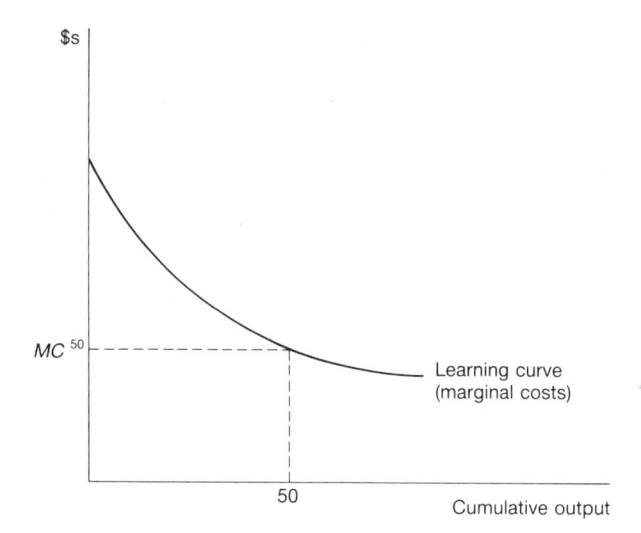

FIG. 5. A learning curve

unit, MC^{50}. Regardless of when the extra chip is actually produced, the increase in total costs will be MC^{50}.

Having made this point it is obvious how a MAR can allow the Japanese firms credibly to announce higher capacities. The MAR credibly ensures them a higher cumulative experience (since their home market is protected) and therefore lower marginal costs. The lower marginal costs imply that it will be profitable to have a larger share of the non-Japanese market as well. In fact according to the estimates in Baldwin and Krugman (1987), in the absence of the MAR there would have been no Japanese production of 16K RAM chips.

In principle the MAR could have improved overall Japanese welfare in exactly the same way as a profit-shifting policy could. That is, the MAR allowed the Japanese firms to commit credibly to building larger RAM-production capacity which in turn forced US companies to scale back their capacity plans. If there had been above normal profits to be made in this industry (there were not), the MAR would have enabled the Japanese firms to grab a larger share of them. Additionally if transport costs had been significant in RAMs (they are not), then the MAR could have improved Japanese welfare by ensuring that more of the world's production was done in Japan so that less of the transportation costs would be borne by Japanese customers.

In actual fact, this is an example of a failed targeting policy. It is instructive to see how so startling a success in winning a share of the market could actually be welfare-worsening. As it turned out, this industry was so competitive (at least during the 16K RAM generation), that no firm seems to have made profits. The MAR may have resulted in the Japanese chip producers grabbing a larger share of *losses* not profits. Furthermore it appears that at least in 16K RAMs the Japanese firms were 10–15 per cent less efficient than US producers, so that the MAR increased the world market share held by the country with the comparative disadvantage. The result was higher prices world-wide which harmed consumers world-wide.

The theoretical criteria by which such policies should be judged are identical to those listed for profit-shifting policies. As we have mentioned, many of the conditions for protection to be welfare-improving were absent in the 16K RAM industry. Japan had a comparative disadvantage in chips and the industry was intensely competitive.

The last caveat we mention in evaluating strategic infant-industry policies concerns the shape of the learning curve. While almost all products face downward-sloped learning curves at some point of their life cycle, extremely few industries have learning curves for which strategic infant-industry arguments apply. For example when a factory is first built some trial-and-error learning is usually necessary to get the kinks out of the production process. As production experience accumulates, the learning-by-doing advances and marginal costs fall. In most industries, this learning relatively quickly irons out the kinks so that the marginal cost curve is flat beyond a certain cumulative experience level. That is, further experience does not reduce marginal costs.

In a few highly unusual industries, such as semiconductors and aircraft, the learning curve is downward-sloped even at the end of the product life. In the case of aircraft this is due to the enormous complexity of the product together with the fact that even the most successful planes involve the production of only a few hundred units. Semiconductors are complex and have product life cycles of only a few years.

Now consider the effects of a domestic MAR on a domestic firm facing a normal learning curve. As before, the restriction implies that the home firm will have greater cumulative production at the end of the product life. But the impact of this additional learning on the firm's true marginal cost is zero. In this case the MAR will not help the home firm compete in export markets, so it will not help the firm to grab a larger share of world-wide profits. Thus one condition for a strategic infant-industry policy to be beneficial is that it must be applied to industries in which significant learning-by-doing is expected to take place right up to the end of the product life. Very few industries meet this requirement.

In summary, many industries face learning curves. Few, however, face the type of learning curves to which the logic of strategic infant-industry protection can be applied.

C. The Calibration Methodology

The logic of strategic trade policy provides a sound theoretical reason for believing that the Brazilian subsidy of the EMB-120 may have constituted a welfare-improving policy. However, this need not be the case as we saw above; indeed we have good political-economy reasons for believing that it may not be welfare improving. In this type of situation, empirical research is essential.

Unfortunately, empirical evaluation of these policies is inherently difficult for three principal reasons. First, there is no general agreement on how to model imperfect competition theoretically (and model choice matters). Secondly, crucial data on firm-specific costs, prices, and market shares are often unavailable, unreliable, or unobservable. Lastly, targeting can result in non-marginal industry changes so standard empirical tools are often of little use. In particular, due to the possibility of hysteresis, small changes in policies can lead to non-standard results in the presence of sunk costs such as the R & D expenditures on the development of an airframe (see Baldwin 1988a).

There really is no solution to the first problem. The researcher must simply work with the most sensible model for the particular industry. Re-evaluating the policy under a variety of theoretical assumptions can improve the credibility of the analysis. However, there is as yet no formal way of choosing between models when they yield different results.

The second and third problems have been addressed by methodology introduced in late 1985 by Dixit (1987) and Baldwin and Krugman (1988). The standard procedure is to specify a partial equilibrium model (that involves a small number of parameters) of the imperfect competition in an industry. Estimates of some of these parameters, such as demand elasticities and learning elasticities, are taken directly from existing industry studies. Other parameters are imputed by 'calibrating' the model to the historically observed base case. This calibration essentially involves choosing the remaining parameters so that the model just reproduces the historically observed prices, outputs, and market shares. This methodology was borrowed from the computable general equilibrium models common in development economics.

The model is then set up on a computer and the researcher runs a number of 'what-if' simulations. In cases such as Baldwin and Krugman (1988), the question asked is: What would the semiconductor industry have looked like without the targeting policy? In particular what would have happened to prices, profits, government revenue, and market shares in the absence of government intervention? In cases where there was no targeting, the researcher attempts to quantify the positive and normative impact of such policies on the industry. Dixit's work (1987) is an example of the latter approach.

While this methodology is far from fully satisfactory, it constituted a big improvement over the existing informal speculation and unapplied theorizing. The methodology has several very attractive features. It is relatively easy to apply and its data requirements are minimal. For many data-scarce industries, calibration would appear to be the researcher's only option. A number of studies have increased the realism of the calibration methodology, most notable are Levinsohn (1987) and Lambson and Richardson (1987). While none of these papers manages actually to evaluate policies, they show how more sophisticated theoretical and empirical considerations can be implemented.

The major drawback with the methodology is that it is essentially estimation with zero degrees of freedom. This problem can be overcome only if sufficient data are available (Baldwin 1988*b*). Thus in some sense the calibration methodology is a second-best approach forced upon us by the lack of readily accessible, reliable data.

2. THE MARKET FOR 30–40-SEATER COMMUTER AIRCRAFT

A wide variety of commuter aircraft are sold, ranging in size from nine to 100 seats. The driving force behind the expansion of this market is booming demand in the recently deregulated US airline industry. The deregulation ended direct government allocation of air routes among airlines. The airlines have responded by running flights more frequently and to more destinations using smaller planes. Also many have adopted a hub-and-spoke routing system which similarly increases the demand for small aircraft. The rise of air travel in the developing world provides an additional source of demand growth. The anticipated market deregulation in European air travel will probably also give the commuter aircraft industry a further boost.

Market segments
Any division of this large industry into product segments is, of course, open to debate. The 30–40-seat range is a product class that is well recognized in the industry. One can argue, however, that somewhat larger or smaller planes are sufficiently similar in size and range to provide competition. On the smaller side a US regulation interferes. The FAA requires a flight attendant on planes with twenty or more seats. Given the importance of the US market, manufacturers have found it profitable to produce 19-seaters

and planes with more than thirty seats. On the upside, the ATR42, a 42-seater produced by Aerospatiale of France and Aeritalia of Italy, might have provided some competition. However as it turned out production and technical problems have kept the ATR42's sales to limited quantities.

In the 30–40-seat range, there are five aircraft currently sold. Two (the Shorts 'flying box cars' 330 and 360) are based on the technology of the 1960s. They are unpressured (and thus must fly in the rougher air below 10,000 feet compared to a cruising altitude of 15–20,000 feet for the other three), fly slower, and have engines which were designed with 1960's fuel prices in mind. We take these aspects, in addition to the fact that their selling price is 30 per cent below the more recent models, as sufficient to exclude them from our market segment. The other three are modern turbo-props introduced in the mid-1980s primarily to service the newly deregulated US market.

Government support

Government backing has been important in the production of all three of the modern 30–40-seaters: the EMB-120, the SF-340, and the Dash-8. Embraer was founded in 1969 by the Brazilian air force which viewed it as necessary for national security reasons. It is still a government-owned enterprise which reinvests all its profits and occasionally receives infusions of additional funds from the Brazilian government. A special clause in the Brazilian tax code effectively subsidizes the purchase of non-voting Embraer shares by other Brazilian companies. On the whole Embraer has been quite successful, having built more than 3,500 planes (mostly the 19-seat Banderainte and a 2-seat, single-engine trainer called the Tucano). There is also some evidence that the EMB-120's success in the US market was due to a subsidy. In the US, the Brazilian firm accounts for 58 per cent of all sales since 1985. However, almost half of this is due to a single sale of fifty planes to Texas Air. According to de Havilland and Saab the price for these EMB-120s was 'ridiculously low' and 'unrealistic'. Furthermore both competitors accused the Brazilians of dumping and violating the OECD guide-lines on export financing of aircraft.

While none of this constitutes hard evidence it seems important to attempt to capture such a subsidy. What we have done is to calibrate the base case on the assumption that the Brazilian government provided a 10 per cent labour subsidy to Embraer. This figure was chosen since it is the optimal subsidy. That is, given that the plane would be produced, a 10 per cent subsidy maximizes the sum of profits net of the subsidy cost. Thus the net loss to Brazil including the 10 per cent subsidy is a lower bound; if the actual subsidy were greater or lesser, the net loss would be even greater.

The Canadian government has heavily subsidized de Havilland in the past; however, the firm was recently sold to Boeing for a nominal price.

While no direct evidence of a deal has come to light, it appears that the sale may have involved an implicit market-access restriction. In any case, either because of such a restriction, or some other reason, the Dash-8 seems to have a 100 per cent share in the non-negligible Canadian market, while its share of the US market is less than half of that. As we saw above in the 16K RAM example, in the case of unexhausted dynamic economies of scale, such import protection can be export promotion.

Saab-Scania of Sweden is a private company that manufactures, *inter alia*, military aircraft. The SF-340 was initially a joint venture between Saab and the US firm Fairchild. Shortly after the first SF-340 was delivered in 1984, Fairchild withdrew from the partnership due to financial difficulties. (If an aircraft ever yields positive net revenue it does so only after three to five years.) The Fairchild end of production (principally the wings) was transferred to Sweden in 1986. The Swedish government extended a 'loan' to Saab which is to be repaid according to the success of the SF-340. Of course a performance-related loan is actually a form of equity participation and should be considered as a strategic subsidy since it is unlikely that a similar loan would have been offered by private sources.

Industry evolution
The first deliveries of the SF-340 and the Dash-8 were made in 1984. The first delivery of the EMB-120 was made the following year. Table 1 shows deliveries and orders as of 1987. One aspect of the time-pattern of sales in Figure 1 is observed for most new planes. Deliveries of aircraft typically follow a front-loaded bell-shaped curve. This is due both to a 'wait-and-see' attitude on the part of purchasers, and to problems of getting production up to capacity on the part of producers.

The EMB-120 was introduced late and has struggled to bring its market share up to that of Saab and de Havilland. Saab has estimated that total sales in this market segment will attain 1,100 over the twenty-year period implying average sales of fifty-five per year. Based on the information in Table 1, we assume that the EMB-120 has 33 per cent of the total market, the SF-340 gets 32 per cent, and the remaining 35 per cent goes to the Dash-8. However these market shares hide the fact that, as far as the open market (the world market exclusive of Canada, Sweden, and Brazil) is concerned, the EMB-120 and the SF-340 are the clear leaders with 39 and 55 per cent respectively.

Table 2 shows that the pattern of consumption is heavily dominated by the US and to a lesser extent Europe. There are two salient points here. First the preponderance of the US market explains why the planes have been designed to compete in that market. Secondly, except in the case of de Havilland, the home countries are negligible consumers of planes, so the issue of domestic consumer surplus can be ignored in Brazil and Sweden.

Table 1. Deliveries and orders by firm

	1984	1985	1986	1987	Total deliveries	Claimed orders
EMB-120	0	11	16	33	60	138
SF-340	11	29	36	32	108	132
DASH-8	2	21	36	27	86	147

Source: Saab Aircraft Division.

Table 2. Consumption by market as of 1987 (%)

USA	57.6
Europe	16.1
Canada	14.6
Sweden	3.1
Brazil	1.4
Rest of World	7.2

Source: Saab Aircraft Division.

A. The Model

The model is a partial, partial equilibrium one. We not only ignore the general equilibrium effects on factor prices and consumer income, but we also ignore the links between the 30–40-seater planes and other aircraft. On the face of it this is what Laura Tyson calls 'patently questionable'. There certainly are many theoretical justifications for the existence of inter-product ties (for example shared management and engineering staffs, common production techniques, etc.). However as noted above, these ties do not seem to dominate the competition in the commuter aircraft industry. In addition to the counter-examples of Saab's success despite its lack of experience and Embraer's difficulties despite its extensive experience mentioned above, we have Fokker which dominates the market for commuter jets (F-100) but is not a serious contender in the turbo-prop market. Also, Piper and Beech have long made small commercial turbo-prop planes but this presence did not give them a dominant advantage in the 30–40-seat market.

This string of counter-examples leads us to assume that although we may be missing some inter-product spill-overs with the partial, partial equilibrium model, we are not missing any dominant factor in the industry competition. In other words, it does not appear that companies undertake the production of an unprofitable plane to boost the success of another of their products.

An important characteristic of aircraft is their considerable durability. A typical airframe is commercially productive for eighteen to twenty-five years (although some Second World War vintage DC-3s still make commercial flights in the US). Consequently we must handle the demand for airplanes as we would the demand for an investment good. In the context of constant returns to scale or static increasing returns to scale, this consideration poses no special problems. However, in the presence of learning-by-doing the problem quickly becomes intractable without additional assumptions. (For a discussion of this see Baldwin and Krugman 1988.) In fact for simplicity we assume that the planes have an infinite service life.

Given these assumptions, the price of an aircraft will depend upon the *stock* of existing planes during the plane's lifetime rather than the flow of production. Thus:

$$P_t = \sum_{i=1}^{\infty} \delta^{t+i} \Omega[Q_{t+i}], \tag{1}$$

where δ is the constant discount factor, Q is the stock of planes, and Ω is the function that relates the existing stock to the marginal revenue an airline would receive from any additional planes. Plainly equation (1) is a standard asset-pricing formula.

The manufacture of aircraft is characterized by two factors. The design and testing of a new airframe involves a large up-front R & D investment. For the 30–40-seaters this is estimated to be \$US220 million. Secondly, the actual production and assembly of the airframe is subject to a steep learning curve. The number most widely quoted for the elasticity of this learning curve is 20 per cent (roughly speaking doubling cumulative output reduces marginal costs by 20 per cent), although this saving appears only to apply to labour costs which are about 40 per cent of the sales price.

The total discounted cost of producing the plane for the producer i is therefore:

$$C^i = F + \sum_{t=1}^{T} \delta^t \left(c^i \left[\sum_{\tau=0}^{t} x_\tau^i \right] x_t^i + z x_t \right), \tag{2}$$

where T is the length of the production run (often twenty years), $c[\cdot]$ is the marginal cost function (marginal costs depend on past production due to learning-by-doing), F is the fixed R & D cost, x is the production per period, and z is the non-labour cost of production.

To model the strategic interaction, we assume that the three firms play Nash in production capacity, x^i. That is we focus on the equilibrium where each firm is choosing its capacity optimally taking as given the capacity of the others. At the optimal capacity, the discounted revenue generated by the marginal unit of capacity over the product cycle just equals the discounted marginal cost. Thus the first-order condition for optimal capacity choice is:

$$\sum_{t=1}^{\infty} \delta^t(\Omega[Q_t] + x\Omega'[Q_t]) = \sum_{t=1}^{T} \delta^t\left(c^i[tx^i] + x^i\frac{dc^i[tx^i]}{dx^i} + z\right). \quad (3)$$

The actual functional forms used were: $\Omega(Q) = \alpha(Q)^{-\varepsilon}$ and $c^i[K] = \beta^i(K^i)^{-\gamma}$.

B. Calibration and Simulation

From a variety of industry studies and interviews with Saab-Scania, it is possible to assign the value of $220 million to F (assumed the same for all three firms), to set T equal to twenty years, and to use a discount rate of 5 per cent (again assumed to be the same for all firms). The average selling price in 1986 was $6 million. Taking the cost of non-labour inputs (engines, avionics, etc.) to be 40 per cent of that, implies that z is 2.4 million, again assumed equal for all three. The learning elasticity is generally estimated to be 20 per cent (this seems to be a well-received number since it is used by Saab, McDonald-Douglas, and Boeing all for entirely different types of airframes). The demand elasticity for turbo-prop general aviation aircraft has been estimated at -2.76 by the US Department of Transportation. (Recall that most of these planes are sold to the US.) Since this category includes commuter, corporate, and pleasure aircraft, the elasticity is somewhat hard to interpret. Certainly we should expect the elasticity for the commuter planes we are interested in to be higher than this figure. Baldwin and Krugman (1988) consider the range -1.57 to -2.57. Baldwin and Flam (1988) consider the range -1.1 to -2.57. Here we take the elasticity to be -1.50.

This leaves us with four unknown parameters—the heights of each firm's learning curve β^i, and the constant in the pricing equation α—and four data constraints—sales of each plane in a typical year (twenty-two each for Saab and de Havilland and eleven for Embraer) and the average price of $US6 million. Using the first-order conditions and the definition of the demand and cost curves, it is simple to find a set of the four unknowns that satisfy the four constraints.

Using these values we can calculate what profits are likely to be in this market. The results for the base case are listed in Table 3. The important result in this table is that it appears that the profit on the EMB-120 is insufficient to cover the subsidy cost, implying that Brazil as a whole will lose from having produced the EMB-120. The present discounted value of this loss is exactly equal to the profit of $71 million net of the $101

Table 3. Base-case results

	Market share (1987 $US m)	Profits (1987 $US m)	Subsidy cost	Total sales (planes)
EMB-120	0.33	71	101	363
SF-340	0.32	42	—	352
DASH-8	0.35	−66	—	385

Source: Author's calculation based on Baldwin and Flam (1988).

million subsidy cost. Moreover, since we used the optimal subsidy in this simulation, any other subsidy level (including no subsidy) would result in a higher loss to Brazil. If we recalibrate and resimulate the base case assuming that there is no Brazilian government export subsidy to the EMB-120, we find that Embraer loses $54 million. Of course this finding can be turned on its head. For instance, if for some reason (say national security or national pride) Brazil absolutely had to produce the EMB-120, a 10 per cent subsidy reduces the net cost to Brazilian taxpayers of having the EMB-120 in production. Secondly, Table 3 shows that the Dash-8 will lose money.

Simplistic Welfare Calculations

We have no need of a simulation to judge the welfare effects by the standard, static criteria of the sum of profits and consumer surplus less the amount of the subsidy. Since only six planes of this class have been sold to Brazil, the consumers in Brazil have been essentially unaffected by the policy. Since profits net of the subsidy are −$30 million, the net welfare effects of the project is estimated to be negative. Thus the net effect of the targeting policy was to transfer income from taxpayers in Brazil to the stockholders and employees of Embraer.

The simplistic welfare calculation, however, misses the point since the Katz and Summers (1988) argument is relevant here. Due, perhaps, to principal–agent problems, US aerospace workers receive a wage that is 20 per cent higher than would be expected given their measured skill level. Although we have no direct evidence on Embraer wages, our calibration methodology identifies what marginal costs Embraer must have been facing to charge the price that they charged, given their market shares and our model's assumptions. However, if as in the US, the Brazilian aircraft worker's wage is greater than it would be in alternative employment, the calibrated cost does not reflect the true social cost of the labour resources—it overestimates the social cost. Consequently a cost-benefit analysis from the social point of view should assign a lower shadow wage to the labour.

As it turns out, we can use the 10 per cent labour-cost subsidy incorporated in the base-case calculations to get a rough idea of what the Katz–Summers point implies quantitatively. Suppose that the Brazilian aircraft workers' wage premium was 10 per cent (only half that in the US). In this case we must add in an additional plus in the social cost-benefit analysis. The 10 per cent wage premium is now a rent gain to the workers. In fact this rent gain exactly offsets the 10 per cent subsidy. Consequently the true social benefit of the project (PDV of revenue) net of the true social costs (PDV of non-labour costs and labour costs evaluated at the social wage) is equal to the $71 million profits. Since this number is positive we see that even a fairly mild assumption on the rent component of Embraer's wage bill could reverse our conclusion that the EMB-120 was a welfare-worsening project.

Furthermore since Brazil imposes extensive capital controls, it is possible that the social value of the foreign exchange earned through the export of the EMB-120 exceeds its dollar face value. Taking this into account would of course tilt our cost-benefit analysis in favour of the project. Of course to do such a calculation it would be important to apply the same shadow price of foreign exchange to the imported intermediate inputs.

What we do next is to take seriously the idea that some of the subsidy is capitalized in the form of workers' experience and skill that are productive beyond the EMB-120 project.

3. A MODEL OF DYNAMIC SPILL-OVERS THROUGH HUMAN CAPITAL FORMATION

Frequently cost-benefit analysis is static. For instance in the case of a subsidy, the typical welfare criterion is the change in profits, plus the change in consumer surplus, less the costs of the subsidy. If this quantity is positive the project requiring the subsidy is advisable, otherwise it is not. This, however, ignores the fact that the economic impact of building a plane such as the EMB-120 may last far beyond the period of production. Workers, engineers, and managers are likely to acquire skills that outlive the project itself. In other words some of the subsidy may be capitalized in the form of human capital. Training and experience that could have been gained only from actually undertaking the project (learning-by-doing), and is beneficial to the economy in ways that extend beyond the project itself, should be treated as an investment. The return on this investment should be appended to the plus column of the cost-benefit accounting.

There are of course innumerable other spill-overs that are for the most part extremely difficult to measure. The value of the learning-by-doing human capital is at least in principle simple to measure. The extra training and experience should be rewarded by the market in accordance with its value (or at least approximately so). Consequently the wage-gap between experienced and inexperienced aircraft workers would provide a measure of the return on the project-related human capital.

To quantify this observation, we find it convenient to cast the decision of whether to undertake the project in terms of dynamic programming. In these terms the planner should subsidize only if:

$$g_t(S) + \delta V_{t+1}(S) > g_t(0) + \delta V_{t+1}(0), \tag{4}$$

where $g(S)$ and $g(0)$ are respectively GNP with and without the project, δ is the discount rate, and $V_{t+1}(S)$ and $V_{t+1}(0)$ are the discounted sum of post-project GNP with and without the subsidy. If the benefits of the project outlive the project itself then $V_{t+1}(S) > V_{t+1}(0)$.

Rearranging equation (4) to build intuition, we get:

$$\delta[V_{t+1}(S) - V_{t+1}(0)] > [g_t(0) - g_t(S)]. \tag{5}$$

According to the calibration results, the reallocation of resources prompted by the undertaking of the EMB-120 resulted in a reduction of value of output by exactly the amount of the subsidy. (That is how it was calculated.)

The project might still have been a good idea if there were dynamic spillovers. These are captured by the difference between the discounted future GNPs with and without the project. This difference consists of the contributions that the workers who got extra experience make to GNP over their post-project working lives. Notice that because we are referring to learning-by-doing it is not possible to claim that the workers would have acquired the skill even without the project. This all says that:

$$V_{t+1}(S) - V_{t+1}(0) = \sum_{t=1}^{T} \delta^t (w - v)(H(S) - H(0)),$$

where w is the experienced workers' wages, v is the inexperienced workers' wages, and $H(S) - H(0)$ is the number of workers who acquired the additional experience.

Defining ϕ as the wage premium on experience ($\phi = (w - v)/v$) and γ as the fraction of the subsidy that gets capitalized (γ is such that $\gamma(S/v) = H(S) - H(0)$) then we have the simple condition that the project is advisable only if:

$$\phi\gamma > \frac{1 + \delta}{1 - \delta^{T+1}} > 1 - \delta.$$

So we get the simple rule that if the fraction of the subsidy which is translated into human capital times the premium on that human capital is greater than $1 - \delta$, then we should proceed with the project. For instance if one-quarter of the subsidy is capitalized and the mark-up is four then the building of the plane is a good idea, despite the profit loss of doing so.

Applying the Criterion to the EMB-120

Although equation (6) provides the most analytically convenient form of the condition, equation (5) is easier to apply to the data. Again calibrating from the data gathered from industry sources, it appears that the construction of the EMB-120 involves approximately 1,500 workers. Suppose that each will put in twenty years of productive work beyond the EMB-120 project. To justify the $30 million social loss (ignoring the wage–rent argument we made above), the value to the extra experience must be at least $1,528 per year per worker. That is, the market worth of those 1,500 workers must be consistently more than $1,500 more than that of workers who did not gain experience on the EMB-120 project.

The size of this number is of course open to debate. Is it likely that the EMB-120 experience will be that valuable for twenty years? To my way of thinking, the number sounds fairly plausible, although of course I acknowledge this to be a conjecture. It would therefore appear that the dynamic spill-overs might justify the project even in the absence of the wage–rent argument. Plainly though, the issue cannot be entirely answered until we see exactly how much the market is actually willing to pay for the experience the EMB-120 workers gain.

4. CONCLUSIONS

This chapter has described the logic of strategic trade policy, and discussed theoretical criteria and an empirical methodology for its evaluation. The empirical methodology (calibration) is applied to the case of the EMB-120, a Brazilian-made commuter aircraft which is exported to the US and Europe. We find that without considering spill-overs, the project resulted in a net loss to the Brazilian economy of $30 million (or about $20,000 per production worker). We considered a model of spill-overs via human capital formation. This enabled us to derive a simple criterion which was applied to the industry. We estimated that the value of the additional training the production workers received from participating in the EMB-120 project would have to be worth more than $1,500 per year in order to justify the subsidy. We also evaluated the project's net social benefit assuming that the workers received a 10 per cent higher wage in building the planes than they would have received in alternative employment. Using this relatively conservative estimate of the shadow wage, we found that the project would have increased the welfare of Brazil by a positive $70 million.

This study is intended primarily as an exercise in developing a methodology rather than as an exhaustive cost-benefit analysis of the EMB-120. The competition in this industry is still under way. It is possible that market developments could entirely reverse our evaluation. Thus it is too early to be sure of any policy conclusions. Yet this chapter demonstrated a genre of methodologies which can be extended and refined to evaluate prospective targeting policies. The novel contribution of this methodology is the fact that it can deal with dynamic economies of scale, and the effect of government backing on the outcome of international strategic interaction among firms.

There are certainly many points on which a more extensive (and more expensive) study could improve upon this one. More detailed information on prices, production, and R & D costs of each of the three firms would improve the credibility of the results and would help improve the precision of our estimates. A more detailed model of the purchasers' behaviour would probably also yield useful insights. Lastly a detailed in-country study of the Brazilian aircraft industry would undoubtedly uncover many additional spill-over effects which could be quantified.

REFERENCES

BALDWIN, RICHARD (1988a), 'Hysteresis in Import Prices: The Beachhead Effect', *American Economic Review*, 78, 4, pp. 773–85.

—— (1988b), 'On Taking the Calibration out of Calibration Studies', mimeo.

—— (1988c), 'Evaluating Strategic Trade Policies', *Aussenwirtschaft*, 43, pp. 207–230.

—— and KRUGMAN, PAUL (1987), 'Market Access and International Competition: A Simulation Study of 16K Random Access Memories', in R. Feenstra (ed.), *Empirical Research in International Trade* (MIT Press, Cambridge, Mass.).

—— (1988), 'Industrial Policy and International Competition in Wide-bodied Aircraft', in R. Baldwin, (ed.), *Trade Policy Issues and Empirical Analysis* (NBER/ Chicago University Press, Chicago).

BRANDER, JAMES, and SPENCER, BARBARA (1983), 'International R & D Rivalry and Industrial Strategy', *Review of Economic Studies*, 50, pp. 707–22.

—— (1985), 'Export Subsidies and International Market Share Rivalry', *Journal of International Economics*, 18, pp. 83–100.

DIXIT, AVINASH (1987), 'Optimal Trade and Industry Policy for the US Automobile Industry', in R. Feenstra (ed.), *Empirical Research in International Trade* (MIT Press, Cambridge, Mass.).

KRUGMAN, PAUL, (ed.) (1986), *Strategic Trade Policy and the New International Economics* (MIT Press, Cambridge, Mass.).

LAMBSON, VAL, and RICHARDSON, DAVID (1987), 'Tacit Collusion and Voluntary

Restraint Arrangements in the US Auto Market' (University of Wisconsin), mimeo.

LEVINSOHN, JAMES (1987), 'Empirics of Taxes on Differentiated Products: The Case of Tariffs in the US Automobile Industry', in R. Baldwin (ed.), *Trade Policy Issues and Empirical Analysis* (NBER/Chicago University Press, Chicago), pp. 11–40.

NORMAN, VICTOR, DALTUNG, SONJA, and ESKELAND, GUNNAR (1987), 'Incentive Problems in Discretionary Trade Policy: Two Examples' (Norwegian School of Economics and Business Administration), mimeo.

VENABLES, ANTHONY (1985), 'Trade and Industrial Policy with Imperfect Competition: The Case of Identical Products and Free Entry', *Journal of International Economics*, 19, pp. 1–19.

—— and SMITH, ALASDAIR (1986), 'Trade and Industrial Policy under Imperfect Competition', *Economic Policy*, 3 (Oct.), pp. 621–59.

10
International Competition and Market Penetration: A Model of the Growth Strategy of the Korean Semiconductor Industry*

Chang-Ho Yoon

1. INTRODUCTION

With shortening product cycles and significant learning effects, industries like that for microelectronic devices exhibit sophisticated dynamic behaviour. Late-comers, including those firms from newly industrialized developing countries, are easily deterred by ever-increasing capital requirements and investment risks. High-technology products have been perceived as a continuing source of long-run comparative advantage of developed countries.

In the 1980s, however, Korea has challenged this traditional view and managed to export goods of high-technology content. Semiconductor devices and passenger cars are the most cited examples of products that have been successfully launched on the world market. This new pattern of intra-industry trade in high-tech products between the developing countries and the developed countries has become one of the important subjects of new trade theory. Empirical issues concerning the role of strategic trade policy and shaping of comparative advantages in developing countries have now been brought out for closer examination (Helleiner 1985). But while new theories of international trade and investment have been well applied to the pattern of trade flow among the developed countries, it is not yet clear if they also have explanatory power in the trade of developing countries.

Krugman (1986) has argued that the new trade theory, emphasizing strategic aspects of government policy and oligopoly behaviour, is likely to be useful in the context of developing countries. An empirical analysis of trade policy experience (along the lines of Dixit 1987 and Baldwin and Krugman 1987) could be undertaken as part of a case-study of the evolution of high-tech industry where externalities and dynamic scale effects are significant. A series of carefully designed single-industry, cross-country case-studies is needed; and for this purpose an extensive application of

---

* I have benefited from comments by Gerry Helleiner, Richard Baldwin, Donald Keesing, and the other participants in the WIDER conference. Preparing an earlier draft, H. Yun and B. Kim helped with the computation. I am grateful to the WIDER, KDI, and the Harvard-Yenching Institute for financial support.

recently developed theories of industrial organization to international trade issues, including the potential for market penetration by developing countries, seems likely to be useful.

This chapter attempts to model the competitive conditions the Korean firms faced and their successful entry into a highly dynamic commodity memory market. Semiconductor memory chips are regarded as among the most important components of modern computer and communication equipment. To compete with the leading Japanese firms, they must be produced at an efficient scale. Competition is essentially dynamic in nature, and an ever-increasing capital expenditure is required to survive. It was surprising that late-coming Korean firms entered this market successfully without any direct governmental subsidy or practices of implicit market restriction. There must have existed a niche for profitable entry even in the later phase of the product cycle. This chapter is largely devoted to an explanation of a dynamic oligopoly in the international market.

By stressing the importance of the competitive aspect of successful entry to the world market, we by no means neglect the importance of the industrial and trade policy of Korea. It is undeniable that the most successful Korean firms are the conglomerates who have led the export growth of heavy chemical products during the past two decades. They are the beneficiaries of past Korean industrial policy and had easier access to capital markets. They benefited from tax and subsidy policies in the 1970s. The past industrial policy of targeting specific industries for export promotion has been largely successful, and provided incentives for the Korean firms to develop their own parts and components even after the government abandoned the targeting policy and introduced a set of policy measures to enhance competition in the domestic market. Increased foreign demand for the final goods reduced the burden of sunk costs associated with the development of capital-intensive intermediate goods. Strategic trade policy at the early stage of industrial development might have strengthened the competitive position of the Korean firms in the 1980s. But these effects have been diffused over time and are hard to measure directly. We shall not attempt to quantify them, since that is beyond the scope of this chapter, but we return to this point in the next section and in concluding comments. Before we examine a model of dynamic oligopoly, we will introduce a brief summary of structural changes in the market environment of the Korean semiconductor industry as background.

2. MARKET ENVIRONMENT OF THE KOREAN SEMICONDUCTOR INDUSTRY AND THE COMPETITIVE STRATEGY

The Korean semiconductor industry has developed rapidly during the past few years. Its share in the world market for 256K chips was 13 per cent in

1987, and the leading Korean firm became one of the dominant suppliers of 1M chips. Such rapid growth was never expected at the initial stage of development. In fact, the Korean government was pessimistic about aggressive private-investment plans in such a highly dynamic, risky business. Strategic trade policy was considered likely to be harmful to the exports of finished electronic products. A government from a small, open, developing economy is not, in general, able to take the burden of a retaliatory response by the developed countries in capital-intensive high-tech industry. The financial constraint would place an unbearable burden on it.

The Korean government seems to have admitted that if foreign dependency on high-tech components continued, Korea might lose its comparative advantage in the related electronics industry. In addition, technical information obtained through purchases of foreign products alone was not sufficient to diffuse microelectronics and information technology throughout the economy. The semiconductor industry has large spill-over effects, and could have been 'targeted' by the government both for import substitution and for export promotion. Instead of targeting, the government attempted to build a small-scale public research laboratory. Because of a budgetary constraint and inefficiencies in public management, it was later privatized and merged with another private research institute.

As is well known, the Korean government had already abandoned policy efforts to promote specific targeted industries by the early 1980s. Most of the previous direct government subsidies, including perferential low-interest loans, had been abolished. A new set of economic-liberalization objectives included a Korean anti-trust and fair-trade law, and gradually increased the scope of import liberalization. The semiconductor industry was no exception. The tariff on imported capital equipment plus insurance fee and transportation increased initial capital equipment costs by 30 per cent for Korean semiconductor firms, and the domestic loan rate of interest has exceeded 11 per cent. In addition, foreign access to the Korean market has been virtually free. When the first Korean firm began to export domestically fabricated 64K chips in 1984, Korea imported $1.15 billion worth of semiconductor products which amounted to 91.5 per cent of total domestic consumption. Since 1981, the annual rate of increase in imports of semiconductor devices has been above 25 per cent, almost comparable to the rate of increase in the domestic demand. Unlike Japan, the governmental role in the development of the Korean semiconductor industry was not important. Korean firms had to stand alone, facing risks associated with the temporal evolution of investment uncertainty. Even conglomerate bankruptcy has always been possible. Their success would depend on their own financing ability and competitive strategy.

Changing Pattern of Export Demand

Until the early 1980s, Korea's main exports consisted of manufactured outputs of relatively low technology content. But after the second oil shock, Korean industrial structure has been steadily changing in a more technology-intensive and energy-saving direction. Diffusion of information-systems technology has been sped up to increase value added in a variety of manufacturing sectors. Rapidly increasing domestic demand for computers and communication equipment signalled the profitability of import substitution of system-like electronic components. Steadily increasing foreign demand for consumer electronics, including colour TVs and VCRs, added further domestic demand for semiconductor devices. Exports of electronic products increased from $2 billion in 1980 to $11 billion in 1987, which amounted to almost one-quarter of the total exports of manufactured goods. Optimistic expectations of the rising domestic demand for semiconductor devices (which turned out to be correct) have reduced subjective investment risks associated with fluctuations in foreign demand, and lowered the expected average fixed cost.

Deepening Dependence on Imported Technology

In contrast to the rapid expansion of exports of processed and assembled products to the United States, imports of capital equipment and parts from Japan have been increasing. If we look at the trade specification index in the electronics industry, it becomes very obvious that Korea imported intermediate inputs from Japan to process and assemble, and exported finished products to the United States (Table 1). Deepening dependence on Japanese technology had been weakening the competitive strength of Korean firms in the export market, and was considered a bottleneck to the further growth of high-tech industry. As the value of the Japanese yen has been increasing since 1985, the cost of inelastic imports from Japan rose dramatically, while Korea improved price competitiveness over Japanese products in the US market. This change in relative prices caused an increase in export earnings and made it profitable to invest in import substitution of what has become more expensive key components of electronics products. System-like components were especially needed to strengthen Korea's comparative advantage in consumer electronics, computers, and other industrial equipment and plants.

Organizational Features and Work Ethic

The leading Korean semiconductor firms are vertically integrated with companies manufacturing consumer electronics and computers. This helps to stabilize demand fluctuations and provides a feedback channel from the

Table 1. Change of trade specification index in[a] electronic products

SITC[b]	1980		1981		1982		1983		1984		1985	
	US	Japan	US	Japan	US	Japan	US	Japan	US	Japan	US	Japan
761	0.79	−0.40	0.99	−0.49	1.00	−0.22	0.99	−0.66	1.00	−0.38	1.00	−0.21
762	0.99	−0.59	1.00	−0.58	1.00	−0.26	0.93	−0.30	1.00	−0.21	0.99	−0.06
763	0.88	0.54	0.89	−0.68	0.85	−0.87	0.88	−0.97	0.93	−0.98	0.97	−0.90
764	0.31	−0.59	−0.06	−0.65	−0.30	−0.63	0.00	−0.67	0.14	−0.59	0.37	−0.51
766	−0.01	−0.39	−0.01	−0.47	0.04	−0.48	0.08	−0.59	0.17	−0.52	0.11	−0.49

[a]Trade specification index (E_{ij}) is defined by H. G. Grubel and P. S. Lloyd (1975) as $E_{ij} = (X_{ij} - M_{ij})/(X_{ij} + M_{ij})$, where X_{ij} = exports of ith industry to j[th] country and M_{ij} = imports of ith industry to j[th] country.
[b]761 TVs, 762 radios, 763 tape recorders, 764 communication equipment and parts, 766 transistors and semiconductors and devices.

Source: Korea Institute of Economics and Technology (1986).

users of systems components. In addition, each of these integrated firms itself belongs to a larger Korean conglomerate, each having subsidiaries in diverse fields ranging from shipbuilding, construction, and electrical equipment to insurance and general trading in a world-wide sales network. A conglomerate's reputation in various established fields makes it easier to get access to low-interest rate credit both in the domestic and international capital market. Conglomerates also make possible the diversification of investment risks and cross-subsidization among the subsidiaries during the initial state of investment losses. Spill-over or external effects of R & D investment are well internalized within the conglomerate itself.

Reinforcing organizational advantages, the work ethic of Korean scientific and engineering personnel seems to have played an important role. As is well known, the fabrication process of very large-scale integrated circuits is not easily describable beforehand. There are many 'black-boxes' to be handled by experienced engineering personnel on the spot. The monitoring and reward system of the hierarchical structure of the American firm is not efficient in handling the incentive problems of repeated moral hazard. The sense of achievement and co-operative work efforts among disciplined scientific personnel (once they form a so-called critical mass) seem to have reduced organizational inefficiency. In fact, the speed of productivity (yield rate) in the production of commodity memory chips turned out to be more than comparable to that in the leading Japanese firms.

Competitive Strategy

In spite of the favourable market environment and organizational advantages, Korean firms are still far behind their foreign competitors in in-house system design, and suffer from backward technology in related fields. Rulings for violations of US patent law turned out to be severe and they have had to pay large sums for licensing fees and royalties. They are also less competent in making a variety of proprietary products, and have always been late-comers, missing the early profitable phase of the product life cycle. When they enter the already mature commodity market, they have to sell at the long-run average cost of the leading competitors. Pessimistic experts and government officials have been afraid of the possibility of suffering from overcapacity in the mature product, and of collapse of the whole conglomerate by too much concentration on the commodity memory market. But Korean firms with relatively large fixed costs and low variable labour costs of fabrication have successfully followed the early Japanese strategy of penetrating the price-sensitive commodity memory market at the lower end of the quality spectrum.

The most dramatic case of aggressive investment in high-tech semiconductor products was a large-scale commitment to developing DRAM (dynamic random-access memory) fabrication capabilities. During the past six years, the Samsung group, together with the Hyundai group and the Lucky–Goldstar group, which are the largest *jaebols* (conglomerates) in Korea, have invested billions of dollars to start production of higher-density memory chips.

So far the strategy is succeeding. The repeated anti-dumping rulings by the US government against the dominant Japanese firms prevented their use of predatory pricing. They were not allowed to price below their average cost of production to squeeze out their rivals. Among the Korean firms, Samsung seems to have demonstrated remarkable growth capacity. Started with less than $5 million in revenue in 1982, this firm reached $300 million in 1987, and is now equipped with a large-scale production facility of 1M DRAM. With virtually no significant experience of comparable research and development in the past, it took only five years to move from making transistor and elementary discrete devices to making VLSI (very large-scale integration) memory products. Korean capacity now can meet more than 6 per cent of total world demand. The rapid expansion of the commodity memory industry also stimulated import substitution of some important equipment and raw materials like lead-frames and silicon wafers, among others.

3. AN OVERVIEW OF THE PRODUCT LIFE CYCLE

The production of high-density commodity memory requires heavy fixed costs, and the greatest portion of initial set-up costs involving design costs and equipment costs is largely sunk cost. Although chips in each generation are near-perfect substitutes, fabrication capacities are each of a completely different character, and the cost of building an MES (minimum efficient scale) fabrication facility is increasing. Apart from the fixed set-up costs, there are variable costs of labour and raw materials. Learning depends on the accumulated know-how from past production experiences. It is expected that the average variable cost of production decreases as the cumulative volume of output increases. In the semiconductor industry, learning takes the form of improvement in the yield rate. The cost of DRAM fabrication falls rapidly over the first couple of years and then more slowly thereafter. The prices of DRAMs also show an initial sharp decline as the firms move down their learning curve (yield curve). Table 2 shows the evolution of successive cycles of prices and production volumes for three generations of DRAMs.

The 16K DRAM replaced the 4K product in 1978, and was overtaken in output by the 64K DRAM in 1981. The effective price[1] of the 256K DRAM fell below that of the 64K DRAM in 1985. The 256K DRAM was

Table 2. Prices and shipments of DRAMs by generations

	1976	1977	1978	1979	1980	1981	1982	1983	1984	1985	1986	1987
Average selling price ($)												
16K	46.4	18.6	8.52	6.03	4.77	2.06	1.24	1.05	1.09	1.32		
64K							5.42	3.86	3.16	1.15	1.03	1.07
256K										3.79	2.31	2.27
1M											31.3	14.2
Total shipments (million units)												
16K	0.1	2	21	70	183	216	263	239	121	49		
64K			150	110	46.3	13	103	371	853	509	404	150
256K							150	1.7	38	201	618	709
1M								47.7	19.9	100	4	44

Source: Dataquest (1987).

replaced by 1M chips in 1988. Leading Japanese firms have been speeding up the replacement process. In fact, the economic life of each successive generation has become progressively shorter. The life of 16K chips was about five years, and that of 64K chips about four years. The life of 256K chips is expected to be about three years. The volume of production increases until the effective price becomes higher than that of the next generation chips, and then decreases abruptly. Since capacity cost is mostly sunk cost, firms will continue producting maximum-capacity output as they move along the learning curve unless the market price falls below the average variable cost of production. Toward the end of the cycle however, price competition becomes intense and destructive. Some of the less efficient, large fabrication lines will therefore be closed and the corresponding exit of the dominant firms will cause a further abrupt discontinuous fall in the volume of production.

In a zero-profits equilibrium with free entry, the most profitable period then must be the early phase of the cycle. The price/cost ratio can be expected to decline steadily as the cycle progresses. But after the effective price of the next-generation chip becomes less than the current one, leading firms preparing for the supply of future memory products will cease production of the current generation chips. Large-scale exit could decrease the industry supply abruptly and a temporary shortage may occur. In the case of 64K chips, excess demand at the price above the long-run average cost reappeared after 1985, the year when massive production of 256K DRAM began to depress market prices. Table 3 shows the estimated market size of successive DRAM products since 1986.

Notice that 64K chips were still demanded for use in personal computers and consumer electronics. The pre-emptive investment race among the dominant firms to enter the early phase of the higher-density commodity memory market outran the development pace in the computer industry, and did not provide sufficient time for consumers to adjust themselves to rapid technical innovation. Only after enough lapse of time can higher-quality final products be marketed at higher prices. In addition, consumers of

Table 3. Market size, 1986–1990 ($m)

Year	1986	1987	1988	1989	1990
64K	417	245	150	—	—
256K	1431	1521	1267	770	366
1M	170	685	1939	2584	2340
4M	—	—	—	210	750

Source: Dataquest (1988).

personal computers, colour TVs, and various kinds of communication equipment are from different economic classes. Products are often vertically differentiated to meet the consumer needs of varying income brackets. It has often been the case that the new product of highest quality is sold at a much higher price than the old one, and at least for some time demand for the existing quality declines only slowly. This partly explains why the prices of DRAMs fall sharply near the end of the cycle and then increase again even after the new generation dominates the market. Market demand for the past-generation chips decreases at a slower rate than the industry supply. Smaller remaining firms can enjoy profits if the fabrication facilities of dominant firms are closed first and become obsolete. Should the larger firms re-enter, the industry supply again will exceed the steadily diminishing demand and the market will collapse. In fact, the large firms never re-entered after the cycle ended. Indivisibility in the operation of fabrication lines implies that smaller, efficient firms will survive the exit game.

The Korean firm started building capacity in 1982 and entered the market in 1984. Until 1984, price–cost margins for the dominant incumbent firms had been maintained well above 1.[2] But the market collapsed temporarily soon after the Korean firm's entry into the late phase of the 64K cycle. Despite substantial initial loss, it survived the exit game. Table 4 depicts the trend of 64K prices and the market shares of the Korean firm. At the beginning of 1988, the 64K price jumped to $1.25 in the US market and $1.15 in Japan.

A similar trend can be traced over the 256K cycle. Starting with less than 3 per cent share in 1986, the Korean share in the world market reached 9.5 per cent in 1987. The average selling price rose from the bottom level of $2.05 in the first quarter of 1987 to $3.35 in March, 1988. In the following sections we will elaborate our analysis further along this line of argument.

4. DYNAMIC COMPETITION OVER THE PRODUCT CYCLE AND WELFARE CONSIDERATIONS

We first consider a world market for 64K microchips with n_U identical representative US merchant firms, and n_J Japanese firms. Their outputs in period t will be denoted by $q_i(t)$ for $i = 1, 2, \ldots, n_U + n_J$. The market price at time t, $p(t)$, is set by these dominant firms and newly entering firms from the other countries are assumed to behave as price takers. We will assume away the existence of captive domestic markets and ignore transportation costs and trade barriers. Firms sell their output anywhere they want at an equilibrium price. Let $x_i(t)$ denote the ith firm's rate of investment for the development of chips of future generations. Since memory chips of each density are near-perfect substitutes, firms expect the length of the product

Table 4. 64K prices and Korean market shares, 1985–1987

	1985				1986				1987		
	I	II	III	IV	I	II	III	IV	I	II	III
Price ($US)	1.65	1.10	0.75	0.85	1.10	1.05	1.05	0.90	0.99	1.05	1.07
Market share (%)	1.9	4.0	5.1	6.1	7.1	8.9	10.6	11.6	16.1	20.4	22.7

Source: Dataquest (1987).

life cycle to become shorter as their competitors accumulate development capacity. Let $k_i(t) = \int_0^t x_i(t)dt$ denote such capacity and $k(t) = \sum_i k_i(t)$. Demand for 64K chips will be assumed to take the following form

$$p(t) = H(k_t, t) Q_t^{-\frac{1}{\varepsilon_p}}, \frac{\partial H}{\partial k_t} < 0, \qquad (1)$$

where $Q_t = \sum q_i(t) + E_t$, and E_t denotes the entering firm's output. Demand may fluctuate as t varies. We assume that at the beginning of the cycle every incumbent correctly anticipates the flow of demand over the cycle. The production capacity for the current-generation chips, K_i is assumed to be installed at $t = 0$. Let F_i denote the associated fixed-capacity cost. Every firm knows that once the capacity is installed, its cost will be sunk. Firms will therefore decide to enter the market only if the total revenue earned is not less than the sum of total variable cost plus capacity cost. But *ex post*, incumbents must behave to maximize the variable profits over the cycle, given the flow of other firms' output and capacity investment for chips of later generations. The sunk cost certainly constitutes an entry barrier.

Following Baldwin and Krugman (1987), let us define one unit of capacity as the fixed capital requirement used to produce one batch of microchips. The firm with capacity K then produces batches at a constant rate K throughout the cycle if fully utilized. The yield of working chips per batch rises with accumulated technical experience through each stage of wafer processing, probing, assembly, and testing.

Suppose the firm produces batches at its maximum capacity until it exits. Let T denote the exit time. The yield rate is defined as a function $h(K, t)$ for $0 \le t \le T$. Let C_0 denote the variable cost required to operate one unit of capacity. Let $C_t(a(t))$ denote the variable cost of producing $q(t)$ units of working chips. Then the average variable cost of production will be $C_0/h(K, t)$.[3] Let $F(K)$ denote the fixed cost. Assuming away the discount factor within the product cycle and suppressing the variables for the other firms, the firm's profits over the cycle $\Pi(K,T)$, can be written as follows.

$$\Pi(K,T) = \int_0^T [p(t)q(t) - C_t(q(t))]dt - F(K), \qquad (2)$$

where $q(t) = Kh(K,t)$. Given the demand function (1), both $p(t)$ and T will in general depend on the other firms' output paths and investment strategies for the development of higher-density chips. Let $N_U = \{1, 2, \ldots, n_U\}$ and $N_J = \{1, 2, \ldots, n_J\}$. Let N denote the set of firms producing memory chips in the market. Let us define $\hat{K} = \{K_i\}_{i \in N}$, where K_i is the ith firm's capacity for 64K chips. In a similar way, let $\hat{k} = \{k_i\}_{i \in N}$, where k_i denotes the ith firm's capacity for higher-density memory chips. Let $V_i(\hat{k}(t))$ denote the

ith firm's current profits from holding capacity for future generation chips. Then each firm i is assumed to maximize as follows.[4]

$$\underset{\{K_i,\ T_i,\ x_i(t)\}}{\text{Max}} \Pi_i(\hat{K};\ \hat{T}) + \int_0^\infty \{V_i(\hat{k}(t)) - x_i(t)\}\, dt, \tag{3}$$

where $\hat{T} = \{t_i\}_{i \in N}$, T_i being the ith firm's exit time. Notice that we assumed away the technological linkage effects between successive generations of DRAM products.

Imagine that the market for all higher-density memory chips is large enough so that the effects of equilibrium output and prices in the 64K market on $V_i(k(t))$ is negligible. Then equation (1) implies that an oligopolistic equilibrium of exit time and capacity choice in the 64K market depends on the investment race in the higher-density market, but not vice versa.[5]

Any firm can produce both 64K chips and higher-density chips or just one type of chip. Although the choice of exit time T_i in a perfect equilibrium depends on the joint investment decision, $\hat{k}(t)$ in the subgame equilibrium of the investment race, our assumption of no linkage effects implies that with free entry into the market for any type of chip,

$$\Pi_i(\hat{K}^*,\ \hat{T}^*) = 0, \quad \text{and} \quad \int_0^\infty \{V_j(\hat{k}^*(t)) - x_j^*(t)\}\, dt = 0 \tag{4}$$

for any i and j at an equilibrium. This follows because if $\Pi_i(\hat{K}^*, \hat{T}^*) < 0$, the firm i will simply not enter the market, and will either invest in higher-density chips or stay out of the memory market. If $\Pi_i(\hat{K}^*, \hat{T}^*) < 0$, the number of firms producing 64K chips must be increased to eliminate excess profits at an equilibrium.

Postponing for the moment an analysis of the investment competition and exit game, let us examine the market over the current product cycle. Since each firm's profit over the cycle is defined as in equations (2) and (3), the equilibrium number of firms within the cycle certainly depends on the way firms compete in the product market. In the case of Cournot competition with high fixed costs, only a few firms can compete. But if firms tacitly collude to maintain high profit margins, the number will increase. In fact, every entering firm must make a guess about the mode of competition over the product cycle, and the best conjecture about the other firm's response to his own output has to be properly taken into account when it decides on its own capacity. To an entrant with large sunk cost, the perceived risk of losing unrecoverable costs could be reinforced by the threat of retaliatory response from the incumbent.

Over the 64K cycle, most of the five leading US and six leading Japanese firms entered in the early 1980s. The Japanese firms started a little earlier and expanded their 64K fabrication capability aggressively. Siemens entered later after the recession period (1981–2). The Korean firm, Samsung, was the last entrant. It seems that until 1984, no joint entry deterrence action had been undertaken by the dominant incumbents. An equilibrium price/cost ratio must have been maintained at a fairly attractive level. This hypothesis can easily be tested by closely examining the actual data on prices and outputs.

Let C_0 be the first unit variable cost. Then in the discrete time version of our model, the average variable cost of production at t is assumed to take the following form.[6]

$$\text{AVC}_i(t) = C_0 \left(\sum_{\tau=1}^{t} q_i(\tau) \right)^{-\mu_i}, \qquad (5)$$

where μ_i is the learning rate. From equation (4), the equilibrium number of firms, output, and prices in an oligopoly market with free entry must satisfy the following condition.

$$\sum_{t=1}^{T_i} p(t) q_i(t) = \sum_{t=1}^{T_i} C_0 q_i(t) \left(\sum_{\tau=1}^{t} q_i(\tau) \right)^{-\mu_i} + F_i(K_i). \qquad (6)$$

Since capacity cost is sunk, every firm stays in the market and produces 64K chips at its maximum-capacity level as long as the market price exceeds the average variable cost. If we further assume the same learning rate, the ratio of the steady-state market shares of any two firms started at the same time from the beginning of the cycle will be the ratio of each firm's initial capacity. Let s_i be the steady state market share, and b, the unit fixed-capacity cost. Then we have for firms i and j entered at $t = 1$,

$$\frac{s_j}{s_i} = \frac{bK_j}{bK_i} = \frac{F_j}{F_i}. \qquad (7)$$

For computational ease, we assume that five identical leading firms produce all of the US output, and six identical firms represent the Japanese industry ($n_U = 5$ and $n_J = 6$). The cumulative outputs and the market shares of each representative firm is shown in Table 5(a). Once we know the learning parameter and the ratio of steady-state market shares, we can compute C_0 and the fixed cost, F_U and F_J from equations (3) and (4). The price/cost ratios for $\mu = 0.28$ and $s_U/s_J = 2/3$ are shown in Table 5(b).

In the early phase of the cycle, the price–cost margin of the representative Japanese firm was significantly greater than that of the representative US firm. As industry moved into a steady growth path after 1982, the profit margin of both types of firms adjusted toward a constant and more similar level throughout the remainder of the cycle (1982–4).[7] With constant market share, price elasticity, and the high price–cost margin, the underlying conjecture parameter seems to have been much greater than in the

Table 5(a). Cumulative output and market shares of the representative firms

		1981	1982	1983	1984	1985	1986
Cumulative output	US	735	7638	35934	99804	130894	148386
(thousand units)	Japan	1572	13078	50150	133039	184940	227928
Market share (%)	US	5.61	6.64	7.62	7.50	6.10	4.32
	Japan	11.99	10.67	9.98	9.73	10.18	10.62

Source: Dataquest (1987).

Table 5(b). Price/Cost ratios[a] of representative firms[b]

	1981	1982	1983	1984	1985	1986
US	2.44	2.04	2.24	2.44	0.97	0.89
	(5.11)[c]	(2.657)	(1.722)	(1.295)	(1.20)	(1.157)
Japan	3.01	2.37	2.46	2.65	1.05	1.00
	(4.31)	(2.286)	(1.569)	(1.194)	(1.088)	(1.027)

[a] Average selling price divided by the average variable cost.
[b] Estimated C_0 and F_u are $224.8 and $20m.
[c] Figures in parentheses denote average variable costs in $US.
Source: Dataquest (1987).

Cournot case. Many potential entrants could well have been attracted if this trend continued longer. Unfortunately, the effective price of 256K chips fell below the price of 64K chips in 1985, and the cycle virtually ended in 1984. The US output of 64K chips dropped by almost 50 per cent after 1985, and both types of firms ceased producing 64K chips in 1987.

Although the price of 64K chips once fell to a bottom level of 75 cents (in the third quarter of 1985, see Table 4), the market price on the average approached the average variable cost of the relatively more efficient Japanese firms. It implies that unless some of the existing firms withdraw from the 64K market, every firm begins to incur a loss. In fact toward the end of the cycle, leading firms faced a non-co-operative exit game and began to seek to outlast competitors. The exit game envisioned here corresponds to the second stage of the original game of dynamic competition we modelled in equation (3), and is itself of a dynamic nature. Sequential rationality implies that under the condition that firms either utilize fabrication lines fully or shut down, those firms with larger indivisible fabrication facilities exit first unless the cost differences with the small-scale firms are great. (See for example Ghemawat and Nalebuff 1985.) In fact, the cost difference may not matter at all since, if it lasts, the small firm could reduce the future average cost by moving down the learning curve. To illustrate our point, let $P(t; Q_t)$ denote the price of 64K chips at time t. Define $\bar{t}_i$ (i = U, J, and S) as follows.

$$\bar{t}_i = \text{Min} \{t | P(t; n_U q_U(t, K_U) + n_J q_J(t, K_J) + q_S(t; K_S)) \leq \text{AVC}_i(t)\}, \quad (8)$$

where $q_i(t, K_i)$ denotes the ith firm's maximum capacity output at time t with capacity K_i. Similarly define t_i^* (i = U, J, and S) as

$$t_i^* = \text{Min}\{t | P(t; n_i q_i(t, K_i)) \leq \text{AVC}_i(t)\}, \quad (9)$$

where $n_S = 1$.

Ignoring other late entrants, let S denote the Korean firm. Let us initialize the planning horizon so that the year 1981 corresponds to 1. Let $n_U = 5$ and $n_J = 6$. The Korean firm must have incurred losses when it first entered the mature market, so $\bar{t}_S = 4$. Table 5(b) shows that $\bar{t}_U \leq 5$ and $\bar{t}_J \leq 6$. As the yield rate improves, the full-capacity output of both the US firms and the Japanese firms must be greater in 1985 than in 1984. The 64K price was \$1.15 when 509 million units were supplied. Had every firm produced more than the previous year's output, the price in 1985 must then have fallen by more than 15 per cent unless the price elasticity ε_P exceeds 2.[8] But with $\mu = 0.28$ and our estimate of C_0, the average variable cost does not fall below \$1 within the conceivable range of cumulative output. It follows that the value of both $\bar{t}_U$ and $\bar{t}_J$ is 5. Similar reasoning shows that $t_U^* = t_J^* = 6$. This implies that even in the absence of the US firms, some of the Japanese firms had to exit by 1986. Notice that in 1987, the industry supply at the average selling price of \$1.07 was 150 million units, which shows that at least five Japanese firms and four US firms must have left the market by 1987. Because of its smaller scale and its late entry, Korean full-capacity output was very small relative to its competitors. On the other hand, the Korean firm moved rapidly down the falling initial phase of the yield curve. In equation (8) with $n_U = 1$ and $n_J = 1$, $\bar{t}_S$ may be greater than 7.

Let $t_U^*(1)$ and $t_J^*(1)$ be the value of the left-hand side of equation (9) when $n_U = 1$ and $n_J = 1$. Suppose $t_S^* > t_U^*(1)$ and $t_S^* > t_J^*(1)$. Let $\Pi_S(\bar{t}_S, t_S^*)$ denote the profits earned from $\bar{t}_S$ to t_S^*. If $\Pi_S(\bar{t}_S, t_S^*) > 0$, then the Korean firm can outlast every competitor.

Beginning from the first quarter of 1985, the leading US firms including Intel and Mostek left the market. The dominant Japanese firms maintained their market share until 1986, but eventually left the market in 1987. The Korean firm started large-scale production in 1984 and survived the exit game during the period, 1985–6. The Korean market share in the 64K market is now well above 20 per cent. Although the size of the 64K market has been absolutely smaller than that of the higher-density memory chips, it provided a good opportunity for the Korean firm to accumulate technical know-how and build its reputation in semiconductor devices. Until the third quarter of 1987, its accumulated shipment of 64K chips reached 83 million units, which is only slightly less than the cumulative output of the representative US firm in 1984. The market price has been steadily increasing since 1985. Having survived the exit game, its investment loss in the 64K market becomes minimal.

Although we do not yet know the value of $\Pi_s(\bar{t}_s, t_s^*)$, the Korean firm still supplied 64K chips in 1988 and broke even. Taking into account the fact that a small-scale re-entry from the US or Japan had not occurred, the Korean firm's learning curve must have been much below those of its foreign competitors. As of 1988, the Korean firm also supplied both 56K and 1M chips and is beginning to make profits. Given spill-over effects or external economies, the positive profit implies that the successful entry without governmental subsidies or market restrictions that might have had harmful effects on other industries is certainly welfare-improving. The fact that efficient Korean firms remain major suppliers in the lower segment of the commodity memory market suggests that their entry contributed to an increase in global welfare as well. The revealed comparative advantage in a vertically differentiated memory market was achieved as an outcome of an intense dynamic competition. In the next section, we explain why oligopolistic competition among the leading firms from developed countries may result in an inefficient outcome and leave a niche for a profitable entry. The investment race resulted in a wasteful shortening of the 64K life cycle and breakdown of the 256K market. The otherwise unsatisfied demands for lower-density memory chips have been met by the profitable entry of Korean firms.

5. INVESTMENT RACE AMONG THE LEADING FIRMS

Despite a shortening product cycle, price/cost ratios have fallen and the cost of building a minimum efficient fabrication facility has been increasing. During the 64K cycle (1981–4), the ten leading Japanese firms increased their annual investment expenditure from $700 million to $2.6 billion and the leading US firms from $1.5 billion to $2.7 billion. In 1985 the price ratio of 256K to 64K chips fell to about 4, signalling a resource shift away from 64K chips to 256K chips. The Japanese firms concentrated more on the higher-density commodity memory market and succeeded in pre-empting the 256K market. Their initial share exceeded 90 per cent, driving out their US rivals. Many previously dominant US merchant firms (but not Texas Instruments and Micro Technology) left the DRAM industry, anticipating Japanese dominance over the coming cycles. The price of 256K chips decreased from $150 in 1982 to $2.31 in 1986. The average selling price of 1M chips dropped from $100 in 1985 to $14 in 1987.

Pre-emptive investment competition often results in excess capacity. Since output is inelastically supplied at each point in time, downward pressure on the market price of the new product is unavoidable and the life cycle of the previous generations becomes shorter. Let $W_i(\hat{k}(t))$ denote the return to the ith firm when every firm holds capacity $\hat{k}(t) = (k_j(t))_j^N = 1$. Then

$$W_i(\hat{k}(t)) = \int_0^\infty \{V_i(\hat{k}(t)) - x_i(t)\} \, dt \quad \text{for} \quad i \, \varepsilon \, N. \tag{10}$$

Let $\hat{k}^*(t)$ denote equilibrium capacity holdings in the subgame of the investment race. Then $\hat{k}^*(t)$ will certainly influence the outcome of the exit game and the initial capacity choice in the 64K market (see equation (3)).

Strategic investment games of this sort have been much investigated in the literature (see for example Spence 1979, and Fudenberg and Tirole 1983, among others). The maintained hypothesis is that in equilibrium, firms invest as fast as they can to reach a steady state. If one firm starts earlier and has superior investment technology, it will exceed its steady-state Nash level to deter investment by the follower. First-mover advantage lies in the credible threat of investing further to reduce the late-comer's capacity in equilibrium. This implies that in a world of perfect information about the other firms' investment technology and rates of return, those firms incapable of competing in an investment race will leave the memory market as early as possible. The survival rate, then, will decrease over time and the memory market will eventually be dominated by only a few giant firms. Establishment of an early equilibrium of this kind partly explains the increasing concentration ratio in the commodity memory market. Among the five leading US firms in the 64K market, only two firms entered the 256K market.

The hypothesis that the number of remaining firms in the DRAM market is decreasing over time has an important implication for the entry process. In an industry with sequential entry the profitability of potential entrants is affected not only by the high current profits of the incumbent, but also by the ease with which further entrants can be deterred. If one of the potential entrants is able to raise lower-cost capital, it could be worth its while taking risks at the soonest possible time. We shall examine this implication later.

Further analysis of the investment competition must begin by relaxing assumptions employed in the existing literature. The assumption of perfect information about rates of return needs to be modified. As pointed out earlier, most of the Japanese firms are vertically integrated from the equipment end to the computer and communication system. This makes outward diffusion from Japan of equipment knowledge and early product information slow, leaving other countries behind in system design and manufacturing of equipment business, thus strengthening the Japanese comparative advantage in electronics-related products. Unlike that of the US manufacturer, Japanese marginal revenue earned in the memory market does not fully reflect the firm's benefit. The actual private benefit from investment in the DRAM fabrication facility is diffused throughout the affiliated companies and is difficult to measure. Spill-over effects make the competitor's rate of return uncertain and costly to figure out.

The firm's return from investment is realized only after the full set of fabrication facilities are completed and the required lead time depends on the level of investment, x_i. Let c_i denote the investment cost per unit time and $(dx_i)/(dc_i) > 0$. Assume that there exists $\bar{c}$ such that c_i does not exceed $\bar{c}$. Let $\tau_i(c_i)$ denote the required time to complete the minimum efficient fabrication capacity, k_0. It is expected that $\tau'_i(c_i) < 0$. For expositional convenience, we assume that only two firms i and j compete in the higher-density memory market, and that each firm's current capacity is such that only one additional fabrication line becomes profitable. In other words, the firm that builds later is not able to recover the additional capacity cost. The value of having an extra fabrication line earlier than the competitor is denoted by V_i and V_j respectively. These values are privately known and each firm has a probability distribution function, $F_i(V_j)(F_j(V_i))$, about the other firm's value which has positive density on an interval of positive value. Since each firm's strategic choice of the investment cost depends on its own value, let us introduce a function $V_i = y_i(c_i)$ such that $y'_i(\cdot) > 0$. Each firm then maximizes $W_i(c_i, c_j)$ defined as

$$W_i(c_i, c_j) = \int_0^{c_i} [V_i - c_i \tau_i(c_i)] \, dF_i(y_i(c_j)) - c_i \tau_i(c_i)[1 - F_i(y_j(c_i))]$$
$$\text{for } i, j = 1, 2. \quad (11)$$

From the first-order condition, we have

$$V_i F'_i(\cdot) y'_j(c_i) - \frac{d\{c_i \tau_i(c_i)\}}{dc_i} = 0 \quad (12)$$

and

$$V_j F'_j(\cdot) y'_i(c_j) - \frac{d\{c_j \tau_j(c_j)\}}{dc_j} = 0, \quad (13)$$

where we have assumed $y_i(c) = y_j(c)$ for the same value of c. To illustrate the possibility of an overcapacity equilibrium, let us assume symmetric distribution and the same investment technology. Then $F'_i(\cdot) = F'_j(\cdot)$ and $\tau_i(\cdot) = \tau_j(\cdot)$. It follows that

$$\frac{V_i}{V_j} = \frac{y'_j(c_i)}{y'_i(c_j)}. \quad (14)$$

Let $y_i(\bar{c}) = y_j(\bar{c}) = \alpha$. Then at equilibrium, (c_i^*, c_j^*), we have

$$y_i(c_j^*) = \left(\frac{V_i}{V_j}\right) y_j(c_i^*) + \alpha\left(1 - \frac{V_i}{V_j}\right). \tag{15}$$

Assume that $V_i < V_j$. Then using the inverse relationship $V_i = y_i(c_i)$, we can easily establish that the probability that the ith firm does not invest $(c_i^* = 0)$ is $F_i^{-1}\left[\left(\alpha\left(1 - \frac{V_i}{V_j}\right)\right)\right]$.

This probability increases as V_i/V_j decreases. If it is commonly believed that V_i and V_j are nearly the same, then it becomes more probable that both firms build extra capacity to reach an equilibrium with overcapacity.

Our simple exercise shows that under uncertainty about the competitive environment, lack of dynamic co-ordination creates an equilibrium with overcapacity engendering downward pressure on the market price of newer products. This will unnecessarily shorten the previous life cycle and drive out the existing firms in a wasteful way.

The early collapse of the 64K market seems due to excessive overcapacity that resulted from pre-emptive investment competition. Dominant firms aimed at reaping the high profit margin phase of the next product life cycle. Implicit collusion disappeared and the DRAM industry became more like a competitive industry with high fixed cost. Toward the end of the 64K cycle, both 64K and 256K chips were underpriced. Some experts estimated that as much as 60 to 70 per cent of the high-volume world-wide DRAM capacity sat idle in 1985. Investment races involved a so-called 'war of attrition' and there existed no mechanism for dynamic co-ordination of investment strategy. Prices fell below the average variable cost of production accelerating the speed of exit. Because of indivisibility in the operation of fabrication lines, production capacities became technologically obsolete and were closed down. As we stated earlier, the demand for 64K chips was still there (see Table 2), but leading firms virtually stopped producing. The imbalance between market demand and industry supply was caused by the inefficient investment race among the leading firms. Unsatisfied demands for lower-density memory chips opened a niche for Korean firms in the quality space of commodity memory products. Until 1985, Korea's cumulative output of 64K chips was negligible and it was never in an advantageous position to threaten competitors. In fact, what looked like a sudden and abrupt collapse in output and employment in the US DRAM industry resulted from the inefficient investment race, and the Korean firm merely corrected the imbalance between market demand and supply (see Table 4).

The semiconductor industry seems to have become increasingly segmented. Those firms having difficulty in financing the aggressive investment race in the commodity memory market left this low-cost, high-volume end of the industry. Some of them strong enough in basic research undertook investment to develop much more R & D-intensive high-value-added products. Examples are custom or semi-custom integrated circuits (ICs), and application-specific ICs. They penetrated the high-value-added niches and participated in the basic creative process of generating new products. Korean firms did not follow this strategy. They relied on US patents and technology licensing and were supported by accumulated technical and business resources in related fields. Large spillover effects made them willing to take risks and decide on an early entering time. Heightened entry barriers in the commodity memory segment were regarded as guaranteeing a fair rate of return, once they had successfully entered the market. Korean firms took advantage of the strategic fact that later potential entrants were bound to face much higher barriers and could be safely deterred.[9] Fortunately for the Korean firms, a series of anti-dumping rulings against the Japanese firms by the US Department of Commerce and the ensuing US–Japan Microchip pact supported high prices in the US market.

6. CONCLUDING COMMENTS

We have developed an argument that even in a high-tech industry a late entrant can survive intense dynamic competition. Without direct subsidy or trade-restricting policies to protect them from foreign competition, Korean firms successfully entered the high-density memory commodity market. Their growth strategy was initially viewed as surprising to those who were not well informed about the technological possibilities and the future demand. It turned out to be right and well tuned to the overall development process of the Korean economy. No delicate central planning could have induced the Korean firms to do what they did. They relied solely upon market forces and their own competitive strength.

As we saw in the previous sections the price-cost margin of the particular chip declines as the product cycle progresses. Leading firms build large-scale capacities at the beginning of the cycle and continue to produce maximum-capacity output along their learning curves until the market price falls below the average variable cost. But toward the end of the cycle price competition becomes intense and not every firm can profitably supply chips. Even though the capacity cost is sunk, the firm would stop production if the revenue from the declining market demand were not sufficient to cover the variable cost. Since the operation of the fabrication line is largely indivisible, only those relatively more efficient and smaller-sized firms can outlast their competitors. Dominant firms take a first-mover advantage at an initial profitable phase but leave the market earlier. A large-scale exit of leading firms retards the speed of decline of market demand and an efficient small firm could stay longer. Although the Korean firm entered the market at a later stage than its competitors, the capacity size was correctly estimated and the learning curve was steep enough to enable it to supply the chips profitably even at the end of the cycle. Technological-linkage effects between the successive generations of chips and spill-over effects on the subsidiaries of the conglomerate firm were other factors contributing to early success from its risky entry decision. Since then Korea has remained as the only developing country that exports higher-density memory chips to the United States.

Given the fact that the Korean firm earned normal profits in the 64K chips, we could have estimated its learning curve and quantified the possible effects of various trade policy measures. Instead we emphasized the successful entry that occurred *without* direct subsidy or market restrictions. But we must not neglect the important role played by past industrial and trade policy in the growth of domestic demand for high-tech memory chips and the accumulation of know-how in the related engineering and marketing areas. Since these effects are diffused over time they are difficult to quantify in our calibrated model.

Throughout the chapter we argued that it would have been almost impossible for the Korean government to collect all the necessary information to simulate the complex incentives operating inside the internal organization of the private firm. Industrial planning often fails in a rapidly changing dynamic environment. In fact, Korea had already experienced a serious governmental failure in promoting the heavy chemical industry during the late 1970s. Difficulties associated with designating an efficient winner in an infant industry where dynamic scale effects necessitate a domestic monopoly power are well known. If, in addition, an ever-increasing capital requirement is likely that might promote the targeted industry, a government from a small, open, developing economy may become even more risk-averse and seek to avoid the burden on limited financial resources placed by aggressive responses from the foreign developed countries. Domestic monopoly power and rent extraction in an intermediate-goods industry could also hurt the growth of final-goods industries.

In the 1980s, the government took a step toward introducing further competition into the domestic semiconductor industry. No incentives were provided to promote the purchase of memory chips fabricated by the domestic firm. At the initial stage, Korean semiconductor firms had to rely upon foreign demand and invested heavily to establish their own distribution channels. It took several years of costly and wasteful competition among domestic electronics firms to reach a mutually beneficial state of altruistic exchange of parts and components that are now produced in the domestic industry. This outcome has been the natural product of continued cut-throat competition and deepening dependency on imported foreign technology from Japan. It has been self-enforcing in establishing long-term relationships among the leading domestic firms. It is yet to be seen whether this implicit co-operation will continue over time. In response, the government planned to initiate an incentive scheme to permit the leading firms to share the cost and diffuse information in R & D activities in the higher-density memory market. The scheme will resemble those already implemented in Japan in the 1970s and the United States in the 1980s. Again it is too early to judge the success of this information-sharing mechanism. It is interesting to note that this governmental response followed only after the successful entry.

As is well known, the world markets for leading items of Korean export are mostly vertically segmented, with the high-quality end dominated by firms from developed countries, and the lower segment of product quality dominated by numerous competitive firms from developing countries. Estimated price elasticities of Korean manufactured export goods are very high while Korean import demand for capital equipment and intermediate goods is very inelastic. The large-scale export of low-technology goods has been threatened by the protectionist movement in the US market, whereas market power in the vertically segmented industry is greater in the firms located in the high-quality end. Realignment of international currencies raised the cost of inelastic imports of capital equipment, parts, and components from Japan.

From the early 1980s, market forces moved in the direction of import substitution of system-like components and strategically important capital equipment. Expanding trade volume made Korean firms introduce modern scientific management techniques and flexible manufacturing systems. Rational anticipation of structural changes in the Korean economy encouraged an optimistic view of the growth of domestic demand for semiconductor devices and induced the leading Korean entrepreneurs to venture into the high-tech industry.

REFERENCES

BALDWIN, R., and KRUGMAN, P. (1987), 'Market Access and International Competition: A Simulation Study of 16K Random Access Memories', in R. Feenstra (ed.), *Empirical Research in International Trade* (MIT Press, Cambridge, Mass.).

BORRUS, M., TYSON, L., and ZYSMAN, J. (1986), 'Creating Advantages: How Government Policies Shape International Trade in the Semiconductor Industry', in P. Krugmen (ed.), *Strategic Trade Policy and the New International Economics* (MIT Press, Cambridge, Mass.).

BRANDER, J. (1986), 'Rationales for Strategic Trade and Industry Policy', in P. Krugmen (ed.), *Strategic Trade Policy and the New International Economics* (MIT Press, Cambridge, Mass.).

DIXIT, A. (1987), 'Optimal Trade and Industrial Policies for the U.S. Automobile Industry', in R. Feenstra (ed.), *Empirical Research in International Trade* (MIT Press, Cambridge, Mass.).
FINAN, W., and AMUNDSEN, C. (1986) 'Modeling U.S.-Japan Competition in Semiconductors', *Journal of Policy Modeling*, 8/3, pp. 305–26.
FUDENBURG, D., and TIROLE, J. (1983), 'Capital as a Commitment: Strategic Investment to Deter Mobility', *Journal of Economic Theory*, 31/2, pp. 227–50.
GHEMAWAT, P., and NALEBUFF, B. (1985), 'Exit', *Rand Journal of Economics*, 16/2, pp. 184–94.
GRUBEL, H., and LLOYD, P. J. (1975), *Intra-Industry Trade. The Theory and Measurement of International Trade in Differentiated Products* (Macmillan, London).
HELLEINER, G. K. (1985), 'Industrial Organization, Trade and Investment: A Selective Literature Review for Developing Countries' (Dept. of Economics, University of Toronto), mimeo.
KRUGMAN, P. (1986), 'New Trade Theory and the Less-Developed Countries' (WIDER, Helsinki), mimeo.
——(1988), 'Multistage International Competition', in M. Spence and H. Hazard (eds.), *International Competitiveness* (Ballinger, Cambridge, Mass.), pp. 289–300.
LEVIN, R. C. (1982), 'The Semiconductor Industry', in R. Nelson, (ed.), *Government and Technical Progress: A Cross Industry Analysis* (Pergamon Press, New York).
MODY, A., and WHEELER, D. (1987), 'Prices, Costs and Competition at the Technology Frontier: A Model for Semiconductor Memories', *Journal of Policy Modeling*, 9/2, pp. 367–82.
NALEBUFF, B., and RILEY, J. (1984), 'Asymmetric Equilibria in the War of Attrition' (Working Paper 317, University of California, Los Angeles).
NEELY, R. (1986), 'A Restructured IC Economy Needs a Restructured Strategy', *Electronic Business*, (Mar.), pp. 84–92.
SPENCE, M. (1979), 'Investment Strategy and Growth in a New Market', *Bell Journal of Economics*, 10/1, pp. 1–19.
——(1981), 'The Learning Curve and Competition', *Bell Journal of Economics*, 12/1, pp. 49–70.

NOTES

1. The effective price is the average selling price per bit.
2. See Table 5(*b*) in Sect. 4.
3. If $h(K, t) = (Kt)^a$ as assumed by Baldwin and Krugman, then $q(t) = K^{1+a}t^a$ and the average-variable cost equals $C_0 K/K^{1+a}t^a$. The constant a determines the elasticity of average variable cost with respect to cumulative output. Following their estimate, we assume that this elasticity is 0.28.
4. We are dealing with the case of no discounting. This enables us easily to compute cost parameters with no additional information on the rate of interest.
5. The game consists of three stages that must be solved backwards, and any

equilibrium must be subgame perfect. Notice that we exclude the possibility of building an additional fabrication line by incumbents after $t = 0$.
6. See n. 2 above. For expositional convenience, we assumed $h(K,t) = (Kt)^a$. Every firm utilizes its capacity fully, and we do not consider a possibility of holding excess capacity.
7. Our results confirm those of a previous study of collusive behaviour in the 64K market, Mody and Wheeler (1987).
8. In Finan and Amundsen (1986), the estimated price elasticity is 1.8.
9. Although we have not examined technological linkage effects, their presence certainly makes the later entry more difficult. In their presence, it could well be the case that firms incur losses in the current period to earn (compensating) profits later. Access to low-cost capital is important for the firm to take a long-sighted view (see Krugman 1988). On the other hand, Korean firms do not seem to have lost money in the 64K and 256K market.

11

Total Factor Productivity in Automobile Production in Argentina, Mexico, Korea, and Canada: The Impacts of Protection

Leonard Waverman and Steven Murphy

1. INTRODUCTION

The automobile industry is a classic example of the use of import-substitution policies. Both developed and less developed countries impose constraints designed to shift production from overseas to the home market. The constraints imposed are numerous: prohibitive tariffs on the importation of finished vehicles and/or parts; quotas and a whole host of domestic content rules. Yet automobile production is a classic example of an industry with substantial scale economies. Hence it has often been argued and demonstrated that these import-substitution policies raise the costs of production, lower productivity, and substantially raise domestic prices.[1]

The main purpose of this chapter is to measure changes in total factor productivity in the auto-assembly industries of three semi-industrialized countries (SIs)—Argentina, Korea, and Mexico—and compare their performance to that achieved in Canada. Rates of growth of TFP are then the measure of performance used here. These rates of growth of course signal little about the level of TFP or unit costs. Levels of TFP are most difficult to measure (see Fuss and Waverman, forthcoming) and have not been calculated here.

Several other issues are addressed. First, we examine how trade restraints and domestic content rules may *bias* measures of total factor productivity and we indicate how total factor productivity should be measured in the presence of trade restraints. Secondly, using costs in Canadian auto plants as a base, I provide rudimentary measures of the unit-cost penalties that would be incurred in these three SIs at per plant capacity levels and utilization rates lower than those achieved in Canada. Thirdly, we provide graphic support for Howard Pack's thesis—changes in total factor productivity by themselves do not signal much about the social performance of an industry. In addition, rapid TFP growth does not mean that the industry is able to compete in world markets. In the 1970s the second highest rate of TFP growth in auto assembly in these four countries occurred in the most autarkic of industries (Argentina). (Korea had the highest TFP growth rate.) TFP is not an end of but a means to development. We also provide evidence for Dani Rodrik's thesis that theory provides no guide as to whether trade liberalization is beneficial for the rate of growth of productivity. While a high rate of TFP growth for Argentina occurred during its trade-liberalization period, consistently high rates of TFP occurred under regimes of trade restraints. The measured rates of TFP growth in the four countries cannot be explained by trade policy.

Automobile assembly began in the early 1920s in Argentina and Mexico, but not until the 1950s in Korea. In 1986, 138,000, 170,000, and 457,000 cars were assembled in Argentina, Mexico, and Korea, respectively. 1986 was a year of peak automobile production for Korea, but 1986 production was well below the peak established in the other countries (1973 for Argentina, 1981 for Mexico). Table 1 provides data on the automobile industries of each of these three countries and Canada—a country we will use as a base against which to judge the efficiency of production in the SIs.

All four countries (including Canada) use a series of tariffs and non-tariff barriers (NTBs) to affect automobile production. The four countries utilize domestic content rules; all except Canada impose very high tariffs on the imports of finished vehicles and (to a somewhat lesser extent) of automotive parts. The import-substitution policies introduced by the four countries have served their purpose: major multinationals have set up assembly operations to serve a share of the small localized market. Entry at small scale has its costs. In 1965, production in each of the four countries was below the minimum efficient level estimated by White (1971) for *one* assembly plant (400,000 cars per year); furthermore the actual output levels achieved in each country were spread over numerous firms and more numerous models.[2]

Canada has the advantage of a twenty-three-year 'Auto Pact' with the USA, a pact which allows duty-free entry into the US market of Canadian finished vehicles and parts which meet the content rules established in 1965. Auto exports from the three SIs are not 'protected' by a pact such as that enjoyed by Canada in sales to the US market.[3] Argentina has never exported cars to North America or Europe; Korean exports to the USA are a recent phenomenon; Mexico is a growing source of parts and a recent source of exported cars to the USA and Canada.

As can also be seen in Table 1, the annual volume of production has fluctuated widely in all four countries, the most in Argentina and Mexico. The fluctuations in these two countries are more pronounced because of the reliance on sales in domestic markets—markets which are susceptible to wide swings in domestic macroeconomic policy and credit conditions, oil price shocks, and pressures on foreign-exchange reserves. Fluctuations in Canadian car output are due to general North American problems of

THE IMPACTS OF PROTECTION

Table 1. Production

	Argentina		Mexico	
	Autos	Comm. Veh.	Autos	Comm. Veh.
1956	326	5 617		39 387
1957	5 461	10 174		41 106
1958	14 310	13 524		38 955
1959	18 290	14 602		51 118
1960	40 144	49 194		49 807
1961	78 274	57 914		62 563
1962	90 648	39 232		66 637
1963	175 338	29 561		69 135
1964	114 617	51 866		90 752
1965	133 734	60 802		96 654
1966	133 812	45 641		113 807
1967	130 297	45 021		126 365
1968	127 965	43 011		143 478
1969	153 047	65 543		165 164
1970	167 000	52 599	136 712	56 108
1971	193 105	60 132	153 412	57 373
1972	200 885	67 708	163 005	66 761
1973	219 439	74 303	200 147	85 366
1974	212 088	74 224	248 574	102 181
1975	185 162	54 874	237 118	119 309
1976	142 072	51 445	212 549	112 251
1977	168 126	67 230	187 637	92 176
1978	133 416	45 744	242 519	141 609
1979	192 011	61 206	280 049	164 377
1980	218 640	63 153	303 056	186 950
1981	139 428	32 935	355 497	241 621
1982	106 886	25 231	300 579	172 058
1983	128 962	30 914	207 137	78 348
1984	137 206	30 117	231 578	112 120
1985	113 788	23 887	246 960	151 232
1986	137 889	32 601	169 567	102 601
	Korea		Canada	
	Autos	Comm. Veh.	Autos	Comm. Veh.
1957			340 381	73 196
1958			297 373	59 045
1959			301 435	66 504
1960			325 785	71 954

Table 1. (Cont'd.)

	Korea		Canada	
	Autos	Comm. Veh.	Autos	Comm. Veh.
1961			323 638	63 285
1962	1 710	67	424 581	80 606
1963	1 063	191	532 243	99 113
1964	216	33	559 603	111 387
1965	106	35	706 810	139 799
1966	3 117	313	684 547	187 667
1967	4 983	1 621	708 281	211 227
1968	11 630	6 027	889 386	260 832
1969	19 494	11 500	1 025 994	300 484
1970	14 487	14 332	923 437	236 067
1971	12 428	10 574	1 083 201	263 564
1972	9 525	9 123	1 135 702	294 382
1973	12 751	13 563	1 216 508	331 799
1974	9 069	21 221	1 171 730	353 852
1975	18 498	18 781	1 027 242	357 895
1976	26 701	22 844	1 119 005	408 847
1977	43 981	41 229	1 120 157	570 927
1978	86 823	72 135	1 107 874	634 092
1979	113 564	90 883	960 614	625 624
1980	57 225	65 910	820 114	503 885
1981	68 760	65 474	796 378	492 853
1982	94 460	68 130	807 645	468 395
1983	121 987	99 032	970 933	554 327
1984	158 503	106 858	1 023 357	811 722
1985	264 458	113 704	1 077 932	856 178
1986	457 383	144 163	1 061 738	792 680

production costs and styling, and are not due to the kinds of foreign-exchange-led macroeconomic pressures which characterize production swings in less developed countries. Moreover the general advanced state of economic development in Canada means that fluctuations in auto output and employment are not devastating to the Canadian economy. For all four countries, output fluctuations are costly. Automobile production is characterized by capital-intensive production techniques with well-defined capacity limits. Fluctuations in output lead to underutilized capital, substantially increasing unit costs of production.

In the following section, I provide a brief history of automobile production in the four countries concentrating on output changes and trade restraints.

1.1 Motor Vehicle Production in Argentina, Mexico, and Canada

1920s to 1950s

Motor vehicle sales and production began early in the twentieth century in Argentina, Mexico, and Canada. By the mid-1920s, American multinationals were assembling cars in each of the three countries. In 1929, these firms assembled in Argentina half the domestic sales of 76,561 vehicles, 197,556 vehicles in Canada, and a small number of cars in Mexico. In Argentina and Mexico the level of local assembly diminished sharply during the Depression and the Second World War. In 1951, eighteen cars were produced in Argentina; the US 'Big 3' did not again assemble cars in Argentina until 1962 (they did remain active in truck assembly throughout the period). In 1958, Ford and GM produced 11,900 units, half of Mexican production.[4] In that same year, *ten* other assembly operations (basically Mexican-owned) produced another 10,100 cars, the largest of which (Auto-Mex) assembled 5,300 Chrysler products (Bennett and Sharpe 1985, p. 50).

Canada had adopted classical import-substitution policies early on (1930s). High tariffs on imported vehicles and parts were combined with domestic content rules (60 per cent for passenger cars and 50 per cent for commercial vehicles), plus a duty drawback scheme for imported parts.[5] In the late 1950s, the Canadian automotive industry was suffering from the excess costs of autarky. Since most models of the US multinationals were produced domestically and sold in Canada, production runs were low, die changes were frequent, and unit costs were high. In 1958, the total Canadian auto-industry output of 297,000 units was divided among four manufacturers and many, many models. Exports were negligible.

1960s

A Royal Commission to study the Canadian automobile industry was appointed in 1961. In the same period, auto-assembly policy was being rethought in Argentina and Mexico. In 1959 and 1960, a new set of fiscal incentives and tariff protection was put into place in Argentina to attract local assembly of autos.[6] The minimum domestic content was set at 60-70 per cent for 1960, rising to 90 per cent in 1964 (Jenkins 1987, p. 46).[7] As in the other countries studied, domestic content refers to the materials and labour, not the equipment or capital, used in production.[8] The combination of prohibitive duties plus incentives for local manufacturing attracted many producers into the Argentinian auto sector. Fifteen firms were in operation in the early 1960s (output rose to 140,000 vehicles per year); clearly no firm was anywhere near minimum efficient scale (m.e.s.).[9]

In Mexico in 1958, 22,000 cars were produced involving some twenty-four different makes.[10] Protection was via tariffs and import quotas, which in essence prevented the entry of fully finished vehicles, but allowed the importation of all parts as completely knocked-down (CKD) kits. The first major initiative by the Mexican government to increase domestic production and the manufacturing of parts was introduced in 1960. Originally, the 1960 plan was to limit the number of assemblers to at most five, to limit each assembler to one model, and one model change each five years. After protests by the existing ten assemblers, the plan as enacted as law on 23 August 1962 placed no limits on the number of producers or models.[11] Domestic local content was set at 60 per cent in Mexico, much lower than in Argentina and similar to Canada. The vertical integration of assemblers was limited to engine blocks and to components produced prior to 1962. All imported parts had to be approved by the government. Finally, the government set quotas for the producers, attempting to carve out market share for the domestically owned firms.

The Canadian Royal Commission on the auto industry produced its report in 1962. In 1965, the USA and Canada signed an historic agreement— the 'Auto Pact' which liberalized motor-vehicle trade between the two countries.

The Auto Pact stipulated the tariff-free entry of Canadian automobiles or original equipment parts into the US market if a minimum of 50 per cent North American (US or Canadian) content was achieved. For tariff-free entry into Canada the 'qualified' manufacturers, the Big 4 (now the Big 3, GM, Ford, and Chrysler, Chrysler having absorbed American Motors in 1989) have to maintain a certain ratio between the net sales value of vehicles made in Canada and the net sales value of vehicles sold in Canada. In addition the qualified manufacturers ensured that in each model year, the value added in Canada would amount to at least 60 per cent of the growth in the value of cars sold in the base year (1964).[12]

Production (assembly) in Canada grew rapidly as did trade. The total number of passenger cars produced in Canada which had doubled between 1961 and 1965 remained flat to 1967, but then increased by over 40 per cent in two years (reaching 1,000,000 vehicles in 1969).

1970s
The 1960s and early 1970s saw very different developments in the three countries. Production stagnated in Argentina in the mid- to late 1960s, and domestic prices remained high. In 1970, a new Argentinian law was passed designed to increase efficiency in the industry, reduce capital outflows, and increase domestic ownership. The attempt at increased efficiency did not succeed.[13] The number of models produced, which had doubled between 1964 and 1972, fell only slightly by 1976. Minimum domestic content was increased in Argentina to 96 per cent (a somewhat contradictory policy for a country attempting to increase efficiency),[14] and export subsidies were greatly expanded.[15] Argentinian production and exports did increase, pro-

duction in 1973 reaching its all-time high (even today) of 219,000 cars and 74,000 commercial vehicles.

In Mexico, output increased by 50 per cent between 1962 and 1964, and continued to rise over the remainder of the 1960s, doubling between 1964 and 1970.[16] Five of the ten assemblers in operation in 1962 exited by 1970 (three small domestic firms, Studebaker, and International Harvester left the industry); one firm—Nissan—entered.[17] Because of the lower domestic content rule, unit costs of production in Mexico, estimated at 50 per cent above those of the USA, were significantly below production costs in Argentina.[18] The Mexican government became concerned that development had not produced efficient world-scale plants. Mexico's entire 1970 production of motor vehicles was near that of one m.e.s. plant, but was split among seven assemblers and forty models, 100 models if two-door and four-door versions are considered as different (Jenkins 1987, p. 110). Another problem was the costs of automotive parts; these imports accounted for over 10 per cent of all merchandise imports in 1968. Imports of machinery and equipment were also large (Mexico did not have to worry about imported oil).

A new Mexican automotive policy was announced in 1969 and formally introduced in October 1972.[19] That policy rejected the imposition of higher domestic content rules based on an examination of developments in Argentina (and Brazil). This decree linked imports to exports in order to acquire the right to sell in the domestic market.[20] At least 40 per cent of these exports had to be parts (to provide the incentives for domestically owned parts firms to expand and obtain scale economies).[21] This policy worked until the Mexican (and world-wide) recession of 1975 and the ensuing reduction in car sales around the world.

1980s
In 1978, an Argentinian government Commission stated that the automotive industry was 'inefficient, excessively dependent on subsidies and producing vehicles at double the unit cost of vehicles on the world market' (Jenkins 1987, p. 290). Argentina tried the 'cold bath' of competition with the aim of improving efficiency. The effective ban on the imports of parts and finished vehicles was removed by reducing tariffs to 45 per cent on cars, 55 per cent on trucks, and 30 per cent on parts.[22] The import content was allowed to be increased to 12 per cent for automobiles and 25 per cent for commercial vehicles (above 1,500 kg). By 1982 a significant rationalization occurred in the industry leaving four firms in the market.[23] Domestic production also increased, rising by nearly 50 per cent in two years (still short of the 1973 peak, however). When domestic sales plummeted in 1981 (due to poor economic conditions—a plight for auto producers everywhere but Japan, Germany, and oil-rich economies), production fell back to near-1978 levels.

Imported vehicles, which had been 500 units per year in 1972 and 1978 hit 60,000 units in 1981 (25 per cent of sales). The import competition period was over. Strict import controls and enhanced domestic content rules were reintroduced. Auto production continued to languish, not even reaching 1981 levels through 1986.

As Mexico's balance of payments deteriorated sharply in the mid-1970s due to payments on external borrowings and increased imports of capital goods,[24] Mexican automotive industry policies again came under reconsideration.[25] In 1978, the government introduced more sophisticated export-promotion schemes, where exports would have to compensate for imported parts, the import content of the domestic parts used, and foreign remittances.[26] Domestic content requirements were raised somewhat by calculating domestic content as 50 per cent of the costs of parts rather than the costs of production, thus removing assembly costs from the calculation.[27] Price controls were eliminated, as were quotas for domestic sales. These export incentives (constraints) combined with the *maquiladora* programme[28] ('in-bond' assembly in Mexico utilizing foreign-made components) led to some increases in exports, but not to the extent predicted. The government announced subsidies for producers of domestic parts, and in August 1980 its 'Engine Resolution' guaranteeing a large part of the engine component market to domestic producers. Between 1978 and 1981, the oil boom led to a substantial 47 per cent increase in auto output. After 1981, the macroeconomic problems of Mexico sharply impacted on the auto-assembly sector as domestic sales sunk. The *maquiladora* programme remained successful.

The Canadian motor-vehicle assembly industry quickly became integrated into the US producing industry. The cyclical problems of the North American auto industry, however, overcame the incentives of rationalization. Canadian passenger-car output peaked at 1,211,000 units in 1973, a level not again reached until 1983. Commercial vehicle production showed more consistent growth, at least until 1978.

Exports and two-way trade in motor vehicles (finished vehicles and parts) grew rapidly between Canada and the USA. In 1966, total Canadian exports of motor vehicles and related products equalled $Can.488 million. In 1973, the value of these exports was $3 billion, and in 1986, $6.7 billion. Until 1982, Canada's balance of current account payments on auto trade remained negative—$1.0 billion in 1974 and $3.2 billion in 1979 because of the imports of parts to be used in the production of motor vehicles. Various duty-remission schemes were introduced by the Canadian federal government in an attempt to encourage more parts exports, schemes which American parts producers considered as export subsidies and against the spirit of the Auto Pact.

The devaluation of the Canadian dollar and the resurgence of the US domestic car market led to large increases in Canadian automotive exports to the USA (they doubled between 1980 and 1983 to $13.4 billion).

Canada's net current account balance in automotive trade with the USA peaked in 1984 at a $5.7 billion surplus. Note that these trade surpluses consisted of large surpluses in finished-vehicle trade ($10.8 billion in 1984) and large deficits in parts trade with the US ($5.2 billion in 1984). Canada has had a large and growing deficit in auto trade with the rest of the world other than the USA since 1980—a $5.7 billion deficit in 1986.

The Canadian automotive industry is a large assembler of semi-finished components, many imported from the USA (or Third World countries) under Auto Pact provisions. Aside from exports to the USA under the Auto Pact, the 'Canadian' automotive industry is not export-oriented (neither is the US industry).

1.2 Korea

The Korean auto industry developed out of the Jeep repair industry which arose during the Korean war. In the late 1950s, domestic production consisted of the assembly of CKD kits of Toyota Corollas (Shinjin Motor Co.). Hyundai began operations in 1967 as an assembler of Ford Cortinas. Asia began assembling Fiat kits in 1970. In 1974, 9,000 cars were produced (plus 19,000 trucks).

In 1962, the government prohibited the importation of assembled vehicles and ordered that majority domestic ownership was a requirement for assembly in Korea. Domestic content requirements were imposed at modest levels and raised as the ability of domestic parts manufacturers rose. In 1969, 19,500 cars were assembled, as were 11,500 commercial vehicles. Auto production in 1974 however was well below 1969 levels. The government orchestrated a change in the industry in 1975 when autos became a chosen growth sector. Capacity additions and growth in domestic demand led to substantial production increases. Motor-vehicle production reached 204,000 units (114,000 passenger cars, 90,000 commercial vehicles) in 1979, an enormous rate of growth in four years. The Korean government attempted to rely on export-led growth for the auto sector, the opposite of the Argentinian case. Domestic demand was discouraged through very high sales taxes on cars (45 per cent) and extremely high petrol prices. In 1979, at the then peak in production, only 89,000 cars were sold in Korea, spread among six models from three producers. Vehicle exports averaged 25,000 units per year from 1978 to 1982. Capacity in 1979 was 231,000 cars and 110,000 commercial vehicles.[29] Capacity-utilization rates were 50 per cent for cars and 75 per cent for commercial vehicles. As a result of these factors, production costs were high: in 1979 the Hyundai Pony was estimated as costing $3,972, as compared to $2,300 for the Toyota Corolla.[30]

The oil price shock of 1979–80 led to a recession in the Korean auto industry as it did in Argentina, Canada, and the USA.[31] Output fell by nearly 50 per cent, capacity utilization obviously plummeting. The 1979 output level was not reached again until 1983. In 1974, the government had anticipated a production level of 500,000 cars in 1980 (Altshuler *et al.* 1984, p. 41); actual production was only 20 per cent of that level. Output began to rise substantially once again in 1983–4.

The Korean government reacted quickly to the 1980 downturn and the 1979 estimates of high unit production costs. Passenger-car production was temporarily limited to the two major firms, Hyundai and Daewoo (50 per cent owned by GM).[32] Kia was given a temporary monopoly to produce light trucks; trucks between 5 and 8 tons could be produced by Hyundai and Daewoo, and Asia alone could produce large trucks. Similar limitations were placed on bus and specialty vehicle production. The aim was to export to North America–Canada chosen as the test market. The Hyundai Pony, an amalgam of imported parts and licensed technology, became the most successful new car ever imported into Canada.[33]

In the 1986 Industrial Development Act the auto industry was selected as an 'infant industry' and entry by foreign firms was forbidden until 1994. In 1987, Kia was allowed to re-enter auto production, as Hyundai and Daewoo would soon be allowed to re-enter large-truck production. Entry into domestic production is still tightly controlled; for example Samsung has not been allowed to establish a desired joint venture with Chrysler.

Restrictions have also been imposed on parts production. Small domestic firms were carefully nurtured by minimizing foreign ownership except in joint ventures, by initially preventing vertical integration by the domestic assemblers, and by establishing increased domestic content requirements and high tariffs. Geber (1985) estimated that two-thirds of the Korean autoparts sector consisted of firms employing 100 persons or less. Recently, larger joint ventures between General Motors and Daewoo subsidiaries have been allowed.

1.3 Summary

The four countries have followed different policies to increase the number of cars manufactured locally. All have used tariffs and NTBs, principally domestic content rules. Some have been more successful than others. The Canadian industry produces more cars than the other three countries combined as a result of the Auto Pact with the USA. Only Korea however has developed successful (at least to this point) indigenous producers. In what follows I attempt to measure the costs of protection—principally the costs of domestic content rules by examining the growth rates of total factor productivity.

2. MEASURING TOTAL FACTOR PRODUCTIVITY: THE IMPACTS OF TRADE RESTRAINTS

2.1 TFP

The relative performance of various country's motor-vehicle industries can be compared by examining changes in total factor productivity (TFP) or cost efficiency (CE) over time. Both TFP and CE measure the real resource cost of production: changes in TFP result from changes in output not accounted for by changes in the physical volumes of inputs; changes in CE result from changes in unit cost not accounted for by changes in input prices.

We can compute TFP growth for country i between periods t and $t-1$ as:

$$\Delta \text{TFP}_{it,t-1} = \frac{Q_{it}/X_{it}(L,M,K)}{Q_{i,t-1}(L,M,K)/X_{i,t-1}(L,M,K)} \quad (1)$$

where Q is output and $X(L, M, K)$ is an *aggregation* formula for combining the inputs—labour, materials, and capital.

The aggregation formula used here is the Tornquist index:

$$\log X_t - \log X_{t-1} = S_L (\log L_t - \log L_{t-1}) + S_M (\log M_t - \log M_{t-1}) \\ + S_K (\log K_t - \log K_{t-1}) \quad (2)$$

where S_L, S_M, S_K are the cost shares of labour, materials, and capital, respectively.

Normally TFP is indexed at 1 in the base year, that is,

$$\text{TFP}_0 = Q_0 = X_0 = 1.$$

The difference in TFP between periods $t-1$ and t for country i can then be expressed as:

$$\log \text{TFP}_{it} - \log \text{TFP}_{i,t-1} = (\log Q_{it} - \log Q_{i,t-1}) - (\log X_{it} - \log X_{i,t-1}). \quad (3)$$

The difference in TFP between two countries i and j in some year t can be measured as

$$\log \text{TFP}_{it} - \log \text{TFP}_{jt} = (\log Q_{it} - \log Q_{jt}) - (\log X_{it} - \log X_{jt}). \quad (4)$$

The expression (4) can be expanded to (time subscripts suppressed):

$$\log \text{TFP}_i - \log \text{TFP}_j = (\log Q_j - \log Q_i) - [S_L (\log L_j - \log L_i) \\ + S_M (\log M_j - \log M_i) \\ + S_K (\log K_j - \log K_i)]. \quad (4a)$$

The difference between TFP in two countries at one point in time is the difference in (the log of) outputs less the weighted difference in (the log of) inputs. The factor share (S_M) is calculated as the average over the time-periods in question.

CE is measured as unit cost (C/Q) divided by an aggregate index of input prices W. Again the Tornquist aggregation formula is used so that the difference in cost efficiency for one country at two points in time is:

$$\log \text{CE}_t - \log \text{CE}_{t-1} = [\log(C/Q)_t - \log(C/Q)_{t-1}] \\ - (\log W_t - \log W_{t-1}) \quad (5)$$

and where

$$\log W_t - \log W_{t-1} = S_L (\log W_{L,t} - \log W_{L,t-1}) + S_M (\log W_{M,t} \\ - \log W_{M,t-1}) + S_K (\log W_{K,t} + \log W_{K,t-1}). \quad (6)$$

Cost efficiency is the inverse of total factor productivity:

$$\text{CE} = 1/\text{TFP}.$$

Similar constructions measure the cost efficiency differences between two countries at one point in time.

2.2 The Impact of Trade Restraints on TFP Measures

It is clear that unrestrained trade does not take place in the automotive sector in the countries under consideration. As described in the first section of this chapter, firms are constrained to use domestically produced inputs (domestic content rules), and tariffs and quotas reduce the flows of imports of finished vehicles and domestic parts, thus increasing domestic production. Export subsidies can increase domestic production rates as well.

In this section, we examine how trade restraints may affect the measurement of TFP (or CE) through the use of aggregation formulae such as the Tornquist index. Basically, the issue is how the restraint in question affects the choice of inputs and thus measured factor shares. What we will demonstrate is that while all trade restraints affect the *level* of costs, only binding domestic content rules bias the firms' choice of the cost-minimizing combination of inputs in such a way as to bias traditional measures of TFP growth.

We begin with a discussion of trade restraints which *do not* affect TFP as conventionally measured: tariffs on imports of cars or parts. A tariff on finished vehicles affects the level of output in the home country but will not distort production possibilities. The domestic firms still attempt to minimize the cost of producing the now higher output level. Figure 1 demonstrates the point. S is the domestic supply curve, D the domestic

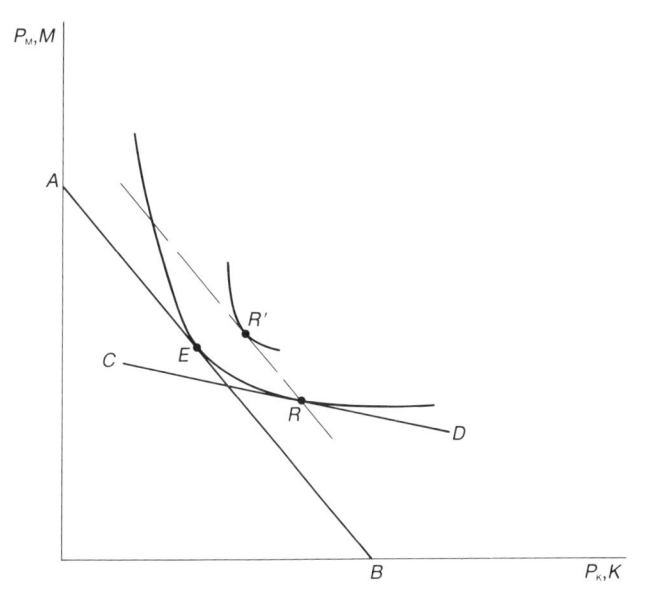

FIG. 1. The effect of a tariff on finished vehicles

demand curve, 0P the world price (plus transport costs) or the world supply curve of cars to this country. Without a tariff on finished vehicles, domestic output is Q_1 and imports Q_1Q_2. A tariff of t per cent on imports of finished vehicles increases domestic production by ΔQ_1. Producers are on their 'supply' curve, costs are minimized whether output is Q_1 or $Q_1 + \Delta Q_1$. Similarly an export subsidy increases the demand faced by the home-country firm and increases output. Again, no bias is imparted to the production side or the choice of technology—conventionally measured cost efficiency is unbiased by a tariff on imports of finished vehicles.[34]

At first glance, it appears that a tariff on imported parts would affect production techniques since it will raise the cost of materials imports and thus the home-country firm's choice of the mix of labour, capital, and materials. However, while this tariff will raise the costs of production it will *not* distort the estimation of the production possibilities (PP) frontier, and thus conventionally measured cost efficiency (total factor productivity) is unaffected by tariffs on imported parts. The firm chooses to be at a different point on this PP frontier from the one it would be on in the absence of the tariff but it is still on the frontier. The firm equates the marginal cost of domestic materials with its marginal product; similarly for imported parts. As a result, conventionally measured TFP (or CE) provides unbiased estimates of productivity (efficiency).

This point is demonstrated in Figure 2. The domestic price of parts is P_D; the landed price of foreign parts is P_D; $P_D > P_F$. Without a tariff on imported parts, the firm faces factor price line AB between imported parts and capital (P_K/P_F), the firm operates at E. A tariff of k per cent per dollar of parts imported changes the price of materials to:

$$P_M = d P_D + (1 - d)(1 + k) P_F,$$

where d = the percentage of domestic parts used.

The tariff shifts the factor price line to CD and the firm moves to a new point such as R. R is a point on the isoquant—the 'frontier' can be estimated, and conventionally measured TFP provides unbiased estimates of efficiency changes.[35]

From this discussion it is clear that those trade restraints which directly affect factor prices (a tariff on imported materials) or output (tariffs on imports of finished vehicles or export subsidies) will not lead to biased estimates of TFP. This is not to say that these restraints have no cost—they do. The point for this part of the analysis is that these restraints do not bias the firm's choice of factor inputs in ways not reflected in input prices; marginal conditions are satisfied, conventionally measured TFP provides a correct picture of the changes in efficiency in production.

Domestic content rules do not directly alter relative prices, but they do affect input choice. As a result, domestic content rules which are binding can bias TFP measures. Simply put, domestic content rules can drive a wedge between marginal product and marginal costs. A binding content constraint means that firms would like to substitute imported parts for domestic parts. As they cannot, we can have a boundary condition where the marginal cost of domestically made parts exceeds their marginal productivity. Using the observed factor shares in an aggregation formula such as the Tornquist index can then provide biased estimates of TFP growth. What is required is the calculation of 'shadow' factor shares based on the domestic content rule in effect.

If the domestic content rule is that *100 per cent* of *all* costs of production must be domestically produced, conventionally measured TFP will provide unbiased estimates. While it would be less costly to substitute imported components, the binding 100 per cent constraint means that the firm is minimizing production costs subject to domestic prices and is at a point such as E in Figure 2.

The Argentinian domestic content rules purport to be near 100 per cent. However, Argentina (as well as Mexico) allows imported machinery and equipment in automotive plants. As a result domestic auto firms can substitute imported capital for both domestic labour and domestically produced semi-finished components. These domestic content rules require that some percentage of labour and materials be domestic—the 'true' domestic con-

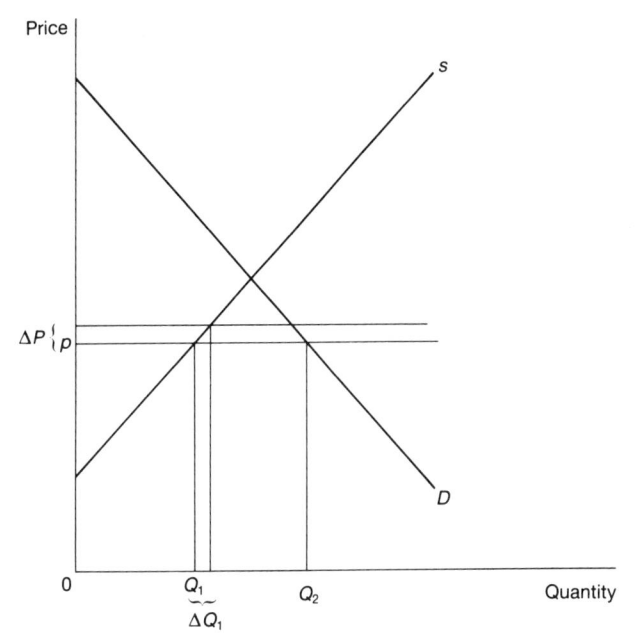

FIG. 2. The effects of a tariff on parts and of domestic contents rules

tent then depends on the proportion of capital costs (depreciation plus the return to capital) in total costs.

Formally, domestic content rules can be analysed as follows.[36]

M^D = quantity of domestic materials used
P_M^D = price of domestic materials used
M^F = quantity of foreign materials used
P_M^F = price of foreign materials used
C = total cost.

Assume that at least a per cent of the costs of production is of domestic origin, that capital costs are excluded from the constraint, and that the constraint is binding.

$$P_M^D M^D + P_L L = a\,(P_M^D M^D + P_M^F M^F + P_L L) \qquad (7)$$

(note that $P_K K$ is not included in the formula since capital costs are excluded from the constraint)

or

$$P^F M^F = ((1 - a)/a) \cdot (P_M^D M^D + P_L L).^{37} \qquad (8)$$

Total costs is the sum of the costs of all factors:

$$C = P_L L + P_K K + P_M^D M^D = P_M^F M^F.$$

Substituting equation (8) into the cost function leads to:

$$C = P_L L + P_K K + P_M^D M^D + ((1 - a)/a) \cdot (P_M^D M^D + P_L L)$$
$$= (P_L/a)L + P_K K + (P_M^D/a)M^D \qquad (9)$$

$$C = P_L^* + P_K K + P_D^* M^D \qquad (10)$$

where $P_{LL}^* = P_L/a$ and $P_D^* = P_M^D/a$.

These observations suggest changes in the measurement of TFP. Recall that changes in TFP are measured as changes in output less a weighted aggregate of factor inputs. The specific form of aggregation used here involves factor shares. Recall from Section 2.1 that TFP was measured as:

$$\Delta \text{TFP} = \log Q_{i,t} - \log Q_{i,t-1} - [s_L (\log L_t - \log L_{t-1}) + s_M (\log M_t - \log M_{t-1}) + s_K (\log K_t - \log K_{t-1})]. \qquad (2)$$

Where there is a binding domestic content constraint the factor shares in equation (2) must be replaced by s_L^*, s_M^*, and s_K and M must be replaced by M^D. For the case of a binding domestic constraint on labour and materials, as derived in equations (8) through (10), these factor shares can be calculated as follows:

$$s_L^* = (P_L^* L)/C, \; s_M^* = (P_M^* M^D)/C, \; s_K = (P_K K)/C. \qquad (11)$$

The labour and materials factor shares which are used in the Turnquist index are 'shadow' factor shares which depend on the domestic content rule.[38]

In the empirical work which follows in Section 4, we will ignore these shadow shares and prices and use factor shares derived from actual data (S_L, S_K, S_M) and actual factor prices to calculate TFP growth thus ignoring the calculations in this section. In the case of Argentinian production, we do measure the bias imparted to estimates of TFP growth when the domestic content constraint is not explicitly accounted for.

Before moving on, it is useful to analyse through the shadow factor shares how domestic content rules may bias production decisions. Here shadow prices refer simply to the impact of the trade restraint. We do not include here any measure of social benefits and costs in these shadow prices. The market price of labour is P_L, the share of labour costs in total costs is $(P_L \cdot L)/C$. To the firm however it is not only the price of labour which matters but the fact that a percentage of labour and materials costs must be domestically sourced. Capital costs need not be domestically sourced. As a result there would appear to be an induced bias to substitute foreign-sourced capital for domestic labour (and domestically produced materials). This bias induced by the way in which domestic content rules can operate can help explain the introduction of means of production which appear, at the surface, to be 'too' capital-intensive given the country's factor endowments. A domestic content rule which specified that a percentage of all costs of production (including capital costs) be domestically sourced would not have this impact on the choice of technology, no matter the number of inputs considered.[39]

3. SIMPLE COMPARISONS WITH CANADA

Before proceeding to estimates of changes in TFP, simple stylized estimates of the differences in cost levels across the four countries can be produced using only data on the average size of plants and on the utilization of capacity. Tables 2(a) and 2(b) present Canadian data on the cost penalties associated with suboptimal scale and suboptimal capacity utilization. These data were calculated in the following way. In other studies (Fuss and Waverman 1988, forthcoming), unit costs of production were calculated in an econometric cost function framework for Canada, the USA, and Japan. These estimates allow the calculation of the average costs for different-sized plants and for varying utilization of fixed capacity. For the Canadian industry, unit costs were calculated for the minimum point on the average cost curve, (m.e.s.), and for outputs less than this size. These data are calculated for four representative years (Table 2(a), Figure 3). We also estimated the costs of under-utilizing capacity from these Canadian data for the same four years (Table 2(b), Figure 4).

These data indicate that operating at a design capacity level of 40 per cent of m.e.s. would result in 12.5 per cent higher unit production (1984)

Table 2(a). Cost penalties from inefficient scale

Size of plant	% Cost penalty			
	1984	1977	1971	1965
100%	0	0	0	0
80%	3.0	3.0	3.3	3.0
60%	6.8	7.1	7.8	7.0
40%	12.5	13.0	14.5	13.0
30%	19.5	17.4	19.4	17.4
20%	23.0	24.0	28.0	24.0
10%	34.5	36.0	40.0	36.0

Note: Based on Canadian data; 100 per cent means the real value per plant at which average cost is minimized.

Table 2(b). Cost penalties from under-utilization of capacity

Utilization capacity	% Cost penalty			
	1984	1977	1971	1965
100%	0	0	0	0
80%	8.4	7.2	8.6	7.0
60%	28.1	24.8	28.5	23.3
40%	82.5	73.8	83.3	68.0
30%	255.0	239.0	256.0	226.0
25%	328.0	303.0	329.0	282.0
20%	462.0	421.0	463.0	382.0

Note: Based on Canadian data. Normal capacity utilization is not 100 per cent due to the necessity of routine maintenance, etc.

costs.[41] A plant operating at a design capacity of 10 per cent of m.e.s. would have unit production costs some 34 per cent above the unit costs of an m.e.s. plant (1984) (Table 2(*a*)). At 80 per cent of design capacity, unit costs are 7–8 per cent higher than at full capacity. If the plant is operated at 60 per cent of its designed normal capacity unit costs rise by nearly 28 per cent (compared to 100 per cent utilization or by 1 per cent compared to 80 per cent utilization). The relationship is highly non-linear—at 30 per cent of normal capacity, unit production costs more than double. These results are caused by the highly capital-intensive nature of auto production in Canada. Therefore the cost penalties are substantial when fixed costs must be covered by a production level which is a small fraction of design capacity. The lower labour costs in the SIs than in Canada and their smaller markets would appear to create an incentive for more labour-intensive production techniques in these SIs mitigating somewhat the cost penalties of under-utilized capital.[42] Two facts work against this hypothesis. First, the Canadian data indicate identical rates of cost penalties of under-utilized capital when the industry was autarkic (1965, before the Auto Pact) and more recently (1984). Secondly, as indicated above, domestic content rules normally do not include imported capital, and as a result a bias can exist to use capital-intensive means of production.

Jenkins (1987, p. 74–5) provides several descriptions of production conditions in Latin American motor-vehicle plants. These descriptions suggest that the capital equipment was largely second-hand, non-automatic, and more general-purpose to allow for lower volumes, smaller scale, and far more model change-over than in the parent MNC's home plant. These observations would suggest that the Canadian data and experience exaggerate the cost penalties incurred in SIs because of inefficient scale and capacity utilization. Data quoted in Jenkins (1987, p. 115) suggest costs of capacity under-utilization far below those given in Table 2(*b*)—a 7 per cent penalty at 60 per cent utilization and a 16 per cent penalty at 40 per cent utilization.

The development of the auto industries in Argentina, Mexico, and Korea shows substantial suboptimal scale and substantial periodic under-utilization of capacity. These data are given in Table 3. In 1965, the Argentinian auto industry operated automotive plants one-sixth the size of the average Canadian plant. In that year capacity utilization in Argentina was 62 per cent, and in Canada 79 per cent. In 1977, Mexican auto plants were 40 per cent of the size of Canadian plants, Korean plants one-fifth as large, and Argentinian plants only one-ninth as large! While both the Mexican and Korean auto industries experienced significant increases in average plant size between 1977 and 1984,[43] Argentinian plant size stagnated at a fraction of m.e.s. Capacity-utilization rates were however relatively high in Argentina, as the industry appeared quickly to rationalize plant size to the small size of the domestic market. Average capacity utilization was lowest in Mexico and rose the most Korea.

Table 3(*b*) provides estimates of the hypothetical cost penalties associated with the scale and utilization values given in Table 3(*a*). In 1965, these data suggest that production costs in Argentina were of the order of 27 per cent higher than production costs in Canada due to suboptimal scale but only 7 per cent higher due to suboptimal capacity utilization.[44]

In 1977, these data suggest that of the three SIs *Argentinian* auto production had the *lowest* penalties relative to Canada due to suboptimal scale and utilization (34 and 5 per cent respectively), and Mexican auto production the highest cost penalties (13 and 71 per cent respectively). The relatively

Table 3(*a*). Measured per plant capacity and capacity utilization
(Canada = 100 in each year)

	Canada	Argentina		Mexico		Korea	
		S	U	S	U	S	U
1965	100	16.8%	79.0%	n.a.		n.a.	
1977	100	11.0%	84.0%	40.0%	41.0%	21.5%	49.0%
1984	100	14.0%	84.0%	50.0%	53.0%	42.0%	129.0%[a]

S: Per plant output as a percentage of Canadian per plant output in that year
U: capacity utilization normalized by Canadian capacity utilization in that year
[a] capacity utilization above Canada

Table 3(b). Cost penalties associated with suboptimal capacity and capacity utilization (relative to Canada)

	Canada	Argentina		Mexico		Korea	
		SS	UU	SS	UU	SS	UU
1965	0	27.0%	6.6%	n.a.		n.a.	
1977	0	34.0%	5.3%	13.0%	71.0%	23.0%	22.4%
1984	0	29.0%	6.2%	10.0%	40.0%	12.0%	−4.0%

SS: The hypothetical cost penalty associated with per plant capacity being different from Canadian per plant capacity
UU: The hypothetical cost penalty associated with capacity utilization being different from Canadian capacity utilization

'good' performance of the Argentinian sector is entirely due to its high degree of utilization of a very suboptimal-size plant.

According to these data, in 1984 the *Korean* auto industry was close to the cost performance of the Canadian sector (again based only on per plant capacity size and utilization), while the Mexican industry performed very poorly (almost entirely due to very low capacity utilization).

4. TOTAL FACTOR PRODUCTIVITY—TRENDS OVER TIME

4.1 Labour Productivity

We begin our discussion of TFP by examining some simple data often used to compare productivity—labour productivity. Table 4 provides data on the number of vehicles (cars plus commercial vehicles) produced per worker employed *in assembly*. These data are however flawed for several reasons. First, the data are susceptible to differences and changes in the degree of vertical integration and domestic content rules. Secondly, and most importantly, any differences in relative factor prices would lead to differences in the desired technology. Countries with lower relative labour prices utilizing more labour (relative to other inputs) would have lower measured labour productivity but not necessarily lower TFP.

The data indicate substantially higher labour productivity in Canada than in the other three countries. Most of this differential likely is an artefact of the relatively high price of Canadian labour, the bias in Canadian auto production to assembly (see Fuss and Waverman 1988), and the very high use of semi-finished components, many imported from the USA.

Table 4. Vehicles produced per worker

	Canada		Argentina		Mexico		Korea	
	Vehicles per production worker	Vehicles per employee	Vehicles per production worker	Vehicles per employee	Vehicles per production worker	Vehicles per employee	Vehicles per production worker	Vehicles per employee
1961	24.1	15.5	8.1	5.6				
1962	28.2	18.8	7.4	5.1				
1963	29.3	19.9	5.4	3.7				
1964	26.9	18.6	7.2	5.0				
1965	28.4	20.1	7.7	5.3				
1966	30.1	21.1	6.6	4.5				
1967	33.2	23.0	7.4	5.1				
1968	43.6	30.1	7.4	5.1				
1969	46.1	32.2	7.9	5.4				
1970	47.0	31.2	7.7	5.3				
1971	46.1	32.1	8.6	5.9				
1972	47.9	33.3	8.4	5.8				
1973	48.4	33.8	8.4	5.8				
1974	44.5	31.6	7.0	5.0				
1975	45.5	31.8	6.1	4.4	13.6	9.9		
1976	46.9	33.6	5.5	3.9	12.6	8.9	7.0	4.3
1977	45.9	33.8	7.1	4.8	11.2	8.1	9.2	6.1
1978	48.8	35.6	7.1	4.7	13.8	9.9	10.0	7.3
1979	41.8	31.4	9.2	6.1	13.9	10.0	10.5	7.4
1980	42.3	30.6	10.5	7.3	13.3	9.5	7.6	5.1
1981	40.2	29.9	9.0	6.1	13.3	9.7	9.0	6.3
1982	41.3	30.3	8.6	5.7	14.4	10.0	14.1	9.4
1983	42.1	32.0	10.3	6.8	9.2	6.4	20.6	11.9
1984	43.8	33.7	10.7	7.1	9.6	6.8	19.3	13.0

These important caveats aside, in 1976 Canadian labour productivity (total employee basis) was 8.6 times as great as that in Argentina, 7.8 times as great as in Korea, and 3.8 times as great as in Mexico. In 1984, Canadian labour productivity was respectively 2.6, 4.7, and 5.0 times as great as that in Korea, Argentina, and Mexico. Labour productivity in Canada, so measured, was identical in 1976 and 1984; labour productivity rose substantially in Korea (post-1980), rose in Argentina, but fell in Mexico. We turn to our constructed series on TFP to see how misleading these 'simple' productivity measures may be.

4.2 Data for TFP Calculations

To calculate TFP we require data on current dollar outputs and inputs and price deflators. These data were not easy to calculate for the SIs (Korea had by far the best data). Details of the sources and construction of the series are given in Appendix A. The most problematic series are materials and capital inputs, the price deflator for materials, and the user cost of capital inputs. Consistent series on the nominal value of materials inputs are not provided in Mexico and Argentina and had to be constructed from several sources. No price deflator for total materials inputs was available: we have used here as a proxy the wholesale price index for domestically produced steel.[45] For Korea and Argentina, no data on the capital stock were available; we constructed series using the perpetual-inventory method. The cost of capital was measured as an *ex post* residual return.[46]

4.3 TFP Comparisons

Tables 5(a) to 5(d) provide data on the growth in real output in the four countries as well as the changes in the number of hours worked, total real wage bill, total real materials usage, and the capital stock. Table 6 provides information on the changing factor shares; Table 7 data on changes in real factor prices; Table 8 data on changes in real unit costs of production (as deflated by the wholesale price index of automobiles) in each of the four countries. Table 9 provides information on changes in TFP. Data are provided as annual rates of change over broad periods (1978–81 is chosen as this was the period of the Argentinian experiment with trade liberalization) since the year-to-year changes are so pronounced that summary analysis is difficult (see Appendix B).

Table 5(a) presents data on trends in output and inputs for Canada. Real output increased rapidly following the Auto Pact in the period 1965–9, relatively substantially over the 1970s, and less rapidly so far in the 1980s. Hours worked have also risen but to a much smaller degree than output; the real wage bill has increased faster (except in the 1980s) than hours worked. Changes in materials have followed changes in output nearly one for one. In the 1970s and 1980s, the change in the capital stock exceeded that of hours worked.

The growth of Argentinian real output was substantial in the 1960s, slower in the 1970s (Table 5(*b*)), and negative in the 1980s (through 1984). Hours worked have fallen precipitously in the 1980s, as has the real wage bill. Throughout the 1970s and the 1980s, the real materials bill has fallen as has real capital stock; according to these values the real capital stock in 1984 was only 70 per cent of its 1969 level.

Mexican data (Table 5(*c*)) were only available for the period 1975–84. The growth in real output in the 1970s was exactly offset by a decline in the 1980s. Hours worked fell 19 per cent over the entire 1975–84 period, while the real capital stock, unlike in Argentina, increased substantially. This experience indicates the capacity added to meet unfulfilled demand and the reduction in labour to meet lower output levels.

Table 5(*a*). Canada

	Change in real output (%)	Change in hours worked (%)	Change in real wage bill (%)	Change in real materials bill (%)	Change in capital stock (%)
1961–9	283.1	66.1	165.7	271.3	68.0
1970s	68.0	7.5	57.9	66.6	19.1
1980s	13.8	27.7	18.4	16.2	36.1
1978–81	−14.5	−20.3	−19.5	−9.7	10.4
1976–84	34.5	21.7	17.8	40.8	51.7

Table 5(*b*). Argentina

	Change in real output (%)	Change in hours worked (%)	Change in real wage bill (%)	Change in real materials bill (%)	Change in capital stock (%)
1961–9	57.5	64.6	210.8	115.4	109.6
1970s	7.8	7.4	31.8	−4.8	−3.8
1980s	−13.3	−48.0	−31.6	−33.5	−27.0
1978–81	−23.1	−28.8	31.7	−32.7	−15.8
1976–84	−3.8	−52.0	4.4	16.5	−39.5

Table 5(c). Mexico

	Change in real output (%)	Change in hours worked (%)	Change in real wage bill (%)	Change in real materials bill (%)	Change in capital stock (%)
1970s[a]	28.2	−11.0	−4.6	70.2	55.0
1980s	−29.0	−17.1	−48.3	−51.8	52.8
1978−81	52.2	11.5	66.3	19.7	162.5
1976−84	7.1	−18.7	−48.4	−47.8	136.8

[a] 1975−9

Table 5(d). Korea

	Change in real output (%)	Change in hours worked (%)	Change in real wage bill (%)	Change in real materials bill (%)	Change in capital stock (%)
1970s[a]	177.1	145.3	195.4	204.5	171.3
1980s	92.8	−26.2	32.6	9.8	35.2
1978−81	28.3	−12.9	24.9	−19.9	116.4
1976−84	434.3	80.9	191.7	234.5	266.7

[a] 1976−9

The experience of Korea is the opposite of the other three countries (Table 5(d)) with real sustained output growth in the entire 1976−84 period.[47] Hours worked, however, have fallen in the 1980s, while the real wage bill has risen. Capital stock growth has been substantial and was especially strong in the 1970s.

Table 6 indicates very different factor shares among the four countries. Canada has a very high materials share, reflecting a US export-orientated assembly operation and imports of semi-finished components (materials). Argentina has a relatively high capital share, reflecting the capital stock in place in the early 1970s for output levels that never materialized.[48] Korea has the lowest factor share in wages; Mexican factor shares are similar to Korea but with a greater share to labour.

Table 7 provides data on the percentage changes in real factor prices (deflated by the wholesale price of output). Concentrating on the 1976−84 period which is common to all four countries, Mexico experienced a 56 per cent real drop in the price of labour; Canada a small drop, while in Korea

THE IMPACTS OF PROTECTION 303

Table 6. Average factor share for given periods

	Canada			Argentina		
	PL	PK	PM	PL	PK	PM
1961–9	0.141	0.114	0.745	0.132	0.234	0.634
1970s	0.124	0.102	0.774	0.136	0.271	0.593
1980s	0.101	0.119	0.780	0.139	0.269	0.592
1978–81	0.107	0.107	0.786	0.152	0.291	0.557
1976–84	0.110	0.110	0.780	0.128	0.286	0.586
	Korea[a]			Mexico[b]		
	PL	PK	PM	PL	PK	PM
1970s	0.066	0.205	0.729	0.172	0.113	0.715
1980s	0.079	0.169	0.752	0.142	0.248	0.610
1978–81	0.070	0.236	0.694	0.156	0.174	0.668
1976–84	0.073	0.185	0.742	0.153	0.185	0.662

[a] Korea: 1976–9.
[b] Mexico 1975–9.

Table 7. % change in real factor prices (real relative to output price)

	Canada			Argentina		
	PL	PK	PM	PL	PK	PM
1961–9	59.9	55.0	8.7	88.9	34.9	−5.3
1970s	46.9	19.7	10.1	22.7	222.3	39.9
1980s	−7.3	3.6	−2.2	31.5	−44.6	15.9
1978–81	1.0	20.1	—	85.0	−21.4	6.7
1976–84	−3.3	−3.2	−2.9	117.4	−17.1	−22.3
	Korea[a]			Mexico[b]		
	PL	PK	PM	PL	PK	PM
1970s	20.5	−12.8	−4.5	−13.0	−1.8	−25.4
1980s	79.7	−59.9	58.7	−47.2	−4.3	31.5
1978–81	43.4	−7.3	56.0	−4.9	−15.7	5.2
1976–84	116.4	−65.0	51.4	−56.0	61.3	3.1

[a] Korea: 1976–9.
[b] Mexico 1975–9.

Table 8. % change in real unit cost

	Canada	Argentina	Mexico	Korea
1961–9	−6.0	2.7	—	—
1970s[a]	4.7	18.1	−3.0	−1.1
1980s	2.9	2.4	7.1	−21.3
1978–81	8.9	1.8	−5.0	9.4
1976–84	0.7	3.5	2.9	−22.0

[a] Korea: 1976–9; Mexico 1975–9.

and Argentina real wage rates more than doubled.[49] In this period, the real cost of capital rose 60 per cent in Mexico, but fell in the other three countries—slightly in Canada, moderately in Argentina, and substantially in Korea.

Table 8 presents data on the change in real unit costs over the period, the deflator used here being the wholesale price of cars. Again, we highlight the 1976–84 period. Korea had the best performance, real unit costs dropping 22 per cent over the nine-year period. Canada experienced near-constant real unit costs. Mexican real unit costs rose slightly by 2.9 per cent over the period, while real unit costs rose the most in Argentina (3.5 per cent). If changes in real unit costs are our measure of performance Korea's achievements were substantial.

Annual percentage rates of TFP are given in Table 9. Over the 1976–84 period, the 'best' performance is in Korea and the worst in Argentina,[50] but in two very different environments. Korea experienced annual TFP growth of 3.3 per cent in a growing industry, Argentina a negative growth rate of 1.8 per cent per year in a declining industry. Mexican TFP growth was 40 per cent of that in Korea as the Mexican assembly industry was hit by domestic macroeconomic problems limiting the sales that the industry had geared up for in the late 1970s. Canadian performance was poor, although 1976 and 1984 were both 'good' years for the industry. This poor performance is somewhat affected by the growth in investment and capital stock, the capacity additions in the Canadian industry aiming at future growth. Still the results are surprising—Canadian TFP performance substantially lagged behind that in Korea and Mexico in the 1976–84 period.[51] Canadian TFP growth was pronounced in the 1960s (during the first years of the Auto Pact) but in the 1970s it lagged behind that of Korea and Argentina.

The 1978–81 period was the period of Argentinian trade liberalization. Domestic sales plummeted in Argentina as they did in Canada and Korea in 1980 and 1981. Argentinian TFP growth, however, was very impressive in the import-liberalization period—an annual rate of growth of 1.8 per cent

Table 9. Annual % of rate of change of TFP

	Canada	Argentina	Mexico	Korea
1961–9	3.11	1.0	—	—
1970s[a]	0.91	+2.9	−4.81	4.06
1980s	−0.94	−1.1	1.67	3.01
1978–81	−2.13	+1.8	1.60	−1.16
1976–84	−0.47	−1.8	1.31	3.31

[a] Korea: 1976–9; Mexico 1975–9.

per year, surpassing that of the other three countries. By comparison, Korea and Canada experienced sharply negative growth in TFP over the 1978–81 period. Looking back at the earlier tables allows us to understand why Argentina experienced substantial TFP growth in this four-year period. The real output of the Argentinian industry did not grow but fell 23 per cent in this period: trade liberalization did not expand sales. However, real materials inputs fell sharply (the import of cheaper foreign parts) and hours worked fell 28 per cent. the TFP growth shows the impact of the loosening of constraints. The story does not end here. First, 1981 was a very poor year for Korean and Canadian auto sectors and 1978 a good year, therefore comparison over this period is somewhat suspect. Secondly, throughout the 1970s, Argentinian TFP growth averaged 2.9 per cent per year, a rate *triple* that of the much larger and more efficient Canadian industry. Yet by the end of the 1970s, Canada was a major exporter to the US market; the Argentinian industry sold no cars abroad. TFP growth is then not a great judge of efficiency or ability to sell in world markets. *Levels* of efficiency and costs are crucial.

Table 10 provides a comparison of TFP growth for Argentina as given in Table 9 and as measured when the domestic content rule is incorporated into the Tornquist index (equations (35) and (36)). The measure given in Table 9 (the conventional measure) did incorporate the domestic price of materials, but not the content constraint. The conventional measure tends to *underestimate* TFP growth in the 1960s and 1980s. The differences are greatest in the 1980s when the conventional measure shows sharply negative annual growth and actual TFP performance was substantially better. Ignoring the domestic content constraint leads to some overestimation of TFP growth in the import-liberalization period, in the neighbourhood of 11 per cent. Note again that in this period TFP grows at 1.6 per cent per year.

In summary, the TFP growth rates are surprising. Since 1970, these data indicate that TFP in Argentina has experienced rapid growth. These data would appear to suggest that rapid learning or technical advance is possible

Table 10. Annual rates of TFP growth—Argentina

	Conventional	Incorporating domestic content rules
1961–9	1.00	1.15
1970s	2.85	2.84
1980s	−1.13	−1.05
1978–81	1.80	1.62
1981–4	−1.02	0.14
1976–84	−1.83	−1.44

in an import-substituting industry, and in one in decline. Canada and Mexico have on occasion had relatively poor TFP performance, the latter in the 1975–9 period, Canada since 1970. Argentina's performance apparently reflects an ability quickly to decrease labour and capital services—an ability seemingly not present in Canada. Yet, the Argentinian capital share exceeds that of Canada, indicating that the reason is not a lower capital/labour ratio in Argentina. What these index-number data cannot indicate is the size of the cost disadvantage existing in Argentina in 1970 or its underlying sources. In addition, capacity-utilization problems, diseconomies of scale, and technical change are all contained within TFP. Further analysis therefore requires comparing unit costs (in a common currency) across countries, and disentangling the sources of country differentials.

REFERENCES

ALMEIDA, J (1982), *A Implantacao da Industria Automobilistica no Brazil* (Fundacão Getuhio Varges, Rio de Janeiro).

ALTSHULER, A., et al. (1984), *The Future of the Automobile* (MIT Press, Cambridge, Mass.).

BARANSON, J. (1969), *Automotive Industries in Developing Countries* (Johns Hopkins Press, Baltimore).

BENNETT, D. C., and SHARPE, K. E. (1985), *Transnational Corporations Versus the State: The Political Economy of the Mexican Auto Industry* (Princeton University Press, Princeton, NJ).

FUSS, M., and WAVERMAN, L. (1988), 'The Extent and Sources of Cost and Efficiency Differences Between U.S. and Japanese Motor Vehicle Producers' (University of Toronto, International Economics Program, Donner Working Paper 87–10, Dec. 1987)

—— (forthcoming), *Costs and Productivity in Automobile Production: A Comparison of Canada, Germany, Japan and the United States* (CUP, Cambridge).

GREGORY, R. G. (1988), 'A Sad and Sorry Story! Industrial Policy for the Australian Motor Vehicle Industry', in A. M. Spence and H. A. Hazard, *International Competitiveness* (Ballinger, Cambridge Mass.).

HELMERS, H. J. (1967), *The United States-Canada Automobile Agreement: A Study in Industry Adjustment* (University of Michigan, Graduate School of Business Administration, Ann Arbor, Mich.).

JENKINS, R. (1977), *Dependent Industrialization in Latin America: The Automotive Industry in Argentina, Chile and Mexico* (Praeger, New York).

—— (1984), 'The Rise and Fall of the Argentina Motor Vehicle Industry', in R. Kronish and K. S. Mericle (eds.), *The Political Economy of the Latin American Motor Vehicle Industry* (MIT, Press, Cambridge, Mass.).

—— (1987), *Transnational Corporations and the Latin American Automobile Industry* (Macmillan, London).

MERICLE, K. C. (1984), 'The Political Economy of the Brazilian Motor Vehicle Industry', in R. Kronish and K. S. Mericle (eds.), *The Political Economy of the Latin American Motor Vehicle Industry* (MIT Press, Cambridge, Mass.).

SOURROUILLE, J.V. (1980), *El Complejo Automotor En Argentina* (Editorial Nueva Imagen, Mexico City).

WHITE, L. (1971), *The Automobile Since 1975* (Harvard University Press, Cambridge, Mass.).

NOTES

1. See Baranson (1969); Jenkins (1987).
2. Note the 1986 production figures given in the preceding paragraph; except for Canada (and possibly Korea) country production levels are well below those required for efficient production in a single assembly plant.
3. Argentina and Brazil recently have signed an agreement permitting manufacturers to rationalize production between these two countries.
4. Production consisted mainly of the importation of CKD kits.
5. Basically duty drawbacks and remissions made the domestic content provisions operational.
6. Jenkins (1987, p. 60) states that 23 firms submitted proposals to assemble cars and 21 produced some vehicles.
7. These content provisions were matched with a set of tariffs which increased non-linearly at a domestic content below 100%.
8. As a result, domestic content rules can alter desired production techniques since imported equipment and capital can be substituted for domestic labour and materials, a point discussed in Sec. 2.0.
9. Jenkins (1987, p. 109) lists 20 models as produced in 1961 and 40 in 1966 when 15 new models were produced. He lists 13 assemblers active in 1964 producing 57 models.
10. The data for Mexico in Table 1 do not distinguish between production of automobiles and production of commercial vehicles until 1970.
11. Jenkins (1987, p. 61) suggests that US government pressure was important in preventing such controls.

12. For commercial vehicles (e.g. trucks), the value added should amount to at least 50% of the growth in the value of commercial vehicles sold in the base year.
13. The law mandated a minimum output per model before a new model could be produced. A model was, however, defined as all variants of a chassis—two-door, van, wagon, etc.
14. Jenkins (1987, p. 114) estimates local content at 92% in 1970.
15. Jenkins (1987) states that the combined export subsidies equalled 60% of the f.o.b. value of cars and 75% for heavy trucks.
16. Bennett and Sharpe (1985, p. 115) report that the value of the production of parts tripled between 1962 and 1964.
17. Chrysler obtained 45% of Auto-Mex (100% in 1971); the domestic assembler of VWs was acquired by VW; the Willy's Overland plant was acquired jointly by AMC and the Mexican government (40%/60%); Diesel Nacional, the assembler of Renault, was taken over by the Mexican government. Jenkins (1987, p. 61) argues that pressure from the Japanese government involving continued access of Mexican cotton to the Japanese market was instrumental in allowing Nissan to enter.
18. See Jenkins (1977, p. 67 ff).
19. Jenkins (1987, p. 112) estimated that local content equalled 64% in Mexico in 1970.
20. In 1971, 15% of import content had to be exported, in 1973, 30%, and in 1976, 60%.
21. While car production itself doubled between 1970 and 1975, the export 'constraint' was underproduced by 40%.
22. Jenkins (1987, p. 197) states that the effective tariff was much higher since a minimum price of $US3.50 per cc. of engine space for cars and per kg. for trade was imposed.
23. GM and Citroën exited, Chrysler was taken over by VW, as was the state-owned IME; Fiat and Peugeot co-ordinated a joint venture (SEVEL).
24. The balance-of-payments deficit on the current account was $726m in 1971 and $3.7b four years later.
25. An inter-ministerial report released in early 1976 suggested an 80% domestic content rule based on the cost of parts as well as forced rationalization, and a mandatory matching of the value of imports with the value of exports.
26. 'Decreto para el fomento de la industria automotriz', *Diario oficial*, 20 June 1977. 50% of exports had to be parts purchased from domestic Mexican firms.
27. This was equivalent to 68% on the old methodology. In addition, domestic content was to be calculated per model, not per plant (or per firm as in Canada). This was expected to lead to the rationalization of production by reducing the number of models produced by each firm.
28. Bennett and Sharpe (1985) discuss how Mexican policy specifically rejected the Canada model, i.e. the Canada–USA Auto Pact of 1965 because of the reliance on exports of finished vehicles and a few parts with minimal manufacture of sophisticated components.
29. *Automotive News*, 7 July 1985.
30. Quoted in Altshuler *et al.* (1984), p. 43.

31. Note how Mexican domestic demand for autos climbed during the second oil shock years.
32. *Automotive News* (4 Mar. 1985, p. 1) suggests that the Korean government would have preferred a single auto-producer but was deterred by GM's 50% ownership of Daewoo. It is interesting to note that the three Latin American countries did not impose limits on the number of producers, even though each announced tentative policies to do so.
33. Korean producers had until 1987 a 9.6% lower tariff on imports to Canada than Japanese or European producers because of the developed-country preference. In 1987 this preference was eliminated.
34. Note that with strong economies of scale, the increase in production will increase the efficiency of production.
35. Note that if the tariff (k) changes, we will see an increase in costs and perhaps a shift in techniques—TFP and CE will still be correctly measured. The 'costs of protection' can be measured. Using the ratio of factor prices without the tariff ($AB = P_K/P_F$) and expenditure level R will allow the calculation of point R'—the output which would be possible at unprotected factor prices; output RR' is a measure of the costs of the tariff. Again if increasing returns to scale are present, the increase in production of parts will increase efficiency.
36. I am indebted to Mel Fuss for assistance in the derivations of the analysis given below.
37. We could just as easily replace domestic materials by foreign materials. This alternative approach is useful (if we know P_M^F) since it can be set to zero and the impact of domestic content rules measured.
38. The calculations assume a binding constraint such that producers would not produce with the same domestic value added without the domestic content rule.
39. An explicit attempt to sign dC/da showed that with two inputs, labour and capital, and with capital excluded from domestic content provision the firm would substitute capital for labour. With three inputs—labour, materials and capital—it could not be proven that $dK/da > 0$.
40. The Canadian data used here include all assembly and parts production so that output per plant is in value terms and cannot be represented here by some physical size of cars produced per year. We refer to the point that minimizes unit costs as a plant of m.e.s. size but this is not strictly true. The data for the SIs include only assembly and thus the comparison of unit size of plants between these countries and these Canada data is not strictly accurate.
41. The calculated cost penalties do not differ much over the period.
42. Baranson (1969, p. 47) states that 'Production volumes in Argentina are low by world standards, which means that Argentina plants can only afford equipment that must be used for a variety of purposes in order to minimize capital costs per unit of output.'
43. In 1986 the average size of Korean plants had increased substantially above 1984 levels.
44. Note, this does not mean that *costs* were this much higher since factor prices were lower, but that, *ceteris paribus*, scale and capacity-utilization differences alone would account for these cost differentials if that same technology were

used in the two countries.

45. Ignoring data on the price of imported materials means that we are approximating the TFP measure utilizing the domestic content rule (see equations (32) and (11)) but not to the correct extent.
46. Normally, the neoclassical *ex ante* user cost of capital is preferred especially in an industry with high fixed costs. To calculate the neoclassical return requires data on capital-asset prices, the real *ex ante* rate of return, and the depreciation rate. These data proved difficult to gather. Moreover, the increased inflation in Argentina in the 1976–84 period made returns calculated by the neoclassical methodology explode. We therefore calculated the nominal residual return to capital over the entire period and the *ex post* return to capital. Through 1975 the neoclassical and residual methodologies gave very similar results.
47. With a sharp downturn in 1980 which is not evident in these data.
48. Another explanation has been advanced earlier—domestic content rules (the strictest of the four) in effect lower the price of imported capital relative to domestic labour and materials.
49. This rise in Argentinian real wages is relative to the wholesale price of automobiles which rose far less than the CPI over the period.
50. Nishimizu and Page (1987) found a 6.49% annual increase in TFP in the Argentinian transport sector for the 1956 to 1973 period.
51. Some might also point to the VER in place against Japan as a possible explanation of poor performance.

APPENDIX A

Notes on Data Sources and Construction of Variables

All data to be analysed in the cost function are denominated in a common currency— the Canadian dollar. Exchange rates utilized to arrive at this common currency were provided by the Bureau of Labour Statistics. The individual country data sources are as follows:

ARGENTINA

(a) Labour

(i) Hours worked and number of workers: La Asociacion de Fabricas de Automotores (ADEFA), *Industria Automotriz Argentina*, various issues; Instituto Nacional de Estadistica y Censos (NDEC), *Indicatores Industriales*, various issues.

ADEFA provides data only on total number of workers (production and non-production) employed and hours worked by production workers. To get total hours worked by all workers the production/non-production worker ratio was utilized from the NDEC data which covers more than just the assembly plants. It should be noted that the total number of workers in the

NDEC data is much higher than that from ADEFA (e.g. 17.7 per cent in 1979). It was assumed that non-production employees worked the same number of hours per week as production employees.
(ii) Total compensation per hour worked: NDEC, *Indicatores Industriales*, various issues; ADEFA, *Industria Automotriz Argentina*. Various issues.
Total compensation per hour worked includes a basic wage rate plus fringe benefits.

(b) Materials

(i) Current dollar materials cost:
Cost of domestically produced materials: ADEFA, *Industria Automotriz Argentina*, various issues.
Cost of imported materials (1961–76): Sourrouille, Juan V. (1980), *Transnacionales en America Latina: El Complejo Automoter en Argentina* (Sacramento, Mexico: Editorial Nueva Images, SA).
Cost of imported materials (1977–84): United Nations, *Yearbook of International Trade Statistics*, various issues.
Domestically produced material inputs were available from ADEFA while imported materials had to be constructed from the sources noted above.
(ii) Materials price index: Iron and steel price index from: Instituto Nacional de Estadistica y Censos, *Precios al Por Mayor*, various issues.

(c) Capital

(i) Capital stock:
Perpetual inventory capital stock computed using straight-line depreciation (10 per cent)
(ii) Current investment figures, 1959–76: ADEFA, 'Datos Basicos de la Industria Automotriz', 5 September 1977; 1977–84 investment available only on manufacturing level. Therefore, we have to take the ratio of the industry to manufacturing. Data are from: Economic Commission for Latin America and the Caribbean (ECLAC), *Statistical Yearbook for Latin America*, various issues.
(iii) Investment price deflator (only available at the manufacturing level from): ECLAC, *Statistical Yearbook for Latin America*, various issues.
(iv) User cost of capital:
We attempted to calculate the *ex ante* neoclassical user cost of capital services: $pk = qk * (r + d)$ where qk is the capital asset price, r is the *ex ante* rate of return, and d is the depreciation rate. qk was obtained from ECLAC as the price index for gross capital formation, d is assumed to be 10 per cent. While a long-term bond rate is desirable, very little information is available on interest or bond rates. Only short-term deposit rates are available from: Central Bank of Argentina, *Statistical Review*, various issues.
Given the problems with data available on interest rates and since we had information on profits and losses for the industry from Sourrouille for 1961–75 and an estimate from ADEFA thereafter, we used the residual method to calculate the user cost of capital.

(d) *Current output and output price*: ADEFA, *Industria Automotriz Argentina*, various issues

(e) *Capacity utilization*: Fundacion de Investigaciones Economicas Latinoamerica (FIEL), *Industrial Survey*, Sept. 1987.

(f) *Number of plants*: Taken directly from ADEFA.

(g) *Product mix*: An estimate of the 'average vehicle weight' of automobiles produced in each year was calculated using data provided by ADEFA.

KOREA

(a) *Labour*

(i) Hours worked and number of workers: 'all employees' data provided by Kyu-Uck Lee, Korean Development Institute (KDI).
(ii) Total compensation per hour: US Department of Labour, Bureau of Labour Statistics, unpublished data

(b) *Materials*

(i) Current materials input: data provided by Kyu-Uck Lee, KDI.
(ii) Material price index: iron and steel price index from: Economic and Social Commission for Asia and the Pacific (ESCAP), *Statistical Yearbook for Asia and the Pacific* (1986) (Bangkok, Thailand).

(c) *Capital*

(i) Capital stock: perpetual inventory capital stock computed using straight-line depreciation (10 per cent) and investment figures from ESCAP.
(ii) User cost of capital. Investment goods price index: ESCAP, *Statistical Yearbook for Asia and the Pacific* (1986) (Bangkok, Thailand). Bond rate: no data on long-term bond rates could be located; therefore the discount rate published in: International Monetary Fund, *International Financial Statistics*, various issues were utilized. No profit figures were available for the Korean automotive industry so the residual method was not used.

(d) *Current output*: Data from Kyu-Uck Lee

(i) Output price index: ESCAP, *Statistical Yearbook for Asia and the Pacific* (1986) (Bangkok, Thailand).

(e) *Capacity utilization and number of plants*: data from Kyu-Uck Lee; Crain Automotive Group, *Automotive News*, 4 March 1985, pp. 1, 8, and 7 July 1986, pp. 1, 20–30.

THE IMPACTS OF PROTECTION 313

(f) Product mix

The average vehicle weight was calculated using data on the vehicle weight of Korean auto imports into Canada and the US from *Automotive News*, various issues and *Wards Annual*, various issues contained in import car specifications tables. This is the best representation of the weight of Korean-produced vehicles that could be located.

MEXICO

(a) Labour

(i) Hours worked and number of employees: Associacion Mexicana de la Industria Automotriz, AC (AMIA), *La Industria Automotriz de Mexico en Cifras* (1986).
(ii) Total compensation per hour: US Department of Labour, Bureau of Labour Statistics. Unpublished data.

(b) Materials

(i) Current dollar material cost: Secretaria de Programacion y Presupuesto, Instituto Nacional de Estadistica, *Encuesta Industrial Anual*, various years.
(ii) Materials price index. Iron and steel price index from Banco de Mexico, *Statistical Review*, various issues.

(c) Capital

(i) *Capital stock*: AMIA, *La Industria Automotriz de Mexico en Cifras* (1986); Secretaria de Programacion y Presupuesto, Instituto Nacional de Estadistica, *Sistema de Cuentas Nacionales de Mexico*, various years.
(ii) User cost of capital. Investment price index and interest rates from: Economic Commission for Latin America and the Caribbean (ECLAC), *Statistical Yearbook for Latin America*, various issues.

No long-term bond rate was available, only three-month deposit available, thus the residual method was used utilizing profit estimates from AMIA.

(d) Current output: AMIA, *La Industria Automotriz de Mexico en Cifras* (1986).

(i) Output price index: Banco de Mexico, *Statistical Review*, various issues.

(e) Capacity utilization: AMIA, *La Industria Automotriz de Mexico en Cifras* (1986).

(f) Number of plants: AMIA *La Industria Automotriz de Mexico en Cifras* (1986).

(g) Product mix: an estimate of the average weight of Mexican-produced automobiles was calculated using data provided by AMIA.

CANADA

Canadian data sources and methods of construction can be found in Fuss and Waverman (forthcoming).

Inter-Country Comparisons
The output price deflators used to convert nominal into real output are indices which are normalized to be unity in a particular year for each country. The same normalization occurs for materials and capital (in Korea).

In order to obtain inter-country level comparisons of cost and efficiency, bench-mark prices must be calculated in a particular year to bridge the individual country price indices.

No data were available comparing actual costs in Canada and Korea, Argentina or Mexico. Therefore, the price indexes from these three countries were bench-marked against the US; and the Canada–US bench-marks from Fuss and Waverman (forthcoming) were utilized to bridge the indexes into Canadian dollars.

(i) *Labour price bridging*
Since the per hour rate of compensation is utilized as the price of labour, no bridging of labour costs is necessary.

(ii) *Materials price bridging*

Argentina
Material price bridged using US/Argentina relative actual materials input costs for 1965 from Baranson (1969).

Korea
Material price bridged using relative actual steel prices for Korea/Japan for 1974 from ESCAP and utilizing the materials price bridge for Japan–Canada from Fuss and Waverman (forthcoming).

Mexico
Materials price bridged using relative actual steel price for 1975 from Banco de Mexico.

(iii) *Capital price bridging.* Since we have used the residual method with information on profits and losses in the industry in Mexico and Argentina, no bridging of the capital price is necessary. The bench-mark for Korea was constructed as follows. We computed the real gross return to capital in each year using the residual method. The year (1982) in which the real return per unit capital most closely approximated the average real return over the sample was determined. For that year the residual return was assumed to be the user cost of capital services. The user cost of capital for other years was obtained by linking the cost of capital index to the bench-mark year.

(iv) *Output price bridging*

Argentina
The output price was bridged using US relative actual output prices of vehicles from Baranson (1969).

Korea
The output price deflator was bridged using 1984 vehicle price comparisons from *Automotive News*, March 1985.

Mexico
The output price deflator was bridged using purchasing power parity calculations for passenger vehicles from: Kravis *et al*. (1982), *World Product and Income* (London: Johns Hopkins University Press, Baltimore).

APPENDIX B

Table A1. Annual Changes in TFP

	Canada	Argentina	Mexico	Korea	
1962	3.9	−7.5	−6.6		
1963	4.1	−10.9	−6.8		
1964	−0.5	7.9	5.1		
1965	4.0	9.2	12.0		
1966	0.4	−6.1	−4.9		
1967	7.4	6.3	7.1		
1968	3.5	−0.5	0.7		
1969	1.5	5.6	5.7		
1970	−2.5	−4.4	−1.2		
1971	3.7	19.6	22.0		
1972	1.5	1.5	1.2		
1973	4.2	8.1	8.0		
1974	2.8	9.3	−6.6		
1975	0.6	11.7	1.1		
1976	−1.5	9.7	15.4	−18.1	
1977	1.3	5.9	0.5	−5.5	9.4
1978	−0.8	−10.0	−15.3	−1.6	4.7
1979	0.5	11.6	10.8	6.5	−1.5
1980	−4.7	9.3	1.5	−4.4	−14.9
1981	−2.1	−9.2	−5.4	2.8	12.2
1982	−0.8	1.3	−1.6	−9.4	
1983	3.3	−0.5	0.3	−10.3	−2.0
1984	−0.2	9.6	−1.8	30.6	−1.5

Index

Adar, Z. 47
Adelman, I. 85
Adler, F. M. 204
Ahluwalia, I. 45
aircraft industry 226–31, 241–9
Albin, E. 44
Alchian, A. 36
Altshuler, A. 308
Amsden, A. 131
Amundsen, C. 278
Anderson, D. 83
Areskoug, K. 221
Argentina 279–82, 283–6, 297, 300, 301–6, 309–10
Atkinson, A. B. 45
Auquier, A. A. 48
automobile industry 279–316
  cost efficiency (CE) 289–95
  domestic content rules 283, 285, 286, 287, 290, 292–5
  international cost comparisons 295–8
  production fluctuation 280–2

Bagachwa, M. D. 129
Bain, J. S. 91, 95
Balassa, B. 5, 113, 121, 144, 174, 220
Baldwin, R. F. 6, 7, 11, 14–15, 112, 121, 142, 225–53, 254, 265
Balogh, T. 129
Bandera, V. N. 222
Banerji, R. 58
Baranson, J. 306, 308, 314
Bardhan, P. 122
Baron, C. 134
barriers to entry 53, 90–1, 95, 111, 228
Batista, J. C. 223
battle of the sexes 227–37
Baumann Neves, R. 223
Baumol, W. 89, 121
Bell, M. 129, 130, 131
Bennett, D. C. 283, 307, 308
Bergsman, J. 222
Bergsten, C. F. 222

Bergstrand, J. H. 121
Berry, R. A. 8, 36, 46–79, 84
Bhagwati, J. 4, 5, 11, 160, 174
Bhuiyan, 141
Blomström, M. 103, 109, 112, 200, 221, 222
Borrus, M. L. 138
Bourguignon, F. 67
Braga, H. 224
Brander, J. A. 1, 177, 225
Brazil
  aircraft industry 226–7, 241–2, 243–51
  changing comparative advantage 209–14
  computer industry 231–5
  FDI 206–14
  MNCs export propensities 199–200
  value added 201–2
Brown, D. 169
Bruch, M. 61, 65
Bulow, J. I. 175
buyer concentration 90, 95

calibration methodology 226, 241–2
Canada 279–84, 286–7, 295–306, 313–14
capacity utilization 2, 31
capital, human 128, 129, 141, 226, 249–51
capital/labour ratio
  and exports 61–4, 70–1
  and firm size 60
capital/output ratio 109
Castana, A. 129
Cavalcanti, L. C. 223
Caves, R. E. 91, 111, 113, 121
Chamberlin, J. H. 91
Chenery, H. 2, 31, 33, 44, 174
Choksi, A. 13
Chou, T. C. 109
Chowdhury, 141
Chuma(n)cero, A. 221

Chung, I.-Y. 146
Clarke, R. 121
Clegg, J. 113, 222
Coase, R. H. 124
Cohen, B. J. 221
comparative advantage 1, 4, 15, 37, 77, 209–14
competition, dynamic 263–70, 274
competition policies 74
competitive strategies 111–12, 259–60
competitiveness 26–8, 210
Condon, T. 175
Connor, J. M. 109
Contractor, F. 44
Cooper, C. 153
Corden, W. M. 126, 128, 144, 158, 174
Cortes, M. 56–8, 60, 73, 84, 87, 131
cost
    efficiency (CE) 289–95
    and firm size 54–6
    see also domestic resource cost; economies of scale
Cournot, A. A. 232, 235
Cox, D. 8
credibility 230–1

Da Cruz, H. N. 129
Da Silva, M. E. 129
Dahlman, C. J. 23
Dasgupta, P. 7
De Jong, H. W. 91, 121
De Melo, J. 111, 175
De Rosa, D. A. 121
Demsetz, H. 89
Denison, E. 129
devaluation 73–4
Devine, P. J. 91, 95, 96, 121
Diamond, P. 45
Diaz-Alejandro, C. F. 2, 61, 66
displacement effects 204
Dixit, A, 4, 8, 175, 177, 227, 241, 242, 254
Dobson, W. 10
Doellinger, Von, C. 223
domestic resource cost (DRC) 27
Dornbusch, R. 175
Dunning, J. 102, 215, 222, 224

Eastman, H. C. 8
Eaton, J. 175, 227
economies of scale 4, 8–9, 155–6
    at low outputs 55
    definition and measurement of 95–6
    dynamic 226, 227
    economic importance of 53–4
    and efficiency 50
    increasing returns 159–61, 168–70
    measurement problems 51–8
    role of 168–71
    see also learning
education 34–5, 39
Edwards, A. C. 175
Edwards, S. 175
efficiency 1–2
    allocative 155
    cost (CE) 289–95
    and firm size 47–8, 50
    gains 212, 213–14
    social and private 53
    technical 155, 156–8, 161–8
    X-efficiency 157–8, 214
employment 2, 33–4, 75
Enos, J. L. 146
environmental effects 127
Escandon, J. F. 86
export
    incentives 170–1
    marketing 9, 78, 176–8, 186, 187–90
    products 178–80, 184–6
    propensities 199, 200, 204
    subsidies 13
export supply capabilities 189
export-promotion organizations (TPOs) 187–90
export/output ratios 61–2, 201
exporting services 189, 190
exports
    capital intensity of 66–7
    country shares 181
    determination of growth of 212–14
    and firm size 48–9
    policy requirements 179, 181, 186
externalities 2, 4, 6, 11, 122–54, 186
    attitudes and motives 128, 141
    case study 135–40

categorized 123–34
defined 122, 123
dynamic 128–32
human capital formation 128, 129, 141
industry pervasiveness 144–5
of location 125–6, 145–6
measurement of 141–3
pecuniary 132–4, 136, 139–40, 143–4
price 139–40
real 127–32, 134, 143–4
and technology change 128–30, 141–2
and technology diffusion 129, 138
and technology transfer 129–30, 136, 141–2

factor prices, related to firm size 47, 77
factor-substitution 37, 39, 78
Fajnzylber, F. 221
Feenstra, R. 112, 121
Fei, J. C. H. 87
Ferguson, P. R. 89
Finan, W. F. 139, 278
Finep 223
Finger, J. M. 82, 121
firm size 46–79
  and development path 69–72
  and factor prices 47, 77
  implication of 9
  optimal 52
  and policy bias 76–9
  primary sector 58–9
firms
  entry 56–7
  free entry and exit 168, 169
  late entry 259, 274
  see also barriers to entry
first-comer advantages 4
Fishlow, A. 222
Flam 247
foreign direct investment 198–224
  in Brazil 206–14
  Hymerian phase 204–6, 207
  Japanese Model 205
Franco, G. H. B. 10, 12, 198–224

Fransman, M. 43, 130, 131
free trade 2–3, 179, 181
Fritsch, W. 10, 12, 198–224
Fudenberg, D. 271
Fuss, M. 279, 295, 298, 308

game theory 90, 111–12
Gan, W. B. 109
Ghani, E. 11, 122–54
Ghemawat, P. 269
Glesjer, H. 48
global industrial organization 198
Gold, B. 51
Goldar, B. 109
Gomez, L. V. 85
Gonçalves, R. 210, 223
Gordon, L. 222
Gray, H. P. 177
Greenaway, D. 112, 113, 121
Greene, W. H. 45
Grether, E. T. 91
Griliches, Z. 28
Grommers, E. L. 222
Grossman, G. 175, 227
growth
  due to TFP 29, 156
  importance of technology 129–30
  social welfare effects 33–4
  and trading regime 32–3, 39
growth accounting 28
Guimares, E. A. 223

Hall, P. 139
Handoussa, H. 31
Harris, R. G. 8, 110, 169
Hason, A. H. 91
Helleiner, G. K. 1–15, 44, 112, 158, 193, 220, 223, 254
Helpman, E. 8, 112, 121, 145, 174
heterogeneity 46–50, 58–65, 65–9
Hill, H. 222
Hirsch, S. 47
Hirsch, W. A. 36
Ho, S. P. S. 57, 84
Hone, A. 193
Hong, W. 68
Horta, M. H. 223

Hufbauer, G. C. 204
Hughes, J. 22
Hymer, S. H. 222, 224

import intensity 60–1
import penetration 109
import-substituting industrialization (ISI) 24, 28–9, 39, 207
import-substitution
 Korea 260
 policies 279, 280
imports, access to 72–4, 76
incentive structures 3, 11–12
income distribution 2, 9
 effects of heterogeneity 66–8
 and firm size 47–8, 71
 impact of growth on 33–4
industrial analysis 90–3
industrial policy 144–9, 215
 Korean 255, 256, 275–6
 Silicon Valley 135–6
infant–industry argument 2, 6–7
information 176, 177, 178
innovation
 and market structure 156
 net benefit of 25–6
 process 24–5
 see also technical change; technology
input/output ratios 59–6
inputs, access to imported 72, 179, 181
investment
 foreign 191
 semiconductor industry 259–60, 270–4
 see also foreign direct investment
Ioshino 222

Jacquemin, A. 89, 121
James, J. 127, 134
James, W. E. 202
Japan 238–40, 266–74
Jenkins, R. 102, 199, 221, 283, 285, 296, 306, 307
Jo, S. H. 221
Johns, B. 222
joint ventures 191, 208–9
Jorgenson, D. W. 28

Kaldor, N. 129
Kamien, M.I. 45, 174
Katrak, H. 109
Katz, J. 23, 27, 36, 43, 44, 129, 130, 224, 226, 248, 249
Katzman, M. 128
Keesing, D. B. 8, 12, 24, 45, 72, 176–93
Kemal, A. R. 109
Kickerbocker, F. T. 222
Kim, L. 129
Kim, Y. C. 31, 39
Kindleberger 224
King, K. 43, 130
Kirkpatrick, C. H. 91, 97, 102, 103
Kojima, K. 222
Koo, A. Y. C. 113
Koo, B. Y. 221
Korea
 automobile industry 279–82, 287–8, 297, 302–6, 311–12
 competitive strategy 259–60
 development path 69–72
 exports 257, 263
 industrial and trade policy 256, 275–6
 investment 259–60
 semiconductor industry 254–78
 technology imports 257
Kravis, I. B. 15, 222, 223
Krueger, A. D. 2, 4, 7, 67, 174
Krugman, P. R. 1, 3, 112, 121, 145, 146, 171, 174, 177, 223, 225, 227, 236, 238, 239, 241, 247, 254, 265, 278
Kumar, M. S. 111
Kuo, S. W. Y. 31, 32, 45, 68, 86
Kuznets, S. 33
Kwon, J. K. 31

labour
 legislation 68
 mobility 129
 productivity 298–300
labour–capital ratios 48
Lall, S. 8, 12, 22, 24, 36, 43, 45, 72, 102, 130, 131, 176–93, 220, 221

Lambson, V. 242
LaMond, A. M. 139
Landes, D. 22, 130, 134
Lavergne, R. 223
learning 4, 6–8, 21–40, 65, 139, 213–14, 260
  by doing 226, 249
  curves 36–7, 38–9, 238, 240–1, 275
  in exporting 177, 178, 180, 189, 190
Lee, K.-U. 71–2, 74, 84, 87, 95
Lee, L. F. 142
Lee, N. 10, 89–121
Leff, N. H. 158
Levinsohn, J. 242
Levy, B. 12, 64, 70–1, 86, 222
Lewis 33
Liedholm, G. 57, 87
linkages 122–3, 138, 142, 275
Lipsey, R. 10, 15, 222, 223
Little, I. M. D. 4, 5, 144
Little, M. D. 56–8, 84, 87
Loertscher, R. 121
Lundberg, L. 121

macroeconomic environment, stability of 33, 158
mad dog strategy 231
Malerba, F. 135, 138
Mansfield, E. 26
Marcus, M. 55–6
Marfan, M. 86
market
  access restriction (MAR) 238–40
  conduct 111–14
  definition 93–4, 110
  imperfections 2, 4, 53, 114, 177
  performance 103–9, 112–14
  structure 10–11, 36, 89–121, 156
market structure–conduct–performance (S-C-P) 89–116
marketing
  buyers–manufacturers co-operation 186
  learning sequence in 182–6
Markusen, A. 136
Marsh, L. 208
Marshall, A. 122

Martin, S. 113
Mascolo, J. L. 224
Mason, R. H. 224
Mathewson, G. F. 121
Mazumder, D. 67
Mead, D. 57, 87
Meade, J. E. 126, 127
Meller, P. 86
Mexico
  automobile industry 279–86, 297, 300–16, 312–13
  computer industry 231–5
  MNCs export propensities 199–200
  value added 201–2
Mill, J. S. 2
Mill–Bastable (M–B) criterion 23
Milner, C. 112, 113, 121
Mishan, E. J. 132
Mody, A. 37, 45, 278
Mokyr, J. 44
Morawetz, D. 193
Morley, S. 222, 223, 224
Morris, D. J. 89, 111, 121
Morrison, C. 84
Mueller, W. F. 103, 109
multinational companies (MNCs), *see* transnational companies (TNCs)
Murphy, S. 279–82
Mytelka, L. 44

Naetke, P. 199
Nakao, T. 109, 110
Nalebuff, B. 269
Nasution, A. 174
Naygar, D. 203, 211, 220
Nelson, R. R. 47, 85
Nelson, R. 28, 45
Newbery, D. M. G. 132
Newfarmer, R. S. 102, 103, 110, 115, 121, 199, 208
newly industrializing countries (NICs) 4
  education 34–5
  initial levels of TFP 33
  product development 24–6
  see also Argentina; Korea; Mexico; Taiwan
Nicholls, W. 128

Nishimizu, M. 27, 29, 30, 44, 45, 174, 309
Nordhaus, W. 45
Nunes, W. P. 221

oligopoly 4, 165–8
openness 201, 202
Ozawa, T. 222
outward orientation 31
  and firm size 69–72
  and growth 32–3

Pack, H. 7–8, 21–40, 65, 85, 130, 144, 146, 154, 160, 174, 279
Page, J. M. 27, 29, 30, 44, 142, 169, 309
Pagoulatos, E. 121
Paine, S. 131
Papageorgiou, D. 13, 174
Park, W. H. 146
Park, Y. C. 175
Phelps, D. M. 45, 222
Pickering, J. F. 113
Pigou, A. C. 122
Pinto, M. B. P. 223
Pitt, M. M. 142
policy
  and heterogeneity 68–9
  see also competition policy; industrial policy; targetting policy; trade policy
policy bias, size related 76–9
Porter, M. E. 56–7, 84
product
  development 24–6
  differentiation 15, 96
product cycle theory 205–6
production function 34–5, 38
productivity 21–40
  see also total productivity factor (TFP)
profit performance 103–9, 111
profitability, and market power 56–7
profits, domestic 170–1
property rights 102, 148
protection 2–3, 48
  impact on automobile industry 279–316

Psacharopoulos, G. 21
Pursell, G. 131

Ranis, G. 128, 131, 134
Rayment, P. B. W. 83
Reid, G. 121
research and development (R & D) 36, 227
Reuber, G. 224
Rhee, Y. W. 12, 131, 193
Richardson, D. 242
Robinson, S. 45, 85, 174
Rodrik, D. 4, 7–8, 45, 155–75, 280
Rosenberg, N. 44, 130, 131, 134
Rosenstein-Roden, P. N. 126, 153
Rowthorn, R. 222
Rutzik 136

Sachs, J. D. 174
Safarian, A. E. 222
Sato, K. 158
Saxenian, A. 135, 138
Saxonhouse, G. R. 129, 130, 131
Scherer, F. M. 54–5, 95, 121
Schmalensee, R. 121
Schmitz, H. 83
Schultz, C. 146
Schumacher, E. F. 83
Schwartz, N. L. 45, 121, 174
Scitovsky, T. 5, 68, 71, 87, 124, 126, 127, 128, 153
Scott, M. F. G. 5, 129
Scott-Kemmis, D. 131
SCP model 89–116
Sekigushi, S. 222
seller concentration 90–1, 94–5, 97–103, 109, 111
Selten, R. 174
semiconductor industry 254–78
  American 266–74
  investment 259–60, 270–4
  Japanese 266–74
  product life cycle 260–3
Sepulveda, B. 221
Serconvich, F. 153
Sharpe, K. E. 283, 307, 308
Sharpston, M. 193

Sharwani, K. 109
Sheldon, I. M. 113
Shepherd, P. L. 112
Shepherd, W. G. 52, 95, 103, 121
Shockley, W. 137
Silber, S. D. 61, 83, 85
Silberston 138
Singer, A. 187
small firms
  contribution to development 49, 75–6
  networks 71–2
Smith, A. 155, 174
Smith, G. 222, 223, 224
Solow, R. 129
Sorenson, E. 121
Spence, M. 271
Spencer 226
Spencer, B. J. 1
Spencer, K. 225
spill-overs 123, 226, 249–51, 275
spin-offs 137–8
Stern, R. 169
Stewart, F. 11, 122–54
Stigler, G. J. 52
Stiglitz, J. E. 45, 121
strategic behaviour theory 90, 111–12
  see also trade theory
Streeten, P. P. 129, 220, 221
Stykolt, S. 8
Suarez, M. A. 223
subcontracting 70–1
subsidies 4, 6–7
  aircraft industries 243, 244, 248–9
  credit 68
  export 13
  public sector 189, 191
Summers 226, 248, 249
survivor test 52–3
Syrquin, M. 44

Taiwan 69–72
Tang, A. 128
targeting policy 227–42
  foreign 237
Tarrago 221
Taylor, L. 138, 174

technical change 21–40
  economic significance of 22–4
  externalities of 128–30, 141–2
  factor in growth 129–30
  review of the literature 22–6
technology
  and export levels 64
  licensing 25–6, 40, 64
  and size 64–5
  transfer 129–30
Teitel, S. 27, 44, 55, 212, 223, 224
terms of trade 32–4
Tham, E. Y. 109
Tharakan, P. K. M. 112, 121
Thoumi, F. E. 27, 212, 223
Tirole, J. 271
Todd, J. 61
Toh, K. 121
total factor productivity (TFP) 8, 14, 23
  in automobile industry 289–95, 300–6
  and firm size 56–8
  and growth 29, 156
  high initial levels 31–2, 33
  measurement 279
  and seller concentration 109
  and trade liberalization 280
  and trade regimes 160
trade
  barriers 133
  free 2–3, 179, 181
  intra-firm 10–11
  liberalization 13, 155–75
  restraint 290–5
trade policy 144–9
  Brazil 214, 215
  and macroeconomic policy 159
  profit-shifting 227–37
  strategic 1, 225–53, 255; evaluation 227–42
  strategic infant-industry protection 237–41
trade theories
  intra-industry 176
  new or strategic 4, 36, 90, 111–12, 177, 254
trading companies 71

trading regime 29–34
  see also import-substitution; outward orientation
transnational corporations (TNCs) 10, 15, 64, 102, 103, 198–206
Tsao, Y. 45
Tuncer, B. 7, 174
Tybout, J. R. 74
Tyler, W. G. 48, 67, 86, 142, 223

United States
  Auto Pact 284
  FDI 199–200, 204–6
  National Bureau of Economic Research (NBER) 4
  semiconductor industry 266–74
  Silicon Valley 135–40
Urata, S. 111, 175

Van Ginneken, W. 134
Vanlommel, E. 95
Venables, A. 225, 238
Vernon, R. 205, 222
Viner, J. 126

Wade R. 25, 87
Watanabe, A. 131, 193

Waverman, L. 7–8, 14, 279–282
welfare
  aircraft industry 248–9
  and industry characteristics 235–7
  semiconductor industry 239–41, 263–70
  trade policies 230
Westphal, L. E. 13, 23, 24–5, 27, 35, 38, 40, 44, 130, 144, 146, 154, 175, 193
Wheeler, D. 37, 45, 278
White, J. T. 222
White, L. J. 121
Willing, R. 121
Willmore, L. 221, 223
Wolter, F. 121
Woo, W. T. 174
work ethic 258
World Bank 4, 5, 48, 187
Wortzel, H. V. 192–3
Wortzel, L. H. 192–3

Yoon, C. H. 7, 13–15, 254–78

Zoninsein, J. 223